What sign are you? This is one of those questions you inevitably ask people, hoping to get to know them better. Whether or not you know astrology, you somehow feel that finding out whether that person is a Gemini or a Libra, or one of the other ten signs, will tell you something about them. This book is a friendly approach to accurately answering that question during those first encounters.

More so, this book is a practical and eye-opening tool for understanding your partner, the boss with whom you've had trouble connecting, or the child that you can always understand better. It opens up greater possibilities of meaningful connections, which will lead to deeper and more harmonious relationships. *A must!*

— *Martha Debayle, entrepreneur,*
international media personality

The Hero's Journey through the Zodiac: The Sun Signs takes us inside the goals, challenges and experience of each Zodiac sign. Not simply a collection of traits, the sun signs each tell a story and Kathie does so eloquently, personally and insightfully. This book is so simple and clear that a non-astrologer can benefit from it, but even the most seasoned astrologer will find new concepts and interesting historical, mythological, literary, and socio-political ideas that illuminate each sign. The many charts and pictures bring her stories to life. In short, this book is informative, fun to read, and full of new perspectives. *I highly recommend it!*

— *David Cochrane, professional astrologer,*
founder of Cosmic Patterns Software

I strongly recommend this exciting new work to all spiritual seekers, as astrology plays a significant role in our evolution. This work transcends the limitations and differences of the various world religions, and focuses on the highest spiritual truths that they all share. It contains keys to self-mastery that are crucial to our growth. In reading my own Sun Sign, I learned more about how and why I live my life.

I've known Kathie for 20 years and benefited greatly from her wise counsel. This work imparts a new and deeper understanding of how the planetary patterns influence our lives. A wonderful gift to humanity!

— *C. David Lundberg, author of*
Unifying Truths of the World's Religions

This book crosses all barriers. No matter who you are, *The Hero's Journey through the Zodiac: The Sun Signs* will spark a new awareness in you, something so profound about your soul, that you will walk away with a deeper understanding of life than you had before you picked it up.

— *Karen Drye, professional astrologer,*
Mystic Visions Astrology

We have deeply appreciated Kathie's astrological insight for the past 25 years. A perfect companion to my own studies in psychology, the *Child*Star* and *Astro*Journey* reports have been invaluable tools for myself and my husband for better understanding the strengths and challenges of each of our children, as well as the nature and timing of their life cycles. We are now using Kathie's reports for the next generation.

It is a delight to see the unique characteristics identified in the reports coming to life in our grandchildren as well. This book will surely provide any seeker of truth with practical tools
for life—their own and their family's.

— *Laura Boise, Montessori teacher, mother of ten children*

The Hero's Journey through the Zodiac: The Sun Signs opens the path to a higher mystical understanding and brings to heart the very vibrancy of the stars! Through its wisdom, you will be drawn to a higher plane of truth.

— *Dr. Neil Kremer, Licensed Acupuncturist*
and Doctor of Oriental Medicine

As I read this rewarding book, my mind often wondered to my own children and to many of the children I have taught throughout my career as an educator. I felt I knew them all better—their strengths, their challenges, and their true potential. Although I hadn't applied all of the practical and spiritual concepts presented here in my parenting and teaching, I rejoiced that I had intuitively applied many of them as best I could.

I am grateful that parents, guardians, and educators who read this book will gain great insight into the true nature and life's purpose of the young ones they love and care for.

— *Randall Klein, Asst. Director of Training*
at Age of Montessori School

The Hero's Journey through the Zodiac is none other than the journey to the Self—a journey of courage to overcome the obstacles that life presents. Having a guide to interpret the signs of the stars along the way, beginning with your all-important Sun Signs, is an immeasurable gift for the seeker, as these give form to the subtle currents of the subconscious mind that control our lives. Kathie's style is infused with allegorical tales, mythological stories, and humorous anecdotes, which help to inspire new cosmic vision and dispel the thick veils of illusion. May this book serve all heroes-in-the-making on their epic journey toward Truth.

— Mark Johnston, young mystic

Astrologers are only as good as their understanding of life. This book is a rare combination of history, popular culture, and mythology in the tradition of Joseph Campbell—an ideal book for anyone who wants to know how to use astrology to lead the life they've always imagined.

— Murray Steinman, astrologer

Kathie García delivers! Whether you are new to astrology or a longtime practitioner, you will find fresh insights in *The Hero's Journey through the Zodiac* to spur your personal quest for inner meaning and outer fulfillment. Kathie offers an original approach, skillfully blending real-life experience with a penetrating and wide-ranging scholarship that encompasses schools of astrology, ancient wisdom, and modern psychology—all done in a way that is accessible, engaging, and resonating with truth.

Peppered with examples from the lives of famous people both modern and historical, the book entertains while it enlightens. *The Hero's Journey through the Zodiac* will reveal positive qualities you never knew you had, and inspire you to make the most of the beautiful journey you are on.

— Gregory Bodwell, Ph.D., Esq.

Navigating one's stars often provides confusion and challenges. Kathie García's wisdom, intuition, and astrological counsel during my life's voyage has helped me make sense out of the senseless. With her vast knowledge, guidance and encouragement the black holes in my earthly road have been filled in or bridged beyond my singular capabilities. I play and replay her recorded sessions to further solidify her messages. She has been blessed by the angels and pays it forward.

— Kathleen M. Kierce, artist

DEDICATION

To all the stalwart souls walking the Way of the Hero—
Love's Journey—at this time of cycles turning

TRANSFORMATIONAL ASTROLOGY™

The Hero's Journey through the Zodiac

THE
SUN
SIGNS

Kathie García

The Three
MAGI

TRANSFORMATIONAL ASTROLOGY™

The Hero's Journey Through the Zodiac
THE SUN SIGNS

Kathie García

Print ISBN: 978-0-9908192-0-2
eBook ISBN: 978-0-9908192-1-9
Library of Congress Control Number: 2014917005
OCLC Control Number: 892 671 049

The Three Magi
P.O. Box 81
Emigrant • Montana
USA 59027

Printed in the United States of America

Cover art by Marius Michael-George
Editing, graphics & layout by Denis Ouellette

For more information & additional copies visit
www.TheThreeMagi.com

~ PART ONE ~
The SUN in the FIRE & AIR Signs
Masculine

~ PART TWO ~
The SUN in the WATER & EARTH Signs
Feminine

ACKNOWLEDGMENTS

Writing *The Hero's Journey through the Zodiac: The Sun Signs* has been so important to my personal journey, which I have not walked alone. I would like to recognize those who have journeyed beside me and shared the creative process that emerged.

My thanks first goes to my son Eugenio García for holding the vision for me, for rooting me on and supporting me in accomplishing my dream. Perhaps I might have seen from the beginning that he would become knowledgeable in publishing and that he would be so instrumental in helping me develop and produce my life's work. Eugenio's natal Moon (mother) conjoins his natal Saturn (career) and Jupiter (publishing) in his Second House (income), sextile his natal Sun and Mercury in Leo (creative leadership), in his Twelfth House (behind the scenes). From start to finish, Eugenio has been a part of this work. Eugenio helped me finance this project, as did my late father, Jerome J. Zuflacht, who never got to see the final result, but who believed in me and in my work, and who supported my growth as no other.

Eugenio's older brother is Eduardo—by two minutes, that is. Their astrological charts are exactly the same. True, some events happen uncannily for both at the same time. At other times, they seem to take turns. But, in the last analysis, no two souls are alike and I read the identical birth chart one way for Eduardo and another for his brother. Eduardo has shown us the way of the Hero even as I was writing this book. Eduardo lives life as an artist and a rising-star chef. (His amazing story is told in the Leo chapter.) His love of life and his gratitude and resolve to make every moment count continue to inspire me, filling me with joy unspeakable.

I made my mark in the astrological world back in 1993, with the publication of *Child*Star*, the first astrological report written expressively to help parents better understand and guide their children through a comprehensive astrological analysis of their charts. My twin sons and their older sister by two years, Indra, were my inspiration. Observing them taught me.

My daughter Indra Fanuzzi (née García) is an Aries (fiery spirit) born with a Grand Earth Trine, which interlaces with a Grand Water Trine, forming a Star of Victory! Practical and productive, compassionate and kind, Indra was helping us all from the time her brothers were born. Her can-do spirit, her wisdom, humor and singular ability to get whatever job done with excellence enriches my life beyond the telling.

Ellie is my youngest daughter, born in 1995. Her star is rising. I thank Ellie for helping me edit many chapters of this book, contributing her unique creative style, her insightful comments, and her youth. My only Water-sign child (Cancer Sun), Ellie's sensitive insights added warmth and dimension, humor and flow. Her knowledge surprised me. She also brought to me the interests of a younger audience—what they were looking for, what would excite them, and grab their attention.

In August of 2013, I contacted my editor, Denis Ouellette. A few years earlier, I had written for his magazine, *Natural Life News*, which he publishes six times a year here in Montana. During that time, I came to appreciate Denis' superb editing skills and our easy collaboration (We're both Libras!) From start to finish, from raw manuscript, to layout, to illustrations, and beyond, Denis' input has proven to be invaluable. His adjustments, artistic knowhow, understanding of publishing—his humor and spiritual insight have accompanied me at every step. Sometimes the words flew off the page, minor edits were done; other times, a chapter was discarded, I started anew.

In early February of 2014, I commented to a group of people at a luncheon that I needed to have my manuscript proofed. Elaine Koepke, who I had seen many times but did not know, felt prompted to call out (somewhat out of character), "I'm a proofreader!" Elaine and I worked together through the rest of that winter, meeting twice a week, going over every word. My writing improved considerably as a result of these meetings! Her sharp eye and love of language, her prior understanding of astrology and the mystical path, and her pleasant demeanor were all a great pleasure.

A heartfelt thanks to Jan Lynch and Holliday Hooks, two special friends who over the years have listened, discussed, and encouraged me to share my unique approach to astrology in book form. Their Capricorn Suns fill in the missing places of my Uranus-based Cardinal T-square—the point of production! When the three of us concur, *aha moments* almost always result!

Then there is my good friend Marjorie Lombard, herself an excellent writer, who in the early days helped me greatly as I was first creating the matrix for this book. Marjorie served as the principal of the Thomas More School for many years, which all of my children attended. She shares my love for children and their families.

My approach to astrology was developed over many years of devotional practice and study of all the world's mystical traditions. I am especially grateful for the Teachings of the Ascended Masters. The beacon light on my path, these spiritual teachings have molded and inspired me in the development of *Transformational Astrology*, which is not a fatalistic omen of prophecy that is set in stone, but a formula for change and an overcoming that can be forged and won—the Hero's journey as he learns to govern his stars.

A special *thank you* to my clients, who are always my teachers. Your lives as seen through your astrological charts have deepened my understanding of a Hero's journey through the Zodiac. As I wrote each section, so many of you flashed through my mind. And thanks to the many others who have spurred me on!

Living with a writer requires patience. There are those days of shutting the door and writing without ceasing; then there are blocks of time with no writing at all. Insights might appear in the wee hours or when burning the midnight oil. Any writer needs encouragement. And so, I thank Manuel García-Castilla, ex-husband, father of my children, and dear friend. Manuel was at my side through all of my pregnancies, helping to make these times blessed. Likewise, through the ups and downs of our relationship, Manuel's devotion to this writing has been constant, always encouraging me, (often with metaphors of being at sea for Manuel was a fisherman in his younger years), *Kathie, este un gran trabajo pero las últimas brazadas son estas—¡termina tu libro! (Kathie, this is a great work but these are the last big waves—finish your book!)* And now it is done!

INTRODUCTION
A WISE MAN GOVERNS HIS STARS

Dear Reader,

The winds of Aquarius are well upon us! The times themselves demand that we accelerate our awareness of our innate reality. Nothing less will do! More than just an updated way to interpret an astrological chart, *The Hero's Journey through the Zodiac* is written for souls living in this unique time of planetary transformation. For not only has the Piscean Age given way to Aquarius, but also larger cycles, some of hundreds of thousands of years, are coming to a close, while others are aborning![1]

Looking at the stars, contemplating periods of evolution so grand as to boggle the imagination, and even when catching the latest news erupting upon the planetary scene, one feels awed with wonder and anticipation and yet comparatively small, seemingly insignificant and, on occasion, understandably apprehensive. What will the future bring? The truth is that we make the times even as the times make us. Every breath of life, every step taken, is part of the cosmic dance! More critical now than ever before comes the choice. Which way will we go, individually and collectively? Will we ride this wave of change—yea, even determine its course—or be overwhelmed by it?

I have always believed that one individual with God can change the world! Imagine a world in which the Hero is not the exception, but rather the rule! Envision a coming age when not just one Christed One will walk the Earth, but many—a time when untold numbers of souls of light, each individual and unique, master their fate and are bonded through love.

In the Piscean Age (roughly the last 2000 years) came grace and mercy, opportunity through faith, and the path of Redemption to bring together and make

---

[1] See *Earth Under Fire,* by Dr. Paul LaViolette, on his research regarding Solar Cycles, their lengths and significance; and on galactic superwaves hitting the earth every 13,000 years; also see my article giving a synopsis of Dr. LaViolette's groundbreaking scientific and astro-archaeological work in *Atlantis Rising Magazine (No. 14) "Galactic Astrology";* astrologer and metaphysician, Dane Rudhyar's work, *The Galactic Dimension of Astrology,* on the history of the evolution to a solar-based Cosmology, he believes that we are now evolving into a Galactic-based understanding. For an introduction to the meaning of the Kali Yuga, in which cycle we are in now according to Hindu Astrology, see Wikipedia.org/ wiki/KaliYuga. In addition to the dawning of the Aquarian Age, a new "great year" or "Platonic Year," which lasts 25,800 years is aborning. See Revealer.com/ platonic.htm.

whole the fragmented parts of our psychology, to heal our diseases and those aspects of our soul trapped in ignorance. It was a time for the salvation—*the self-elevation*—of individuals and the whole planet to planes of beauty and truth. (See the Sun in Pisces chapter for more on the Piscean Age and the role of Jesus, called the Piscean Avatar.)

Although there exists some controversy among astrologers and metaphysicians as to exactly when the Aquarian Age began (or will begin), by the end of the 1990s, I realized, not only from world trends and headlines, but also from the lives and concerns of my clients, that the Piscean Age was indeed coming to a close.

What are the signs of Aquarius? We see technological advances exploding upon the world scene and the awakening of souls across the globe to a higher understanding as if shaken from the slumber of centuries. We hear cries for freedom worldwide—global uprisings and the ousting of dictators and oppressive forms of government—and the rethinking of intolerant and prejudicial cultural norms. We observe the negative consequences occurring on a social level when freedom is mistakenly understood to mean license.

Significantly, Aquarius brings opportunities and challenges for greater soul freedom. Secret inner teachings that were guarded for centuries are now available, as happened when the Dalai Lama went into exile in India, bringing to the world an appreciation of Tibetan Buddhism. Previously guarded mystical teachings of both East and West are being made public, along with their counterfeit versions in a world of increasingly greater global connectivity and "noise." We are reaching new frontiers in medicine and science, such as the growing acceptance of intuitive and energetic forms of healing. We are noticing the popularization of Astrology and concurrently the opening of an up-and-coming frontier—long held in abeyance lest it be grossly misapplied—of the power of sound combined with meditation for the healing of body and soul—both personal and planetary.

With Aquarius come the children of the New Age, generation after generation of souls, whose minds and hearts are further advanced than those who have come before them. Without these children and other souls destined to take their place on the stage of life during this epic period, Aquarius could be derailed! Without the right education of their minds, hearts and souls, the promise of a Golden Age could be delayed or even lost.

Aquarius brings the return of the Mother—the feminine energies of God such as beauty, economic and physical well-being, the wisdom that comes from understanding, and the gifts of the Holy Spirit—not to just a chosen few and not to just the women, but to all who would receive her love. With this mighty onrush of love, the most powerful force in the Universe, comes judgment—for love exposes and consumes all unlike itself!

Teachings on the nature and manifestation of the Mother energy in the different signs in the Aquarian Age are threaded throughout *The Hero's Journey through the Zodiac*. See how this applies particularly for the Sun in Cancer, Scorpio and Virgo.

Aquarius has indeed arrived and we are fast becoming transformed into men and women of this new era. But I cannot help but wonder how many among us have successfully fulfilled the requirements for graduation from the previous era—indeed, even from the Age of Aries that preceded it—that mandated loving God with all of our heart, mind and soul, and loving one's neighbor as oneself? How many of us ensoul the compassion of a Buddha and detachment from worldly ambitions? For it is written that he who would save his life (ambition to gain material possessions or accolades of this world) will lose it, and that he who would lose (sacrifice) his (worldly) life to follow the Christ Presence will save it![2]

How many have, during the last two-thousand-year cycle, seized that pearl of great price for which, it is written, a man sold all that he had—the priceless wisdom and the spirit of truth that stirs a man's soul and transforms his understanding?

Cycles of change bring new windows of opportunity and challenges. It is also true that the mastery gained during one cycle allows us to grasp the opportunity of the next, like graduating high school and moving on to college. Seen from another perspective, what is not accomplished during one cycle can handicap one's progress in the next. So much has been gained, but so much has been distorted or lost! How many among us have arrived on time, ready to take our place as men and women of this new age?

In considering such vast periods of time, one has to step back to get the broader picture. We can identify the trends and events marking the end times (the last few centuries) when the imminent closing of one age sets the stage for the next. With the discovery of Uranus, ruler of Aquarius (with Saturn) in 1781, coinciding with the American and then the French Revolutions, with their cries for liberty heard around the world, we saw the predawn entrance of the Aquarian Age. Even Christopher Columbus' discovery of the New World, in 1492, was instrumental in paving the way for a land of liberty and justice for all! Notwithstanding that this same discovery resulted in the loss of life and disaster for many native populations and that the ideal of liberty and the responsibility it entails is yet to be realized, the way was opened for future generations on a global scale.

Is time itself accelerating, causing the dates of the larger cycles to be other than what would be calculated on the calendar? Perhaps. But if we are to

---

[2] Luke 9:24, Matthew 16:25, Mark 8:35

grasp the Aquarian torch of love and freedom, we must as individuals and as a people be healed of the wounds of the past, some open and raw, others scarring the soul's sensibilities. Pisces brings us that unguent. Let us bear in mind that, although Pisces may have taken a back seat, this sign of self-mastery has not disappeared from the Zodiac (or from our experience)—not at all! More so, I do believe that the dawning decades of Aquarius—those of the 21st century and possibly even into the next century—contain elements of the Piscean era, even as the night, increasingly less perceptible, slowly recedes as the dawn grows into light. Consider, then, that all the outer planets have passed or will transit through Pisces during the first half of this century.[3] At the time of this writing alone, Neptune and Chiron are both in Pisces.

Especially during these powerful Piscean transits, I see much grieving, a deep soul desire not only to be healed, but also to bind up the wounds of a planet where brother has been set against brother, where so much blood has been shed, often in the name of God, where loss and sorrow have tried the soul. But Pisces is also a sign of great joy and miracles, of faith and forgiveness—all of which are but reminders of who we really are and of our higher calling! Let us then be comforted that a window in time remains open to transmute the errors of our past through love and forgiveness even as we accelerate into the Aquarian consciousness. In *The Hero's Journey through the Zodiac,* you will find many keys for embodying the wisdom of Pisces and for receiving the Holy Spirit in Aquarius.

This extraordinary time of cycles overlapping has been described as a kind of cosmic harvest. It is a time in which it was foretold that the tares of the righteous, or "right-use" of light, would be separated from the chaff of evil among mankind and within ourselves. For long and complex is the history of the intermingling of light and darkness on this planet. Now the fields must be purified and prepared for what is to come!

We see this cosmic reckoning take place in Earth changes as the planet literally bursts at the seams, unable to avoid upheaval, as the new wine of Aquarius may not be placed into the old wine skins of Pisces. While some go through actual hurricanes, earthquakes, and the devastation of wars, others undergoing the same astrological influences struggle to keep peace within their marriages and families, or within their own psyches. Solutions abound, but to see them and to implement them properly, and on time requires greater awareness, more love, and new levels of caring and cooperation across the globe. We must come to realize our interde-

---

[3]At the time of this writing (2014), transiting Neptune and Chiron are both in Pisces. Neptune's transit in Pisces began in the spring of 2011, on the heels of the seven-year transit of Uranus in this sign. It lasts until 2025, when this generation of youth will come into adulthood. The attention to the tides of the sea and to the availability of water is a physical manifestation. Saturn enters Pisces in 2023, for an almost-three-year-stay. Pluto will enter Pisces in 2043, for the first time in 245 years, remaining until 2068.

pendence, not only with one another, but also with the elemental life forces—fire, air, water and earth—on the planetary orb that sustains us. Understanding the Hero's (your) journey through the Zodiac can help!

Even as we must be transformed into men and women of Aquarius, the healing sciences themselves, of which Astrology is one, are changing. And so I developed *Transformational Astrology* to help fulfill this need and guide those seeking spiritual self-realization and soul freedom in this age. *Transformational Astrology* has emerged in response to and seeks to awaken an Aquarian approach—one of love, compassion, and spiritual maturity—that the promise of Aquarius, an age of divine love and soul freedom, not be derailed!

The Hero's Journey through the Zodiac, focuses on the *Sun Signs*, imparting a foundation of understanding that is suitable for a novice as well as for the Transformational Astrologer. Even the soul knowing virtually nothing of Astrology will discover vital clues and insights into the understanding of himself and his world. And those who have studied Astrology for many years, whether amateurs or professionals, will find fresh understanding and a new way of approaching astrological study that provides unique and timely keys for men, women and children during the Aquarian Age.

Aquarius represents a coupling of the best—of the old (Saturn) and of the new (Uranus), and so, the concepts I present in *Transformational Astrology* are for the most part classical, but the interpretation of them is new, insightful and multi-dimensional. I have weeded out any elements of fear of the future (Saturn) or mistaken interpretations of the nature of Uranian freedom in our present and future lives. Esoteric and Kabbalistic viewpoints and principles figure strongly in my work. I feel they help us to see beyond the outer life into that of the soul! Due partly in response to Pluto coming upon the world scene (discovered in 1930) and exposing the darker elements of the subconscious and unconscious minds, profound insights and advances in psychology have come forth and psychological approaches to astrological study have sprouted. We saw tremendous breakthroughs as many professional astrologers, particularly those practicing in the first half of the twentieth century, fought for Astrology to be recognized and practiced as a science, rather than a dubious form of fortunetelling.

Especially Western astrologers introduced the importance of figuring free-will choice into the equation in chart preparation and interpretation—an indication of Aquarian-Age thinking. Astrologer Liz Greene's insightful works are greatly influenced by Jungian archetypes. Astrologers Alan Leo (influenced by Theosophy), Dane Rudhyar (creator of Transpersonal Astrology), Isabel Hickey (*Astrology, A Cosmic Science*), Kabbalistic Astrologer Z'ev Ben Shimon Halevi (*The Anatomy of Fate*), and more recently, Jhampa Shaneman and Jan Angel (*Buddhist Astrology*) and others, have brought transcendental and spiritual dimensions into their analyses. Several astrologers are mentioned in *The Hero's Journey through the Zodiac* in relation to their particular thoughts and approaches. For instance, the perceptive viewpoints of medical astrologer Eileen Naumann are referenced often. Also discussed are details related to the events and nature of several well known astrologers as reflected by their sun sign. You can read about Dane Rudhyar in *The Sun in Aries*, Alan Leo in *The Sun in Leo*, and Grant Lewi in *The Sun in Gemini*. Building upon these traditions, we add yet another dimension, that of the soul on the path of self-transformation in the dawning decades of Aquarius.

While certain mystical communities have cropped up throughout the millennia across the globe where select individuals have accelerated on the path, now many more souls are destined to take up these initiations in the Aquarian Age—more than we have seen since ancient times on the advanced civilizations of Lemuria and Atlantis. *Transformational Astrology* provides a roadmap! Are you ready to go **through the wormhole**—the dimensional shift (as described in *Star Trek* and spoken of by mystics), in the acceleration of consciousness, without which it is impossible to travel from one dimension to a higher one? A man once cried out to me, "Kathie, I am falling through the cracks!" "No you are not," I replied, "You are flying between dimensions!" By altering his perspective, he turned around his trepidation and his circumstances as well. We live in a time of unprecedented change and opportunity. We had best learn to fly!

WHAT YOU'LL NEED TO KNOW

The Hero's Journey through the Zodiac shares the mystical viewpoint that your soul is not a passive victim thrown helter-skelter into random embodiments—not at all. Rather, your soul (and your Higher Self) chose a specific moment for your birth because of the complex combination of planetary patterns active then (influencing the development of your character as well as historical trends) to be precisely what you needed to realize the divine purposes unique to you in this lifetime.

Astronomical as well as mythological insights into the constellations and planets are woven throughout this book. Through them we gain significant clues as to their effect and meaning in our lives. But the astrological sun signs are more than mere constellations, clusters of stars, placed around the elliptical Zodiac. Just like the physical body that a man wears as a vehicle for his soul in his evolution in time and space, the planets also have physical bodies, influential energy, and spiritual essence.

Metaphysics is, by definition, the study of the spiritual cause behind the physical effect. The energy en-souling each sign and planet is seen as emanating from a greater spiritual source. Like the rainbow rays of colors you see when peering through a prism, every sun sign is another expression, a frequency, of the One Light that translates to our experience as different aspects of understanding and of beingness ever evolving.

What is this original source? Even as our galaxy has a galactic center, so the metaphysical and the physical manifestation of the center of our galaxy was the subject of great interest to ancient astronomers and astrologers. Modern esoteric traditions speak of a point called the *Great Central Sun,* reflected in each one's divine presence, the center of the entire Universe. This is seen as the ultimate source and storehouse of God's energy, which disseminates throughout the Universe.

Kabbalists often refer to *Ein Sof*—the infinite, literally, *that which is boundless,* the name Kabbalists use to refer to God transcendent, in His pure Essence—God in Himself, apart from man—as the original point from which descend the sephirot positioned on the *Kabbalistic Tree of Life*.[4] Rabbi Moses Luzzatto, an 18th century Kabbalist writer, mystic, teacher, poet, and playwright, wrote that the Creator issued the sephirot as channels or veils through which:

> *His bounty might be transmitted to man restraining that bounty to the extent that the worlds not disappear because of the too great intensity yet providing a sufficient amount of it to ensure their continued existence. He therefore made ten vessels in order that the bounty in traversing them would become sufficiently densified that the lower creations could bear it.*

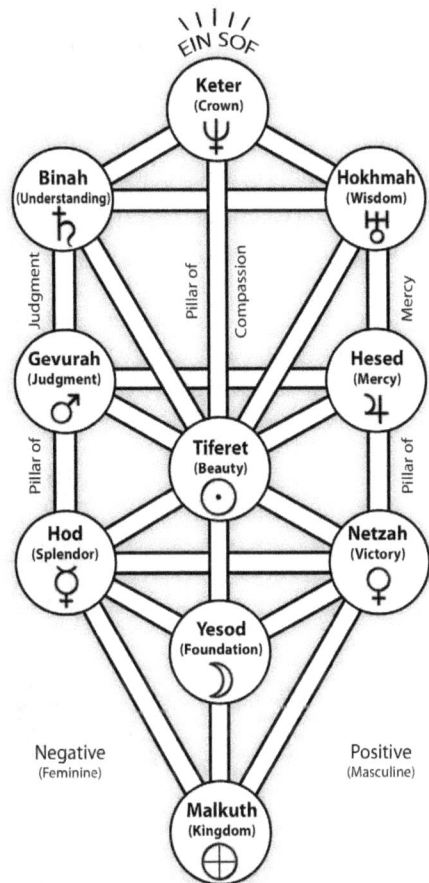

The Kabbalistic Tree of Life—
The descent of the Infinite Light into the ten Sefirot or transformers (shown with corresponding planets)

Likewise, spiritual leader and messenger Elizabeth Clare Prophet (who also references Luzzatto) taught that the Master El Morya speaks of the twelve solar hierarchies (the Sun Signs) as, "transformers that step down the intensity of the light of the Great Central Sun for the lesser evolutions in the far flung worlds that they might drink of the Cosmic Communion Cup without being consumed by the unmitigated Light of the Sun."[5]

The astrological configurations present at birth for souls during the dawning days are Aquarius are particularly meaningful for each soul, for soul mandalas or groups, and for all of civilization itself. So much makes sense when reincarnation is taken into account and thus we are able to experience and evolve through different aspects of ourselves. Thus, in each embodiment, we are able to balance particular karmas and to attain mastery in the ***corresponding chakras associated***

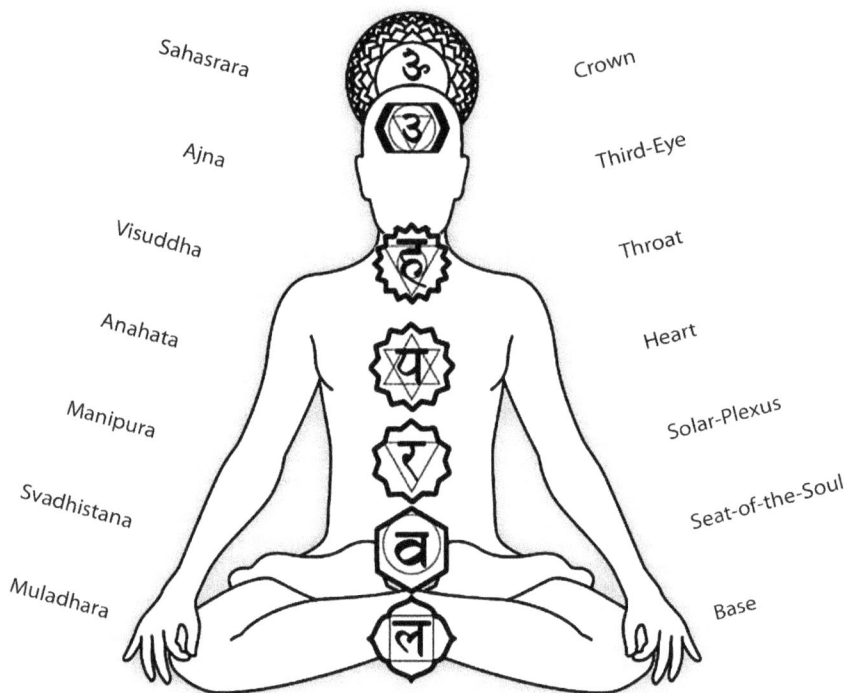

The seven chakras
(Sanskrit equivalent on left)

[4] See www.JewishVirtualLibrary.org.

[5] Elizabeth Clare Prophet produced, *Mystical Paths of the World Religions, (Part 14) Keys from Judaism—The Kabbalah and the Temple of Man: The Sefirot: Emanations of God.*

with our sun sign, or perhaps fulfill a specific calling outpictured in the shining qualities of that sign. (These are listed on the chapter divider pages.)

Moreover, we must meet with other individuals and groups intrinsic to our life plan, in definite settings and on time! *Transformational Astrology* avoids psychic interpretations and probings. Nonetheless, the natal chart offers many clues as to where you have been and what you are dealing with in the present life. Regardless, we live in the now! The natal chart certainly does not reveal all that we are, but speaks to plenty of what we are dealing with and must become in this life.

Einstein once said, "If you can't explain it simply, you don't understand it well enough." He also wrote that it takes complex mathematics to come to a few simple conclusions. Astrology is a complex art and science with a particular vocabulary that must be learned in order to master it, but its premises and conclusions are simple.

I begin all of my astrological sessions with the question, "How can I serve you? What is upon your heart?" Most of my clients wish to gain greater insight into the forces at play in their lives and world: "What is happening to me?" "How long will it last?" "What are the lessons that my experiences contain?" "How can I meet them victoriously?"

Although it is true that many, when they know better, can do better, it is also certain that we must meet even difficult and trying challenges head-on. Others will take a more proactive role, especially through the application of spiritual practices, directing positive energy through the science of the spoken word, using invocations and affirmations to counteract any negative astrological portents, so these can be turned around, the karma transmuted, before they can even manifest in the physical plane.

In this first volume of *The Hero's Journey through the Zodiac*, we explore the meaning and interpretation of the sun signs as the soul evolves in consciousness. We introduce the soul as the individual, the Aspirant and Hero-to-Be—all different cycles of the soul moving through the stages of development in each of the twelve signs of the Zodiac. This is you in your actuality and, if you choose, in your becoming! The would-be Hero is the man (or woman)—often a young adult—who first begins to look beyond materialistic ambitions and sincerely dreams of finding his mission in life. He may be actively engaged in a mission. He looks for greater meaning and understanding in his life, but has not as yet fully committed himself to the path of Overcoming. The Aspirant is the one who aspires for union with God. He strives for self-mastery, but is still in the midst of balancing his karma. He walks the mystical path of self-transformation—the selfsame path that the saints, adepts, and heroes of East and West have demonstrated over thousands of years! The Hero-to-Be is another name for the Aspirant as he gets closer to realizing his goal. The Hero is our name for the self-realized man or woman. Here we will see what it takes to gain self-mastery in each of the sun signs.

What attracts me most to Astrology is its potential for accelerating powerful self-transformation. By interpreting the nature and timing of cycles in the life of a client, I have found that we often can diagnose quickly what a psychologist may take months to uncover, thereby opening the way for proactive change. A dire forecast can thus be turned into a positive one. Challenges can be met victoriously. Positive potential can be enhanced and one's reason for being fulfilled! It is my hope that the wisdom of timeless teachings in conjunction with the window-to-the-soul astrology when rightly interpreted, can help facilitate a return to love and compassion in both our intimate and interpersonal relationships. Let us all graduate from dysfunctional, discordant patterns into a higher unity, so that together we may do more for humanity than any of us could do alone!

Interpretation of cycles within cycles and of overlapping frequencies requires an intuitive and multidimensional approach that takes into account many factors, not least of which is the essence of the person himself. Aside from the necessary study of Transformational, Classic, and Kabbalistic astrological approaches, the *Transformational Astrologer* must endeavor to become an instrument of the Higher Wisdom, maintaining a state of peace and harmony. He must seek to confirm, but never replace, the soul's Inner Guide—never making a decision for the client that the client must come to by himself.

The alchemy of self-transformation occurs in stages. Intrinsic to *Transformational Astrology* is that the interpretation of a chart depends first and foremost upon the consciousness of the inquirer—a point only a spiritually attuned astrologer can rightly discern. Contradictions often make sense, for consciousness changes over time. What is true for one may be (rightly) fanciful for another. For instance, the way we see the world as a child differs from our perception as adults. Sometimes we must return to the child-like consciousness to remember profound truths we may have lost along the way. In other ways, innocence must evolve into a mature inner sense—now, perception must be coupled with spiritual responsibility! Likewise, what may appear to be, and in fact is, fanciful and imprudent for a certain person or a person in a certain phase of growth, such as giving without care for tomorrow, may be exactly the right formula for another, more advanced individual, or for the same person at a later time of greater spiritual maturity, in which he has attained the faculty of discernment.

Then again, a soul may experience a religious conversion or spiritual rebirth. The moment comes when he realizes he cannot continue without a set of definite spiritual values. He begins to search for a teacher, or perhaps has a chance meeting or a conversation is overheard that stimulates his mind, calls to his attention, shakes his heart, and changes the course of his life forever! As he pursues the path of self-mastery, the interpretation of his chart changes. What once represented an obstacle, while it still exists (such as a square, an opposition, or an intense conjunction in the natal chart, or a planet placed in a sign considered to be unfavorable for its expression) now becomes a launching point of power and creativity!

THE SUN SIGN—THE POINT OF BECOMING

Our adventure begins with the Sun Signs. Of all positions in the chart, the Sun represents your evolving sense of self. It is the most important influence and carries the most weight in our birth chart. In working with thousands of clients, I have observed in many who are consciously on the spiritual path that their opportunities for self-mastery come under the aegis of the sun sign into which they are born. *The Hero's Journey through the Zodiac* is full of keys for those seeking greater self-mastery. He who we call the Hero will epitomize the perfection of the qualities of the sign of his birth and (through his many embodiments journeying throughout the Zodiac and even in this current life, being tested on all signs through transits and other planetary influences) ultimately becomes the master of all!

In reading this volume, you are embarking on an adventure that continues to grow through the other ones. Your first inclination may be to turn to and read about your own sun sign, or perhaps that of a friend, a child, or a loved one. You are, of course, welcome to do so, but I still recommend going back and reading this book from the beginning. While every sun sign can be understood in and of itself, it is best explored in relation to the other signs and as a part of the greater whole. Take Aries, for example. As the first sign of the Zodiac, we can see that Aries, the I Am Sign, includes the potential of every other sign, even as all men are said to be part of Adam's soul.

You will want to understand all twelve signs since each one deals with another step along the Hero's Journey. After all, every sign is placed somewhere on your natal chart and therefore figures into your life. Moreover, as we pass through the months of the year, we experience the energies of each sun sign. Observe how in late March and April, with the Sun in Aries, your patience can be strangely lacking! We find ourselves being argumentative and wondering why. We deal with, for a month, what the soul born into that sign deals with every day!

But the Arian who learns to be free of arrogance and pride eventually becomes our teacher, for who among us is free from ego and pride? In Cancer, as the summer rolls in, we all are more emotional than usual, and in Scorpio, curiously, we almost always feel self-concerned. (Of course, for our friends in the Southern Hemisphere, the seasons but not the signs are reversed.)

NOTE: Because of changes in the Earth's rotation—earthquakes, tidal coupling with the Moon, and other disturbances—causing the Earth either to speed up or to slow down, plus leap years, time zones, and other factors, sun-sign ingresses (the exact day and time when the Sun enters a particular sign of the Zodiac) may change slightly from year to year. If you were born on (or on a day before or after) the date listed here, you will have to consult an ephemeris or have your natal chart cast to establish your sun sign. (See list of sun-sign dates at the end of this Introduction.)

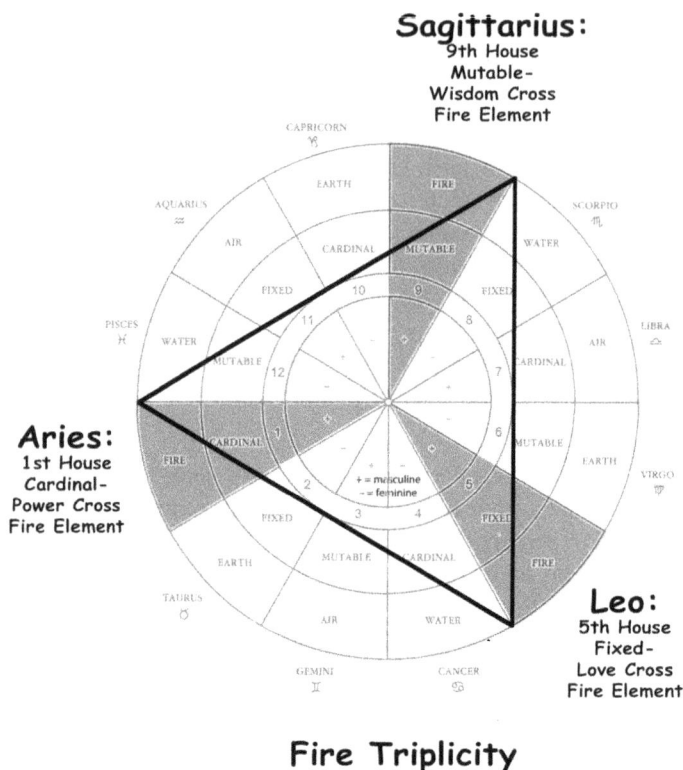

Sagittarius:
9th House
Mutable-
Wisdom Cross
Fire Element

Aries:
1st House
Cardinal-
Power Cross
Fire Element

Leo:
5th House
Fixed-
Love Cross
Fire Element

Fire Triplicity

UNDERSTANDING THE TRIPLICITIES

Astrological signs are usually presented in sequence. This is valuable since we see a thread of evolution occurring. For example, the man who is heart-centered in Aries becomes the selfless builder in Taurus; whereas, the man who is proud in Aries is apt to be greedy in Taurus. Also, we come to understand each sign as a reaction to that preceding it—Librans typically see "me" in terms of "we"; whereas, Scorpios can become overly self-concerned. We refer to the signs in sequence and in polarity throughout the book. Nonetheless, I have divided the Sun Signs and the book itself into two major sections according to the Elements: Part One includes the Fire and Air signs, which are energetically masculine or positive; Part Two includes the Water and Earth signs, which are energetically feminine signs and receptive. The elements are called the *Triplicities* in traditional Astrology because three of the twelve signs belong to each of the four elements. Aries, for example, is not only a Fire sign, but is also the first sign of the Fire Triplicity. Each sign in the Triplicity is related to, and tells us something of, the other two. The elements correspond to the expression of the sign. Fire signs (Aries, Leo and Sagittarius) are masculine and fiery in temperament. They have a correspondence to spirit. The Air signs (Gemini, Libra and Aquarius) are also masculine

Air Triplicity

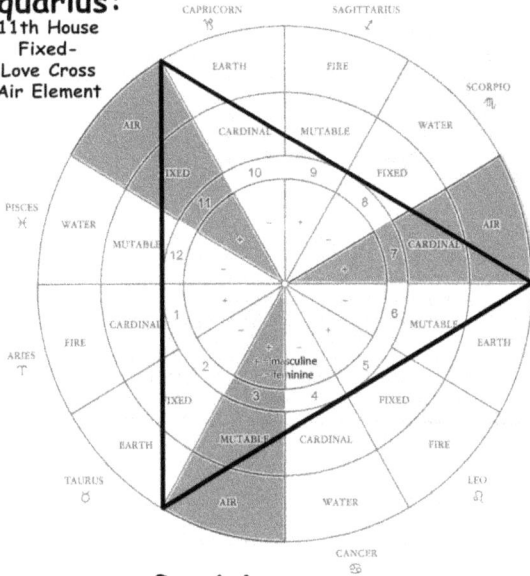

Aquarius:
11th House
Fixed-
Love Cross
Air Element

Libra:
7th House
Cardinal-
Power Cross
Air Element

Gemini:
3rd House
Mutable-
Wisdom Cross
Air Element

Water Triplicity

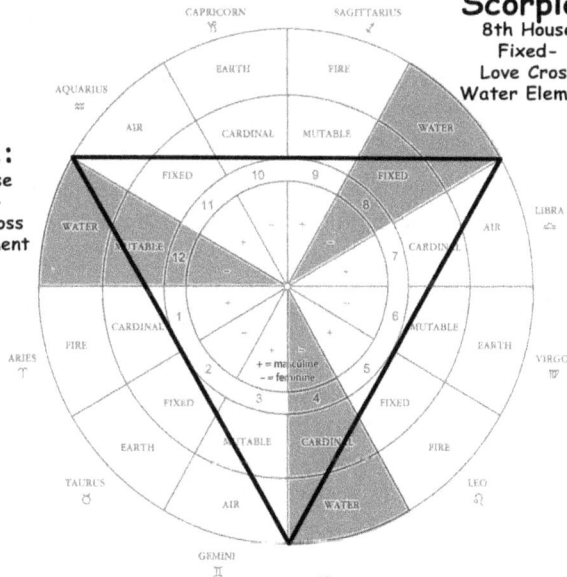

Scorpio:
8th House
Fixed-
Love Cross
Water Element

Pisces:
12th House
Mutable-
Wisdom Cross
Water Element

Cancer:
4th House
Cardinal-
Power Cross
Water Element

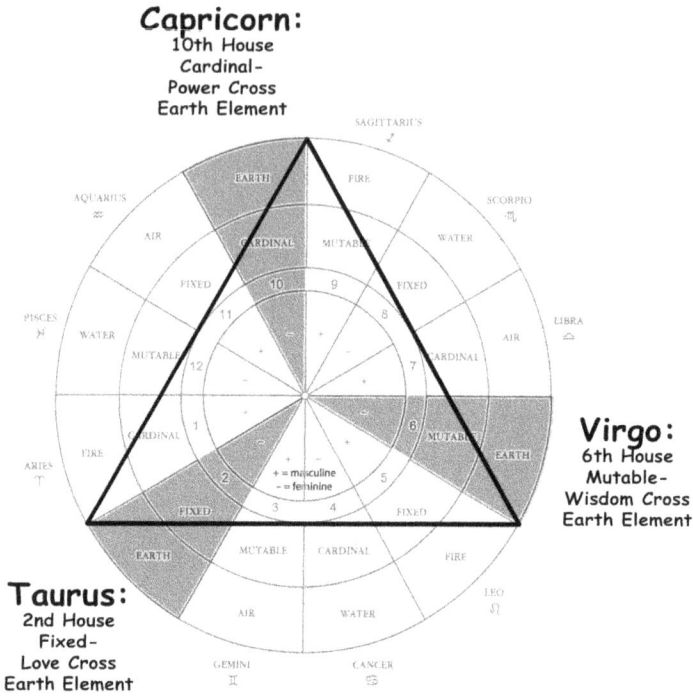

Capricorn:
10th House
Cardinal-
Power Cross
Earth Element

Virgo:
6th House
Mutable-
Wisdom Cross
Earth Element

Taurus:
2nd House
Fixed-
Love Cross
Earth Element

Earth Triplicity

(positive, +). They correspond to the mind—the winds of the spirit. The Water signs (Cancer, Scorpio and Pisces) are feminine and receptive (negative, -); they represent the flow of the emotions. Finally, the Earth signs (Taurus, Virgo and Capricorn) are also feminine and receptive, but rather than corresponding to the emotional plane, correspond to the densest of them all—the physical.

Reading all three signs in a particular element in sequence can help the reader to get a feeling for the nature of that element.

UNDERSTANDING THE QUADRUPLICITIES

Each sign belongs to one of three crosses, known to traditional astrologers as the *Quadruplicities,* since the Four Elements—Fire, Air, Water and Earth—are represented on the four points of each cross. Each cross denotes a different dynamic or modality, a mode of activity, and way of approaching life, three forms of adaptability to changing circumstances. In *Transformational Astrology,* the crosses are called Cardinal-Power, Fixed-Love, and Mutable-Wisdom.

The Cardinal-Power Cross (Capricorn, Cancer, Aries and Libra) describes the opportunity to master time and space and focuses on the basic grid of daily existence represented by the First, Fourth, Seventh and Tenth Houses of the astrological chart—myself (Aries/First House), my partner (Libra/Seventh House), my home, my mother and family (Cancer/Fourth House), and my father, my career and reputation (Capricorn/Tenth House). This cross, which we also refer to as *The Cross of Right Identification*, describes the individual's perception of who he is and his relationship to God, which is reflected in the most fundamental and important relationships of his life.

Those squarely on the spiritual path—especially when born with the Sun in one of the Cardinal-Power signs (or any aspirant when passing through an Aries, Cancer, Libra or Capricorn cycle)—can expect important lessons, tests and initiations in the use of power, whether wielded by them or in response to others, usually in terms of changing circumstances involving important relationships and offices, and demanding some sort of decisive action.

In *The Hero's Journey through the Zodiac*, you can gain different dimensions in your understanding of this cross when you read about the Sun in Aries (Fire on the Cardinal-Power Cross), the Sun in Libra (Air on the Cardinal-Power Cross), the Sun in Cancer (Water on the Cardinal-Power Cross) and the Sun in Capricorn (Earth on the Cardinal-Power Cross).

Cardinal-Power-Cross Quadruplicity

Capricorn:
10th House
Cardinal-
Power Cross
Earth Element

Libra:
7th House
Cardinal-
Power Cross
Air Element

Aries:
1st House
Cardinal-
Power Cross
Fire Element

Cancer:
4th House
Cardinal-
Power Cross
Water Element

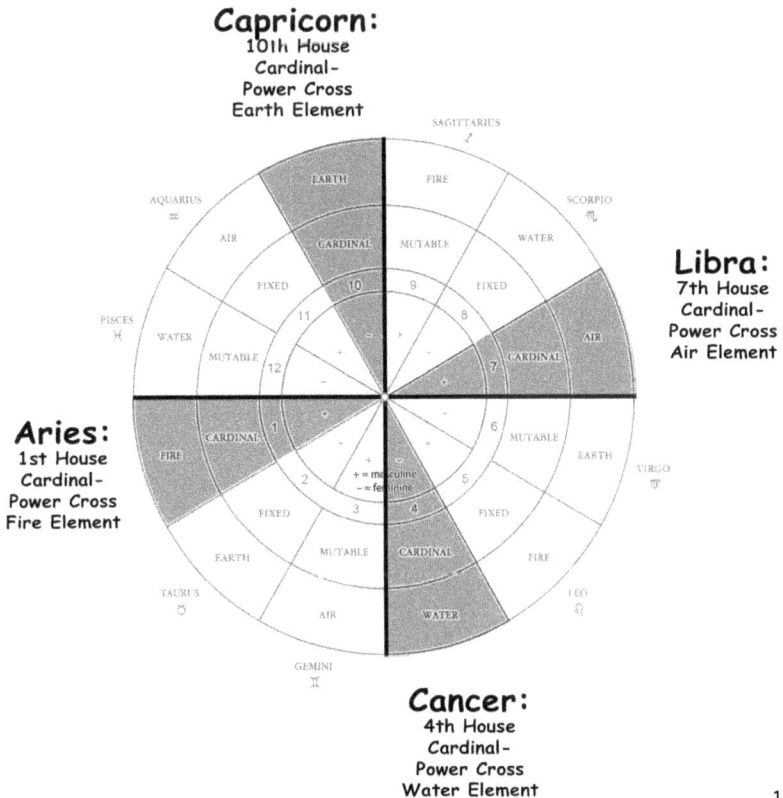

Fixed-Love-Cross Quadruplicity

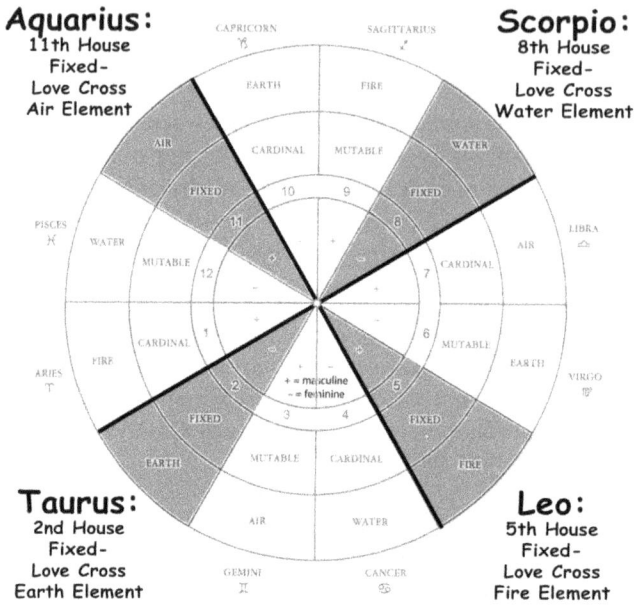

Aquarius:
11th House
Fixed-
Love Cross
Air Element

Scorpio:
8th House
Fixed-
Love Cross
Water Element

Taurus:
2nd House
Fixed-
Love Cross
Earth Element

Leo:
5th House
Fixed-
Love Cross
Fire Element

The Fixed-Love Cross (Taurus, Scorpio, Leo and Aquarius) relates to our capacity to love and create, and also to the blocks we have put up and must dissolve, where we have shut others out due to fear. This cross tells much about our economy, our values, our income, and the give-and-take of life. On the Fixed-Love Cross, we discover insights into the conflict of will-versus-desire, its myriad expressions, and the keys to its overcoming.

On the Mutable-Wisdom Cross (Gemini, Sagittarius, Virgo and Pisces), we learn that we all are simultaneously both students and teachers on different rungs of the ladder of life. Here we see the impulse to vanquish ignorance, but also the tendency to justify ignorant mindsets. On the path, the Mutable-Wisdom cross describes what must happen so that the lower, rational mind can transcend itself into the higher mind—that knowledge can be translated into wisdom.

Cardinal-Power sign people are action oriented. They are dynamic, in charge, active and very involved in material life. The Fixed-Love signs anchor what the cardinal signs initiated. They preserve and sometimes they destroy. They are often resistant to change. The Mutable-Wisdom signs are the most flexible. They pick up information quickly, but do not necessarily retain what they have learned and are often very impressionable and prone to change their mind.

Like learning to become fluent in a language and then, artistically self-

Mutable-Wisdom-Cross Quadruplicity

Sagittarius:
9th House
Mutable-
Wisdom Cross
Fire Element

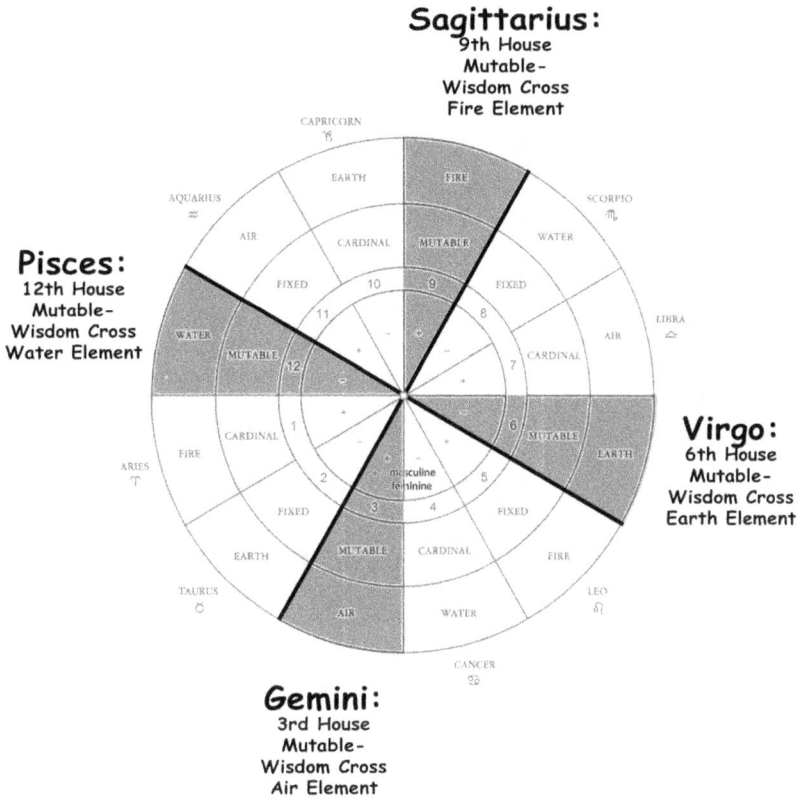

Pisces:
12th House
Mutable-
Wisdom Cross
Water Element

Virgo:
6th House
Mutable-
Wisdom Cross
Earth Element

Gemini:
3rd House
Mutable-
Wisdom Cross
Air Element

expressive, a master of communication, as you become increasingly more familiar with the astrological building blocks, your creativity and your understanding in Astrology increases exponentially. In *The Hero's Journey through the Zodiac,* we explore traditional meanings of the *Triplicities* and the *Quadruplicities* and the deeper meaning behind their symbologies that you can apply today in your own life.

For example, Cancer is a water (emotional) sign on the Cardinal-Power (active) Cross. Cancer relates to the mother and the home, a place of care and sustenance. Even in nature, the mother—the most personal (water) of all relationships—is busy (Cardinal) taking care of her brood! Gemini is called a double Air sign because it is an Air sign on the Mutable Cross, which relates to the Mind and the transmission of thought, and therefore, has a correspondence to the Air Element. Unless the rest of the chart adds other more grounding elements, Geminis often live in their heads! Even if you are already familiar with astrology's terminology and divisions, you will find new nuances of meaning in this book.

SPIRITUAL KEYS, CHALLENGES & LESSONS

The spiritual keys I present in each sign are valid for all the signs. In Taurus, for example, I write about *Kavannah*, a Kabbalistic concept that is best translated as *right attitude*. This is what Taurus is all about—will motivated by love. We all, however, need right attitude regardless of our sun sign. Without *Kavannah*, a person is not teachable, being either willful or will-less. *Kavannah* is willingness to be God-taught, represented by the Tree of Life's central pillar of Compassion. In the Virgo, Sagittarius and Scorpio Sun Signs, I speak of the importance of forgiveness, without which spiritual progress is impossible. Each of these signs offers a different insight into how and why to forgive and their respective blocks to forgiveness. What is true for one is true for all, but Sagittarians, for example, will deal more directly with the fires of resentment, Virgos with a gnawing sense of injustice, and Scorpios with seething anger. The tests of love knock at each one's door, but differently garbed!

In *The Hero's Journey through the Zodiac* we will touch upon (and explore in greater detail in future volumes) the significance of the planetary rulers of a particular sign and their corresponding houses on the astrological wheel. Gemini and Virgo, for instance, are both ruled by the planet Mercury; Gemini corresponds to the Third House of communication and transportation, and Virgo relates to the Sixth House of work and service. Aries, ruled by Mars, is *esoterically* ruled by Mercury. What is the difference between them?

Virgo and Pisces are both related to the Solar-Plexus chakra. Pisces is a Water sign. Virgo is an Earth sign. Reading about one adds to the understanding of the other. And we all, regardless of sun sign, need to learn mastery over our emotions. For those committed to a higher walk with God, so much changes and yet some of the challenges the soul has encountered will be the same, but greater in intensity. It may take much experience before the Leo Aspirant embraces humility or the Virgo devotee overcomes his tendency to be anxious, or the Libran seeker clearly discerns the difference between the mind's reasoning and the heart's intuition.

In life, even more so once the seeker is squarely on the path, the soul accesses greater Light, so he comes in contact with a corresponding greater darkness. *The Hero's Journey through the Zodiac* offers teachings to help aspiring souls recognize, deal with, and avoid, as much as possible, the traps so subtly laid, and the pitfalls that threaten every devotee. Personal stories, lessons learned from observing the lives of famous people, insights into the meaning of the chakras associated with each sign, psychological insights and Kabbalistic and other esoteric principles—all these will help the reader to bring forth the consciousness of his loving Higher Self and to recognize and overcome the elements of the shadow self that oppose him.

Once the Aspirant sets his sights on the goal of self-transcendence, he traditionally measures his progress by means of tests and initiations, some of which will be stepping-stones and others greater milestones. Even as the chakras are associated with certain signs, as are the ten *sephirot* on the Kabbalistic Tree of Life, so are the initiations on the path. For instance, all Aspirants will one day meet what Saint John of the Cross referred to as *the dark night of the soul*. This initiation has a certain correspondence to Libra, the sign associated with the Holy Spirit through a balanced heart. Regardless of your sun sign, you will benefit from reading about *the dark night of the soul* in Libra.

THE AQUARIAN-AGE CHILD

Nothing is higher on my priority list than the future of all children in the Aquarian Age. We must make the best of their time of great promise and beware of watering down the intelligence, squelching the spirit, or distorting the psyches of tomorrow's leaders. The words written in Proverbs ring true today: *Train up a child in the way he should go: and when he is old, he will not depart from it.*[6]

I am a Montessori teacher, the mother of four, and grandmother of two. I wrote the first-ever astrological software report for parents in 1993, called *Child*Star*. One mother of ten children has often told me how invaluable these reports have been for her and her husband in raising each of their children. I also wrote *Astro*Journey*, a forecast report for older teens and young adults, with a separate section for their parents, to help guide these souls and their parents during this critical period of their lives.[7]

Every sun-sign chapter discusses the child, his nature, upbringing, and special needs, and takes into consideration those souls aborning in the Aquarian Age. In learning about the child, you can learn much about your own inner child as well. In reading about the child in the different signs, remember that no two souls are alike. I have been blessed with twin sons. They were born two minutes apart and while they have exactly the same chart, I read the chart one way for Eduardo and another way for Eugenio. Although some uncannily similar events have occurred in their lives, they are very different. Some qualities obvious in one child do not appear for years in another. For example, in The Sun in Aries section you can read about the quiescent Aries child whose inner fire is atypically quiet in his earlier years, like a volcano, which lies dormant until it erupts, activated by a passing transit, such as Uranus on his Ascendant.

---

[6] Proverbs 22:6

[7] For a free chart, send e-mail to kathie.garcia@thethreemagi.com. Astrologers can purchase the software for these reports at www.TheThreeMagi.com. For a single report, go to www.TheThreeMagi.com.

THE HERO GOVERNS HIS STARS

Lastly, think of the teachings you read of and the discoveries you make as ever expanding. Truly, as I write, new dimensions of understanding are continually opening up to me. Such is the Hero's journey, full of wonder and romance! The wise man governs his stars. He understands the timing of the cycles, the nature of where he has been, his current circumstance, and what lies before him. His choices are illumined by his comprehension of the roadmap of his destiny, the twists and turns of his karmic script, its heights and depths, the moments for beginning as well as those of ending, which open up new horizons. Aware that the past and the future meet in the present, he changes his past by altering his present, and thus reconfigures his future—he is the master of his destiny!

KATHIE GARCÍA & THE THREE MAGI—

SOUND THE OM!

Before we begin, I would like to invite you to enter my office of The Three Magi, the dedicated space at my home here in Paradise Valley, Montana. The Magi of biblical fame bore their gifts to the child Jesus and a timely warning of King Herod's threat to the newborn babe. They understood astrology and astronomy as sacred sciences and used their calculations to time and navigate their journey to Bethlehem. In the tradition of the ancient Magi, we welcome you on your journey to follow your own star appearing!

A big brass Tibetan gong stands in my entryway. I now hand you the mallet and invite you to sound the gong three times. As the monk who sold this to me said, years ago, the sound will put your mountains into alignment! To entone with the clearing vibrations, let us sound the OM together: *Ommmm! OMMMMM! OMMMMMM!*

Please come in and take a seat. I offer an invocation that we may be blessed and inspired, and that your most pressing questions will receive illumination during this session. We sense a dimensional shift. The space around and within us feels enlivened. Glancing out the picture window, you see the tall, snow-capped Emigrant Peak. (If you are fortunate, you might see a bald eagle soaring before it.) There is a sense of spaciousness and freedom.

Your eyes glance at the items on my desk. Next to my ephemeris sits a figurine of a monk studying, a picture of clouds that appear to be large angels, and a cloth Cinderella doll, a gift from my daughter when she was six. We all know Cinderella's story. Born into a well-to-do, loving family, her mother died when she was small and her father remarried. He soon also died, leaving Cinderella to her wicked stepmother and her two stepsisters. Jealous of the girl's (outer and inner) beauty, they delegated her to the attic, mocking her and treating her as a servant. But no matter how they mistreated her, they could not take from Cinderella her sweet disposition. Now, when you take up this doll and turn it upside-down, *voilà!* The poor Cinderella is transformed into the princess, wearing a gold crown and holding a wand with a star.

For me, the doll serves as a reminder that karma can be severe—life's challenges can come upon us suddenly and sometimes tragically. But regardless of the harshness of our karmic circumstances, we all have a date with destiny awaiting us. If Cinderella had become cynical and depressed, I doubt that the prince would have noticed her at all!

In the Aquarian Age, no one need be a victim of his stars or the karma they represent. Life is full of challenges. There is no good or bad astrology—it's all good! This is because it is your journey, your opportunity, and your victory in the making. *The Hero's Journey through the Zodiac* is for the soul desirous of cracking the code, of leaping beyond seeming limitations, and of governing his stars and thus realizing his dreams. It can be done! You can turn what looks like a breakdown into a breakthrough, enhance your potential, and be in the right place at the right time, fulfilling your reason for being! *Transformational Astrology* will help you get there.

The Hero's byword is love. With courage and the spirit of adventure, let us begin!

APPROXIMATE DATES OF THE SUN SIGNS

ARIES	**March 20 ~ April 19**
TAURUS	**April 20 ~ May 20**
GEMINI	**May 21 ~ June 20**
CANCER	**June 21 ~ July 22**
LEO	**July 23 ~ August 22**
VIRGO	**August 23 ~ September 22**
LIBRA	**September 23 ~ October 22**
SCORPIO	**October 23 ~ November 21**
SAGITTARIUS	**November 22 ~ December. 20**
CAPRICORN	**December 21 ~ January 19**
AQUARIUS	**January 20 ~ Februay 18**
PISCES	**February 19 ~ March 19**

NOTE: The exact day and time when the Sun enters a particular sign of the Zodiac may change slightly from year to year. If you were born on (or on a day before or after) the date listed here, you will have to consult an ephemeris or have your natal chart cast to establish your Sun Sign.

~ Part One ~
The SUN in the FIRE & AIR Signs
Masculine

Sagittarius:
9th House
Mutable-
Wisdom Cross
Fire Element

Aquarius:
11th House
Fixed-
Love Cross
Air Element

Libra:
7th House
Cardinal-
Power Cross
Air Element

Aries:
1st House
Cardinal-
Power Cross
Fire Element

Leo:
5th House
Fixed-
Love Cross
Fire Element

Gemini:
3rd House
Mutable-
Wisdom Cross
Air Element

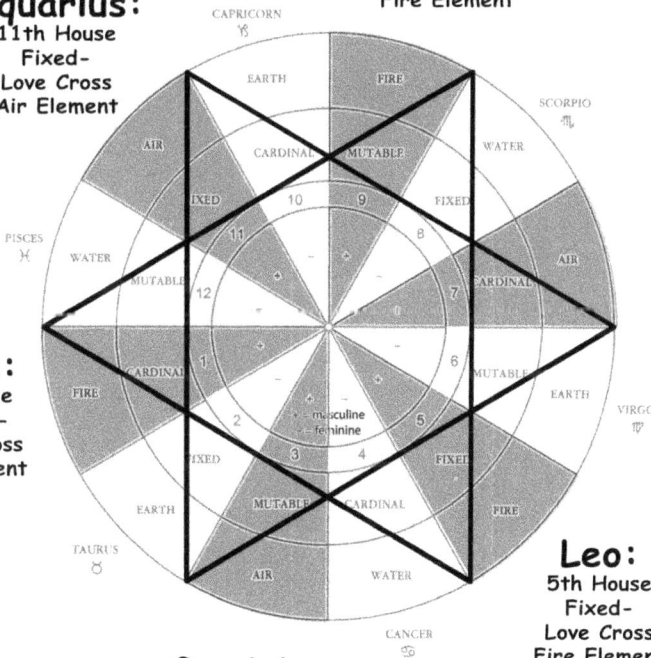

CAPRICORN ♑
EARTH
FIRE
SCORPIO ♏
AIR
CARDINAL
MUTABLE
WATER
FIXED
10
9
FIXED
11
8
PISCES ♓
WATER
AIR
CARDINAL
MUTABLE
12
7
1
6
MUTABLE
CARDINAL
FIRE
EARTH
VIRGO ♍
2
5
masculine
feminine
FIXED
3
4
FIXED
EARTH
MUTABLE
CARDINAL
FIRE
TAURUS ♉
AIR
WATER
CANCER ♋

♈ ♊ ♌ ♎ ♐ ♒

1. ♈ Aries

Symbol	*The Ram*
Born	March 20 ~ April 19
Archetype	*The Son*
Key Phrase	*I Am*
Element	**Fire**
Cross	**Cardinal-Power**
House	**First:**
	Me, myself & I
Ruler	**Mars**
Esoteric Ruler	**Mercury**
Polarity	**Libra**
Chakra	Heart
Anatomy	Head, face & eyes

Spiritual Qualities .... **Self-knowledge & dominion, courage, speaking truth, acting fearlessly**

Vulnerable to .... *Pride, arrogance & ego, impatience & anger, impulsiveness, non-cooperation*

Must Acquire .... **Humility, heart's wisdom, self-discipline, patience, listening skills, self-control, tempered passion**

Jesus • Johann Sebastian Bach • Elizabeth Clare Prophet • Wilbur Wright • Mary Pickford

THE SUN IN ARIES

Man, Know Thyself

—Socrates

THE SEARCH FOR SELF

Aries is the first sign of the Zodiac. At zero degrees on the Zodiac wheel, Aries is the gateway to the First House and the entire chart. The sign on the First House cusp (the Ascendant, determined by the precise moment of birth) colors the individual personality. In Aries we must answer the first and most basic of questions: Which me do I choose to be? Which me do I choose not to be? That's the nuts and bolts of the Arian riddle. Astrology deals with relatedness—our relationship to one another, our relationship to influences and happenings occurring in our immediate environment and outer world; our relationship to energies reaching us from even the most distant points of our solar system—and most importantly, our relationship to spirit. Our central point of reference is, of course, "me." In *Transformational Astrology*, the interpretation of the entire chart hinges upon the perception of whom we think ourselves to be—our current state of self-awareness. We all, regardless of birth sign, deal with the conundrum of self-definition. For the soul born in Aries, however, the search for self is at the core of all he does.

The beginning, the middle and the ending of the Arian person's search for self all revolve around one thing—the relationship of the Self with God. By knowing himself as *he really is,* man can know God. In Genesis it is written that a man cannot know God and live, but I believe that means that once a man knows God, he cannot live as he did before, for he is transformed! The more a man understands his true nature, the better he can understand and relate to others. Mystics of all faiths believe this truism, captured in the powerful Hebrew prayer called *The Shema*: *Hear, O Israel, the [LORD] is our God, the [LORD] is One.*[8]

One Spirit, many manifestations: as above, so below.

Jesus certainly was knowledgeable about the Jewish mystical principles that in later centuries became the core teaching of Kabbalah. When one of the Pharisees asked him when the kingdom of God (the consciousness of Heaven) should come into manifestation, Jesus answered: *The kingdom of God cometh not with observation: Neither shall they say, Lo here! or lo there! For, behold, the kingdom of God is within you.*[9]

THE ARIAN HERO

Jesus likely was an Aries, born around the time of the Spring Equinox.[10]

On the Cardinal-Power Cross, Aries occupies the position of the Son, the fusion of the Father (Capricorn) and the Mother (Cancer). Jesus addressed God as *Abba,* an affectionate and reverential Aramaic word, which means *father.* Throughout his ministry, in parables, teachings and simple declarations, Jesus spoke continually of himself in relationship to the Father, as when he said: *My Father worketh hitherto, and I work.* [11]

And, I can of mine own self do nothing: as I hear, I judge: and my judgment is just; because I seek not mine own will, but the will of the Father which hath sent me.[12]

At the very prelude to Jesus' Palestinian mission, when he went up from Galilee to the Jordan River to be baptized by John the Baptist, we read:

And straightway coming up out of the water, he saw the heavens opened, and the spirit like a dove descending upon him. And there came a voice from heaven, saying, Thou art my beloved Son, in whom I am well pleased.[13]

The term, "son of God," did not originate with Jesus; Jewish literature abounds with the term. In the second Psalm of David, we read: *I will tell of the decree of the [LORD]: He said to me, 'You are my son; today I have begotten you.'*[14]

In the Aquarian Age into which we have already embarked, not one but millions of souls, receive the opportunity to walk the Earth as Christed Ones. People around the world are awakening in spirit and in love from a centuries-long slumber. This is the real purpose of globalism, that we might embrace the culture of the Divine Mother and together lay the groundwork for the Aquarian Age; an era of Universal Brotherhood, freedom and opportunity characterized by the feminine qualities of loveliness, beauty, comfort, wisdom, self-discipline and abundance.

---

[8] Found in Deuteronomy 6:4, *Sh'ma Yis'ra'eil Adonai Eloheinu Adonai Echad.* Many Jews consider *The Shema* to be their most sacred prayer; it has deep spiritual and mystical meaning.

[9] Luke 17:20-21 (KJV)

[10] For a detailed discussion on the engineering of Christmas Day by Constantine, and Jesus' more probable birthday, see, *Marking Time,* by research astronomer Duncan Steele, and the section, "The Birth of Jesus," by Noel Tyl, in his book, *Prediction in Astrology.*

[11] John 5:17

[12] John 5:30

[13] Mark 1:10-11

[14] "Thou art my Son; this day have I begotten thee." Psalms 2:7

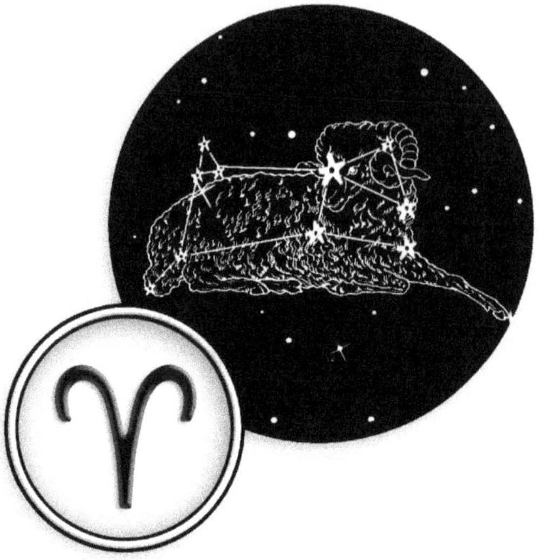

Aries:
1st House
Cardinal-
Power Cross
Fire Element

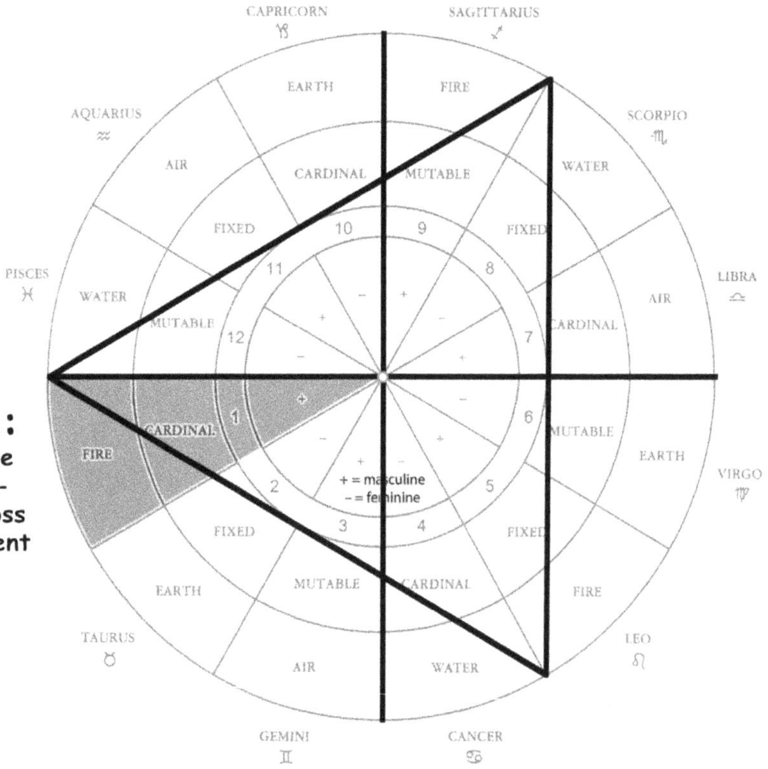

SELF-REALIZATION ON THE CARDINAL-POWER CROSS

Language, which divides into units called words, cannot justly describe that which is infinite, ever transcendent and ever expanding. Men cannot describe God, nor are our brains capable of comprehending such magnitude and eternality. But we cannot be silent, for even while walking the Earth clothed in flesh, all men experience at some time in their lives awe-inspiring moments of sublime revelation when they contact God—perhaps in a flash, a vision, in the eyes of a child. The mystic is he who would sustain that thread of contact; he is willing to let go of all that would interfere or block this up-lifting communion.

When Astrology is understood as sacred science, its symbology offers a map, an invaluable tool to the seeker on the way. The circle of the chart represents the whole of Cosmos; its circumference and divisions mark the cycles of that which is infinite and boundless in the framework of a defined period of time in the lives of men. Thus, Astrology attempts to better understand the working out of Spirit individualized in the lives of men through cycles of time. The first and major divisions of the circle, the vertical and horizontal lines dividing the circle first in half and then into four quadrants are the lines forming the Cardinal-Power cross, the basic framework of the chart and of our lives. In each heartbeat, the light descends from spirit (Capricorn/Crown chakra-Father) *in a figure-eight, flowing spiral* to the Mother (Cancer/Base chakra), where it rises once again through the Heart chakra (Aries and Libra-Son and Holy Spirit) before returning to spirit to begin the cycle anew. This cosmic drama outpictures itself in the basic areas of everyday life.

Capricorn is associated with the entrance of the soul into incarnation, his relationship to God through his interactions with authority figures and his contribution to life through his chosen career. Cancer is associated with a person's home, family, community and nation. Aries is associated with his developing sense of self and Libra with his marriage and important partnerships.

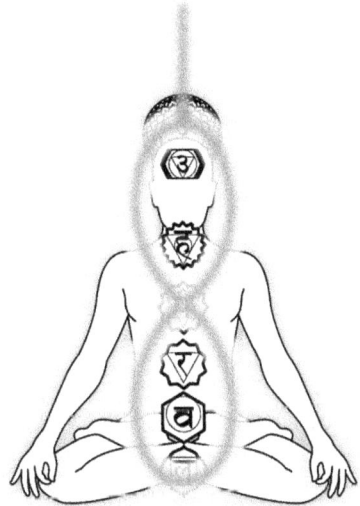

Crystal cord, figure-eight flow with Heart chakra nexus

WHAT IS IDENTITY?

Aries is a Fire sign. Fire relates to spirit and to identity. What is identity, if not a flame endowed with awareness of self? The Sun is exalted in Aries. You might say that the individual born at the beginning of springtime has an extra dose of solar energy available to

29

him. But is he the Sun or the recipient of its rays?

Experiencing the Fire element in the physical body, Aries Sun types are understandably energetic, *fiery* and impulsive by nature. The Aries child zips across the street before you can blink an eye! His parents may be hard pressed to give him the example of patience he so sorely needs as they deal with their own exasperation over their difficulty in controlling their son, who cannot as yet control himself! It is precisely this disciplining of self, this conscious controlling of the life energy available to us each day, the daily exercising of the power of solar radiance, that primes the Arian person's pump, awakening his inner resourcefulness and native creativity.

As the Sun in Aries person gains experience and matures, his sense of self naturally changes, sometimes dramatically so, affected by and setting up a chain of events in his life. He meets different parts of himself in varying aspects of his potential that become apparent in his response to events, personal or in the world in which he lives, that challenge and encourage him, opening him up to new possibilities. At times, these bring him into confrontation with tumultuous aspects of his own psychology or karma. Throughout it all, he becomes more and more acutely aware of who he really is and who he is not, although he must shed many masks before glimpsing the real man.

Aries is the sign of the ego, with all its trappings, for good or for ill. The ego is often more pronounced in Aries than in any other Sun Sign. Self-confident, the Aries Sun character tends to be self-motivated, on the ball, and direct in speech and in manner—a trailblazer forging new ground in his field. Fire and cardinality charge him with enthusiasm and a powerful drive to create, to think, to do! But until he is free of pride and self-importance, he may adopt a false persona very convincingly, in some cases wielding tremendous authority—for a time, a cycle, or even for lifetimes!

THE NATURE OF THE CHOICE

The deciding factor for the Sun in Aries type—who represents the "I" in us all—is the choice. Aries belongs to the Cardinal-Power Cross, where opportunities for transformational growth manifest through changing and challenging circumstances requiring quick decision and decisive action.

Joshua, who followed in Moses' footsteps, challenged the Israelites: Choose you this day whom ye will serve. At the heart of every choice is revealed the nature of the soul's relationship with her own divine reality and/or unreality. Will she serve the truth o error?[15]

---

[15] Joshua 24:15

With each choice he makes, the Aries Sun person either feeds the ego or exercises the native power of his real self. A simple example would be whether to lie or tell the truth, especially if telling the truth would result in difficult consequences. If he chooses to lie, no one may ever know, but his identification with the mask invariably grows. As the momentum of living a lie strengthens, the soul drifts further and further from its true self.

How can the Aries individual be in the right place at the right time, doing the Will of God to the best of his ability? Only by attuning to the heart's wisdom can he be certain as to which way is the right way. He must be centered in the nexus of the Cardinal-Power cross, the place where the energies of Father and Mother, meet—the point of the Heart chakra! Yet being fiery in spirit, he tends to be impulsive, too often acting without thinking. Aries rules the head. Like the Ram, Aries' symbol, the Arian individual can be very headstrong and hardheaded! He thinks he's right—in his mind he *knows* he's right—and so will disregard, decimate through argument, or simply thrust aside much of the well meaning advice that is offered to him. In almost all cases, experience proves to be his best teacher. When the Ram has hit his horns enough times that it hurts, he finally accepts that he must look before he leaps! Even so, for no one does the expression, "I learned by the school of hard knocks," hold truer than for the Sun in Aries person.

What about Arians who recognize their weaknesses but have not yet conquered them nor fully capitalized upon their strengths? Especially in the Fire signs (Aries, Leo and Sagittarius) the line separating healthy self-confidence and initiative from egoism and conceit is not always easily discernible. So much of what we do is caused by emotional programming and responses rooted in childhood experience or in past lives. Therefore, to effect permanent, positive self-transformation almost always involves connecting with the soul at the level of the inner child. This is where *Transformational Astrology* can prove to be an invaluable tool.

Even so, a healthy ego is better than no ego! It would be foolhardy to demand of the Aries child (or those of any sign) to surrender his ego when he is still creating his sense of self. We praise the child and support his sense of achievement. Children, however, have no difficulty grasping at a very young age that there lies within them "a little me" and "a great me," and that they can choose which me they want to be![16]

The wise parent allows the Aries child room to make age-appropriate decisions; the natural consequences of his free will choices teach him to use power responsibly.

---

[16] See *The Little Me and the Great Me,* by Lou Austin (The Partnership Foundation, 1957).

Stripping the ego of its pretentious masks can be scary! Courage, the kindling of the inner fire of the heart, is a positive Aries trait. But can we be courageous if we are not afraid? The true Aries individual is anything but faint-hearted. His courage, strength and fortitude are apparent, especially in acute situations requiring a strong, reassuring presence, emergency action, and the intelligence to take on-the-spot action. Arians often find themselves on the scene, somewhere, somehow, when they are needed for some unforeseen crisis, great or small.

MEDICAL & MYTHOLOGICAL CLUES

As the I Am principle, Aries represents the quest to realize one's higher potential. The constellation of stars called Aries, appearing in a formation that the ancient Greeks thought resembled a ram's head, is visible from the Earth. The ancient Egyptians associated the constellation Aries with the god Amon-Ra, who they depicted as a man with a ram's head. Egyptians came to recognize Aries as "Lord of the Head."

Even in modern astrology, Aries rules the head. Especially if the Sun is impacted by hard aspects at birth, or by transit, Arians are especially prone to head injuries, headaches and the like. Arian children, even when toddlers, being so actively energetic and not tending to look before they leap, tend to bump their heads. So much so that the medical astrologer Eileen Naumann urges parents of Arian children to assure their child is wearing a helmet in sports, when cycling or when horseback riding.[17]

Aries rules fevers and burns. Naumann points out that natives of this sign tend to get acute fevers with symptoms that come on suddenly. While the sudden onset of high fevers can be startling to their parents, Naumann adds that these youngsters usually bounce back amazingly quickly!

THE PIONEER

The Aries personality strives to give expression to the energy he experiences through concerted action. Determined to make the goal, he energetically removes obstacles encountered on the way, whether circumstantial or psychological. Not prone to dawdle or delay, his catch phrase might be, "Just do it!" or "Do it now!" As he conquers his world, he develops strong self-esteem. Others respect his can-do spirit and dauntless gusto. Because he likes to do his own thing, in his own way, he may opt to be an entrepreneur. He characteristically pioneers new

---

[17] See MedicalAstrology.medicinegarden.com/2009/04/medical-astrology-sun-in-aries/.

[18] See http://en.wikipedia.org/wiki/Dane_Rudhyar.

ideas. If he works for another or as part of a team, he somehow makes his way into a position where he enjoys much personal latitude and creativity and can legitimately, at least in his area of expertise, call the shots. Unafraid of competition, he embraces the challenge to show he is the best!

An Aries person's résumé or biography typically, and at times remarkably, is accentuated by the phrase "the first to..." or "founder of...." Aries people get the ball going! Consider the brilliant Aries musician, poet, artist, historian, philosopher, theoretician, author and highly influential astrologer, Dane Rudhyar, born Mar 23, 1895, in Paris. In 1917, the Metropolitan Opera House in New York City played some of Rudhyar's original musical compositions, the first polytonal musical pieces to be performed in the United States. Some years later, Rudhyar pioneered modern *Humanistic Astrology,* which effectively shifted astrological interpretation from being primarily event oriented to being person centered. With Rudhyar, astrological symbology gained depth and new perspective. He incorporated metaphysical beliefs, Jungian psychological concepts, the influence of cultural nuances and the individual in question's free will choices. Rudhyar emphasized 'potential becoming'—the working out of probability and possibility—more than fated happenings. He founded *The International Committee for Humanistic Astrology.*[18]

Wilbur and Orville Wright's historic first successful flight of a powered airplane—at Kitty Hawk Beach, North Carolina, December 17, 1903. This flight was the first time that a powered, heavier-than-air machine achieved controlled, sustained flight with a pilot aboard. It flew forward without losing speed and landed at a point as high as that from which it started.

In *Transpersonal Astrology,* Rudhyar digs even deeper, addressing world transformation and "the vision of a total transformation of the whole person." Such a *transpersonal* vision, he insisted, demanded a *transpersonal* astrology.[19]

Wilbur Wright, the elder of the two famous Wright Brothers, was born with the Sun in Aries on April 16th, 1867. He and his brother, Orville, are both credited for together making the first successful airplane; they were the first to successfully carry out a "heavier-than-human flight," on December 17th, 1903. In *To Conquer the Air*, literary historian, James Tobin, notes that while they worked closely together, Wilbur initiated the project in 1899–1900, during which time he wrote of "my machine" and "my plans."[20]

Tobin further states that, "it is impossible to imagine Orville, bright as he was, supplying the driving force that started their work and kept it going from the back room of a store in Ohio to conferences with capitalists, presidents, and kings. Will did that. He was the leader, from the beginning to the end."

Of the great Aries organist, violinist, harpsichordist and composer, **Johann Sebastian Bach**, born March 21, 1685 (Julian; March 31, Gregorian),[21] in Eisenach, Germany, Beethoven once wrote, "My heart beats sincerely for the sublime and magnificent art of that first father of harmony."[22]

The Austrian composer **Franz Joseph Haydn** was born on March 20, 1732 (Julian; March 31, Gregorian). Papa Haydn, as he was called, pioneered new frontiers; he became known as the "Father of the Symphony" and the "Father of the String Quartet." Credited as being "the Engineer of the Classical Form," Haydn's work exerted a tremendous influence upon future great composers. Although Bach and Haydn have very distinct musical styles, one senses the vibrancy, boldness and strength of Aries in the works of both composers. We feel uplifted and energized when listening to the music of these two Arian musical giants.

---

[19] See http://www.khaldea.com/rudhyar/fromhtot_3.shtml, Dane Rudhyar, *From Humanistic to Transpersonal Astrology*.

[20] James Tobin, *To Conquer the Air*: *The Wright Brothers and the Great Race for Flight* (Free Press, 2004)

[21] Some sources cite March 21, 1685, while others March 31, 1685. The former do not take into account changes made when switching from the Julian to the Gregorian calendars. Either way, Bach was an Aries. NOTE: In 1582, Pope Gregory XIII introduced the Gregorian calendar as a reform to the Julian calendar. Great Britain and the British Empire (including its American colonies) adopted the Gregorian calendar in 1752. To make the change, it was necessary to advance the Julian calendar by 11 days (Wednesday, 2 September 1752, was followed by Thursday, 14 September 1752). Throughout this work, the Gregorian dates have been used in chart preparation and analysis. Sources, except where otherwise noted: ASTRODATABANK (Astro.com) and Astrotheme (Astrotheme.com). Note: All charts in this book are Geocentric, using the Placidean House System.

[22] Letter to Kapelmeister Hofmeister

Then there's the actress, ***Mary Pickford***, born Gladys Louise Smith, on April 8, 1892, in Toronto. (See her natal chart below.) With her Sun and Jupiter in fiery Aries (enthusiasm), Mary made up for her 5'1" stature with her natural pluck and gusto. She became known as "Little Mary," "America's Sweetheart," and "the Girl with the Curls." Although she did star in a handful of "talkie" films, Pickford made her greatest mark earlier, during the silent-film era. She appeared in 52 feature productions throughout her life. Mars, which rules Aries, is exalted in powerful Capricorn in Pickford's chart and forms part of a Grand Earth Trine involving both the Moon in Virgo and Mercury in Taurus. Strong Earth positions are particularly useful for talented performers who become producers and successful businesspersons. "Little Mary" was both. Moreover, Uranus (innovation) in Scorpio—sextile her Moon in Virgo (resourcefulness), but bisecting the Grand Trine by opposing Mercury in Taurus—becomes the point of vision (Scorpio) for investing in the future of filmography. She was co-founder of the United Artists film studio and one of the original 36 founders of the Academy of Motion Pictures, Arts and Sciences. She was recognized by the American Film Institute as 24th among the greatest female stars of all time and, in true Aries fashion, is known to be a pioneer in early Hollywood.

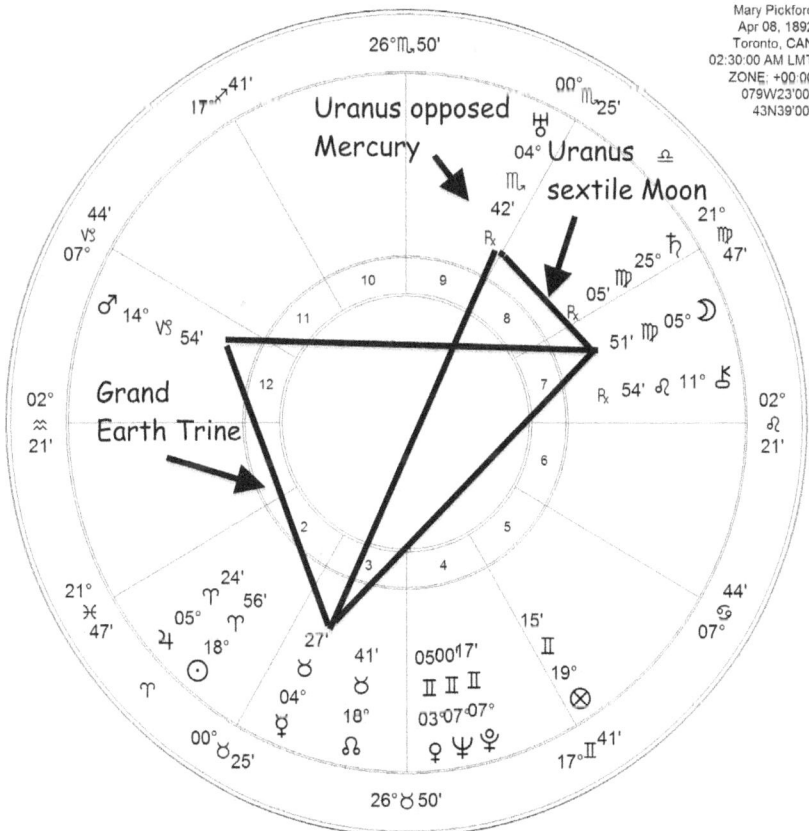

MARTIAN ENERGY

Mars rules Aries. Called *the planet of action through desire,* Mars endows those born under its influence with an energetic can-do, roll-up-your-sleeves-and-get-the-job-done-now spirit! Unless Saturn's restraining influence figures strongly into his astrological picture, the Aries individual tends to be understandably impatient. Many persons born into this self-motivated sign naturally take the lead, oftentimes the leap, opening the way for others to follow. Solution oriented, upfront, bold and ambitious, they typically take more to getting a project successfully off the ground than keeping it going. The Aries child typically jumps to the head of the line. He may have a hard time surrendering first place when it's someone else's turn to kick the can! While many Aries children (and adults) thrive on competition, another type simply knows he does it best—why bother wasting time and effort with someone less able? In fact, he may be right, but such stances feed his pride. One way or another, life molds and mellows him, perfecting his abilities and tempering his heart through patience.

In its negative manifestation, Martian energy is highly combative. We all can recognize Mars' underside when we wake up on the wrong side of the bed, snappish, edgy and ready to pick a fight! Whether in the personal astrology or that of the world, chances are that Mars is making headlines. While none of us are immune from negative Martian energy, Arians deal with the Red Planet's emanations in greater measure and all the time! Natal Mars in the Arian person's natal and progressed charts and by transit is frequently the major dynamic in his daily forecast. Until these spirited individuals learn to tame the beast, Martian energy takes them for quite a ride; in effect, they become their own worst enemies. Difficult planetary aspects to the Outer Planets (Uranus, Neptune and Pluto), especially in the charts of Arian children, teenagers and young adults, or of persons unsettled by trauma and emotional imbalance can upset the apple cart, oftentimes resulting in unwise or compulsive actions lest controlled. Mars in sextile or trine (harmonious aspects) to other planetary positions is a more positive influence, imparting the enthusiasm and spirited drive to act resourcefully and assertively, with self-confidence and decisiveness. Nevertheless, even the more harmonious aspects to Mars can prove troublesome, sometimes even abetting the ego in its charades!

Living in the present with an eye toward the future, for most Arians the past is prologue and gone. Nor are they prone to delay or to dawdle. Arians tend to be physically active. Sports or vigorous daily exercise help the Arian personality actively channel his abundant energy without being overbearing and so maintain health and happiness. Even a brisk walk helps him let off steam, lest he be too large, too loud, too confrontational. One very successful self-made Arian businessman once considered giving up his daily practice of brisk jogging every morning at daybreak as a worthy sacrifice during the Lenten Season. His astrologer's advice: "Don't do that to your wife!"

Arians characteristically get uncomfortably testy and argumentative when asked to conform to someone else's way of doing things. Although they may gain the admiration of others as they rarely wait around for instructions, the same self-initiative can be problematic when working closely with a partner or as a member of a team. Even the more cooperative type Arian upsets others when he quite naturally acts without first consulting those in his circle. Why dilly-dally when there is so much work to be done? Arians generally feel greater inner peace when they respect others whose modus operandi may be slower, more contemplative, and cautious or less dynamic—not everyone was born an Aries!

Learning how to control his forceful reactions typically takes considerable effort for the soul born into this powerful Sun Sign. Every person born with the Sun in Aries will inevitably attract persons and situations that test and tax his patience, expose his impatience, and spark his ire and indignation. All such encounters grant him the opportunity to discover how he might acquire greater self-control. He tends to take things personally and will too often react in fighting mode, verbally or physically! Flashing cheeks and a quickly beating heart in most cases are warning signals—breathe, take a run, calm down! When he must step up to the plate and take on a formidable challenge or foe—though his heart pound—as long as he remains centered, he is strengthened by the powerful and peaceful presence of love. Until he gains mastery in using his mind to control his explosive reactions, the person born in Aries is apt to be hot-tempered and easily provoked. He may tersely justify an excessively blunt demeanor, defend his sense of righteous indignation or feign indifference. Anger's manifestations are too many and varied to possibly list—some are more obvious, while others, like passive-aggressive apathy, are harder to discern. The cause is almost always pride. Consciously, but more often subconsciously, pride masks insecurity, pain and fear.

Aries people typically feel compelled to get in the last word. George, a gregarious Aries father of four makes no bones about it: "I love to argue with my wife and kids. We get it out! Why not? In the morning we all love each other again." Some Arians pride themselves on being forthright to a fault. An extremely articulate and accomplished Aries athlete, born in early April, once confessed, "My mouth is my worst enemy!" Elena, an active Aries woman in her midlife years, took on an uncharacteristic femininity and most likely saved her marriage when she discovered that preserving the nest of love is sometimes more important than proving that you're right. Sharply telling someone their faults, supposedly for their own good, without taking into consideration their feelings, with rare exceptions, shatters the peace and creates alienation and hurt or invites a fight. A certain abrasive arrogance, so typical in the Aries person, can be hard for him to shake because he doesn't think he's brash; rather, he insists that he is just stating the truth! The Aries Sun's life is transformed when he recognizes and embraces that the route to happiness comes through tempering his speech instead of lashing out at the world around him. For many born under this Mars-ruled sign, controlling their temper is far easier said than done.

In some cases, the consciously caring and thoughtful Aries Sun person faces another's anger without having directly provoked the confrontation. Unpleasant as the circumstance may be, it may provide a mirror of realities he could not otherwise fathom, manifest a returning karma, or provide a conflict that is necessary to expose truth and reach resolution. All is opportunity. Nothing happens by chance.

When the Aries Sun person's ego and/or his cause—his declared mission—take a solid beating, he may experience deep pain and searing resentment. He may seem defeated and be temporarily down, but once he reconnects with his inner strength, once he remembers who he really is, he comes up fighting with love and more love, and then more love still!

THE QUIET ARIES CHILD—QUIESCENT FIRE

Although many Aries children manifest self-confident bravado, others tend to be gentler, quietly good-natured and even uncharacteristically timid. Despite their quieter disposition, they, too, tend to be impulsive with a strong independent streak. Even the more compliant children of this powerful Fire sign may be argumentative, a manner in many young Arians that seems to defy all correction to the contrary! Parents and teachers can help the shy Aries child bolster his self-esteem by providing him with the tools he needs to build his natural skills and abilities. Interactions with his peers challenge him to be at peace with being who he is and with doing what he believes is right, even if this means not conforming to the norm. Notwithstanding, even the quiet Aries child's inner fuse will be lit, usually sometime in adolescence, triggered perhaps by a strong planetary transit; suddenly, the previously quiescent fire appears!

THE ARIES SUN PERSON IN CLOSE RELATIONSHIPS

Born at the time of the Spring Equinox when night and day are of equal length, the Aries person nevertheless often finds achieving balance with others a challenge. He insists on blazing his own trail by himself. A lifestyle of self-reliance may have come about as a way of surmounting trying circumstances. Not surprisingly, many Arians grapple with a feeling of aloneness even when surrounded by family or friends. The moment arrives, however, when the Aries individual who lifted himself up by his own bootstraps discovers that his self-reliance gets in the way. This one who felt so alone and on his own reaches a point in his journey when he must learn to love another and in so doing consider needs other than his own. Not only must he learn to give of himself in greater measure, but he must also learn to receive graciously. He must let himself be loved. In essence, to feel whole, he must learn a few lessons of his natural polarity, Libra. We all need one another, and the only true compass is the heart.

What the Aries Sun person will not or cannot see about himself is sometimes revealed to him through close relationships with others. While the process may prove painful, the lesson if rightfully understood, often proves invaluable in his understanding of himself and the consequences of his choices. Diego is a strikingly handsome Aries man. When in his late twenties, he pursued the object of his affection, the beautiful and vivacious Clara, and had little difficulty winning over her heart. While Clara agreed to marry him, there was a catch — the minister of her church disapproved of Diego's chosen faith. Diego severed all connections with his church and joined hers, attending services and prayer vigils daily. The quirk of the story is that when Diego recreated himself to please Clara, she no longer felt attracted to him! Well, he learned the futility of faking being who he was not — as good a lesson in self-gnosis as any.[23]

He picked up the pieces of his broken heart with a truly Aries resolve: "I will not enter another intimate relationship until I know who I am!" Fortunately, Diego's story ended — or began — happily several years later when he met and married the woman of his dreams.

In order for love to flourish in their lives, Arians need to curb an innate tendency to dictate to others what to do. Some Arians are downright bossy. Others push people away by an arrogant demeanor; many become tiresome when they talk mainly about themselves. True, a certain Aries type is a real go-getter. Enterprising, considerate and clever, he is out there to help and serve others and so he succeeds by exercising a degree of natural dominance without becoming too overbearing. Needless to say, Arians do best when paired with someone they respect who can keep abreast with them, or better yet, someone who inspires them to strive to do better. Nevertheless, because he often feels essentially self-sufficient, the Aries individual may have to work at entering the give-and-take, the unavoidable art of compromise (without compromising his own integrity), which sets the rhythm of a healthy relationship. By learning to be more understanding of others, including their shortcomings, he is less apt to take their actions personally and more prone to remain centered rather than to spring into reactionary battle mode. Sometimes Arians would be wise to give Mars a back seat, while letting Venus, the planet of love, take center stage.

All these Aries Sun qualities are modified, amplified, revealed, or redefined when the entire chart, person, stage in life, and current situation are taken into consideration. In addition, particular astrological cycles that can be defined and which reflect upon past, present and future circumstances must be taken into

---

[23] Self-gnosis: self-understanding, leading to spiritual self-transformation.

account. Of course, all depends upon spiritual maturity or lack thereof; an Arian in whose chart the Sun is square Mars would predictably be hot-tempered, conceited and impatient. Another more spiritually aware individual or even the same man, humbler and wiser years later, might experience the same influence as charged energy that he wields lovingly and responsibly.

A young Aries woman born with an interlaced Grand Water and Earth Trine (great compassion coupled with practical know-how) worried so much about her friends and family during her teenage years that her challenge was more about finding and defining herself (rather than pruning an overly bombastic ego). As she matured, she never stopped caring, but she did cease worrying. She found that in meeting her owns needs she could better serve others. She became Aries at its best—positive, upbeat, and dynamically proactive. At the same time, she was also mindful of the importance to allow others to make and learn through the results of their own choices.

A fundamental factor in the shaping of the Aries soul's sense of self is his childhood perception of his relationship with his parents, especially with his father, and his perception of his parents' relationship to one another. When the Aries person feels secure with both father and mother, he displays an inspiring self-confidence and gusto for life. No challenge seems too great —except perhaps that of handling routine! Giving up is not in his vocabulary. The Aries teenager particularly can be affected by domestic discord or loss, as when a parent is taken from him and more so when parents separate or divorce. He may for a time lose his bearings and sense of direction. In many cases, the outer circumstance is but a reflection of a soul theme that has gone on for lifetimes seeking resolution, the tip of an undefined iceberg. In time, he picks up his life and charts his course anew having learned a basic Aries lesson—the only one he can control is himself!

The Aries Sun parent can be authoritarian in a no-nonsense, "this is the way it is," manner but still tend to be positive. He typically does not make decisions for his children but rather allows them to discover the consequences of their freewill choices. Asked to what he owed his success in life, a Leo man matter-of-factly said of his Aries father, "My dad refused to see failure in me."

THE SUN IN ARIES HERO-IN-THE-MAKING

Knock, and He'll open the door.
Vanish, and He'll make you shine like the sun.
Fall, and He'll raise you to the heavens.
Become nothing, and He'll turn you into everything.

—Rumi, Sufi Poet

The time arrives in an Aries individual's journey when he wills to move on to triumphs not worldly in nature. The illumination of his heart is at first exciting. He jumps at the thrill of starting out on a new adventure; but it's also a bit disturbing—his emotions strangely tumultuous as he enters terrains outwardly unknown, if inwardly familiar. Once again, the soul born under the sign of the Son questions, "Who am I?" Once again he faces how, through his choices, he has fashioned the person he thinks himself to be. He knows he is not who he thought himself to be, he knows not who he really is or will become.

The Arian who would embrace the mystical path begins by confronting and sorting out the illusions he has held about what is real and what is unreal within himself. Not all are ready or desirous for such an encounter, not yet willing to commit to what may appear to be a frightening and risky undertaking, entailing too great a sacrifice. Some come to the gate, tarry for a season, and then return back to their everyday lives. Many enter in for a time, but then detour to go pick up a piece of self, pay a karmic debt, fulfill their responsibilities with families or friends, or perhaps to satisfy some personal unfulfilled desire. Nonetheless, once he forges his resolution, the Aries Aspirant tends to be disciplined, committed and undaunted in his determination to do whatever it takes to reach the goal!

PATIENCE OBTAINS ALL THINGS

The Catholic saint, mystic and Carmelite nun, Teresa de Ávila, was born on March 28, 1515 (Julian; April 7; Gregorian), in Gotarrendura, a municipality in the province of Ávila, Spain. Drawing primarily from her own experience, St. Teresa wrote extensively about the successive stages of spiritual development. She explains that especially in the earlier stages of the Aspirant's path many he knew, neither willing to accept nor able to understand his choice, will likely reject him. He therefore benefits by surrounding himself with like-minded friends set on the spiritual path. The spiritual community supports him during this vulnerable time when others readily point out his weaknesses and problems, which tend to be many as he struggles to find his footing. The right Teacher or guide is especially vital at the beginning of his journey when he can so easily become discouraged, distracted, confused or detoured.

As Arian souls gain greater mastery over the Heart Chakra, thought and action become one. The prominent 16th century Spanish mystic *Teresa de Ávila*, (March 28, 1515–October 4, 1583), taught—"The important thing is not to think much, but to love much."

As he advances he becomes more secure, but the testing of his soul and his resolution to carry on become progressively more challenging. St. Teresa describes a time that may last for many years, in which the habits, emotional patterns, desires and momentums of the instinctual, selfish man war against the nature and identity of the emerging true Spiritual Self.

St. Paul referred to this confrontation of light and darkness within the Aspirant as "the warring of the members." The false ego does not disappear overnight. So closely identified is the Aries person with his "mask" that if it were to be ripped off in a second, he would feel lost and in danger of assuming other, more insidious facades. Although the recognition of aspects of one's self working against one's own good may come in a flash, an epiphany or in a startling revelation, the dismantling of the old man and the putting on of the new is a step-by-step, dynamic process of surrender to love. As the devotee expands the flame within his heart through prayer, meditation and decrees (focused affirmations), spirit's fire within him quickens his understanding, but its intensity may be disquieting. This is because the frequency of the light he has invoked stirs up pockets of darkness or density within his psyche. And yet prayer brings him peace.

For the sincere Aspirant, Teresa de Ávila advises:

> *Let nothing disturb you. Let nothing frighten you. All things are passing away. God never changes. Patience obtains all things. Whoever has God lacks nothing. God alone suffices.*

THE PASSION OF THE PATH

Mystics of East and West have likened their yearning for God with the passionate ardor of a lover seeking his beloved. She appears and then is lost from sight, sometimes for long, long periods of time that seem endless. The marriage he yearns for is in truth the marriage of his soul with his own Divine Presence. Such a union rarely happens at once—he could not withstand it. Rather, it occurs gradually; in increments he merges with his lost love.

In the Zohar, the chief text of Kabbalah, a wise man compares the Torah to a beautiful maiden wooing her lover (he who would know her innermost secrets). Secluded in an isolated chamber of the palace, she alone knows of the lover's existence. We read:

> *She knows that whosoever is wise in heart hovers near the gate of her dwelling place day after day. What does she do? From her palace, she shows her face to him, and gives him a signal of love, and forthwith retreats back to her hiding place... he is drawn to her with his whole heart and soul, and with all of his being. In this manner, the Torah...discloses herself to her lovers, so as to rouse them to renewed love.*

PURGING THE HEART OF PRIDE & AMBITION

Circumstances in which the Aries Aspirant finds himself seem orchestrated to expose the serpent of pride hiding in the garden of being. This is what the Greeks called *hubris*, a noxious weed that must be purged lest it sabotage the seeker's best efforts to advance forward. Merriam-Webster defines hubris as, "exaggerated pride of self-confidence." In everyday talk, we recognize this quality when we remark that someone is "full of himself" rather than full of the true spirit recognizable in a man who is humble. Merriam-Webster supports their definition with the example, "His failure was brought on by his *hubris*," and a quote from Simon Winchester's, *The Professor and the Madman* (1998): "When conceived it was a project of almost unimaginable boldness and foolhardiness, requiring great bravura, risking great *hubris*."

This point is key for the Aries soul striving for self-realization today. During the dawning decades of the Age of Aquarius, few Aspirants will be secluded in monasteries and hidden retreats. Rather, most seekers on the upward path must maintain spiritual integrity while simultaneously fulfilling secular roles in life. The Aries Sun person tends to be ambitious. Does he need to let go of his ambitions when on the spiritual path? Yes and no! His challenge is to complete his chosen line of dedication and labor with excellence, whatever that may be, while maintaining the vision of his greater goal, oneness with God. He must strive to not get overly caught up either in material or in spiritual ambitions.

Situation after situation affords the Aries Aspirant the opportunity to acquire greater and greater self-control. He learns to refrain from reacting angrily when others disapprove of his actions or speech, when he doesn't get what he wants, when he wants it—or even when he gets what he doesn't want! Unexpected events and confrontational type encounters test his ability to remain centered and unmoved. And so, he strives to be patient despite his native impatience. He pauses to listen to another's point of view despite his tendency to be opinionated. He determines to be honest yet forbearing, ready to speak truth when truth need be said, yet loving enough to keep silent, candid but never brutally nor unnecessarily blunt. In the meekness of humility, he accesses the source of the power pulsating within his being. In turning the other cheek and refraining from entering into needless battles that would only sap his light, he taps into the powerful presence of peace. The Aries seeker of reality begins to put on the Real Man.

The soul with the Sun in Aries is abetted in his daily transformation of the self into the Self (with a capital S)—the selfish ego into the Selfless Ego—by learning to recognize that when he allows himself to get piqued by little things, when he mistakenly thinks himself to be a law unto himself, when he engages needlessly in heated arguments, he is dangerously on the wrong side of the Arian fence.

As the intensity of his trials increases, so does his faith. As opposition to his mission mounts and more and more is required of him, his determination to give all he's got (and all he is and can become) increases.

MASTERING THE HEART CHAKRA

As the Aries seeker gains greater conscious control over the powerful life force pulsing within his being, he is less prone to be rash, having learned that not all initiatives require immediate resolution. Some are best left for another time (and perhaps for another person) to resolve. Even tragedies and seemingly avoidable conflicts sometimes are part of a larger drama and a greater good—many things simply work themselves out over time. But forbearance is not timidity. He knows by virtue of his very nature that, "he who hesitates is lost." Major turning points in his life may occur suddenly and unexpectedly, requiring that he act quickly and decisively now!

That he not err, the Aries Aspirant must develop balance and become more and more sensitized and attuned to the inner heart—he must master the heart chakra. As he meditates upon the spiritual heart the Aries Aspirant becomes aware of blocks and barriers he has construed to shut love out. These, he realizes, must be dissolved by love's consuming fires!

One Aries woman, a devotee of many years, relates how she obeyed what she calls *an inner directive* to knock on the door of a certain woman's home whom she barely knew. She intuitively understood only that they were to work together somehow in some as yet unknown capacity. Summoning that courage so characteristic of the Aries Sun person, she made the trip, found the woman's home and knocked on the door. No answer. She knocked again and again. Finally the woman appeared, still clad in her bedclothes. Over a cup of tea, they discovered the work in store for them. That meeting set the direction of both of their lives from that moment forward. When asked, "How did you know the message was real?" she replied, "My heart spoke to me very clearly."

I OF MYSELF CAN DO NOTHING

To love God is to be hated by the world. He who has determined to strip himself of all that is less than love challenges those still caught up in the wiles and illusions of the ego. Although in past ages those seeking self-transcendence were the exception to the rule, Aquarius is the Age of the return to love and the return to the Mother. Many souls desiring initiation into the inner mysteries are entering Aquarius' golden gates. Seeking the Mother's wisdom, they welcome love's chastening through her, as they become self-disciplined men and women, free of lesser energies and the weight of past negative karma. Only thus can the Aquarian Age evolve into a Golden Age of Peace, an era when love binds the majority of Earth's people to their own divine reality and to one another.

The ego does not relinquish its hold upon the soul without a fight! The Arian Aspirant's personal confrontation with his own shadow can be particularly intense. As the Arian Aspirant comes to distinguish light from darkness, Christ from antichrist, love from anti-love, he fervently invokes the strength and courage to expunge darkness from his person and from the world. He prays for humility and for peace, for he increasingly realizes, as did David when facing Goliath, that "the battle is the [LORD]'s."[24]

That the battle be won, the devotee's heart, like that of David of old, must be one with God's own heart. The more he advances, the closer his tie to his own Divine Presence, the more ferocious is the assault upon him and upon his mission. Sill, he strives to be the Adept, the Steadfast One who like Jesus proclaims, "All power is given unto me in Heaven and on Earth."[25]

And yet, he also knows, "I of mine own self can do nothing."[26]

Divested of the ego's pseudo identities, railings and temporal ambitions, the Arian soul who would exchange the lesser self for the greater Self declares, "God in me is the doer and with God nothing shall be impossible!"

As the Aries Aspirant gains greater spiritual maturity, taking on more and more of the Hero's inner strength, steadfastness, love and faith in divine purpose, he becomes a force of tremendous positive change in the world. Consider the successful Aries businessman, astute in the ways of the world, but incapable of being corrupted by money or power. Consider the Aries politician who likewise can represent truth without being intimidated or swayed by the powers that be. Consider also the enthusiastic Aries educator who adheres to high standards of learning for the youth. Then there is the Aries spiritual leader who sets an example through his courage, who disciplines, guides and inspires, but remains humble in heart, bowing to the Light within all he meets and serves.

"YOU CAN ASCEND!"

Elizabeth Clare Prophet was born April 8, 1939, in Red Bank, New Jersey. Spiritual leader of the Summit Lighthouse and the Church Universal and Triumphant, Guru Ma, as her followers knew her, truly lived the life of a soul born in Aries who would be Hero at the dawn of the Aquarian Age.

Prophet taught that the true core Teaching of both East and West had been lost, buried, distorted, even intentionally misrepresented. In a world increasingly materialistic, but on the verge of a great spiritual awakening, she brought

[24] 1Samuel 17:47
[25] Matthew 28:18
[26] John 5:30

forth *The Lost Teachings of Jesus* and *The Lost Years of Jesus,* and revealed the common thread of truth inherent in the world's mystical traditions. She spurred souls worldwide to complete the karmic cycles of the concluding Piscean Age and thus be able to enter the Aquarian Age and prepare the world for incoming souls of great light.

Although Mars rules Aries *exoterically*, Mercury is Aries' *esoteric* Ruler. When the soul born in Aries is stripped of pride and the masks of the Ego and is vested in his Higher Self, thought (Mercury) and action (Mars) are one—seamless, instantaneous, precise and direct.

In Prophet's teaching style, in her daily interactions with others, and in her role as Messenger for the Great White Brotherhood, the teaching rang clear.[27] The vibration elevated the listener into higher dimensions of gnosis (knowledge of spiritual things); yet the meaning was at once practical and action-oriented. This courageous Arian pioneer of the New Age taught that yes, Jesus was the Son of God. He performed many miracles. He was and always will be the Savior; his mission was to remind those who had forgotten who they were of their true identity and destiny. He gave his life that all might be saved. He demonstrated the Transfiguration, the Resurrection and the Ascension—love's victory over death.

Elizabeth Clare Prophet brought Jesus' message back updated, not some via dolorosa, but a joyous path. After all, Jesus never said that he was the *only* son. Indeed, he taught that those who would follow in his footsteps would do all that he had done and more. Therefore, you can conquer your astrology, transmute your past negative karma and reap the benefits of your positive karma. And, as Jesus and others who have followed in his footsteps have done, you can fulfill your divine plan and destiny—you can Ascend!

But, Prophet explains, there is an exchange for you cannot gain your victory bowed down by negative karma. To transmute our karmic burden and enter the New Age consciousness we need to expand our understanding of karma in our lives. In the traditions of the East, the soul's karmic debt binds him to the wheel of rebirth for lifetimes unending. Nonetheless, Prophet taught that karma is more than just the simple equation that what you have sowed you will reap. Karma is the very essence of life; all you are is the result of all you have been. It

---

[27] The term "Great White Brotherhood" refers not to race but to the aura of white light that surrounds these immortals beings, known as the Ascended Masters, who have risen from every race and walk of life. Messengers are trained and anointed by the Ascended Masters to deliver divine teachings, messages and prophecies to guide mankind. To learn more, see SummitLighthouse.org/Teachers/Mark-and-Elizabeth-Prophet/Messengers-Mark-and-Elizabeth-Clare-Prophet.html.

[28] Paraphrased from excerpts in, *The Path of Personal Christhood,* by Elizabeth Clare Prophet. See www.TSL.org/2010/01/video-the-path-of-personal-christhood-part-1,- and www.TSL.org/2010/01/video-the-path-of-personal-christhood-part-2.

is said that the past cannot be changed, only the present and the future. But you can change the past by learning to invoke the *Violet Transmuting Flame* (the action of the Holy Spirit, which acts as a cosmic eraser transmuting your karma and removing your burdens). There are no free tickets into heaven. The path of Personal Christhood is arduous. Self-transformation, like anything worth striving for, is hard work. But the reward is great![28]

THE MISSING KEY—THE MEANING OF I AM

What is the inner meaning of the phrase, I AM? The question is an Arian one. In the Torah is written that God revealed his name to Moses—I AM THAT I AM. Therefore, when we say, "I AM," we are saying, "God in me is." In giving the following Heart Meditation by the Ascended Master St. Germain, dictated through the Messenger Elizabeth Clare Prophet, remember that when you say, I AM, you are saying, "God in me is..."

> *I AM the Light of the Heart*
> *Shining in the darkness of being*
> *And changing all into the golden treasury*
> *Of the Mind of Christ.*
>
> *I AM projecting my love out into the world*
> *To erase all errors*
> *And to break down all barriers.*
>
> *I AM the power of Infinite Love,*
> *Amplifying itself*
> *Until it is victorious, world without end!*

How wondrous to behold the spiritually transformed Aries individual in whom thought and selfless action are one! His heart is one with God's own heart. His consciousness, being and world are in perfect alignment with divine purpose. No longer is he ruled by volatile Mars, but rather, by Mercury—"the diamond shining mind of God."

The mystery that the Aries Hero, not at the end of his journey but freed into his next one, discovers and declares is that he is conceived in love. Secure within himself and in control of the life force flowing within him, rather than being controlled by it, he declares, "God is in me and I Am in God—I Am That I Am!"

2.

♌

Leo

Symbol . . . . **The Lion**

Born . . . . July 23 ~ August 22

Archetype . . . . *The Knight*

Key Phrase . . . . *I Love*

Element . . . . **Fire**

Cross . . . . **Fixed-Love**

House . . . . **Fifth:**
Creative self-expression, children, romance,
drama & entertainment, recreation
& sports, financial speculation

Ruler . . . . **Sun**

Esoteric Ruler . . . . **Sun**

Polarity . . . . **Aquarius**

Chakra . . . . Seat of the Soul

Anatomy . . . . . Heart, back & spine, vena cava

Spiritual Qualities . . . **Leadership of the heart, magnanimity, gratitude & joy, creative self-expression, valor, loyalty, love of children, sacrifice**

Vulnerable to . . . . . . *Pride & vanity, emotional density &
hardness of heart, ingratitude &
carelessness, self-righteous anger*

Must Acquire . . . . **Soul-sensitivity, gratitude &
a humble heart, patience & care**

Napoleon Bonaparte • Queen Elizabeth • Mario Moreno • Lucille Ball • Eduardo García

THE SUN IN LEO

Your vision will become clear only when you can look into your own heart. Who looks outside, dreams; who looks inside, awakes.

—Carl Jung (July 26, 1875)

LOVE'S RADIANCE!

Leo is the sign of kings whose symbol is the Lion. Even persons of this sign born into humble circumstances walk with a noble bearing. A Fire sign on the Fixed-Love Cross, Leo imparts fire of heart! Leos typically glow with self-assurance, *joie de vivre,* and generosity of spirit. Powerful and yet playful, they like having fun and enjoy making others happy. A large, magnetic, and charismatic auric presence makes it easy to spot the Leo in a crowd. People sense a radiance beaming from his chest area. His smile lights up the room!

Leo represents the soul, the recipient of *solar* awareness. The soul feels compelled to express that love in which she was conceived.[29]

In so doing, the soul taps into and brings forth the power potential of her original source in Spirit. Leo relates to the Seat-of-the-Soul chakra, which is located midway between the navel and the base of the spine. Here the soul abides. This chakra is the point of equilibrium, the center of the life force, or *chi*, which from here is distributed throughout the physical body. The soul senses that she is in her comfort zone, a kind of cradle, when nestled in the Seat-of-the-Soul. However, this is one of those lower chakras in which the soul's—and the planet's— negative karma is stored in what is called esoterically the electronic belt.[30]

Eventually the soul, like a knight on a quest, must clear away the thorny karmic hedges and make its way up to the Heart chakra and then to the upper chakras—the Throat, Third Eye and Crown. The Heart chakra is the ultimate distribution point of the light of the sacred fire that descends from the Divine Presence (the Father) through the Crown chakra, and which then rises from the

---

[29] The soul, in its relationship to Spirit, is feminine in nature whereas a soul may refer to a person in a male or in a female incarnation.

[30] "The electronic belt is the negative forcefield or spiral of density that surrounds the lower portion of man's physical form and is created through the misqualification of energy. Extending from the waist to beneath the feet, the electronic belt is similar in shape to a large kettledrum and contains the aggregate records of an individual's negative thoughts and feelings." From *The Enemy Within,* by Elizabeth Clare Prophet, p. 219.

Base-of-the-Spine chakra (the Mother). But to reach the Heart, the soul must set its sails and bravely leave its abode to journey through the Solar Plexus chakra, a vortex of powerful emotional energies. There the soul must meet, resolve and transmute aspects of self that are in turmoil, wounded, and therefore reactive and unpredictable.

CARPE DIEM—SEIZE THE DAY!

Having strong wills, Leos can work—and love—with unparalleled drive and conviction. They do not typically work laboriously or slowly. However, they often seem to wait until the last minute while other, more plodding, cautious and industrious types often feel exasperated at the Leo person's seeming ignorance of the work at hand. But then in a flash, a snap of the fingers, they spring into action and it is done—with excellence! Many Leo students approach their studies in a similar manner. In Leo we see perhaps a less dynamic but more creative and ingenious twist on the Aries motto, *do it now!*

One Leo executive woman's gold ring bore the inscription *carpe diem—seize the day!* Even while still in the Seat-of-the-Soul chakra, the soul intuitively grasps what escapes the mind. While the mind analyzes and deduces, seeking to find meaning and answers, knowledge and information, the soul intuitively knows. For example, when we take a soul reading of someone or something as a first impression, this prompting from the soul is almost invariably correct.

So, Leos typically get hunches; they wait until they feel thus inspired and then move into action. *They just know!* When my Leo son, Eugenio, was thirteen years old, he said, out of the blue: "Mom, I want to meet your cousin who lives in New York." I had not seen that cousin for over a decade, but knowing how important it was that I take Eugenio's inner promptings to heart, I assented. A date was made; a meeting happened. The cousin ended up taking an interest in my sons and became a major influence, mentor and guide for Eugenio. Most Leos have great confidence in the soul barometer and so, in love, in money, and in life in general, they are known to take risks, which often pay off—but not always! In any event, they gain experience and mature spiritually. As Leos become more attuned with the heart, as they access the light of the upper chakras, they intuitively check their soul readings with the wisdom of the heart!

LOVE'S TRANSFORMING FIRES

Leos express the soul's desire to love and to be loved. All of us have a chance to love, somewhere, somehow. Love is simple; karma is complex. To love is to unlock the soul's hidden treasures, reach heights that seem to touch heaven itself, experience inexpressible joy—but to love is also to risk being hurt and humiliated. The Leo personality instinctively masks his seeming imperfections—

CAPRICORN
SAGITTARIUS
AQUARIUS
SCORPIO
PISCES
LIBRA
ARIES
VIRGO
TAURUS
GEMINI
CANCER
EARTH
FIRE
AIR
WATER
CARDINAL
MUTABLE
FIXED
+ = masculine
– = feminine
Leo:
5th House
Fixed-
Love Cross
Fire Element

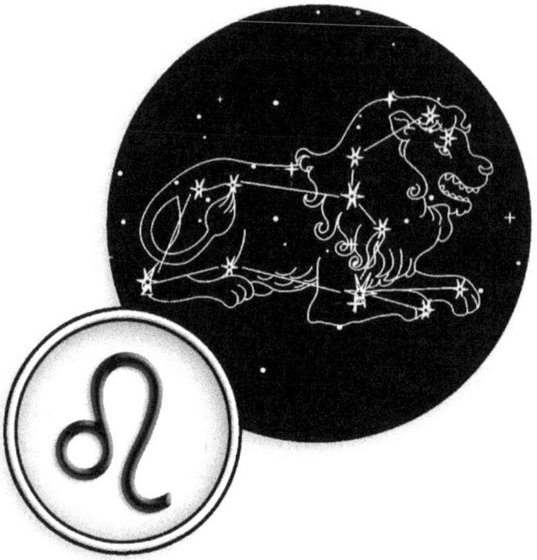

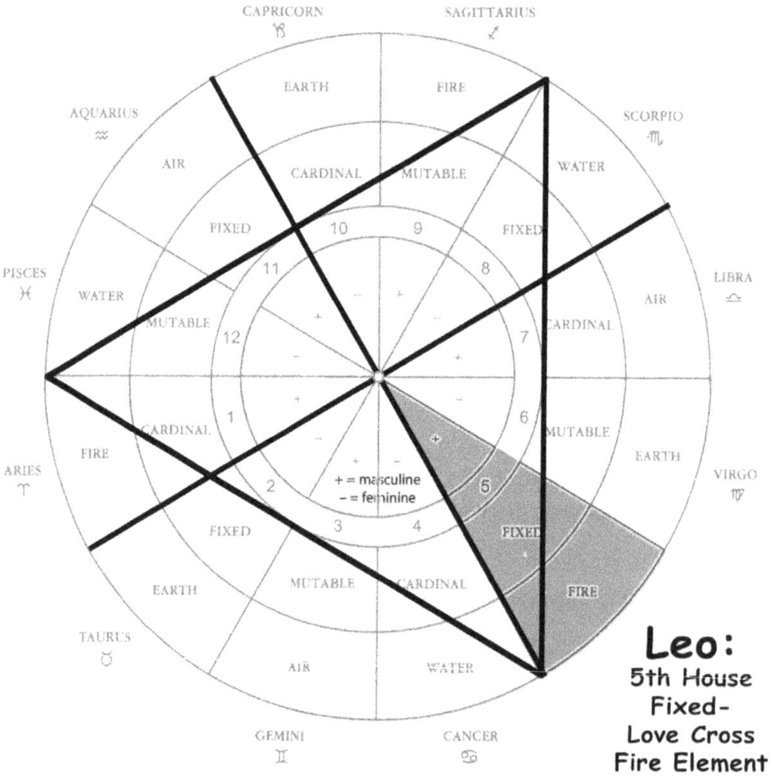

after all, Leo lions are natural-born leaders who stand tall, proud and fearless! But to love, the Leo soul must be willing to be vulnerable and unafraid of having his weaknesses exposed. If he chooses to shut out love, the rushing fount of creative energy will no longer be available to him. If he would love and be loved, he must be willing to open his heart and submit his soul to love's transforming fires.

The Leo type, if he dares, is destined to discover, become, and hence teach others one of love's great mysteries. Only when he resolves to love with all his heart and with all his soul will the means to unravel this riddle be revealed to him.

LEO — THE ANCHOR FOR THE AQUARIAN AGE

We understand Leo to be the fiery polarity of Aquarius and therefore the anchor for the Aquarian Age. When we think of Aquarius we think of love, divine love — the love between the soul and the Divine Presence, between the Zadek[31] or Guru and the disciple, and between close friends. But Aquarius is an Air sign and as such can be aloof and impersonal. Leo balances Aquarian detachment with personal warmth and the carefree joy we see in the little child.

Indeed, the consciousness of the Hero in Leo is that of a little child.[32] Unpretentious, humble, full of awe and wonder, devoted to father and mother, he lives in the moment, celebrating life with every pulse of his heart! The gift of Leo (second Sign in the Fire Triplicity) to the self-realized man in Aries (first Fire sign) is that of magnificent, creative self-expression and the bringing forth of love in the grand tapestry of colors, sounds and textures that we call Life!

LEO RULES ENTERTAINMENT

Most Leos are very aware of their effect upon their audience, as if the eyes of the world were upon them — indeed, they usually are! The Leo person wears his heart on his sleeve; you're inspired by his largesse of heart, his magnanimity, and his romantic idealism. Blessed by the Sun, he strides with the appearance of one endowed with an extra dose of good fortune. Anything but dull, Leos do make life fun — but oh, watch out! Mr. Leo can convince an Eskimo to buy a refrigerator in winter! It's not that he's out to trick you, but if he is convinced that you need it, so are you. Leo children pick up early in life that one of their most valuable assets is their irresistibly sweet smile. They seek center stage. While they

---

[31] Tzadik/Zadik/Sadiq (*tsa-dik,* "righteous one") This is a title given to personalities considered righteous, such as Biblical figures and, later, to spiritual masters. See www.Wikipedia.org/wiki/Tzadik.
[32] "And said, Verily I say unto you, except ye be converted, and become as little children, ye shall not enter into the kingdom of heaven." Matthew 18:3

do sulk when ignored or thwarted, they don't tend to sit in puddles of emotion; they know the value of putting on a happy face. After all, the show must go on!

The Lion's sign is ubiquitously present in the charts of celebrities: "The Queen of Comedy," Lucille Ball (born August 6, 1911); Robert De Niro (August 17,1943), sometimes called the greatest actor of his time; Spanish singer and actor Antonio Banderas (August 10, 1960), whose mixture of Leonine charm, good looks and daring made him the perfect choice for portraying the legendary swordsman Zorro in *The Mask of Zorro* and *The Legend of Zorro*. And the list goes on!

CANTINFLAS—PLAYING THE (UNLIKELY) HERO

The Mexican comic actor, screenwriter and producer, Mario Moreno, popularly known as *Cantinflas,* was born on August 12, 1911. Cantinflas starred in 50 films and became a household name for generations of Mexicans and Mexican-Americans. Mexicans identified Cantinflas with their national identity! Moreno said that his greatest desire was to see a world of greater peace and tranquility. His artistic goal was always to make people laugh and to add joy to their lives. Many Leos have that special quality of making you laugh at jokes that aren't even funny—it's not the content, really, but the sparkle. Somehow, in the laughter, you relax and awaken joy within yourself that you had forgotten about in the hustle and bustle of life. An intuitive, rich use of language, peppered with body language, gestures, and facial expressions, often subtle, underplayed but understood in the common cultural code, is so much a part of Mexican culture. It is a cultural art form so curiously particular to that land that outsiders have difficulty grasping its nuances. Cantinflas brought this rich tradition to life with great humor and ingenuity.

Growing up in the rough-and-tumble neighborhood of Tepito, in Mexico City, Mario Moreno had street smarts. He started out working in a traveling circus where his clownish antics became part of his signature performance. In a variety of roles—fireman, barber, priest, bricklayer, shoeshine man, impoverished *campesino* (peasant farmer), lifeguard (who barely knows how to swim), street vendor, or slapstick bullfighter thrown into the ring—Cantinflas often plays the poor man, often of little if any formal education, who nevertheless is blessed with a resourceful nature, a rich imagination, and most of all, a singular combination of innocence and astuteness! Cantinflas uses his wits and his way with words to artfully make his way through life and outwit those who put obstacles in his path. The colorful characters he plays capture the soul and hearts of his people in all their complexity. Cantinflas gets away with his outrageous antics and poorly thought-out schemes by virtue of his big and tender *Leo* heart. Childlike himself, he is loved by children to whom he often plays the loving godfather. And again in a Leo-like posture, despite the slapstick silliness and absurdity, which paint him the fool, he inexplicably ends up the hero—and what Leo doesn't? He is not only forgiven for the countless mishaps his senseless behavior creates, but he is also honored and loved! He has often been compared to both Groucho Marx and Charlie Chaplin, who once called him the best actor alive!

Moreno, who helped write many of his own scripts, always had a social message targeted to a world he envisioned of greater love and humanity. He used humor to expose corruption and injustice, but somehow kept everyone applauding him. For example, he supports a common disgust for policemen who abuse their power and privilege, in roles where he confounds and mocks them, but then he turns around and plays the police agent 777, uniform and all, who wins the day; he honors the bravery of good policemen.

His characteristic way of using language to confute, confound, bewilder, speak truth, and expose social injustice, indirectly but precisely, always won hearts and left you wondering, "What did he say?" He became so popularized that *La Real Academia Española* decided to include in its dictionary the verb *Cantinflear* (to speak like Cantinflas) and *cantifleado* (the state of having been stumped by someone confounding you by speaking as did Cantinflas). See Moreno's natal chart with analysis.

Mario Moreno "Cantinflas" captured Mexico's soul and touched the hearts of her people. He used film and Leo charm and appeal to make people laugh while being a catalyst for political and social change.

The hero is a part that Leos love to play, especially Leo men, who, like Cantinflas, embroil themselves in dangerous plots and dramas aimed at rescuing a helpless woman or child. A key life lesson in Leo can be learned from Cantinflas' heroic roles. Especially Leo men need to beware of falling into the trap of playing the hero, rescuing the damsel in distress, which often includes a jealous (if ex) lover or husband. This not only ensnares him in endless dramas but also can lead to falling in love (through Leo's Achilles' heel of pride and vanity) with women who cling to him as *"my hero!"* Interestingly, Cantinflas has roles, such as that in *El Bolero de Raquel (Raquel's Shoeshiner)* and *El Bombero Atómico (The Atomic Fireman)* where, after his heroics win the day, the story ends happily, but he wipes a tear, smiles, and returns to his life, while those he rescued move on with their own. (When he does win the pretty woman, she is more likely attracted to his inherent goodness.)

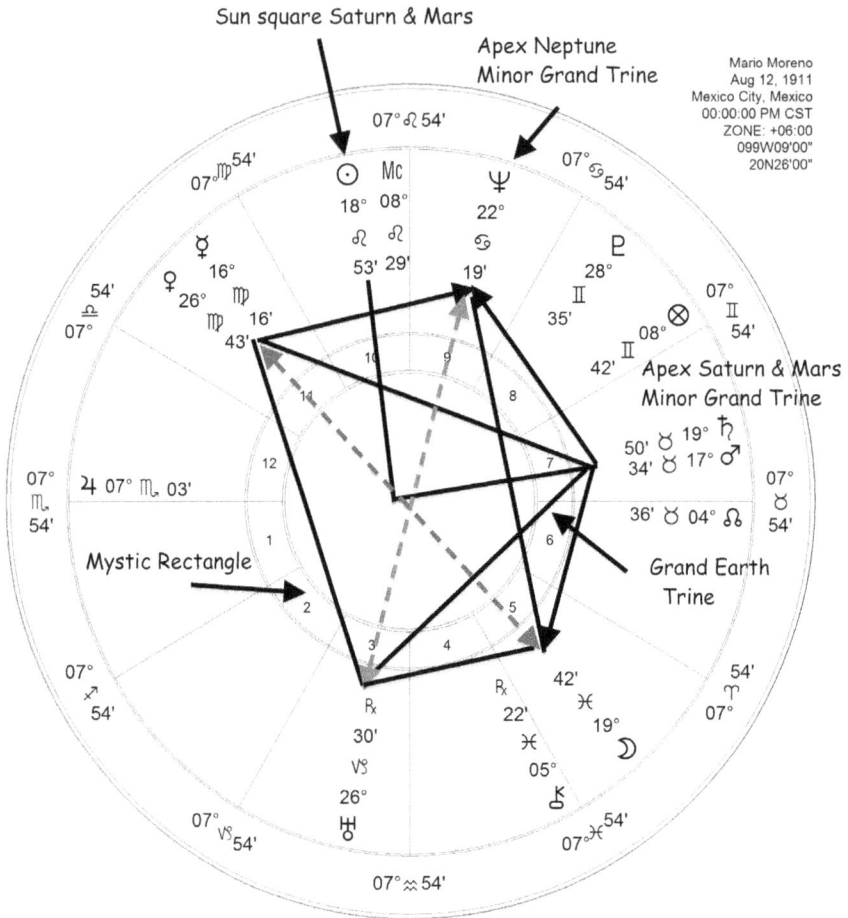

Sun square Saturn & Mars

Apex Neptune
Minor Grand Trine

Mario Moreno
Aug 12, 1911
Mexico City, Mexico
00:00:00 PM CST
ZONE: +06:00
099W09'00"
20N26'00"

Apex Saturn & Mars
Minor Grand Trine

Mystic Rectangle

Grand Earth
Trine

[33] Moreno's natal Leo Sun highlights his positive spirit, natural leadership and play-ful personality. The Sun is also tightly square Mars conjoined Saturn in Taurus—he was born into humble circumstances and had no easy rides. But this challenging coupling is part of Grand Earth Trine (fortitude, persistence, productivity) involving Mercury in its ruling sign, Virgo (a way with words), widely conjoined Venus (art), all trine Uranus (novelty) in Capri-corn. The Moon—which describes the energy of the mother, emotions and *el pueblo* (the people)—aspects almost every other planet in Moreno's chart. Like his character Cantinflas, he was caring, loving and personal. His Moon in compassionate Pisces trines Neptune; both are sextile Mars and Saturn. Neptune, which rules Pisces, is in Cancer, the apex planet of a second Minor Grand Trine. These multiple trines and sextiles denote Moreno's rich imagi-nation and charitable nature, his ability to resourcefully and imaginatively utilize his natural gifts to bring forth his dream (Neptune) of a more loving world. Note the Mystic Rectan-gle—the tension of the crisscrossing oppositions awakens awareness of conflict and need for change while the sextiles suggest intelligent, innovative solutions.

Leos are natural-born leaders. Moreno began as a pioneer in Mexican cinema and emerged as a business leader, taking a daring role in his country's often dangerous and tangled labor politics. Cantinflas was seen as a spokesperson for the downtrodden, a key player in the people's early struggle against the dominance and control of the PRI political party over labor. Moreno was a political force in the shaping of Mexico's future.[33]

TAKING CENTER STAGE

Famous Leos leave an unforgettable presence, as if they were destined to play a part and play it well, whatever their field of endeavor. Consider the following examples: "King of the Wild Frontier" folk hero, frontiersman, and congressman, Davy Crockett, born August 17, 1786; Annie Oakley, the sharp-shooting star of Buffalo Bill's Wild West Show, born August 13, 1860; Helena Blavatsky, the riveting and enigmatic founder of the Theosophical Society, born August 12, 1831; Guy Ballard, American mining engineer and founder of the I Am Movement, born July 28, 1878; Amelia Earhart, the first woman to fly solo across the Atlantic, whose life and career became legendary when she disappeared and was never found while flying over the Central Pacific Ocean in 1937, born July 24, 1897; Chef Julia Child, who brought French Cuisine to America, born August 15, 1912; and the dignified, iconic and much esteemed Jacqueline Kennedy Onassis (better known as Jackie), born July 28, 1929.

Leo is the sign of rulers, leaders, despots, dictators and showmen. Leo political personalities are noted for their charismatic presence, at times being treated almost as if they were movie stars: Venezuelan Simón Bolivar (July 24, 1783), Cuban Fidel Castro (August 13, 1926), Venezuelan Hugo Chavez (July 28, 1954), Bill Clinton (August 19, 1946), Barack Obama (August 4, 1961), and Mexican Felipe Calderon (August 18, 1962).

LOOK AT ME!

Leos are so likeable! But like him or not, you're not likely to ignore him. Even quiet, private Leos exhibit an understated but noticeable magnetism. Most Leos like getting attention, even as they enjoy lavishing attention upon another.[34]

With theatrical gestures peppered by comical antics, or with lavish pomp

---

[34] Especially when the Leo Sun is posited in the Fourth, Eighth, or Twelfth Houses, the natural houses of Cancer, Scorpio or Pisces, or when the Moon or rising sign is in more modest Virgo, we sometimes see a shy or overly self-conscious Leo personality. Sometimes when such souls reach maturity and obtain a degree of material or social success, their light begins to shine more radiantly. A buoyant sense of humor often is the first sign of this type of Leo stepping up to the plate!

and ceremony, or simply due to a magnetically attractive nature, the Leo personality commands: "Look at me!"

Or sometimes he has people talking about him because he insists, "Don't look at me." Beyond the pangs of abandonment and neglect, nothing hurts the Leo soul more than being denied the opportunity to express his love. When little lion cubs feel ignored, they're likely to see to it that they attract negative attention—in their minds, it's better than none at all!

Six brothers, ages fourteen to twenty-seven, were once chosen to represent their community at the State Fair. The seventeen-year-old, who happened to be a Leo, (unmistakable bright eyes, regal gait and warm, engaging smile) opted out: "I don't like these public events where everyone's eyes are on you," he remarked. "Well," a friend retorted, "everyone will be searching the crowd to find the missing brother." Looking as if he had been caught red-handed, he replied, "Okay, then, I'm in!"

APPLAUDING THE MASK

The Leo person may be quite caught up in himself—not necessarily in the narcissistic way of Scorpio, nor in the *me first* way of Aries, but simply because he hasn't realized yet that he is the beneficiary and the instrument, not the source, of the glorious solar energy pouring through him each day. Leo is ruled by the Sun. As the planets revolve around the Sun, he knows himself to be the center of his universe—an assumption confirmed by the fact that people tend to gravitate around him. While others might withdraw, he comes alive in the spotlight and thrives when entrusted with a position of command and authority. All else being equal, the Sun in Leo person in a managerial or leadership role is often at his creative best as he comes up with ingenious policies whose results speak for themselves while quickly implementing solutions others somehow missed. Self-possessed and with an unshakeable will, others believe in him and follow his lead because he believes in himself. In the Aquarian model—where people work in teams rather than in the old boss/underling relationship—the Leo team leader must actively engage his heart. He must be friendly and personable so his lead will not stir up jealousies or disempower his team members.

Acutely aware of the impressions they make, Leos often create convincing personas, behind which they may hide to further their ambitions. An 18-year-old Leo confessed, with a tinge of cynical awe and sad self-awareness, "When I become who I'm not, even my best friends applaud my mask." Leos typically like being liked—flattery is their Achilles' heel. Especially the younger, less spiritually mature Leo is vulnerable to this subtle form of pride. He loves getting praised and he can also dish it out—with flowers to match. But in his heart of hearts, the soul born with the Sun in Leo knows that nothing less than being genuine will do. A 27-year-old Leo man, in describing who he had to be in order to attract the woman he envisioned one day marrying, remarked, "I want to be a sincere man."

"THE BIONIC CHEF"—AN HONEST MAN

Thirty years old and feeling at the top of his game—life was good—my son, Eduardo García (August 4,1981), an avid outdoorsman, was hiking through the Montana woods one perfectly beautiful October morning when, in curiosity, he touched with his knife what appeared to be a dead baby bear and suddenly—he was electrocuted! (What he did not see was a mesh of live electrical wiring that had, in all probability, killed the bear and which sent 2400 volts of electricity through him!) With nine searing exit wounds, Eduardo somehow summoned the will to get to his feet and to walk three miles to get help. He was airlifted to the University of Utah Hospital. When he was rolled into the ICU Burn Unit, his nurse thought, "He looks like death with a heartbeat!" Miraculously surviving this encounter, which nearly claimed his life, and which would cost him his left hand—he would go through twenty-three surgeries to put his body back together—Eduardo determined that he would beat the odds that he might live to motivate others. I flew down to Salt Lake City to be with Eduardo the morning after the accident. (His sister Indra arrived on the scene when he was airlifted from Livingston and had not left his side.) From his hospital bed the next day, he spoke softly but resolutely, "I left behind the man I was on that forest floor, and I took up the man who I really am and am becoming—and I am an honest man!" Such simple declarations speak of the heart's in-

Chef Eduardo García's recipe for living life with a smile: "Never forget that as long as your heart is beating, you have the ability to write the story of your life. Decide to be positive and keep it up. Take advantage of every second of every day of your life and give whatever you do your best shot!"

tent, clear of all that would detour, delay, or misuse the ineffable power of love that the Leo person possesses to transform the soul and change the world!

Eduardo had always been on the go; as a classically trained chef working on yachts he had travelled near and far, and his personal warmth, kindheartedness and upbeat spirit had touched many souls. But somehow this life-changing event intensified within him *the will to be*, to squeeze the pulp, as he put it, out of every moment—and, through his example, to motivate others to do the same. Humble and charming, Eduardo's greatest joy is seeing others overcome adversity and win with a smile on their faces! On a nationally televised show, he was asked about learning how to cook with a prosthetic hand. He playfully explained, "I can grab things out of an oven and not get burnt. I don't cut my fingers anymore. I'm rockin' it!" Eduardo realized that even though he had to do it differently, "It was doable—that takes you away from the focus of *Woe is me!* to *Whoa, it's me!*" Eduardo epitomizes the Leonine positivity, indomitable will, and creative genius that lives life as art—key attributes helping natives of this sign to live to the fullest and reach their goals while jumping hurdles along the way!

SOUL SENSITIVITY & A HUMBLE HEART

The heart loves; the soul chooses. The Leo person must acquire soul sensitivity and a humble heart if he is to become the Leo Hero. Leos protect themselves from pain by hardening their hearts. The logic goes, "If I don't care, it won't hurt me." Such a tactic actually works to a certain degree and, in some traumatic situations, might serve as a survival mechanism against the unbearable grief of a broken heart; nevertheless, the karmic consequence of such a decision is that the heart becomes increasingly unfeeling and the soul insensitive. When Leos elect to harden their hearts, they are no longer sensitive—not to others or to their own Divine Presence. In such a state, the Leo individual may be uncharacteristically cruel, thoughtless and unappreciative.

In shutting out pain, Leos cannot receive the great solution—the peace born of faith, the healing balm that eventually results from embracing and courageously bearing the pain of love. When he elects to close the door to his heart, the debris of negative energy amassing around the heart weighs upon his soul, resulting in a kind of emotional density. For the moment, the soul's senses are silenced and the sun is obscured.

QUEEN MOTHER, MOTHER COURAGE

Lady Elizabeth Angela Bowes-Lyon was born on August 4, 1900. Throughout her life, she shone with Leonine dignity. Her charm, valor and captivating presence were legendary. Although born into the sign of Royalty, she did not covet the throne. When the smitten Prince Albert came courting and proposed, she refused him not once, but twice! She felt that entering royal life would mean that she would "never, ever again be free to think, speak, and act as I feel I really ought to." Leos are often quite adamant about what they will and will not do, a defining characteristic especially strong during their youth. Nevertheless, people born under the influence of the Sun in Leo often feel the call of inner obedience to duty. Once they make up their minds—and as a rule, they will allow no one to decide for them—they step up to the plate quite resolutely, as if to say *this was my choice all along*! And so, when Lady Elizabeth assented to marry Prince Albert and thus become the Duchess of York, she devoted herself fully and lovingly to her office. When the Duke of Windsor, King Edward VIII, abdicated the throne in 1936, his brother Albert took his place as King George VI, and Elizabeth became Queen.

Queen Mother Elizabeth (as she later came to be called to distinguish her from her daughter, Queen Elizabeth II) supported the King and boosted the morale of the people during the perilous times of World War II. When advised by the Cabinet to leave London or to send the children to Canada where they would be safe, she refused to go, even during the Blitz, when London was under siege from the Nazis. She declared with characteristic Leo backbone, faithfulness and resolve, "The children won't go without me. I won't leave the King. And the King will never leave." While her bright manner earned her the title of "the smiling Duchess," the Queen Mother was also known to possess "an indomitable spirit." Beneath the winsome smile and endearing personality, Leos can be quite set on their course of action. So popular was the Queen with the people that Hitler once called her "the most dangerous woman in Europe."[35]

When the Queen Mother visited Iran in 1975 at the invitation of Shah Mohammad Reza Pahlavi, the Iranians thought it strange that she spoke to everyone in the same manner, regardless of status or importance. True, the Leo personality may be prone to glamour; he may seek to impress others and through this weakness may be misled, even beguiled, by outer glitz; nonetheless, some Leos, like the Queen, enjoy wealth and are lovers of beauty and art, but are unimpressed by outer status or appearance. They relate easily to people of many different backgrounds, being endowed with a special quality of soul universality.

BLINDED BY THE SUN

While he can be downright bossy, even condescending in his native sense of superiority, the Leo individual is often curiously blind to his own weaknesses. An old astrological saying explains the Lion's propensity toward psychological

---

[35] For a synopsis of Queen Mother Elizabeth's life and contribution to her country, read www.TheGuardian.com/uk/2002/mar/30/queenmother.monarchy12.

blind spots: "The Sun is so bright that to look at it you have to cover your eyes." Some things he doesn't see; some things he doesn't want to see. Some things he won't be able to see until he recognizes and dissolves the recalcitrant arrogance that protects him from pain, but prevents him from truly loving.

Leos can be incredibly stubborn—for good or for ill. They don't want to be told what to do. Leo children (and some Leo grownups who refuse to grow up) pout when they don't get their way. What seems simply an infantile emotion emits a surprisingly heavy vibration, uncomfortably hard to endure for anyone close enough to experience it. Soul energy is deep, powerful, and charged with emotion. When qualified with negativity, the weight can feel terribly ponderous. In Leo adults, such childish tantrums typically prove very damaging to intimacy.

Normally affectionate and attentive, the Leo person when riled has been known to roar with anger, feign apathy, be petulant, or become cruelly cold. (Leos who feign indifference and boredom are masking their hurt.) Dignity and honor are not old-fashioned attitudes for these natives of the Sun. Their very posture demands respect!

The Lion gives out orders better than he takes them. Regal and proud, he's not about to abdicate his throne! The Leo child typically has bouts of resistance, insisting, "Don't push me!" But when he loves and respects his parents, he can be the most devoted of all children. Despite his imperial demeanor, the person born in Leo has a tender, soft side. Underneath the armor of a seemingly perfect personality, he's sentimental and a touch naïve. His open-heartedness gets him into trouble over and over again.

The Leo mother watches over her brood like a fierce lioness protecting her cubs. The Leo father can be tough in his expectations, but his playful nature endears him to his children. Leo parents need to guard against being overly indulgent with their children. Leos can be incredibly unaware of their tendency to dominate others, as if they were kings and all lesser mortals needed to submit. As children they are challenged to obey, as team members to work in cooperation with the group, and as parents and spouses to avoid being overly domineering.

WHO WROTE THE BOOK OF LOVE?

Leo governs the heart. Engagingly warm-hearted, loving and kind, Leos do not usually live in their heads, but rather in their hearts. Leo is the sign of romance—the expression of joy at the discovery of one of life's greatest treasures. Flowers, great food, fun outings, theatre and sports events and, oh, the declarations of a beating heart—plus, as exemplified in Leo actor, director, film producer, and businessman, Robert Redford, that self-confident, charismatic smile and Lion-like mane of hair! Who could resist the Leo in love? They can be gallant, sweeping the object of their affection off his or her feet. One 24-year-old Leo man advised his mother on how to keep her relationship with his father fresh: "Mom, when you look in the mirror, always think, this is my first date with the man I love!"

A certain type of Leo epitomizes the chivalrous knight or the courtly lady. Romantic and idealistic, these Leos hold to high moral standards and expectations. They typically put off marriage if their partner comes up short, perhaps wisely; but often, unfortunately, for perfect people don't exist. Another kind of Leo is more the conqueror than the knight—rather than love's radiance he emits a powerful, sexual magnetism. He laps up the adulation laid upon him and is typically subject to one of pride's most dangerous illusions—glamour! Money, expensive clothes, outer beauty, fancy cars, and expensive jewelry mean more to him than the heart's sincerity! Let the Leo native beware that drugs and alcohol can dull the soul's senses while at the same time enhancing selfish and narcissistic behavior.

Young Leos especially are vulnerable to such amorous detours. Most Leos mature out of what amounts to a *Don Juan* phase, but often only after having broken a heart (or many) along the way. They must then overcome the torturous guilt experienced within their own souls when they awaken and realize how they have hurt others—and themselves! At last, older and wiser, they seek and strive to be worthy of a lasting and solid relationship and often prove to be the most devoted of companions.

Astrologer Alan Leo, himself a Leo, born August 7th, 1860,[36] claimed that in his Sun sign could be found the weakest and the strongest of individuals. He explains that some natives of this sign possess considerable self-control over their naturally ardent feelings. These people are able to influence many people by their ability to "combine the practical with the philosophical and the ideal with the real." On the other hand, those Leos who "turn their forces downward," being led by their strong passions and sympathetic natures, may become "weak, dissolute characters."[37]

Alan Leo's observations hold true today. Sexual energy, esoterically called the Kundalini or the sacred fire, is very potent in this sign, for Leo is the sign of creation. Fervent in love, romantic and good-humored, souls born under this fiery love sign must learn to manage their intense tempers and passionate natures. They must discipline the life force or risk becoming enslaved to it.

When we put on the mask of non-reality in Aries, our soul's capacity to truly love in Leo is compromised. So, to the extent that he is selfishly absorbed in his own needs, even the most amorous and gallant of Leos will, consciously or perhaps subconsciously, woo to his own personal advantage. For him, the ends justify the means. Perhaps he is consciously scheming or subconsciously handling

---

[36] Alan Leo was born William Frederick Allan. He later took the name of his Sun Sign as a pseudonym.

[37] See *Astrology for All,* by Alan Leo (L.N. Fowler & Co., Ltd., 1971)

his uncertainties, but often he believes his convictions justify his actions. Leos in love can be excessively loyal. They feel deeply wounded at the loss of love, regardless of whether a break-up is the best decision for them or not. While they may hold on too tightly, once they walk away they do not usually look back. Whatever the case, experience will teach the Leo that in the long run selfish attitudes will boomerang back against him. Being willful, he's apt to learn "the heart way" the hard way!

THE PROUD CONQUEROR

Napoleon Bonaparte, born August 15, 1769, is a classic example of great Leonine qualities gone awry. Napoleon is considered by many to be one of the greatest military commanders in history. Rising from obscurity to become the self-proclaimed emperor of Europe, his exploits were such as to become the stuff of legends. Although small in stature at 5-foot-7, portraits of Napoleon reveal his Leo-like strength, majesty, and sense of invincibility. He was surrounded by admirers and popular with the people; his victories were celebrated with due pomp and ceremony. Biographers have called

Napoleon Bonaparte is regarded as one of the greatest military leaders in Western History., "Power is my mistress," Napoleon once said to the politician Pierre-Louis Roederer, "I've done too much for her conquest to let anyone abduct or even covet her." But this proud attitude set him up for defeat. *(Jacques-Louis David, 1802, oil on canvas)*

---

[38] Napoleon's natal chart is fascinating. It is dominated by a challenging Sun-based T-square (extreme focus on self): Jupiter in Scorpio (intensely passionate vision) opposes Uranus in Taurus, and both planets square the Sun (ego) in the Tenth House of command (if his 11 am birth time is correct). Here we see Napoleon, the visionary, the strategist, the bold leader—commanding, authoritative, and highly self-centered. As often happens in the charts of those thrust into extraordinary scenarios, the ends of this tense T-square tie into fortuitous trines. Uranus in Taurus, Mars in Virgo (the general's position), conjoined Neptune (the myth), and Pluto powerfully placed in Capricorn, form a galvanizing Grand Earth Trine. Saturn in Cancer, Jupiter in Scorpio, and Chiron in Pisces form a Grand Water Trine. These two interlaced Grand Trines approach being a Grand Sextile, an unusual configuration

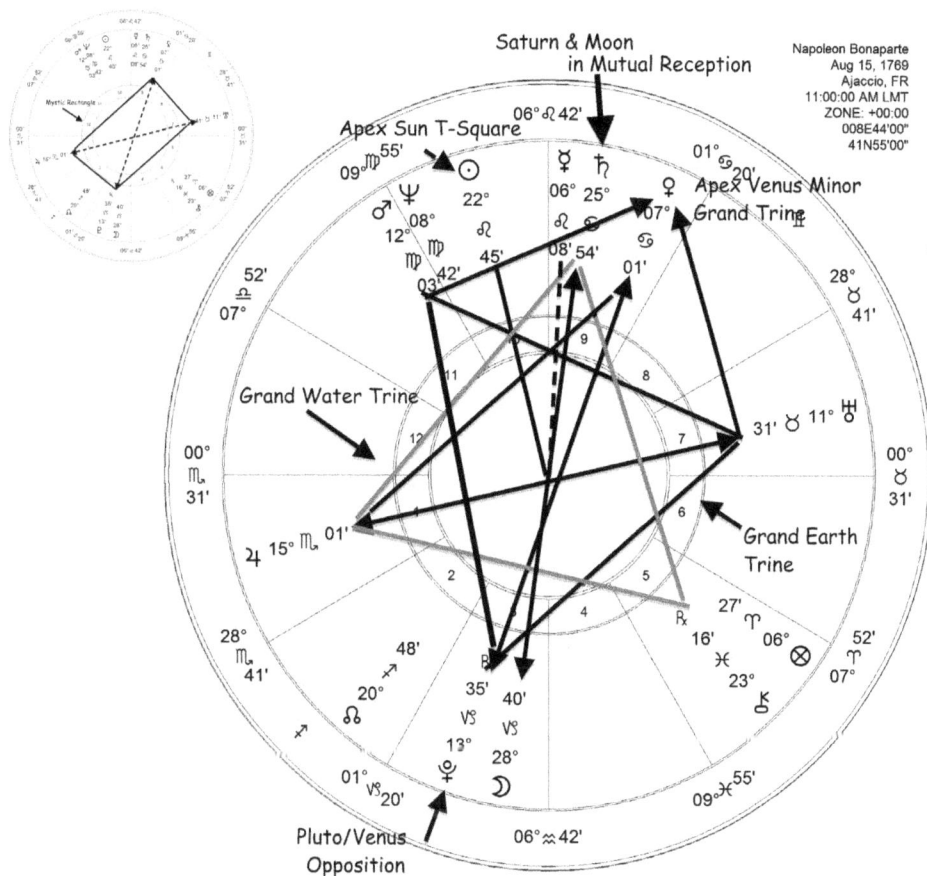

Napoleon Bonaparte
Aug 15, 1769
Ajaccio, FR
11:00:00 AM LMT
ZONE: +00:00
008E44'00"
41N55'00"

Saturn & Moon in Mutual Reception

Apex Sun T-Square

Apex Venus Minor Grand Trine

Grand Water Trine

Grand Earth Trine

Pluto/Venus Opposition

his rise to power meteoric. His ambition knew no bounds. Beyond any errors in military campaigns, he made a fatal Leo mistake—he proudly began to believe himself to be the origin of his power, and so, he met his Waterloo. Whatever exploits destiny puts before the Leo-born individual, no conquest is greater than that of gaining mastery over the lesser self. The Leo individual would do well to learn from Napoleon's example: *Be humble, lest you be humiliated!*[38]

suggesting genius. A Mystic Rectangle (see insert) formed by the crisscrossing Jupiter/Uranus and Venus/Pluto oppositions heightens tension, conflict, daring and vision. Note that Saturn in Cancer opposes the Moon in Capricorn—a weighty influence, these planets are nonetheless stimulated by being in mutual reception (each planet is placed in the opposing planet's ruling sign). Here we see Napoleon's reaction to the trying circumstance of his birth: Corsica had just been taken over by the French; his relationship with his mother (Moon), who was very influential in his life, but who was also quite harsh (Saturn); a degree of hardness within himself, a lack of mercy toward others; the many tests of power that marked his life. This complex astrological picture helps us understand Napoleon's meteoric rise and eventual fall from power and ultimate exile—not inevitable, but a consequence of his blindness that his ambition and pride had gotten out of hand.

DISSOLVING HARDNESS OF HEART

Although they may be keenly sensitive and truly compassionate, Leos typically deal with hardness of heart to a greater or lesser extent. Some natives of this Fire sign just don't get it! Others, assessing the feedback they receive in interpersonal relationships, may in the course of their lives come to desire greater soul-sensitivity.

An actual dialogue that took place between an empathetic Piscean woman and her Leo friend illustrates the point. She just couldn't grasp why he didn't understand her sentiments. Finally, she asked him, "Are you capable of sensing someone else's feelings?" The Leo man replied, "No, I sense my own feelings." Piscean woman: "End of conversation!"

What are the symptoms that the Leo person has closed his heart? You will know when his expression is cold and heartlessly matter-of-fact, when he is careless with his or others' possessions and even with his/their money, and when vanity creeps into his consciousness. Regardless of circumstance, hot cheeks, a heated bristling of the spine, the bursting forth of self-righteous anger, or even an intense burning sensation within the physical heart (distinguishable from the warmth of the heart that loves), are all warning signs of pride's presence. Promiscuous behavior often reflects brooding and perhaps buried anger. A cold heart can become a cruel heart, as if to punish life for inflicting upon him the pain of the loss of love! This is when the Leo native must catch himself, let go of his fear of appearing vulnerable, and open his heart. The fear of pain must be conquered by the desire to love selflessly.

To open his heart to love, the Leo person must ask himself when he first willed to harden his heart so as to not to feel pain. Perhaps he does so habitually, or perhaps he reacted this way during a crisis he may recall. However, more often the cause lies at a forgotten point in time, perhaps in his childhood or during a past life. To the extent that he has become insensitive to others, the answer will elude him. Only the mercy of divine love can dissolve the encrusted substance that has calcified within his feeling world over time. The Sun in Leo person must will this change and consciously work with the soul, his inner child, comforting and assuring him step-by-step so he will not lose the way. Purifying the soul's intention and releasing its inner power-potential is painful, but there is no other way. To neglect such a labor is to risk not only the atrophying of beauty within the soul, but also to hazard actual problems with the physical heart. Purifying the spiritual heart on time helps prevent or minimize the onset of heart *disease* or heart *dysfunction,* so common to natives of this sign.

---

[39] "But Jesus said, Suffer the little children, and forbid them not, to come unto me: for of such is the kingdom of heaven." Matthew 19:14

SUFFER THE LITTLE CHILDREN...[39]

Leo rules children. Aspects to the Leo native's Sun, plus any planets in the Fifth House and to a lesser extent, the house upon whose cusp Leo is posited, can reveal much about his children. Certainly, there is no greater expression of creativity than the co-creation of life with God. One day it will be recognized that the child's soul is very much involved in the gestation process.

Childlike himself, the Leo person's *dharma*, his life's work, often involves children and their affairs. He must recognize the difference between being child-like, spontaneous, looking at life with wonder—that special quality of joy in being connected to the higher worlds, and being childish spoiled and petulant. To be a parent or a mentor of youth in some capacity is to know the meaning of self-sacrifice, a spiritual quality of love in Leo. The loving Leo parent opens his heart, allowing it to be purged of selfishness. Giving gladly without thought of reward, he sacrifices his own pleasure, curbing his freedom when necessary in order to love a child that needs his care.

As is often the case with royalty, little Leos often take the good things in life for granted and benefit when taught as children to give thanks and show appreciation for the gifts of life and for what others do to help them. Leo children need to be taught to be courteous and polite. The cultivation of good manners and gratitude during childhood is an essential key to his future happiness. "Please" *IS* the magic word, because you are teaching the child to recognize that what he receives is given in love and not through obligation. Learning to say, "Thank you," will teach him to curb his sense of entitlement. Hence, he will acquire appreciation and respect, not only for his elders, but also for himself. While he thrives on well-deserved praise for his efforts, the young Leo is often particularly hurt by adult criticism. Being treated with respect and courtesy gives him the example he needs.

Leo rules romance. Even young lions can be quite chivalrous! One Leo High School Senior had the biggest account in his town at the local florist. When he was in 6th grade, he began his first job as an entrepreneur (many Leos prefer to be their own boss), earning 50 cents a shot by writing love letters for his friends. One read:

Dear Sally,

You are in my thoughts night and day. I cannot concentrate in Math class, thinking about how I will finally get to see you at recess. I can't wait for the recess bell to sound.

Till then, your friend,
Shorty

The picture of the boy Krishna, putting his hand into the butter pot and helping himself, can serve to remind the parent of the Leo child (or any child) to not be overly severe, but to allow the child's soul to flower! Sometimes the neighbors reacted angrily when they discovered that Little Krishna had been at it again, stealing their butter! But soon they came to see that the boy's presence brought them so many blessings, that they would put out their butter jars so he would visit their homes and take generously. Like Krishna, the Leo child's love and laughter bring joy and happiness, blessings and warmth.

Most Leo children are outgoing, friendly and generous. Playful and funny, they tend to be the center of attention. Even the more subdued Leo child expresses strongly charged emotions. Young Leonine reactions can be sharp and indignant and at times disturbingly and surprisingly cold. He tends to be strong-willed and determined to accomplish whatever he sets his mind on doing. But he can be stubborn, willful and impervious to advice.

Leo children often do well and benefit when participating in youth programs where merits can be earned and true leadership skills developed. Many Leo young persons enjoy caring for and playing with younger children. Leo is the sign of amusement and recreation. Most Leo children enjoy parties and gatherings. They respond to lessons that make learning fun! Of course, life is not all fun and games. The Leo child may need to learn to do the job or finish his work, simply because it needs to be done.

Many Leos feel a special connection with animals and pets. Caring for a pet may prove to be a vital aspect in the Leo child's education and happiness. In addition to his soul's connection with animals and nature, he grows by learning to care for and be responsible for his elemental friend.

Although he tends to be strong, the Leo child also has a more hidden, fragile side. He is not one generally to hold grudges, but trust, once broken, is not easily repaired with this child.

LEO & THE LION OF JUDAH

Leo has long been associated with the Lion of Judah. In Genesis we read the story of Judah, the patriarch Jacob's fourth son. Judah founded the tribe of Israel bearing his name. Now, the symbol of the tribe of Judah is the Lion, dating back to the dying Jacob's blessing upon Judah recorded in Genesis.[40]

Judah signifies "praise of God." Although Judah was not without error — he sold his brother Joseph into slavery[41] — in the end, he learned his lesson and was repentant. Twenty years after betrayal by his brothers, Joseph, then a ruler in Egypt, was not recognized by his brothers when they came to collect grain during the seven-year famine. When Joseph threatened to keep the youngest brother Benjamin in Egypt, Judah confessed his earlier crime and begged to be taken as a slave in Benjamin's place. Joseph then revealed his identity to Judah and his other brothers and all were reunited.[42]

When transferring his inheritance from Reuben, the first born, who lost the blessing due to his sins, to Judah, Jacob prophesied:

> *Judah, you are he whom your brothers shall praise; Your hand shall be on the neck of your enemies; Your father's children shall bow down before you. Judah is a lion's whelp; From the prey, my son, you have gone up. He bows down, he lies down as a lion; And as a lion, who shall rouse him? The scepter shall not depart from Judah, nor lawgiver from between his feet, until Shiloh come, and unto Him the people shall adhere. (KJV)*

The Lion, then, is a symbol of might,[43] majesty and dominion. Jacob prophesied that the Kings of Israel would come through Judah's lineage. And that eventually so would *Shiloh*, a name associated with the coming of the Messiah.

Astrologers throughout the centuries have described Leo's stars as prophesying the coming of the Promised One. The constellation Leo consists of many stars, among them Regulus, one of the brightest stars in the night sky.[44]

Regulus is derived from a Latin word for king and is sometimes known as, *Cor Leonis*, meaning "the heart of the Lion," because it stands in the breast of the Lion. Then there is *Denebola*, on the tail, which means "The Judge," or "The [LORD] who cometh." *Al Giebha* (Arabic) on the mane, means "the exaltation." Another star, *Michir al Ahad* (Arabic), means "the punishing" or "the tearing of the Lion," while yet another, *Zosma*, on the hind part of the Lion's back, means "shining forth."[45]

David, who slew Goliath, wrote the Psalms and became the greatest King Israel has ever known, also descended from this tribe. Jesus hailed from the lineage of David and the Tribe of Judah. Jesus is referred to as "the Son of David"

---

[40] The blessing of Jacob upon his twelve sons appears in Genesis 49:1-47.

[41] Genesis 37:26

[42] Genesis 44:18-34

[43] The meaning of the Hebrew word "Shiloh" is derived from a Hebrew root word, pronounced, *shaw-law*, which means *to have peace*, i.e., something that the world has never truly known, and will never know, "until Shiloh come; and unto him shall the gathering of the people be." Genesis 49:10

[44] Regulus is actually a star system, consisting of 4 stars organized into two pairs. NOTE: Today, the stars of the constellations are not necessarily within the Zodiac sign because tropical Zodiac signs are different from constellations, but the individual stars (such as Regulus) do describe different facets of each sign, so I have included a discussion of some of the fixed stars in various constellations.

[45] *The Glory of the Stars*, by Raymond Capt

seventeen times in the New Testament. In Hebrews it is written, *For it is evident that our [LORD] sprang out of Juda.*[46]

And in Revelation, Jesus is called *The Lion of the Tribe of Judah.* Jesus is seen as the ultimate fulfillment of Jacob's prophecy.[47]

Universal Brotherhood is a major theme of the Aquarian Age. Judah is associated with the Sign Leo, Aquarius' polarity. In proving he was truly repentant, Judah confirmed, *I am my brother's keeper.* The first mention of brothers in the Bible was of Cain killing his brother Abel. In Genesis, the [LORD] asked Cain, *Where is Abel thy brother?* And he said, *I know not: Am I my brother's keeper?*[48]

Today, more than ever before, people around the world must put aside their hostilities and learn to live as brothers!

THE LION THAT ROARS

The Lion can be ferocious, stealthily stalking its prey before killing and devouring it. In Leos, who can sometimes be ruthless, fierce, and self-serving, we see the lesser instincts of the lion as the individual's shadow self, sometimes called the dweller-on-the-threshold—the selfish underside of the Leo person's Real Self. The apostle Peter admon-

Hercules and the Nemean Lion

---

[46] Hebrews 7:14

[47] "Until Shiloh comes: The leadership prophecy took some 640 years to fulfill *in part* with the reign of David, first of Judah's dynasty of kings. The prophecy took some 1600 years to *completely* fulfill in Jesus. Jesus is referred to as Shiloh, the name meaning, *He whose right it is* and a title anciently understood to speak of the Messiah." See www. EnduringWord/comment-aries/0149.htm.

[48] Genesis 4:9 and Genesis 44:31–34

[49] 1 Peter 5:8

[50] See www.Theoi.com/Ther/LeonNemeios.html

ished, *Be sober, be vigilant, because your adversary the devil, as a roaring lion, walketh about, seeking whom he may devour.*[49]

The ancient Greeks associated the constellation of Leo with the Nemean Lion, killed by *Heracles* (known as *Hercules* to the Romans) as the first of his twelve labors.[50]

The fearsome lion was enormous, its coat so strong that it was impervious to weapons. It stalked and plagued the land causing havoc and destruction. The eighteen-year-old Heracles killed the lion by strangling it with his bare hands. Significantly, after Heracles destroyed the beast, he skinned its hide with the lion's own claws, since no man-made instrument could pierce it. He then made a lion-skin cape, using the lion's head as his helmet and the skin as a cloak, which became one of his distinguishing features. The Greek goddess Hera afterwards flung the lion amongst the stars to create the constellation Leo.

This first labor of Hercules can be interpreted as a life-or-death confrontation, in which he who would be Hero in Leo must grapple with and destroy the terrifying beast created by the human ego. He must summon all his might, ingenuity, and courage to defeat the monstrous beast of pride, symbolized by the savage man-eating lion.

THE LEO SOUL'S MOMENT OF TRUTH

A time arrives, a cycle in fate, an earned opportunity, when events conspire to awaken the Leo soul. Something happens—the soul is aware that he is trapped—enough! The superfluousness of the ego, the glamour, the applause, and the outer signs of power and prestige suddenly lose their sheen and allure. The Leo soul may leap, "this is the moment I have desired for so long," or he may refuse to budge, musing, "It's warm and cozy here in my little cocoon." Sometimes the mother needs only to tug at the bed sheets to rouse her son, "Good morning, it's a new day, time for school!" But often the Leo soul may need coaxing because he wants to keep dreaming or perhaps because he dreads what lies ahead.

The Lion can be lazy, set in his throne or den. "Let someone else do the work!" he roars or yawns. Denial sets in. Emotional density may prevent him from seeing the obvious. Hardness of heart makes him insensible to advice. Sometimes only a traumatic event suffices to bring the Leo's soul to the inevitable fork in the road where he must choose life over death. Self-help groups call this "hitting bottom." In mystical circles there is the saying that, "the only way out is up!"

Astrologer Alan Leo held high hopes for the Leo Sun person, even for those who had squandered their light and lost their way. He wrote:

> *But the true spiritual fire is ever burning within and phoenix-like they will rise from the dead ashes of themselves to greater and nobler things. For this sign is known by astrologers*

*as the House of the Sun, and it is through this sign that the rays
of the Sun become most powerfully charged with spiritual life
and energy.*[51]

LANDMINES IN THE LION'S DEN

The Leo person desirous of self-transformation needs to be increasingly alert, for he will be faced as never before with whatever is within him that opposes his victory. Once committed to walking the spiritual path, the way of self-mastery, the Leo individual will discover, as do all the Fire signs, that his enemy is pride and its bedfellow is fear. Flattery, a most dangerous allure, is a form of pride to which he is particularly prone due to his love for attention.

Eventually, the universal law of Mercy shatters the Leo's illusion of grandiosity so that he might return to truth—a sobering lesson, but better for the soul than to be mocked by its own self-aggrandizement. To accelerate consciousness tainted by pride is a recipe for disaster! Ancient spiritual teachers and gurus would often test the level of a spiritual seeker's pride to determine his readiness.

A 13th century Kabbalistic tale related by author Perle Epstein tells of such a teacher:

> *"When someone insults you, do you still feel injured?
> When you receive praise, does your heart expand with pleasure?"*
>
> *The would-be disciple thought for a moment and replied, somewhat sheepishly, "Yes, I suppose I do feel hurt when injured and proud when praised."*
>
> *"Well then, go out and practice detachment from worldly pain and pleasure for a few more years. Then come back and I will teach you."*[52]

Spiritual detachment is quite an accomplishment for any of us, but, as Alan Leo explains, when Leo persons seek Enlightenment, they make rapid progress, being by nature sensitive to spiritual influences. He writes, "Their faith becomes marvelous and the whole of their life seems to be devoted to doing good to others."

The objective of the Aspirant seeking union with God is that his soul be one with his Higher Self as much as possible. The Kabbalist, Halevi, notes that the demands of the outer world and the pulls within a man make it almost inevitable that he will have moments of slipping out of the consciousness of Self (Gamut) into that of the confines of the ego (Kamut.) In *The Way of Kabbalah*, Halevi writes: "Therefore, Kabbalists do not condemn a man for forgetting who he is, where he is and why he is there, but set it as a constant aim to be in the Present as much as possible."

Although giving and receiving praise is appropriate and right at times, as when encouraging the child or showing gratitude for a job well done, the Aspirant reaches a stage in which he no longer is in need of such accolades. The Leo Aspirant is more likely to stay tethered to his path when he gives glory to God for each accomplishment. Doing so does not minimize his merit and joy in his accomplishments in any wise. As the Master Jesus responded when a man ran up to him, and addressed him as Good Teacher, *Why callest thou me good? There is none good but one, that is, God.*[53]

FOOL'S GOLD OR SOLAR RADIANCE?

Even once squarely on the path, the Leo Aspirant needs to beware of the lure of romantic intrigues and infatuations, of glamour's titillating pull, of a desire to play the hero and a need for applause and approbation. Life can become very complicated when he allows himself to be detoured by these temptations.

As the Leo Aspirant advances on his journey, his capacity for service and for personal sacrifice increases, as does his joy. But the faces of pride become more difficult to discern, sometimes cloaked in supposed virtues, such as spiritual zeal. When his personal dragons rear their ugly heads, the Leo Hero-in-the-Making must stop and destroy them—a daring venture for which the courageous heart of the Lion is well suited. Let him be ever mindful of the Leo lesson so evident in the case of Napoleon—who in many ways exemplified the best of Leo—that pride goes before the fall!

The prerequisite for entering higher realms of understanding is a balanced heart and detachment from the worldly concerns of the ego, even as one is actively engaged in service to an as yet imperfect humanity.

SPIRITUAL SURRENDER UNTO LOVE

For the Leo Aspirant to come to the point of willingness to let go of the Ego's attachments and fears is difficult. Only by increasing the fire of love within the heart can he emerge victorious in this test of Will versus Desire. But once he resolves to release in love all his worldly attachments, he is filled with the light of his own Presence. He discovers he wants not any of those things he once held so dear, so essential. In this act of spiritual surrender, the Aspirant sacrifices none of his reality, only aspects of his unreality he has mistakenly come to claim as being parts of himself! Now he can be divested of soul fragments not his own.

---

[51] *Astrology for All*, p.26
[52] Perle Epstein, *Kabbalah: The Way of the Jewish Mystic* (Shambhala, 1988)
[53] Mark 10:18

Lost soul fragments are restored to him — aspects of self flung to far-off reaches of the universe, buried in the unconscious or perhaps in some distant past, given away foolishly or unknowingly.

As he advances on the path, the Leo Aspirant's soul senses become increasingly refined and his will ever more attuned to Spirit. Dedicated and resolute, he is unmoved by temptation, fearless, and yet sweetly humble. He is so heart-centered that his loving presence inspires other souls to transcend their limitations, to come up higher, and to be all that they really are and can become! He begins to know the unbroken connection spoken of by the saints in their direct communion with God. At a further stage, he will be directed from the heart to the tests, initiations, wonders, and mysteries of the Secret Chamber of the Heart in which abides the Threefold Flame of immortal life. Such is the course of the Leo seeker destined to manifest himself as the Lion of the tribe of Judah!

GRATITUDE — THE LEO ANTIDOTE

The antidote to so many of Leo's ills, and therefore, to the soul, is so simple as to hardly be believed! On the Fixed-Love Cross, we must transform our attitudes and motivations. And what is the grandest attitude of all, if not Gratitude? Gratitude and humility are so akin that one springs forth from, and depends upon, the other. He who is grateful celebrates life regardless of circumstances. Knowing that in every adversity can be found a hidden blessing, the Leo Aspirant sees the glass as half full rather than half empty. His attention is ever upon the Sun of his spiritual Source, whose blessings he extols in a positive and gracious expression of life's many gifts.

When we pass through adversity, such as a natural disaster and come out intact, we are so grateful to be alive! In that moment, we experience heightened awareness. Beyond the adrenalin rush, the static energy of the soul is stimulated and joy and awe are experienced.

In achieving this fine balance between steadfast self-awareness in the One and tender regard, the Leo seeker may gradually acquire a remarkable inner attunement. Once the way is cleared, the soul finally reconnects with the "Hidden Man of the Heart," and the light of the Sun, his birthright, pours upon him like a fountain. At last, he can be trusted with the most powerful force in the Universe, that of Divine Love.

Leading by example and living to serve, the soul becomes the Hero, who in Aries affirmed, "I Am That I Am," and in Leo adds, "I Am Grateful!"

3.

Sagittarius

Symbol	***The Centaur***
Born	Nov. 22 ~ Dec. 20
Archetype	*The Archer*
Key Phrase	*I Seek*
Element	**Fire**
Cross	**Mutable-Wisdom**
House	**Ninth:**

Travel, foreigners & foreign affairs, higher education, philosophy & the pursuit of truth, the courts, aunts, uncles & in-laws, publishing

Rulers	**Jupiter & Neptune**
Esoteric Ruler	**Earth**
Polarity	**Gemini**
Chakra	Throat
Anatomy	Hips

Spiritual Qualities .... **Quest for truth & enlightenment, prophecy, prayer**

Vulnerable to ...... *Resentment, revenge & retaliation, fanaticism, exaggeration, not finishing, impatience with detail, overly blunt, mental pride, restlessness*

Must Acquire .... **Patience, steadfastness, attention to detail, wisdom, forgiveness, open mindedness to opposing viewpoints, listening,** *Virya!*

Pope John XXIII • Judi Dench • Walt Disney • Caroline Myss • Mark Twain

THE SUN IN SAGITTARIUS

If you can dream it, you can do it!

—Walt Disney (December 5th, 1901)

FIRE OF MIND!

Sagittarius, the third sign of the *Fire Triplicity*, imparts fire of mind! Fire impels the soul to act in Aries (Fire on the Power Cross), to love in Leo (Fire on the Love Cross), and to know in Sagittarius (Fire on the Wisdom Cross). Sagittarians tend to be positive, outgoing, philosophical, free-spirited and candid. An inborn impulse toward self-transcendence tests the Sagittarian soul's ability to stay anchored in the here-and-now. His thoughts seem boundless; notwithstanding, he must contend with the reality that he is born of flesh and blood, in time and space, carrying the load of not only his personal karma, but also that of the times into which he is born. And yet, it is precisely this tension between the immense magnitude of the ideal he envisions and the constriction of his imperfect conditions that goads him to explore and discover more. And so, he stretches his mind, unleashes his imagination, and reaches beyond what seems possible in order to vanquish the bane of ignorance upon his soul—indeed, upon the souls of humanity.

The Sagittarian personality is not usually possessive or overly attached, neither to things nor to knowledge. Inwardly he knows that when the cup is full, it must be emptied so that it might be filled again. To know completely is to not have a reason to search further. He may enthusiastically seek teachers and experiences to expand his horizons. He may then teach, preach, publish, or zealously proclaim the truth he has discovered—only to realize, as Socrates admitted, that with all his knowing, he knows nothing! To be sure, the highest rung of the ladder in this world is the lowest in the next—*ad infinitum!*

THE SAGITTARIAN HERO—HERALD OF OPPORTUNITY

Afire with the Word and enlightened by the Divine Mother's wisdom, the Sagittarian Hero at the dawn of the Aquarian Age goes forth to proclaim the opportunity for souls of light to grasp the Torch of Freedom. The fervor of his dedication and the joy of his countenance, the unwavering strength of his conviction and the comforting presence of his kind and loving heart elicit the ancient question and its answer—*Do you believe?*[54]

He knows that souls upon Earth have long waited for the convergence of cosmic cycles to receive keys to enlightenment, such as the Aquarian Science of Invocation and the miraculous violet transmuting flame, that their souls might be freed at last from the karma binding them to the wheel of rebirth![55]

For in the Aquarian Age of Love, not only a few daring seekers, who in centuries past set themselves apart from the majority of men, but now also the many will take up the ancient path of Initiation unto the Ascension in the Light!

THE QUEST

The symbol of Sagittarius is the Centaur, with the head, chest and arms of a man and the body of a horse. The Centaur is about to launch his arrow symbolizing the quest for superconscious (transcendental) awareness, while the horse represents the animal nature of man. The soul born under this sign must gain access to the Higher Mind so that he can tame and master his lower nature. For many, especially younger Sagittarians or those who are still in the early stages of their journey, life at times feels like a roller-coaster ride of highs and lows. One moment, he reaches for the sky; in another, he's back in the confines of the flesh. Nonetheless, Sagittarians tend to be honest and straightforward. Aiming their arrow high, unshackled by the past, they embrace the future with optimism and faith.

Sagittarians are mission-oriented, even when they're not quite sure of where they're headed! The Sagittarian soul senses that he was born to fulfill a specific purpose. He experiences life as a journey, a veritable quest. Reaching for the stars, he hardly knows the meaning of limitation. How else could he attempt endeavors that others consider foolish and unattainable, the meanderings of a dreamer? Heeding his conscience often means ignoring the many voices that would deter him from his goal.

Being fiery by nature, most Sagittarian Sun types don't take well to routine, unless these daily motions have taken on a ritualistic meaning or have been endowed with significance as a means toward a desired end. A particular quality of faith acts as an active agent in the lives of most Fire sign people. Knotty circumstances rarely squelch the Arian's impulse to *do it now*! The Leo personality seizes the day by acting on hunches, often making an intrepid move at the last moment. The Sagittarian's positivity is often ratified by a certain degree of good fortune, typically taken for granted. Somehow he knows that help will arrive on the scene and that things will always work out!

---

[54] One of many instances in the Bible referring to belief (faith) and unbelief is when Jesus has just cast out a demon from a boy. The disciples ask why they were not able to accomplish this, to which Jesus answered: *Because of your unbelief: for verily I say unto you, If ye have faith as a grain of mustard seed, ye shall say unto this mountain, Remove hence to yonder place; and it shall remove; and nothing shall be impossible unto you.* Matthew 17:20

[55] See final chapter, *The Aquarian Science of Invocation.* The action of the violet flame is the application of the frequency of the Holy Spirit.

Sagittarius:
9th House
Mutable-
Wisdom Cross
Fire Element

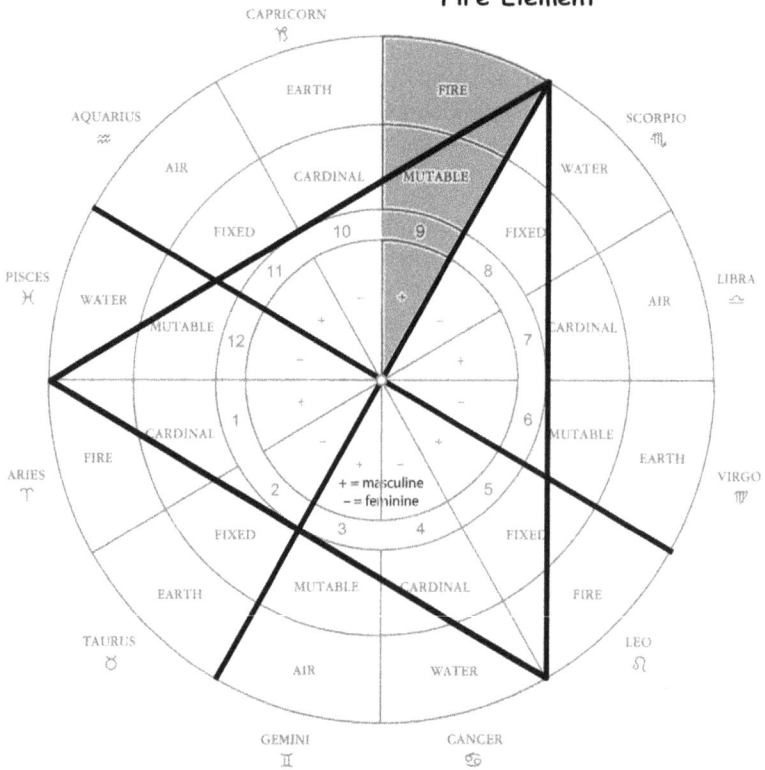

Co-ruled by Jupiter (planet of expansion) and Neptune (planet of dreams and dreamers), the Archer will travel far and wide in search of the truth. Sagittarians often fulfill their destinies in some role related to theology and religion, philosophy, higher learning, history, psychology, law, writing and publishing, or the arts—one of the Jupiter-Neptune related fields of study and accomplishment that frame civilization. They are often involved directly or indirectly with universities, religious bodies, law firms or publishing houses. Many Archers embrace a particular credo or a religious, ethical, or spiritual philosophy. Some delve into sports, which for them becomes a fitting metaphor for spiritual striving. Sagittarius governs (as does Jupiter) foreigners, foreign lands, international commerce and other foreign affairs, all of which often figure strongly into the Sagittarian person's life and calling.

We also find Archers working as broadcasters, disc jockeys, advertising agents, and in sales. Whatever their field of endeavor, they will seek effective means to transmit and share knowledge in the hopes of inspiring, teaching, persuading and/or influencing people. They believe so fervently in what they are saying, in the product they are selling, or in the truth they espouse that their listener tends to believe also. Sagittarians are happiest when engaged in an occupation that serves as a medium for creatively expressing their own personal values and beliefs, or perhaps for seeking the significance of history or the portents of tomorrow. They will usually choose personal independence rather than working primarily for the sake of making money. Many among them, whether consciously or unconsciously, would follow a lifestyle that allows them to legitimately continue being a gypsy—always on the move and living life to the fullest!

In those inevitable ordinary and monotonous periods between escapades and creative projects, the Sagittarian individual typically displays a marked restlessness and may seem distracted, almost bored. He may space out from the here-and-now. In the meanderings of his rich imagination—like the knight holed up in a castle, who dreams of fighting dragons—his mind may be a thousand miles away. Then again, it was Sagittarian Walt Disney who said and proved that, "All of our dreams can come true if we have the courage to pursue them," and "It's kind of fun to do the impossible!"

Transformational Astrology recognizes that only a thin line may separate an individual's perceived strength of character, native to his Sun Sign, from being seen as a weakness. So, whereas the Sagittarian is certainly abetted by a healthy belief in his own abilities, a thirst for knowledge, and a bright and resourceful mind, he is susceptible to believing he knows more than he actually does. Moreover, he tends to be restless and impatient. Perhaps he is brilliant, but even so, of greater value many times is not the goal he aspires to attain, but the humility he must acquire along the way! Sometimes, the lessons of failure that challenge him to look within and re-evaluate the way he does things reveal that the core of his loss came not so much due to lack of creativity nor of effort, but to pride and a tendency to get distracted or to somehow leave unfinished what he has begun.

KESHET — THE RAINBOW OF PROMISE

In Kabbalistic Astrology Sagittarius is associated with the month *Kislev* and is called *Keshet*, which in Hebrew means rainbow. Jewish tradition teaches that the first rainbow seen after the Flood, symbolizing the sealing of God's promise to Noah to never again destroy the world by water, happened during Kislev. As recorded in Genesis, God refers to the rainbow as "my bow."[56]

Like Pisces (month of Adar), Sagittarius is said to be a sign of joy, a time when miracles happen. Chanukah, called the *Festival of Lights*, a happy time, is celebrated during the Sagittarian cycle.[57]

Jupiter and Neptune rule both Pisces and Sagittarius. Natives of both these signs typically are highly idealistic, sometimes foolishly or extraordinarily hopeful and optimistic. Pisceans typically resist establishing boundaries on their faith and Sagittarians resist limiting their hopes and ideals.

The rainbow of promise, the joy of Sagittarius, is reflected in the positive dispositions of so many born during this time.

FIRE ON THE WISDOM CROSS

Sagittarians tend to learn quickly. Life for them is the best classroom. Some things can be told, others can be studied, but only through life's experiences can one really know! The Air quality of the Wisdom Cross fans the flames of their mind, characteristically full of ideas. They are enthusiastic thinkers and great storytellers of colorful yarns. One of the most popular of American storytellers, Mark Twain, was born Samuel Langhorne Clemens, on November 30, 1835. In Twain's natal chart, the Sun in Sagittarius in the First House (of "me") was conjoined Mars (action), also in Sagittarius, in the Second House (of income).

Despite a characteristic good sense of humor, Sagittarians are by nature serious thinkers. They ponder the issues of their day and are vociferous in letting their opinions be known. Mark Twain's most colorful and classic characters, the

---

[56] "I do set my bow in the cloud, and it shall be for a token of a covenant between me and the earth." Genesis 9:13

[57] Chanukah commemorates the Maccabees' military victory (165 B.C.E) over the much larger Syrian army, after which they rededicated and purified the Temple that had been desecrated and could thus worship freely. But then another miracle happened. There was only enough oil for the eternal light to burn for one day; miraculously, the oil replenished itself for eight days, by which time more oil had been secured.

[58] See *How to Tell a Story,* by Mark Twain, at www.ClassicLit.about.com.

protagonists of novels bearing their names: *Huckleberry Finn, Tom Sawyer, Prince and The Pauper,* and *Joan of Arc*, are all teenagers seeking to be free and to be instrumental in freeing others. A master of what he called the humorous story, Twain makes us laugh at the youth, pluck and folly of his heroes and the adventures they fall into.[58]

Twain's protagonists reveal stark truisms about the societal prejudices and pressures of their day. They have a deep moral sense and a natural faith, which Twain contrasts with the often rigid and hypocritical ways of the world into which they are thrust. Certainly, Sagittarians have a strong sense of right and wrong. Not only do they see the need for rules and order, but also they often are in positions and professions where they are instrumental in applying them, such as the judge, the psychologist, or the teacher. But the urge to be free is native to their constitution. They may feel very constrained by conventional limits. Twain paints his heroes with an innate goodness despite their circumstances and naughtiness.

In Chapter One of *Huckleberry Finn*, Huck lets us know that although the good widow Douglas adopted him, he resists her efforts to "sivilize" him:

> *The Widow Douglas, she took me for her son, and allowed she would sivilize me; but it was rough living in the house all the time, considering how dismal regular and decent the widow was in all her ways; and so when I couldn't stand it no longer, I lit out. I got into my old rags and my sugar-hogshead again, and was free and satisfied.*

HALF-FULL OR HALF-EMPTY?

Being mutable (liable to change), Sagittarians are far more impressionable than they tend to realize. Like their polarity, Gemini, they are subject to picking up others' thoughts and confusing them with their own. Sagittarians' receptive and ardent nature puts them in danger of passionately airing false impressions they have accepted almost unthinkingly. When natives of this sign make mistaken assumptions about people and circumstances, whether the cause is a negative mental projection, a prejudice they may harbor, or a tendency to jump to conclusions, they can lash out with furious anger! It took one Sagittarian woman, Zoë, several encounters and lost friendships before she realized, during an astrology session, that her tendency to spew out resentment, thus alienating those with whom she had formed close relationships, was based on a habit she had of picking up on negative thoughts and acting upon them.

Zoë's assumptions were erroneous, but even if they had been correct, while resentment is certainly understandable, it is not justifiable. The danger of the Mutable-Wisdom Cross is the tendency to justify ignorance. Resentment and its corresponding reaction to seek revenge are misuses of the Sagittarian light and therefore manifestations of ignorance. Like Zoë, Sagittarian souls desirous of peace must come to terms with any tendency they might have to entertain gossip, to allow resentment's destructive fires to occupy their minds, and to act precipitously. Sagittarian resentment due to pride is the number-one misapplication of spiritual energy in the Fire signs. Not only does it harm the person to whom it is directed, but also the Sagittarian's mind is agitated and piqued! That he not be moved by such psychic static, the Sagittarian soul must learn to oust accusatory and negative thoughts from his mind the moment they appear on the radar, replacing them with strong, positive affirmations. Additionally, he must develop and sustain a momentum of forgiveness.

THE THROAT CHAKRA—THE POWER OF THE WORD

Gemini and Sagittarius are both associated with the Throat chakra. Natives of both signs feel compelled to find and communicate truth. Natural philosophers, most Sagittarians are at home with profound and abstract concepts, which they translate effectively in the here-and-now in practical and understandable terms. They rarely are at a loss for words! But how can language structure that which is boundless, making it accessible to the minds of men? How can the scaffolding of words not be confused with the awe-inspiring meaning they attempt to convey? As the poet Khalil Gibran beautifully expressed, *For thought is a bird of space that in a cage of words may indeed unfold its wings but cannot fly.*

Self-help author Dale Carnegie (November 24, 1888) believed that public speaking helps develops healthy self-esteem. Carnegie's book, *The Art of Public Speaking,* reads like a Sagittarian primer for success:

> Live an active life among people who are doing worthwhile things, keep eyes and ears and mind and heart open to absorb truth, and then tell of the things you know, as if you know them. The world will listen, for the world loves nothing so much as real life.

Sagittarians are known for telling it like it is. Although they typically take pride in being frank, they can be tactlessly blunt and arrogantly opinionated, a mindset they typically justify and therefore do not readily change, for in their minds, they are simply stating the truth! A reflex action exists between the Solar Plexus and Throat chakras. (Note that the Solar Plexus chakra is associated with Virgo and Pisces, the other Mutable-Wisdom Cross polarity.) The Throat chakra is the body's power center. The Word is the command to come into manifestation! We read in Genesis, "and God said, let there be light! And there was light!" The careless use of words, through idle conversation, accusatory statements, coarse language and other misuses of the Throat chakra—result in karmic consequences that effectively dissipate the speaker's ability to rightfully exercise the power to create. The Sagittarian native especially needs to beware of the knee-jerk reaction of telling people off. If he would be an instrument of enlightenment and truth, he best guard his mind, his feelings, and by extension, his tongue!

Andy was 16 years old when he came for an astrological consultation. His main concern was his relationship with his father. Andy's father had been a caring and responsible parent, working hard and providing his family with all they might need. Andy protested his dad's failure to realize that his son was no longer a little boy. According to Andy's account, his father was forever telling him what to do. Andy's gripe was not unusual for a teenage boy in America today. As the astrologer, I admonished Andy, "Your dad is a hard-working Capricorn. Apparently, he runs the family like his manages the office staff. So, that's what he is dealing with. *But you, you have such a big mouth*! Andy, there's no excuse speaking to your father that way!" Andy looked stupefied. "How did you know? Did my mom tell you?" I replied, "You're a Sagittarian. You need to learn to master your Throat chakra. Your dad has his tests and you have yours!" Andy understood. He felt less justified in lashing out at his father. Getting this perspective actually helped clear the way for father and son to mend their relationship.

SAGITTARIUS & THE LIVER

Since ancient times, Sagittarius has been associated with the liver. The tendency to be angrily reactive increases when the liver is diseased, even as anger creates toxicity in the liver. The liver is typically the Archer's weak point, but he can turn it into his strength. All people, but especially Sagittarians, can gain greater dominion over their stars by maintaining a healthy lifestyle of right nutrition and plenty of exercise. On the move, traveling and adventuring, enjoying life's gifts and pleasures, Sagittarians oftentimes ignore the details of a healthy diet. A toxic liver may be a wake-up call! Indeed, Sagittarian initiative rarely lets up with age, so a fit body is a must. Here's a Sagittarian rule of thumb: learn to manage the Jupiterian tendency of this sign to overdo, overthink, overwork, overeat, overspend, over-party, talk too much, and so on and so forth!

THE CHALLENGE OF COMPLETION

The Archer directs his arrow! Where? Somewhere out there! Fire sign people (Aries, Leo and Sagittarius) are known to take risks. Setting out on a journey whose course is unknown is preferable to sitting around waiting for the map to be drawn! Sagittarians love exploring. They are attracted to foreign lands and cultures, typically taking some adventurous or unbeaten path. Many Sagittarians seek jobs, professions, or alliances that offer them the opportunity to travel or otherwise expand their horizons. They characteristically create a lifestyle that allows them to be successful, while rising above the banality of everyday living, somehow managing to keep their head in the sky and their feet on the ground!

That the arrow must meet its mark sounds simple enough—Sagittarians tend to be direct, self-confident and on-target. However, for many Sagittarians, keeping focused and finishing what they have begun turns out to be a lifelong aspiration. So many things capture their interest that they are prone to leave one work undone to begin another. Another reason why completing cycles can be so difficult for the Sagittarian Sun person is due to his inborn tendency to think big—too big! He finds out over and over again that he has taken on far more than he can handle. His is the sign of the Visionary. Although he may be unusually adept at grasping the big picture and seeing the future now, he tends to brush aside the planning for the steps that it will take to get there.

Generally speaking, Sagittarians at the university are in their element. The energetic pursuit of knowledge in an environment full of diversity and movement suits them—after all, this sign rules higher education. Nonetheless, getting through those required basic college courses can be especially wearisome for them. The mindset that, "I know more than this professor. Why should I waste my time sitting in this classroom?" is often later regretted. Quitting before graduation may pay off for some, as it did for the brilliant Sagittarian film director, screenwriter and producer, Steven Spielberg (December 18, 1946), who dropped out of Cal State Long Beach to make films. But it too

Steve Spielberg stimulates our imaginations and our minds whether bringing us into other galaxies or prehistoric times, wild adventures, a story of the horrors and heroism of war, or into the heart of a Hero, such as Abraham Lincoln.

often happens that the Wanderer one day finds himself seeking employment from the Taurean Tortoise, who may have been less talented, but more steadfast and who went through the steps to attain the degree to get the job. Even successful Sagittarians boasting PhDs, and there are plenty of them, wrestle with impatience in some area of their life.

Already the winner of three Academy Awards, Spielberg re-enrolled at CSU in 2001, finishing his course load and receiving his degree in Film and Electronic Arts in 2002. Going back and completing an aborted cycle, even when not necessary, can be of utmost importance to the Sagittarian soul's sense of accomplishment. Spielberg explains:

I wanted to accomplish this for many years as a "thank you" to my parents for giving me the opportunity for an education and a career, and as a personal note for my own family— and young people everywhere—about the importance of achieving their college-education goals. But I hope they get there quicker than I did! Completing the requirements for my degree thirty-three years after finishing my principal education marks my longest "post-production schedule." Now I can eagerly look forward to joining the graduates at this year's Commencement ceremonies.[59]

The Sagittarian Sun person's reputation suffers when he fails to follow through on his promises. By breaking goals down into manageable segments, Sagittarians have a better chance of completing their cycles and can avoid getting caught up in schemes so grandiose as to be impractical.

The Sagittarian challenge can be compared to the thrust-for-a-purpose necessary to make a winning goal. Determining to dismiss those inevitable moments of discouragement or even sheer exhaustion, when he is apt to throw in the towel, he needs to garner his will, focus his energy, and rev up his spirit!

How to make your dreams come true? Walt Disney advised, "Get a good idea and stay with it. Do it and work at it until it's right."

TAKING THE REINS

Sagittarians tend to be physically active and energetic. Unlike Geminis, their polar opposites, they are not multitaskers by nature, preferring instead a direct course of action and typically working on one project or dream at a time! For Sagittarians, physicality is not a limitation but rather a challenge they embrace. When they train their bodies and discipline their minds to outstretch the body's normal limitations, they feel empowered.

Many natives of this sign become avid athletes, dancers, or active outdoorsmen. Sagittarians characteristically feel a soul connection with horses. In learning not just to ride, but also to relate effectively and compassionately to the horse, they gain sensitivity and patience. By slowing down and paying attention to details that they otherwise would have missed, they find they can achieve their goal faster. As they seem to be controlling the animal, they are, in reality, discovering how to control themselves. The Archer in them takes command over the horse! A certain integration of their spiritual, physical, emotional, and mental worlds takes place, helping them to mature with a greater degree of competence,

---

[59] See www.Calstate.edu/newline/Archive/01-02/020514-LB.shtml. Spielberg was able to use an independent study option to fulfill the college course requirements.

self-assurance and balance. Sagittarian children especially benefit by learning how to ride and care for horses.[60] Learning horsemanship often helps them acquire degrees of self-mastery and soul-sensitivity, both essential for worldly and spiritual success.

DON'T FENCE ME IN![61]

Natives of this fiery sign often express reluctance to be committed, not wanting their wings to be clipped. A certain type of Sagittarian balks at authority and societal restraint, blatantly refusing to be fenced in. As a child this type may be quite challenging to raise. The Sagittarian child needs somehow to learn that when he cooperates, he earns the freedom to spread his wings and do many wonderful things.

Many Sagittarians may feel fenced in by relationships; nevertheless, most of them, even those who are fiercely independent, will concede that the pros of a close or otherwise important relationship strongly outweigh the cons. Even so, settling in, which would be sweet comfort for a Cancer, for this adventurer might feel more like a ball and chain—his or her partner had better be up for the ride! A Sagittarian couple, both born on December 13th but fifteen years apart in age, lived together for four years and had a son before deciding to make their love official. They got married atop a mountain and their first home was a teepee beside a running creek. Certainly, a Sagittarian match made in heaven!

As is true of all the Fire signs, intimate relationships challenge the Sagittarian to develop a greater capacity to love—to match the fire of his spirit with a tender regard, his zest for life with patience, his adventuring with a grateful sharing, and his frankness with kindness.

THE GOSPEL OF WEALTH

The American industrialist and steel magnate, Andrew Carnegie, born November 25, 1835, is an archetypal example of Sagittarian success. A self-made man, he thought big, fulfilled his dreams, and was faithful to his principles. When Carnegie retired in 1901, he was 66 years old and the richest man in the world. He became a philanthropist—Sagittarius rules philanthropy—dedicating the rest of his life to what he called, "the Gospel of Wealth." Carnegie expressed a great

---

[60] I recommend the 1979 movie, *The Black Stallion*, starring Mickey Rooney and Kelly Reno, which depicts this principle as the young boy, Alec, stranded on a remote island with an Arabian stallion, forges a bond with the horse.

[61] Bing Crosby sang, "Don't Fence Me In."

[62] See www.Gutenberg.org.

love for mankind. He believed that those who had been blessed with wealth were morally obligated to give back to society what they had received and so he donated 90% of his wealth to good causes. (Over 2,500 well-built libraries, in large cities and small towns, bear his name.) Raised in humble circumstances, how did he make his millions? The more evolved Sagittarian perceives not only the past, but also the future. He knows that the only thing permanent in this world is change. Historian John Ingram had this to say about Carnegie: "I think Carnegie's genius was, first of all, an ability to foresee how things were going to change. Once he saw that something was of potential benefit to him, he was willing to invest enormously in it."[62]

Andrew Carnegie (1835–1919). This steel magnate thought big, worked hard, became the richest man of his day and then gave it all away.

A CYCLE DONE IS A CYCLE WON!

Sociable and outgoing by nature, Sagittarians are also somewhat introspective. Although they tend to see the brighter side of life, at times they sense that the weight upon them is more than they can possibly bear. Idealists by nature, the morning headlines or some stark reality or perceived failure can threaten to bring down their normally upbeat spirits. Nonetheless, experience reveals to them that when they feel the heaviest and the most prone to giving up, victory is often right around the corner! At these moments, the Sagittarian soul is more aware that positivity is a choice. As Dale Carnegie wrote in *How to Stop Worrying and Start Living,* "Two men looked out from prison bars, one saw mud, the other saw stars." Sagittarius is the ninth sign of the Zodiac, preceding crystallization in the Power Earth sign of Capricorn. When the Archer feels most tempted to give way to discouragement is often when he must double his forces to complete the cycle, whether the task at hand be great or small. A cycle done is a cycle won!

Sagittarius represents the judicial system and the courts of law. True Sagittarians are passionate defenders of justice, expressing strong and oftentimes bold opinions about what is right and what is wrong. Many of them feel a calling to courageously defend truth, personally and if need be, in courts of law or by

Historian Joseph Ellis has called Founding Mother ***Abigail Adams*** one of most extraordinary women in American history.

promoting the passing of necessary legislation. Once engaged in a cause, they are not likely to give in or to give up the fight! Sometimes justice is served here on Earth—sometimes it is not. Regardless of which way the wind may blow, the Sagittarian soul must find his peace.

UPWARD & BEYOND

Sagittarius is the sign of victory—limitation is simply not in the Archer's vocabulary! The Sagittarian Hero-in-the-Making sees the good even in adversity or seeming failure. He refuses to be stymied by obstacles strewn in his path. Beethoven, born December 16th, 1770, wrote what many believe to be his finest symphonies after he had gone deaf.

American patriot Abigail Adams was born November 11, 1744 (Julian; November 22, Gregorian). That day, the Sun was at 30 degrees Scorpio, which is the same as 00 degrees Sagittarius—she was born on the Scorpio/Sagittarius cusp. Abigail Adams is considered, along with the Founding Fathers, to be a key player in the United States' fight for independence. Adams embodied the Scorpio fighting spirit along with Sagittarian wisdom and love of freedom. She once wrote to John Adams, her husband and the fledgling nation's Second President (born November 10, 1725, Gregorian):

> *A people fired with love of their country and of liberty, a zeal for the public good, and a noble emulation of glory, will not be disheartened or dispirited by a succession of unfortunate events. Like them, may we learn through defeat the power of becoming invincible.*[63]

British statesman Winston Churchill, born November 30, 1874, spoke with the impassioned and yet matter-of-fact tone common to Sagittarians. His formula for victory, "Never give in—never, never, never, in nothing great or small, large or petty, never give in." This determination was qualified by the touch of

Judi Dench starred as Juliet at age 25 (with John Stride as Romeo) in director Franco Zeffirelli's 1960 stage production.

nobility and fair play characteristic of the Sagittarian spirit, and so he added, "except to convictions of honor and good sense."

THE QUINTESSENTIAL SAGITTARIAN WOMAN

English film, stage and television actress Judi Dench (December 9, 1934) has been called, "Britain's leading actress" and "the greatest Shakespearean actress of her generation." The list of honors awarded her in the entertainment industry is six pages long![64]

She is a multiple winner of Academy Awards, Golden Globes, Tonys, BAFTA (British Academy of Film and Television Awards), and Laurence Olivier Awards.[65]

In addition, she has been appointed an "Officer of the Order of the British Empire," a "Dame Commander of the Order of the British Empire," and a "Companion of the Order of Honour."[66]

She has received honorary degrees from a number of universities, including an honorary doctorate from Sterling University for her contributions to the Arts.

Although she assumes the role of powerful Queens so convincingly (she won an Oscar for her portrayal of Queen Elizabeth in *Shakespeare in Love*), she is known off stage for her vivacity and positivity, her straight answers, and her compassionate and playful nature. One interviewer commented, "She can make you believe anything." You believe in her characters because she believes in what

---

[63] Excerpt from a letter written by Abigail to John Adams on September 6th, 1776

[64] See www.IMDb.com. (IMDb is an acronym for Internet Movie Data Base.)

[65] *The Olivier Awards* are named after the British actor Laurence Olivier and are recognized internationally as the highest honor in British theatre.

[66] *The Order of the Companions of Honour* was founded in June, 1917, as a reward for outstanding achievements in the arts, literature, music, science, politics, industry, or religion. *The Most Excellent Order of the British Empire* was established on 4 June 1917. It is an order of chivalry.

she is portraying. Unlike natives of serious Scorpio, the sign preceding Sagittarius, Archers are not typically stuck on perfection, but rather have a broader sense of the value of the entire experience. In her autobiography, *And Furthermore,* Dench relates many amusing and unexpected happenings behind the scenes and on stage, some of which brought rage or tears to others, but which elicited a hearty laugh from her. After all, the show must go on! In 1960, early in her career, her parents came to see her perform on the Old Vic stage in Shakespeare's *Romeo and Juliet,* directed by Franco Zeffirelli:

> *Daddy famously got so carried away when I cried out to Peggy Mount, "Where are my father and my mother, Nurse?" that he called out from the stalls, "Here we are, darling, in row H!"*

Sagittarians are known for going way beyond expected limitations. Dench continues to prove that age need not be a limiting factor to an accomplished actor. In an interview published in *The Observer*, journalist Tim Adam asked Dench, then 77 years old, whether she ever allows herself the satisfaction of feeling like she has done enough. "I hope not," she replied with a smile. "It might well feel like enough for someone else. But it always feels like nowhere near enough for me."[67]

At the time of this writing, Judi Dench is 79 years old and is dealing with macular degeneration caused by age. Stating, "I will never stop!" she has adapted by asking others to read her script to her. She recently earned her seventh Oscar nomination for her role in the film, *Philomena*.

Dench's chart shows her as being a pioneer in her field, a very determined woman, who set new precedents by her refusal to settle for less.

THE SAGITTARIAN CHILD

The rapidly advancing Aquarian technology of communication is a gift of the Mother, in order that we might be united and that truth will be available to all people in all lands. Simultaneously, the Aquarian themes of freedom and the liberation of the soul advance across the globe, exposing ignorance, agitating ancient hatreds, and stirring up fears that must be vanquished. Into this creative explosion arrives the Sagittarian child, whose mind is apt to be far advanced of the thinking of his parents' generation. Nevertheless, like any child, he needs discipline, love, education, and guidance.

The Sagittarian child loves to travel, physically and figuratively. Colorful tales with religious themes, heroic deeds and far-off lands capture his attention and ignite his sense of mission! He can become engrossed in a book or a movie or perhaps, like the young Walt Disney, he will take off into the world of his imag-

---

[67] See www.TheGuardian.com for Judi Dench's *Skyfall* interview.

ination. One of five children, Walt grew up in a family that knew the hardships of poverty. His father was severe and Walt had to work hard to help out his family. He would dream of a happy place where children could really be children! Even as a child, Walt loved art. By the time he was a teenager, he began selling his sketches of the animals on his father's farm to neighbors and friends.

Young Walt was also fascinated with trains. When he was 14 years old, Disney took a summer job selling snacks and newspapers to passengers traveling on the Missouri Pacific Railroad. The job seemed more of a Sagittarian escapade than anything else. Walt reportedly ate much of the candy himself, and he lost the soda bottles when the train car in which he had stored them was detached from the train. He would take breaks in which he offered the crew fruit from his father's farm in exchange for learning how to operate the train! Later, in *Disneyland*, this hard-working Sagittarian dreamer tried to recapture the feeling of freedom he experienced when aboard the train.

Then there is the more mellow Sagittarian type, who, as astrologer Alan Leo put it, "is quite content to have someone else shoot his mental arrows for him." As children, these souls especially need help in getting started, staying focused, and completing their tasks and studies on time. But many Sagittarian children would learn better while riding a bicycle or on horseback than sitting at their desks most of the day. Little Archers especially can be quite rough-and-tumble. It is not unusual for restless, daydreaming Sagittarian children to actually fall out of their seats; others give away their Sun Sign by drumming their fingers on their desks. Sagittarian youngsters are natural explorers. They characteristically delight in outings, and many have a natural love of nature and the outdoors. Sagittarians have been called the Indiana Joneses of the Zodiac—when adventure calls, they're off! They generally do better at school when their studies are punctuated with plenty of fresh air, movement, and exercise.

Young Sagittarians do not take readily to restrictions on their freedom. Even as babies they let their parents know that they do not like to be stuck in a playpen! Participating in extracurricular activities, such as sports, dramatic productions, rodeos, celebrations, and student government are all excellent ways for these youngsters to learn the value of teamwork and the importance of playing fairly and by the rules.

Even more important than book learning for Sagittarian children is an exposure to a variety of diverse environments and experiences: the park, the marketplace, the mountains and the sea. Horseback riding comes naturally to many of them. Archery is another favorite Sagittarian skill worth acquiring! The arrow in the Centaur's hand must reach the mark! The spirited Archer may need to be reminded in more ways than one that he must finish what he begins, whether it be putting away his toys or completing his homework and chores. He needs to experience bringing his projects to completion, getting the ball in the net, and making that goal. Especially if Mercury is in Sagittarius (less so if it's in Scorpio or Capricorn), he may tend to skip the details in his work or become easily distracted. Disney was noted for keeping his eye on every last detail; in his chart, Mercury was in Scorpio!

Sagittarian young people are generally outgoing and well liked. Many are quite jovial and funny! Nonetheless, they are notorious for being too blunt—the old "foot-in-mouth" syndrome! They benefit greatly when raised in an environment where courtesy and consideration are emphasized.

Judi Dench's childhood seems tailor-made for a Sagittarian child with a destiny in the arts. Her father, Reginald Dench, was a doctor for actors. So young Judi got to travel with "mum and dad" immersed in the wonderful world of theatre—loving the sets, trying on costumes, and singing along as mum played the piano. Dad was known to be a great storyteller and children flocked to him. Dench writes that even as a child she was hot-tempered and loquacious. One teacher reprimanded her that she needed to learn to be quiet!

The Sagittarian young person has an inborn sense of fairness and will defend a friend or a cause he believes in. When he feels he has been wronged (disciplined, mistreated, or hemmed in), he may openly express his resentment and may even want to get even! When the Sagittarian soul's youth is marked by victories and when he learns the need to forgive and be compassionate, there is no longer room for resentment!

In his autobiography, Andrew Carnegie reflects upon the days when he was a young lad growing up in Dunfermline, Scotland. Noting that from his grandfather (and from the stars!) he inherited the ability to shed troubles and to laugh through life, Carnegie offers young people this advice:

> *A sunny disposition is worth more than fortune. Young people should know that it can be cultivated, that the mind like the body can be moved from the shade into sunshine. Let us move it then. Laugh trouble away if possible, and one usually can, if he be anything of a philosopher, provided that self-reproach comes not from his own wrongdoing. That always remains. There is no washing out of these "damned spots." The judge within sits in the Supreme Court and can never be cheated. Hence the grand rule of life, which Burns gives: "Thine own reproach alone do fear."*[68]

SAGITTARIUS & THE SPIRITUAL PATH

What happens when the Sagittarian soul arrives at a crossroads? He has been searching and asking why for some time. A major alteration in life direction may come about as a result of discovering a belief system that he believes holds the key to enlightenment and freedom. The Wanderer becomes the Aspirant en route to becoming the Sagittarian Hero. While he is apt to maintain his outward good-humored manner, his choices and direction are apt to change dramatically. As his understanding quickens, the Sagittarius Aspirant, like the converted Saul of Tarsus, may enthusiastically attempt to convert his own, but others close to him may be shocked and confused.[69]

If the relationship is intimate, the friend or spouse may angrily blame the Sagittarian's new way of thinking for changing him, and hence want nothing to do with him or with his message. It does not always work out this way, of course, but for Sagittarians, forks in the road involving confrontations of this sort are almost inevitable.

He who would earn his victory in Sagittarius must be undeterred even when men revile him, obedient without question to the Teacher guiding him, but most of all to God within himself. Indeed, Sagittarius has been called the Sign of the Voice of Conscience. He must be the disciplined one, fiercely passionate in his resolve, so that doubt not worm its way into his mind or the dust of discouragement settle upon his soul. For once committed to the Higher Way, all death and hell conspire to thwart his mission, to detour, overwhelm or discourage him.

PRAYER, PROPHETS & PROPHECY

Sagittarius is the sign of prophecy and of prophets—messengers of the Divine Word. Sagittarians are naturally receptive to divine guidance in their lives, perhaps calling the connection truth, intuition, or a certain prompting they feel. Sagittarius rules prayer. This dialog allows the soul to connect with the Divine Presence and superconscious awareness. As the Sagittarian devotee builds his momentum of prayer and invocation, the light rises up and increases within him. For the Sagittarian devotee, the miraculous is the way things naturally work when a student on the path gets his limited thinking, distorted manifestations, and inordinate desires out of the way.

MASTERING THE THROAT CHAKRA

The Sagittarian seeker of self-realization in the Aquarian Age must become adept with the Spoken Word—he must master the Throat chakra. The Throat chakra is the soul's command center, bearing a direct relationship to Divine Will. The Sagittarian Aspirant answers the call: "Thou must prophesy again before

---

[68] See www.Gutenberg.org.
[69] Saul was en route to Damascus to persecute the Christians when he was converted by a mystical experience with Jesus in his ascended light body. Saul, now Paul, set on his mission, began by preaching to the Jews in the temples what had been so dramatically revealed to him. But he was stoned, reviled and thrown out. See the Book of Acts.

many peoples, and nations, and tongues, and kings."[70]

However, as long as the workings of pride remain within him, he is in danger of being the voice of lower spirits and of promulgating error and perhaps even unintentionally broadcasting false teaching. On the Mutable-Wisdom Cross, the spiritual faculty of discernment becomes increasingly essential as the Aspirant advances on the way. He comes to realize that anger, anxiety, sadness and other emotional imbalances cause him to lose his connection! One of the first require-ments on the spiritual path is to act rather than react, challenging for Sagittarians with passionate temperaments!

The Sagittarian Aspirant gains mastery by using his mind to control his emotions. The need for disciplined self-awareness becomes vital to his progress, for he cannot risk losing his momentum in an unguarded moment. By learning to govern his emotions, he becomes less apt to blurt out words that inadvertently hurt another. He practices guiding the direction of his thoughts and words pur-posefully and compassionately. He refuses to lend an ear to gossip. As the Psalmist wrote, *Let the words of my mouth, and the meditation of my heart be acceptable in thy sight, O [LORD], my strength, and my redeemer.*[71]

GOING WITHIN

Being restless and somewhat impatient by nature, the Sagittarian Aspi-rant typically finds quiet meditation challenging. Assuming an upright and atten-tive posture with his inner eye focused on his heart and his God-Presence helps him to be alert yet still. With patience he can master meditation even when in mo-tion.

The intuitive healer, international speaker, modern mystic, and five-time *New York Times* bestselling author, Caroline Myss, was born on December 2, 1952. Myss portrays the spirited thrust and enterprise of the Sagittarian woman with a message that she is determined to get out. Myss' output of books, CDs, and workshops is prolific and yet, in the midst of so much to say and share, she teaches about the importance of silence. This is from her book, *Entering the Castle—Finding the Inner Path to God and Your Soul's Purpose*:

> *Contain your experience within the divine so that it does not escape you but rather shapes you. Be silent. Silence helps focus the busy mind—the mind that always has to be oth-erwise engaged lest it become introspective and allow the soul's voice to override its own. The silence I am describing is a silence that you use to contain the grace you receive when you enter the Castle of your soul. This quality of silence allows you*

to engage in discernment. You carry this silence within you, even when you are with others. It allows you to hold your center amid the chaos of your life; it keeps you clear so that you do not do or say things you will regret or make decisions out of fear.

THREE SAGITTARIAN DRAGONS

On the road to enlightened understanding, the dust of ignorance gets stirred up before the truth it has eclipsed for so long can be clearly seen and understood. All the Mutable-Wisdom Signs (Gemini and Sagittarius, Virgo and Pisces) are vulnerable to duality (as symbolized in Sagittarius by the centaur— half man and half beast). But the Sagittarian Aspirant cannot progress with one foot in this world and the other in the next! If he would be *in* this world, but not *of* it, he must vanquish three inner dragons that are standing in his way: one takes the form of discouragement, the other of resentment, and the third of fanaticism— all three originate in pride.

Sagittarian seekers of the Way must expect their faith to be tested— again and again. The "throw-in-the-towel" syndrome awaits the Archer at every corner and when he least expects it. Weariness overshadows him; his mind is assailed with a hundred reasons why he should give up. This crisis in faith tumbles him into the temporary abyss of uncertainty. With the fire and vigor of invincible faith, he must summon his courage and pull up the parts of his mind that he has allowed to descend into the perfidious terrain of doubts and misgivings. The Sagittarian spiritual warrior comes to realize and accept, as one Sagittarian mother of four exclaimed in the midst of a trying circumstance: "Giving up is not an option!"

The Sagittarian Aspirant will almost certainly know moments when the fires of resentment sear through his mind. Situations seem set up to extract such a reaction from him. He must determine that his mind and psyche be free from even the slightest, subtlest, and most apparently innocuous vibration of resentment. If not extinguished, the fire of resentment can lead to depression and feeling helpless, or to thoughts of settling the score by taking power into his own hands! If he elects to retaliate for a perceived injustice, he effectively poisons his mind, keeping the original injury freshly alive. In effect, he becomes a prisoner of memory. For his mind to soar freely, it must be released from the pounding thoughts of vindication. To self-justify revenge is nothing short of insanity; it is written: *Vengeance is mine sayeth the [LORD]!*[72]

---

[72] "To me belongeth vengeance, and recompense; their foot shall slide in due time: for the day of their calamity is at hand, and the things that shall come upon them make haste." Deuteronomy 32:35 (The Song of Moses) and "Dearly beloved, avenge not yourselves, but rather give place unto wrath: for it is written, Vengeance is mine; I will repay, saith the [LORD]." Romans 12:19

Forgiveness does not mean making a wrong into a right. It simply surrenders ultimate judgment into the hands of a Higher Power. Forgiveness is a healing process; it takes effort and, in most cases, time. When the Sagittarian Aspirant truly forgives, he effectively releases the one who injured him from responsibility for his happiness and retakes the reins on his life. He comes to know that through forgiveness comes peace, without which life is torment. He may then counsel, write about, or somehow help others to communicate compassionately and will find peace through what he has come to appreciate—that as we free another, we ourselves are freed.

Unless spiritual pride is rooted out of the Sagittarian Aspirant's consciousness, what initially appears to be earnest zeal too often turns into fanaticism. The fanatical mindset is not aflame with love and truth, but with arrogance and hatred. Even the sincere Sagittarian devotee is not immune to the danger of fanatical self-righteousness. Therefore, he must be diligent in swiftly weeding out pockets of pride and prejudice as he finds them, replacing them with humility and forbearance. Tibetan mystics call this process of objective self-observance "mindfulness." By practicing mindfulness, the Sagittarian seeker gains skill in quieting mental, emotional, and physical agitation and restlessness. With his mind at peace and in balance with his heart, he strengthens his auric forcefield and wards off the negative influence of aggressive thoughts permeating the atmosphere or directed toward him (from within or without).

VIRYA!

Buddhists have a name for the perfecting of zeal—*Virya!* Mahayana Buddhists teach that without *Virya* there can be no enlightenment: without Virya there can be no forgiveness. *Virya* is vital for the one becoming the Sagittarian Hero. What, then, is *Virya*? The *Dhammasangani* defines it as:

> *The striving and onward effort, the exertion and endeavor, the zeal and ardor, the vigor and fortitude, the state of unfaltering effort, the state of sustained desire, the state of not putting down the yoke and the burden, the solid grip of the yoke and the burden, energy, right endeavor—this is Virya!* [73]

When the Sagittarian Aspirant is tempted to give in to suggestions that he has carried on too long, labored in vain, outspent his resources, or burdened his loved ones—whatever reason may be goading him to forsake his dream, let him determine to be led only by the spirit of victory. Then, taking a long, deep breath and setting his eyes toward Heaven, let him exclaim with power and conviction: *Virya! Virya! Virya!* until his victory is won.

---

[73] Buddhist scripture.

THE SAGITTARIAN HERO

Pope John XXIII, born Angelo Roncalli on November 25, 1881, was a forerunner of the Aquarian Age. As pope, and in the many years of service before he entered that office, he did much to clear the way for men to lay down their ancient prejudices, vendettas, and hatreds, and to come together in love. In true Christian and Sagittarian spirit, he welcomed all with open arms, regardless of their faith, or lack of it! Affectionately called *il Papa Buono,* the Good Pope, John XXIII was known for his candor, cheerful personality, deep devotion, selfless courage and his tell-it-like-it-is sense of humor.

Before he became pope at the age of 76, Cardinal Roncalli spent twenty-five years as a papal diplomat for Bulgaria, Turkey and France, and six years as archbishop of Venice. Motivated by his great love for humanity, fearlessly determined, and as astute as he was compassionate, Roncalli was instrumental in saving the lives of tens of thousands of Jews during the Holocaust. John XXIII turned around the Catholic Church's centuries long condemnatory thinking toward Jews, claiming that Jews as a people were not guilty of killing Christ and respectfully calling Jews, "the people of the Covenant with whom God first spoke." The changes wrought by Pope John XXIII and Vatican II, a council he called whose purpose was to seek truth and rid the Church of injurious practices and thinking, amounted to what many claim to be a revolution within the church with worldwide implications.

We see in Pope John XXIII an example close to our times and to our hearts of the Hero in Sagittarius. Having conquered the beast of pride, the Sagittarian Hero is unshackled from the magnetism of the lower nature. Forgiveness is his shield, so that the poison of resentment never need soil his garments. He perceives the future and comprehends the meaning of the past. A true prophet, he is ever hopeful, knowing that negative prophecy is but a warning that can yet fail if only the people will take heed and change in enough time. He is Victorious! Although he captures vistas of greater glory, he knows that in order to transcend time and space, he must fulfill its requirements—he must finish what was begun in the *maya* (the illusion) of *mater* (the physical plane). The Sagittarian Hero, the Enlightened One, thus becomes the Teacher in whom compassion takes the form of imparting to mankind the keys to unlock their inner Wisdom—so that souls on Earth might be free!

4. Ⅱ

Gemini

Symbol	***The Twins***
Born	May 21 ~ June 20
Archetype	*The Sage*
Key Phrase	*I Think*
Element	**Air**
Cross	**Mutable-Wisdom**
House	

Third:

Short distant travel, commutes, siblings, relatives & neighbors, early education, teaching & writing, literature, transportation

Ruler	**Mercury**
Esoteric Ruler	**Venus**
Polarity	**Sagittarius**
Chakra	Throat
Anatomy	lungs, breath, oxygenation of blood, ribs, nervous & respiratory systems

Spiritual Qualities . . . . . **Wisdom, pursuit of Will of God, mastery of the Word, union of Twin Flames**

Vulnerable to . . . . . . *Envy & jealousy, inner & outer schism, gossip & lies, excessive analysis & criticism, disconnection from feelings, superficiality, non-commitment*

Must Acquire . . . . . **Discernment, spiritual attunement, integrity, union, mental clarity & focus**

John F. Kennedy • Anne Frank • Padre Pio • Jacques Cousteau • Marylin Monroe

THE SUN IN GEMINI

Wisdom is the principal thing; therefore get wisdom;
and with all thy getting, get understanding.

—Proverbs 4:7

THE GEMINI RIDDLE

The familiar adage, "man proposes but God disposes," sums up the Gemini riddle. To seek, to discern, to know and to manifest Divine Will is the way of the Gemini Hero.

Of course, in the scheme of things, we all eventually meet that fork in the road between divine intent and human reason. However, the choice of whether to embrace or to willfully ignore the spiritual Law written upon his heart becomes the life-theme of the soul born with the Sun in Gemini. The very course of his life depends on his recognition (or non-recognition) that he must give answer to this election—one way or another.

Gemini represents our use of the Word, the Divine Logos, and is associated with The Throat chakra. In the ancient scriptures of both East and West, it is written: "In the beginning was the Word, and the Word was with God and the Word was God."[74]

Man, made in God's image, releases the power of sound that can create and destroy worlds.

And yet he knows it not, even as he ponders not the measure of his breath or the number of his days or the sun that shines down upon him every day. Man is more than he thinks himself to be—*aha*—therein lies the rub! Man thinks so much and yet he thinks not! For what purpose is he endowed with the Breath of Life? The answer is so simple and yet so elusive. The answer escapes him because it lies within a dimension outside the range of normal thought.

GEMINI THE TWINS

The constellation Gemini contains 85 stars visible with the naked eye. The Gemini symbol of the two pillars, easily identified in the night sky, indicates the two in one, a theme occurring repeatedly in diverse manifestations throughout the Gemini soul's personality and life circumstance.

The Zodiac describes the relationship of the macrocosmic to the microcosmic world and the relationship of individuals to one another. Gemini represents the relationship between brothers. The Romans called Gemini *The Twin Brethren*, with its two brightest stars named *Castor* and *Pollox*. They associated *Castor* and *Pollox* and the principle of brotherly love with the foundation of their city. The Greeks called the Gemini Twins, *Dioscuri*, the sons of Zeus. The Hebrew name for Gemini is *Thaumin*, meaning "united."

In astrological analysis, Gemini tells the tale not only of our relationship with our siblings, but also to cousins, close relatives and even to neighbors. People born with the Sun in Gemini or with strong Gemini placements (or with planets in the Third House, ruled by Gemini) often find their lives very much affected by siblings or close relatives. Especially when a planetary transit or progression passes over the Sun (or Mercury, Gemini's ruler, and any planet in the Third House), an issue with a sibling, relative, or neighbor may crop up. These relationships often revolve around some karmic circumstance, whether it appears to be a burden or a blessing.

Gemini represents not only twin brothers, but also Twin Flames—two distinct souls created male and female from a single electronic blueprint, both endowed with individuality, complementary to one another, but also separate and unique. Indeed, the Sanskrit name for Gemini in Hindu Astrology is *Mithuna*, represented by a man and a woman. In the *Dendera Zodiac*, Gemini is represented by the figure of a man walking hand and hand with a woman.[75]

The principle of the dichotomy and union between siblings and also between man and woman is echoed in Astrology: while Gemini is said to be ruled *exoterically* by Mercury, the planet associated with brothers, Gemini is *esoterically* ruled by Venus, the planet representing the love of Twin Flames.

Twin brothers symbolize the dual nature of man, being spiritual in origin, but on the other hand clothed in flesh; having the spark of eternity within his heart, but being mortal. The brothers, as Cain and Abel, one selfish and murderous, the other righteous, dramatize the meeting of the Sons of God with the Fallen Angels and the Nephilim,[76] and the battle within man to separate himself out from all that is not of the light, so that he might return to a state of purity and higher consciousness and thus fulfill his destiny to one day take his place among the stars.

---

[75] The sculptured *Dendera Zodiac* is an Egyptian bas-relief on the ceiling of a chapel dedicated to Osiris in a temple on the west side of the Nile.

[76] In Genesis 6:1-4, and the Book of Enoch, we read of the seed of light mixing with that of darkness. The term Nephilim appears twice in the Torah, in Genesis just before the story of Noah's ark, and in Numbers 3:33. Often translated as "powerful giants," Nephilim literally means, "fallen ones."

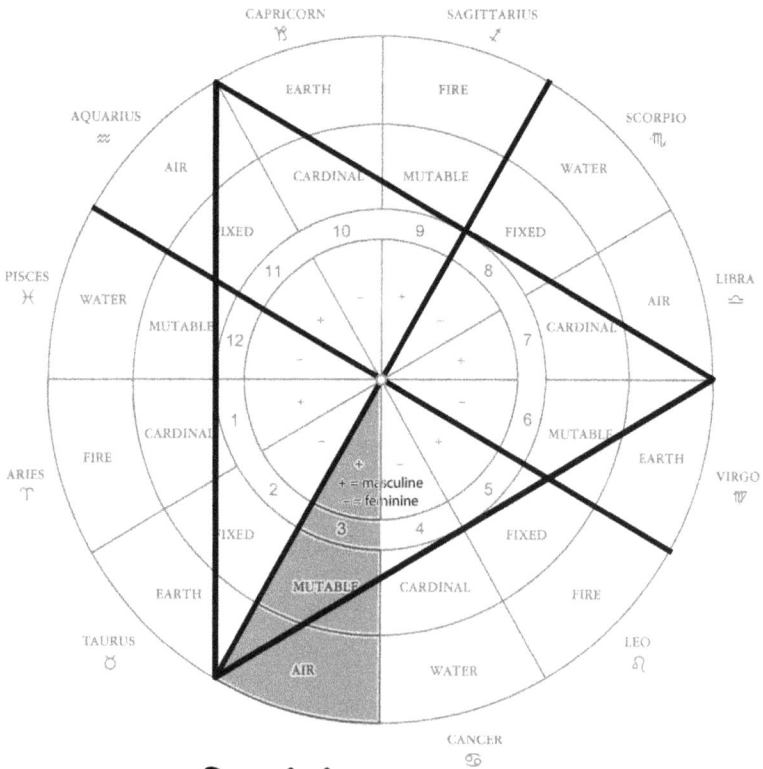

Gemini:
3rd House
Mutable-
Wisdom Cross
Air Element

Some of Gemini's stars speak of brotherhood and unity; others speak of peace—still others of pain. The star *Hercules*, for example, means "He who has come to suffer." *Propus* (Hebrew) means "the branch spreading," *Al Gizura* (Arabic), "the palm branch," and *Dira* (Arabic), "the branch,"—all symbolizing a time of peace.

Gemini, then, can be interpreted as prophesying a time of peace, preceded by a time of judgment and travail—the suffering preceding the victory of man as demonstrated by Jesus Christ, Gautama Buddha, and all the great Lights of East and West—the many Heroes, both celebrated and unsung, who have walked the path of the Ascension.

GEMINI & *SIVAN*

Sivan is the third month in the Hebrew calendar, thus corresponding to Gemini, when Moses is said to have received the Ten Commandments. The two stone tablets upon which they are written are represented in the Kabbalistic *Tree of Life* by the two outer pillars or columns, the right one being positive and masculine (Mercy) and the left negative and feminine (Judgment) in their energy. The masculine gives; the feminine receives. The right hand of the human body is associated with the sephirah *Hesed* (Love/Mercy) on the right column, the left hand with the sephirah *Gevurah* (Justice/Judgment) on the left column.

The integration of the masculine and feminine columns is seen in the middle column, sometimes called the Way of Compassion (like the Buddhist "middle way"). This third column, and the sephirah *Tiferet* (Beauty/Compassion) represent perfect balance, circuitry and wholeness, allowing love to flow freely. And so, *Sivan*—Gemini—is seen as a time of duality, with the potential for unity—of the two separate halves becoming one.

Kabbalists meditating upon the Tree of Life during *Sivan* remember the words of Rabbi Akiva,[77] who explained that the whole *Torah* is captured in the words, "Thou shall love thy neighbor as thyself."[78] (These words were echoed by Jesus himself in Mark 12:29-31.)

Gemini is the first sign of the *Air Triplicity* (Gemini, Libra and Aquarius). Unless there is harmony between brothers, how else can the Age of Aquarius become the Age of Brotherhood?

---

[77] Akiva ben Joseph, widely known as Rabbi Akiva, was a *tanna* (teacher) of the latter part of the 1st century and the beginning of the 2nd century. He is referred to in the Talmud as *Rosh la-Chachamim (Head of All the Sages)*.

[78] Leviticus 19:18

THIS WAY

Along the winding path of a Japanese tea garden appears the sign with arrows pointing in opposite directions and the simple phrase, "This Way." Geminis are not alone in experiencing the crisis of choosing among multiple opportunities, all seemingly desirous and not one obviously better than the others. But the soul born in Gemini typically is beset continually throughout his life with the necessity of choosing which way to go. Life challenges him to develop the discriminatory faculty of intelligence—yes this, not that—in his most important as well as in his everyday choices.

Figuring out which way is the right way sometimes requires a period of dedicated and deep inner work (a spiritual exploration of the mind and psyche) and soul searching! Paulina was 28 years old. She had suffered for weeks from that pounding headache common to those stuck in a classic Gemini dilemma, uselessly racking her brain while trying to resolve which option she should take. The question at hand was of great importance to her. Moreover, the happiness of two other persons was at stake—she had to figure this one out sooner rather than later! She came for an astrological consultation, anticipating that the stars somehow would reveal the answer. And so, she asked, "Who should I marry, Juan or José?" My answer was simple and to the point: "If you do not know, do not marry either of them. After all, marriage is a serious commitment."

Geminis become confounded when they do not know nor can discern right choice. Interestingly, many people experience this perplexity when the Sun transits through Gemini each year. In Paulina's case, an understanding of her psychology through her astrology helped reveal *the cause and core* of her problem. Paulina's parents had divorced, shortly after which her father died. Juan, thoughtful and intellectual, represented her mother, while Jose, emotional and wildly independent, reminded her of her late father. In effect, she had internalized and attempted unsuccessfully to harmonize and resolve her parents' very different approaches to life, as well as their love/hate feelings for each other. I advised her, "Forgive your mother, and get through the steps of grieving the loss of your father. Once you are healed of this inner division, you will be more likely to attract the one man with whom to spend your life." That day marked a major turning point in Paulina's journey.

Natives of this sign have been accused of being superficial, fickle, faithless and flighty. Although it is certainly not generally the case—this accusation may seem to be an injustice and for some Geminis an affront—there is some truth behind the popular warnings to avoid dating a Gemini lest one get hurt! But as was the case with Paulina, who sincerely sought to know the right answer and who did not want to break either of her suitor's hearts, the fact of the matter is that many Geminis simply do not know which way to go although they wish they did!

Geminis caught in a dilemma such as Paulina's naturally ask the astrologer which love—job, investment, purchase, school, etc.—is the right one? Oftentimes I find that the best answer to this question is another question: "Why don't you know?" When the Gemini soul is unable to resolve his indecision, he must look beyond the surface; like Paulina, he is likely to discover that his inability to determine which way to go is due to an underlying condition in his psychology. When he discovers what condition in consciousness is causing him to go in circles, the right answer appears. An astrological analysis can usually diagnose the fault, but the Gemini must be patient and do the work to resolve the rift.

In most cases, outer circumstances are but the tip of the iceberg, situations motivating the Gemini soul to dig deeper. But regardless of how entrenched the condition may be (perhaps the soul has been beset with the problem for lifetimes), with true understanding all can change in the twinkling of an eye!

WHO CAN CATCH THE WIND?

An Air sign on the Mutable-Wisdom Cross (Air), Gemini is the most mentally receptive of all the signs. People born with the Sun here are "mercurial" by nature—they tend to be inquisitive, mentally alert, restless and somewhat highstrung. They are motivated by an ever-present and active curiosity. The malleability of this influence makes them highly impressionable. They learn quickly, but can change their point of view as quickly as the wind might blow in a different direction. Their interest is easily piqued but can just as easily be lost. So many thoughts play within their minds, so many diverse options present themselves to them at a time, and so many things attract their attention, that they must necessarily turn off several of the many "radio stations" playing in their mind so they can hear just one clearly.

An innate objectivity and impartiality is invaluable in helping Geminis sort out multiple possibilities. When they become skilled in prioritizing their goals and working out the details of their varied interests, they are more adept at juggling several activities at once and tend to accomplish a great deal. They benefit from learning to quiet their minds. Without such tools, not only their desks, but also their minds tend to become cluttered and unmanageable.

FREEDOM TO CHOOSE

Astrologer Alan Leo called Geminis, *the non-conformists of the Zodiac*. Gemini astrologer, Grant Lewi (June 8, 1902), whose work has had a profound effect on astrological thought, introduced an approach to forecasting, which takes into consideration individual free-will choice. In, *Astrology for the Millions*, first published in 1940, Lewi writes about those born with the Sun in Gemini:

> *Into strange paths leads the Gemini's desire to be him-self, to think for himself, to do for himself, and ultimately, in its highest form, to become his best self. It takes him a long time to learn that he can't be anything except himself...*

> *If his life gives him sufficient scope to be himself, Gem-ini stays settled. The more his concept of what it means to be himself diverges from the early, sensational, rebellious, adven-turous urges, toward intellectual excellence and a sense of so-cial responsibility, the higher Gemini gets in the world, for his sense of what constitutes his best self is not limited.*

MAKE HASTE SLOWLY

Geminis typically are busy doing this and busy doing that. They can be quite knowledgeable, but until they stop to consider *who* they are and *why* they do what they do, they are apt to skim on the surface of things. Until they con-sciously focus their attention their minds tend to flit from one idea to another. Even the more anchored natives of this sign would do well to heed the words of an Eastern adept that once advised, *"Make haste slowly,"* and *"Meditate while in motion!"*[79]

Gemini rules the lungs and the body's respiratory and nervous systems. Air is infused with *prana*, a Sanskrit term meaning *life force*. Air and its energy permeate everything. When Geminis get scattered or distracted, they can exhaust themselves by thus dissipating their energy. Yoga and other practices that teach deep, conscious breathing can often help natives of this sign to heighten their awareness, calm their beings, and rid themselves of even deep-seated fears. Gem-ini also rules the hands and fingers. Natives of this sign are often dexterous and manually agile. Their speech is peppered with hand gestures. They often speak, type and write quickly (Especially when Mercury is in Gemini, less so when Mer-cury is in Taurus or Cancer). Gemini children can be especially fidgety. Working with their hands in some way, especially when handling clay or some other mal-leable, earthy substance, usually helps them to settle down.

In Gemini, the understanding of the right relationship of the material world to the spiritual world is experienced through the successful handling of everyday details and the management of time. Gemini governs all documents, files and contracts, scheduling and ticketing, plus the making and keeping of dates, reunions, and appointments. Managing everyday duties is a Gemini exercise in multi-tasking and juggling, oftentimes more challenging than one would think! Sometimes, natives of this mercurial sign do need to slow down so that they can hurry up! The minutiae in today's world seems endless, the appointments innumerable, the communication constant. Once these skills are mastered, Geminis will excel at calculating schedules, making appointments, arranging transportation and sorting out whatever.

In essence, the Gemini person outpictures who he thinks he is—his connection to (or his ignorance of) his Source—through the decisions he makes on a daily basis.

FOREVER ON THE MOVE

The Capuchin priest and mystic, Padre Pio, was born Francesco Forgione on May 25, 1887, in Pietrelcina, Italy. As a young man, he suffered severe respiratory problems (to which many Geminis are prone in varying degrees). Padre Pio moved to the monastery at San Giovanni Rotondo in 1916, with hope that its fresh mountain air would help ameliorate his chronic ailment. Except for a brief period of military service, he would stay there for the rest of his life.

But Geminis are forever on the move. How did Padre Pio manage to stay put in one place for so long? According to many well documented accounts from diverse places around the world, he bilocated.[80] (So Gemini!) He would appear in his finer, etheric (spirit) body somewhere distant while his body was sound asleep in his friar's cell at the monastery. Thus, he was able to extend his ministry to those in need, many of whom experienced miraculous cures. Those who told of receiving an out-of-body visitation from Padre Pio witnessed to a strong perfume of flowers filling the room during and immediately after these appearances.

MASTERING CONNECTIVITY

The working out of events, the weaving of the tapestry of one's life-story and the mastery of time is an exercise in connectivity. Mastering connectivity means being in the right place at the right time for the right reason. Synchronicity,

---

[79] El Morya in *Supermundane: The Inner Life, Book 1,* Nicholas Roerich (1938); also *Festina Lente*, "make haste slowly," is an ancient adage and an oxymoron (a figure of speech with apparently contradictory terms that together make sense).

[80] Bilocation is considered to be a spiritual gift from God whereby a person can be in two places at once.

when things almost magically seem to coincide in time and space, like bumping into your long-lost friend from Paris at the Empire State Building in New York, is a close cousin to connectivity. And although synchronicity appears to be more the work of fate and less a matter of conscious choice, the Gemini soul's attunement with (or ignorance of) inner promptings play a vital part in getting him to (or keeping him from) those important crossroads in his destiny.

An older Gemini man, a Master Montessori Teacher, spoke of his life's work as having evolved through a series of connections—one thing leading to another. Missing a beat is oftentimes no more grievous than dealing with the inconvenience of having to wait for the next train, but for Geminis, the consequences of not arriving on time or of moving too quickly can sometimes mean losing the ride for good or landing far afield of where they wanted to go. Geminis, both young and old, often practice and excel at making split-second decisions by participating in certain sports or activities, such as tennis, ping pong, and even card games, where all can be won or lost depending on their alertness and ability to think on their toes.

While Sagittarius is the sign of "the big picture," Gemini, its polar opposite, represents "the small steps"—the connections that, like pages in a book, all add up to the story of a life! Sagittarian types discover that for their dreams to come true, they have to focus on the details. Geminis, however, can get so caught up in detail that they lose sight of the greater goal, like focusing on words and forgetting they are part of a sentence, which is part of the overall story. When Geminis get too wrapped up in detail they typically become trapped in micromanaging. It is in handling their everyday affairs effectively, managing to be in the right place at the right time, making a connection that is perhaps unforeseen, that the story of the soul with the Sun in Gemini unfolds!

The timing of connections—in meetings and departures, within the twisting labyrinth of opportunity and karmic circumstance, in communication and misunderstandings, and in free-will choices—is often a key element in the story of the Gemini person in love.

Laura, a freelance photographer from Buenos Aries, moved to San Francisco when she was 24 years old. There she fell in love with and became engaged to Armando, a man 20 years her senior. For Laura, a double Gemini, travel was a way of life. Armando, a successful jeweler and a Taurus, was a stay-put kind of guy. Laura bitterly broke off the relationship when she found out that he was seeing another woman. Two years later, when she was visiting relatives in Europe, Armando managed to contact her and begged her to reconsider. She hesitantly agreed, but thinking to test his sincerity, insisted that he meet up with her in Argentina in three weeks' time. She coquettishly had him wait for her. When she arrived a week late, she learned that Armando had returned to San Francisco the day before, after waiting for her for days.[81]

Thus, the engagement ended. Laura ended up marrying and gave birth to three children. After nine years in Buenos Aires, she returned to San Francisco with her family. They bought an apartment in an upscale neighborhood. Three months later, she bumped into Armando. It happened that he, too, had moved—into the apartment building next door! Armando and Laura knew the old spark was still there, but now she was married; it was a no-can-do situation. They spoke occasionally. The years passed. Laura became estranged from her husband and they divorced. She was then free, but Armando was married. True to her conscience and overriding her strong feelings for this man she loved, Laura avoided an affair. She was then fifty and he was seventy. Laura moved back to Argentina. Armando suffered a stroke soon afterwards. It was hard for him to move, but he managed to scrawl on his notepad "L" for Laura.

It is not always easy to know the Will of God and even in knowing to act upon that awareness. Did pride and dishonesty destroy the possibility of a life together for Armando and Laura, or was their relationship not fated to be in this round? Only they can know for sure, for the lesson is theirs alone. But if we consciously strive to always be in tune with Divine Will for us, despite opposition or doubts, the chances of our being connected in time and space increase dramatically.

COMMUNICATION—"COMING INTO UNION"

Gemini and its polar opposite, Sagittarius, both represent communication and education—man's need to understand and to teach, to impart and to acquire knowledge and/or information. The destiny and indeed the karma of many a Gemini soul revolves around the written and spoken word. Broadcasters, writers, reporters, tour guides, schoolteachers, advertisers, editors, and lecturers are all engaged in Gemini/Sagittarius- type occupations. Transportation is another Gemini area whose usage continually affects the nature and speed of our daily lives and our interactions with one another. Gemini occupations include postal clerks and deliverers, chauffeurs, taxi cab, truck and bus drivers.[82]

Texting, tweeting, e-mailing, and all manner of devices designed to facilitate communication and connection are Gemini-related.

Natives of this mercurial sign are usually glib and loquacious. They often excel in mastering foreign languages, as well as their own, and can be entertaining salespersons. Many are skilled in research and fact-finding. They distinguish themselves by their logical, analytical arguments, and by their engaging wit and wisdom.

---

[81] This true story between Laura and Armando took place in the early 1970s, before computers and e-mail.

[82] Airplane pilots, mechanics, and so on, are ruled by Aquarius.

Unless their natal Moon, Mercury or Venus is in a Water sign (Cancer, Scorpio or Pisces), natives of this sign usually appear to be somewhat impersonal. This is due to the aloof, double-Air influence of the sign. The truth, they reason, needs no justification. However, criticism devoid of love is not truth at all but rather a form of ignorance. In such cases, observations made and conclusions drawn are often best kept unspoken. Learning to speak with discrimination, an awareness of their tone of voice, and a tactful choice of words helps Geminis communicate more compassionately.

Like the ancient Roman god Mercury, Geminis can be mischievous and not necessarily reliable in their roles as deliverers of the word, whether the message be their own or that of another. Mercury, also known to the Greeks as Hermes, was thought to be both quick and cunning. According to legend, he sometimes outwitted the gods themselves on behalf of mankind. Like Mercury, Geminis tend to have a way with words. Surely, language brings us together but words also divide us, through gossip and lies and through propaganda or misleading advertisements, even when negative thoughts and matrices may not be of our own making, but are mistakenly allowed to take hold of our minds. Articulate though they may be, Geminis need to be sure that their communication is honest and forthright, never deceitful nor manipulative.

Gemini rules speech, so most people with their Sun sign here love to talk. The occasional verbally inhibited native of this sign may channel the never-ending movement of his mind in some less obvious manner—perhaps on blogs in cyberspace, or in prolific writing, in music where his instrument tells his story, or even in some physical activity demanding constant motion such as bicycling. Even so, his reticence to communicate may be related to pockets of psychological fear and, if so, can often be remedied. Anyone who has been struck with stage fright or has experienced "the cat getting his tongue," as well as he who blurts out words he later regrets, has known firsthand the relationship between the gut and the mouth, between emotion and speech—between the Throat and the Solar Plexus chakras.

EVERY WORD COMMANDS YOUR ATTENTION!

Literature, politics, and entertainment can provide an ideal medium for those Geminis desirous of getting their message out. Witness comedian Bob Hope's wit and humor (May 29, 1903), politician John F. Kennedy's stirring speeches (May 29, 1917), and western actor John Wayne's affected yet popular drawl and dry humor (May 26, 1907). Consider Ralph Waldo Emerson's legacy of poetry and philosophy (May 25, 1803), and finally, the intricate plots and engaging cases of detective Sherlock Holmes and his assistant, Watson, as presented by the prolific Sir Arthur Conan Doyle (May 22, 1859).

What better example of the Gemini orator than American revolutionary

Patrick Henry, born May 18, 1736 (Julian; May 29, Gregorian), whose passionate, persuasive speeches roused his countrymen to take up arms in the name of freedom! His famous cry, given in a speech to the Second Virginia Convention in 1775, became a slogan for those willing to risk their lives for the cause: "Give me Liberty or give me death!" Thomas Jefferson attested to the powerful impact of Henry's speeches. Virginian freedom fighter, George Mason, said: "Every word he says not only engages but also commands the attention, and your passions are no longer your own when he addresses them." Patrick Henry had tried his hand as a farmer (his first wife's dowry included

Patrick Henry (1736–1799)

10,000 acres of land) and as a shopkeeper—all to no avail. Politics was his destiny and the rightful stage for his gift of eloquence and drama. Revolutions are prime times for radical Gemini thinkers to make their mark!

The opening lines of the Declaration of Independence (drafted primarily by Thomas Jefferson in June of 1776, when the Sun was transiting though Gemini) claim man's inalienable right: *to life, liberty, and the pursuit of happiness.* (In Jefferson's original draft, *the pursuit of happiness* read *the pursuit of property.* In other words, every man has a right to seek prosperity, regardless of his social status at birth.)

THE FATHER OF ECONOMICS

While the colonists were fighting to win their independence from Great Britain, Scotsman Adam Smith's writings, which advocated sovereignty for the colonists, were kindling a revolution across the Atlantic.[83]

Adam Smith was born on or about June 14, 1723 (Gregorian), in Kirkcaldy, a small town just north of Edinburgh.[84]

---

[83] Smith maintained that England should give up the colonies as a matter of economic necessity.

[84] Adam Smith's baptism was registered at the church in Kirkcaldy, Scotland, on June 5, 1723, so he was probably born around June 3 (Julian, adjusted to Gregorian, June 14).

Regardless of the exact date, Smith's destiny, as one of the key figures of the Scottish Enlightenment, and his lifelong search for truth during this revolutionary time can be seen in his chart.[85]

But he was not a rabble-rouser; he was a philosopher and a non-

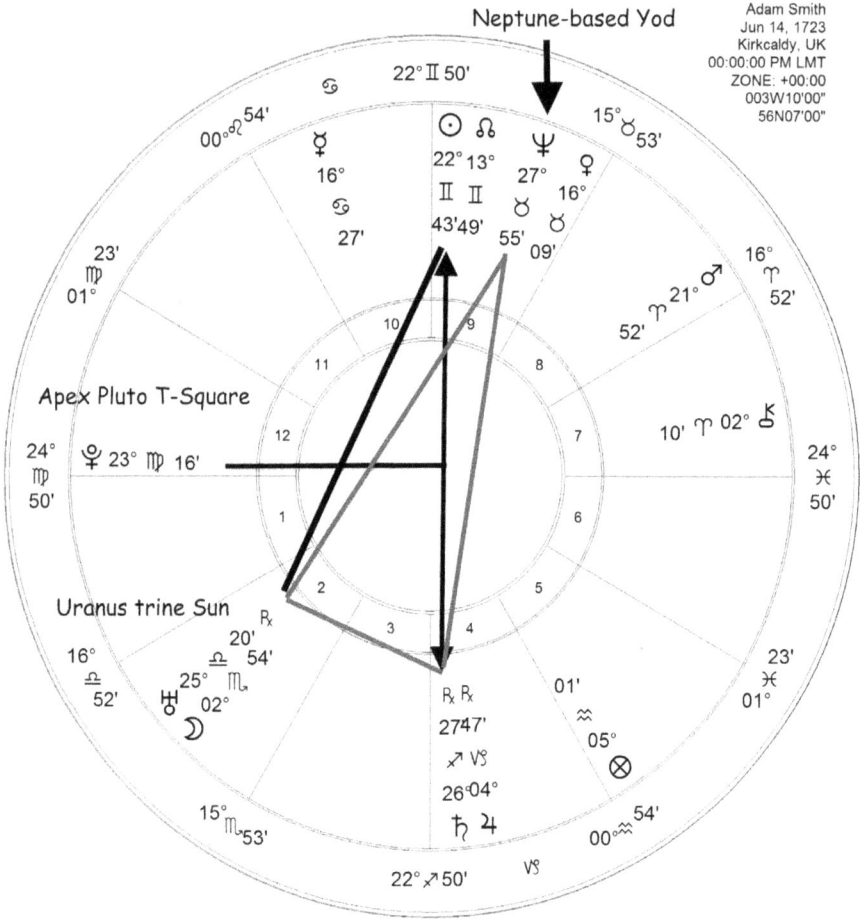

Neptune-based Yod

Adam Smith
Jun 14, 1723
Kirkcaldy, UK
00:00:00 PM LMT
ZONE: +00:00
003W10'00"
56N07'00"

Apex Pluto T-Square

Uranus trine Sun

---

[85] Smith's Sun in Gemini trined Uranus (revolution) in Libra, while forming part of a Mutable-Wisdom Pluto-based T-square. Saturn in Sagittarius opposed his Gemini Sun, both of which squared Pluto in Virgo. Gemini and Sagittarius, in speech and with pen, encapsulated the intense discussion and passionate oratory of the times, exposing (Pluto) injustice (Virgo), and proclaiming truth (Gemini/Sagittarius). And Neptune in Taurus (economy and values) was the catalyst planet in a Yod, focusing the need to answer the question of how honorable economic exchange could occur between free men.

conformist who worked within the system, which he thought to be limited and inadequate, in order to change it. In 1751, Smith became Professor of Logic at the University of Glasgow and in 1759, he took the Chair of Moral Philosophy. Smith believed that personal freedom was the key to prosperity. That same year, he published *Theory of Moral Sentiments,* which set the moral foundation for his later work on Capitalism. Smith maintained that individual freedom is rooted in man's nature to be self-reliant and self-commanding.

Smith is often called the Father of Economics. In 1776, the year that America declared her independence from Great Britain, he published *An Inquiry into the Nature and Causes of the Wealth of Nations.* With its shortened title, *The Wealth of Nations*, it is required reading in most economics courses to date! Many consider *The Wealth of Nations* to be the most groundbreaking and seminal work ever written on free-market Capitalism.

THEIR PENS WERE MIGHTIER

Harriet Beecher Stowe (June 14, 1811) and Anne Frank (June 12, 1929) are examples of Gemini female writers whose work influenced social thought on a large scale.

Stowe had strong abolitionist opinions, but she lived in a time when a woman's power was limited and behind the scenes. Anne Frank was still a child whose education and life were threatened by virtue of being a Jew during the Nazi occupation of the Netherlands where she lived. Stowe wrote *Uncle Tom's Cabin,* published in 1852, in order to persuade her readers to take a strong stance against slavery. She brought her message home by personalizing the horrors of slavery through the dramatic lives of the characters and families depicted in her novel. *Uncle Tom's Cabin* had such a widespread and powerful impact on people's feelings and thought that legend tells of President Lincoln greeting

Abraham Lincoln with Harriet Beecher Stowe—"So you're the little woman who started this Great War!" Uncle Tom's Cabin was the best-selling novel of the 19th century and the second best-selling book of that century following the Bible. In the first year of its publication, 300,000 copies were sold in the United States and one million in Great Britain.

Stowe at the White House in 1861, saying, "So you're the little woman who started this Great War!"

Annelies Frank's journal, published posthumously as *The Diary of Anne Frank,* brought to the world a most personal account of what life was like for a young Jewish girl and her family in hiding from Nazi terror in WWII. Although she died in a Nazi concentration camp, Anne's aspiration to be a writer did come true. On April 5th, 1944, she wrote:

> *I know I can write... I want to be useful or bring en-*
> *joyment to all people, even those I've never met. I want to go*
> *on living even after my death! And that's why I'm so grateful to*
> *God for having given me this gift, which I can use to develop*
> *myself and to express all that's inside me!*

THE GEMINI CHILD

The Gemini child was born to learn. Of all children, he is apt to be the most inquisitive, always asking questions, curious about this and that. Unless his teachers and elders remember that he is born into an Air sign on the Wisdom Cross, they can easily become exasperated! Gemini children typically like to write and to share their observations. (Many journalists, reporters and teachers have strong Gemini placements in their natal charts.) Why not help this child record his questions in a little book, and then research the answers together? Later he may be interested in working on the school paper.

While Sagittarius rules higher education from high school to graduate degrees, Gemini rules early education, from primary through middle school. An astrological adage states that there is nothing sadder than the Gemini child denied the benefit of a good education. Gemini children typically love to read from an early age; they enjoy learning a broad range of subject matter in detail. A good book can be like a treasured friend to children of this double air (mind) sign.

Questioning and quick-witted, the Gemini child is a classic candidate for the Socratic Teaching Method, named after the classical Greek philosopher, Socrates.[86]

Meant to invigorate the mind and to stimulate amazement rather than de-mand passive acceptance, this teaching style asks questions that help the inquirer examine, rather than memorize, and deduce logically rather than accept someone's conclusions. It also considers meaning and truth from a philosophical and moral standpoint as well as a factual one. By asking questions not easily answered, and which may expose flaws in thinking, Socrates intended to help the inquirer access the truth already known at the level of the soul.

---

[86] Socrates lived circa 470–399 BC.

Maria Montessori's approach to early-childhood education is also directed toward stimulating the child's innate potential. In the Montessori classroom, the teacher is but an assistant to the child's inner guide. All Montessori lessons and methods of presentation are designed to help the child in his own self-discovery. Better to teach him *how* to think, using classical educational and Montessori methods, rather than dictating to him *what* to think!

Essential to the young Gemini's success is the ability to focus and complete the task at hand. As he grows he can practice making lists, prioritizing his diverse activities, and categorizing his paraphernalia to help him keep his mind and his world in order. Gemini children seek variety in everything—clothes, food, books, and experiences! Some Gemini youngsters are so "airy" that they seem unaware of their physical environment. Many have trouble staying still. Most learn at a fairly brisk pace. Working with their hands helps them steady their nervous energy and restless minds. A nutritionally balanced diet (with fewer sweets) helps this child feel grounded and less apt to dissipate energy.

Some Gemini children are chatterboxes. They often are exceptionally witty. Teaching Gemini children to be lovingly truthful in word and in action helps set their sails aright for the rest of their lives.

Born mimics, Gemini youngsters are highly impressionable and need good role models. Discernment is advised in the selection of books, movies and the Internet, since little Geminis will copy (often verbatim) what they see and hear.

Some young Geminis are quieter than others; they tend to be serious students. Others are reminiscent of Curious George (that mischievous yet adorable monkey created by Margaret and Hans Rey, whose curiosity gets him into all kinds of trouble!) Although Margaret was a Taurus and Hans a Virgo, their charts were loaded with Gemini placements and their lives with Gemini-type adventures. Carrying the illustrated manuscript (Gemini) of *Curious George*, they escaped Paris on self-made bicycles (Gemini) only hours before the city fell to the Nazis.

Various modes of transportation catch the Gemini child's attention— scooters, bicycles, skates and skateboards! Teenage Geminis may spend much time working on bikes or cars, or whatever helps them get from one place to another swiftly.

WHAT ONE CAN DO, ALL CAN DO!

While we think of the relationship between brothers as binding, a special loyalty determined by bloodlines and familial traditions, we also recognize that contention is common between siblings. According to Freudian analysis, almost all of us are prone to sibling rivalry simply by having to share our mother's affection.

The first mention of bloodshed in the Bible occurs between brothers, when an enraged Cain kills his brother out of jealousy that Abel's offering "was more acceptable unto God." Cain could have conceivably learned from his more righteous brother. But envy and jealousy quickly disfigure the mind. Envy is so insidious that it has been called, "the green-eyed monster."

The Gemini soul can come to terms with and ultimately transmute any propensity he might have to envy through the awareness that, although all men are created equal, they have through their deeds and unknown karmic circumstances positioned themselves on different rungs of the Ladder of Life. Nevertheless, even though, *one star differeth from another star in glory,*[87] what one man can do, all can learn to do!

DUALITY—THE GEMINI CONUNDRUM

A double-minded man is unstable in all his ways.[88]

When the Sun passes through Gemini, June brides abound. Perhaps less known is that many divorces also take place at this time! Having been separated from God and from one another by freely partaking of the knowledge of relative good and evil, man is also prone to division—one from another and also within his own mind and psyche. To master such seeming contradictions is to successfully be in the world but not of it. When all the parts work together harmoniously—when the dual nature of the Gemini soul is unified—he exemplifies integrity.

Duality is represented in all the Mutable-Wisdom Signs: the Gemini Twins, the Sagittarian Centaur, half-horse and half-man; the Piscean Fish swimming in opposite directions; in Virgo an innate understanding of perfection struggles with man's imperfect state.

Geminis are particularly susceptible to duality, which the ancients rightly called "division within the members." Psychological dysfunctions such as compulsive lying, schizophrenia, the hearing of voices, bipolar disorder or depression are often symptoms of an inability to resolve opposing or contradictory inner states. Occasionally, the non-resolution manifests itself in outer events rather than in obvious internal mental states. Witness the Gemini "serial dater," who leaves relationships as soon as they get serious or who is unable to find or stay with the right partner, as in the case of Paulina, above.

Geminis are on the Wisdom Cross (along with Sagittarians, Virgos and Pisceans). What over time can manifest as a Jekyll-and-Hyde identity dichotomy

---

[87] Corinthians 15:41
[88] James 1:8

begins with a small justification; that is, finding some excuse to make a wrong right—some rationalization by which the individual ignores the inner voice's warning, saying to himself, "Just this once won't hurt." Geminis particularly need to guard against mental projections. They may hear the inner echoes of the astute fallen angel, inciting Eve through subtle intellectual arguments, to partake of the Tree of Knowledge (of relative good and evil). "Don't worry," the serpent whispers, "you will not *surely* die." Eve was beguiled but could have done better! Never before or since has such a judgment been handed down—the exile from Paradise and the loss of immortality!

Marilyn Monroe, born June 1, 1926, aspired to be a serious actress, but she could not shake the sexy-clueless-blond image that she adopted so successfully. She captured Gemini's duality when she said, "I'm two people, really."

The soul born in Gemini has a very special opportunity to repair and restore fragmented aspects of his being. The solution to the many types of inner schism so common in this sign is always a return to wholeness. Outer circumstances are but the tip of the iceberg. But regardless of how entrenched the condition may be—perhaps the soul has been beset with the problem for lifetimes—with true understanding, all can change in the twinkling of an eye.

EMBRACING THE MISSION

At a certain point, the soul in Gemini ceases to dance on the surface of things. He senses that he was born to fulfill a higher goal and will seek to conform his life to that end. He may dedicate himself to some worthy outer cause, as did the French sea explorer, naval officer, scientist, filmmaker, inventor and ecologist, Jacques Cousteau (June 11, 1910).

Among his many credits, Cousteau co-developed the Aqua-Lung, the forerunner of today's deep-sea diving equipment. Destiny brought him to work with the element of breath and with lungs—both represented by his birth sign—in a most unique and meaningful way! Known by many as *Le Commandant*, for his service in WWII, Cousteau's Aqua-Lung was used to remove enemy mines in the water after the war. His greater mission, however, was to increase mankind's awareness of the underwater world that surrounds us so that its waters and sea life might be better appreciated and preserved!

BECOMING THE GEMINI HERO

"Midway in our life's journey, I found myself astray in a dark wood in which the straight way had been lost." Thus begins *The Inferno*, part of the classic trilogy, *The Divine Comedy*, by Italian poet, writer, moral philosopher, and political thinker, Dante Alighieri (birth date in question).[89]

Brilliantly constructed, *The Divine Comedy* is incredible in the complexity of its meaning, style, hidden codes, and its entertaining portrayal of the path of Redemption. Dante's story is that of the journey of a soul who awakens to realize his use of free will has led him far astray. He yearns to return, but he is lost, terrified and in need of a guide. Indeed, to awaken from the slumber of ignorance can be terrifying, but it is the first step home.

The awareness that a Higher Will is guiding his life and that he has, through his own free will choices, gone his own way and must find his way back home, is the beginning of freedom from struggle for the Gemini Aspirant. A silence opens up and he can hear what he was not listening to before. The desire to restore an ancient harmony within his being becomes stronger. He gradually, or sometimes suddenly, attempts to bring the many facets of his life into alignment with his emerging understanding. Now he makes a firm *commitment* to the spiritual path, its disciplines and its requirements, and to his Teacher or Guru. He values the commitment his Teacher has made to him. Strengthened by the flow of love's current between them, he humbly recognizes that the commitment of the Teacher—whose power lifts him temporarily from the labyrinth of his own karmic condition, while guiding, instructing, disciplining and working with him—is far greater than his own. And so, in this relationship, whose binding tie is reflected in the Gemini Aspirant's approach to life in general, he learns the meaning of love on a new level. His multiplicity of interests and thirst for learning continues, but all lesser things come under the one umbrella of his sacred vow.

THOU SHALT DECREE A THING & IT SHALL BE DONE![90]

Right from the start, the Gemini soul on the path of overcoming learns the power of the Word to create and to destroy. He becomes increasingly more adept in the use of the Throat chakra in devotional prayer and powerful spiritual affirmations, and in sharing the wisdom of the ages. The more power he wields through the spoken word, the more imperative it becomes that he refrain from gossip and idle conversation. Particularly if unresolved schisms exist within him, he must learn how to guard his mind against "the voices of the night"—negative thoughts cluttering the conscious mind. Although his natural ability to reason objectively and analytically helps him discern and communicate truth, he is vulnerable to accepting these accusatory mental projections due to his habit of being excessively critical. He needs to guard against voicing criticism, which picks apart, shatters and divides, rather than heals or justly exposes.

---

[89] Dante was born in Florence, Italy. The exact birth date is unknown, generally believed to be on or around May 31, 1265 (Julian; June 11, Gregorian). Dante alludes to being born a Gemini in *The Divine Comedy*.

[90] "Thou shalt also decree a thing, and it shall be established unto thee: and the light shall shine upon thy ways." Job 22:28

As he obtains greater mastery with sound, the Gemini Hero-to-Be learns to intone *fohatic keys,* which are particular combinations of words, tones, pitches, which generate energy and frequencies that release and quicken the light of the chakras. These are similar to the use of *kias,* Japanese for "spirit shouts," used in martial arts to focalize and project power.

Padre Pio (1887–1968) shown here as a younger priest with the stigmata (the open wounds of Christ) which he bore for 50 years.

Padre Pio often spoke of the importance of prayer. "Prayer is the best weapon we possess," he said. "It is the key that unlocks the heart of God." One of Padre Pio's favorite expressions was, "Pray, hope, and don't worry." He explained, "Worry is useless. God is merciful and will hear your prayer."

GEMINI TESTS ON THE WAY

Geminis are especially vulnerable to a ploy not uncommon in spiritual communities called 'divide and conquer'—a test of solidarity of purpose and of love—in which brother is pitted against brother. Divide and conquer can be deadly, effectively dismantling the relationship between persons meant to strive and work together. The wise spiritual seeker born in this most mutable sign avoids acting upon hearsay and gossip, so often the seed of division and conflict.

Even the most dedicated and sincere Gemini devotee, who may have walked the spiritual path faithfully for many years, nevertheless finds that if he has not made his peace with himself or with another, if there be an absence of forgiveness within his being, he will not be able to advance beyond a certain point.

As the Gemini Aspirant advances to higher levels of initiation, the tests confronting him become more difficult and the choices less obvious. The inner battle can become intense and unrelenting. As the veil is rent and he gains access to higher worlds, he also perceives darkness as never before. Padre Pio bore the stigmata, the wounds of the Christ, and had continual communion with God's absolute Love. But his battle with demonic forces was very real. The Gemini Aspirant finds he must continually test the spirits.[91]

How can he discern whether he is hearing the voice of God or that of demons masquerading as sacred beings? Padre Pio offered this rule of thumb: imposter spirits tend to elicit a feeling of joy and attraction followed by great sadness (because when they depart, they have taken something precious from us), whereas in the presence of angels, masters, and other ascended beings, one is apt to feel true humility and great peace.

Despite the Gemini Aspirant's great devotion, knowing and then accepting the Will of God does not always come easily; the right way that he perceives may go against his desires. He can justify almost anything through shrewd argument. At times, he is tempted to sever his relationship with his Teacher, whose demands may appear to be contrary to his own inclinations.

Nonetheless, he keeps his promises; he obeys the higher calling. He increasingly understands that when he surrenders his will to divine Will, he experiences a newborn freedom and creativity that he has never known before. In effect, he enters superconscious awareness. He comes to know and seeks to sustain the Holy Spirit, the Divine Presence described in the Bible as a rushing, mighty wind and the breath of spiritual fire, which empowered the disciples on Pentecost. The 18th century Italian rabbi, scholar and Kabbalist, Moses Hayyim Luzzatto, described the Holy Spirit as "bestowed enlightenment." The preeminent Jewish philosopher and Torah scholar, Maimonides, taught that the Holy Spirit transforms a person, who then is able to perceive things generally inaccessible to the mind.[92]

As he cleaves more and more to this basic Law of Living, he will in some way become a teacher of this path to others. Apart from any outer triumph, he realizes inwardly that his destiny is that of being an instrument of a Plan, divinely conceived and guided, which may impel him to shift gears dramatically. At the point of transformation he may abandon prior aspirations, (often to the consternation of those around him), to pursue what now appears to him to be not only a more meaningful way — but also, indeed, the path to his salvation.

THE GEMINI HERO — THE SAGE

The Gemini Hero has mastered being in the world, handling a multiplicity of detail and functioning on several tracks of awareness, yet not feeling overwhelmed. Perhaps it took years, if not lifetimes, for him to be so engaged, and yet to remember always who he is, why he is, where he is, and where he is going.

---

[91] "Beloved, believe not every spirit, but try the spirits whether they are of God: because many false prophets are gone out into the world." 1 John 4:1

[92] Moshe ben Maimon, known as Maimonides, lived from 1135 to 1204.

He asks not, "Should I do this or should I do that?" When beset with multiple options, he asks inwardly, "What, [LORD], would you have me do?" His heart attuned with the Will of God, which he knows to be his reason for being; he has learned to listen to the inner voice, and not confuse it with so much noise and seemingly good advice. He walks with simplicity and with self-confidence. He is as a fountain of Wisdom from which many draw guidance. He has become the Gemini Sage.

5.

♎

Libra

Symbol . . . . *The Scales*

Born . . . . Sept. 23 ~ Oct. 22

Archetype . . . . *The Advocate*

Key Phrase . . . . *I Balance*

Element . . . . **Air**

Cross . . . . **Cardinal-Power**

House . . . . **Seventh:**
Marriage & other partnerships, divorce,
agreements, the law, open enemies

Ruler . . . . **Venus**

Esoteric Ruler . . . . **Uranus**

Polarity . . . . **Aries**

Chakra . . . . Heart

Anatomy . . . . . . Kidneys, adrenal glands, skin

Spiritual Qualities . . . . **The Holy Spirit through
the balanced heart, integrity, higher intuition,
defender of truth, beauty, understanding
of others, endurance**

Vulnerable to . . . . Idolatry, dishonesty, intrigue
& betrayal, unwise liaisons, fear of conflict, peace at
any price, mental vacillation, being a social butterfly

Must Acquire . . . . **Peace in the eye of the hurricane,
balance in all things, higher understanding,
glaring honesty, inner & outer
resolution, core sense of self**

Ghandi • Margaret Thatcher • Nicholas Roerich • Catherine Zeta-Jones • Luciano Pavarotti

THE SUN IN LIBRA

When I despair, I remember that all through history the way of truth and love has always won. There have been tyrants and murderers, and for a time, they can seem invincible, but in the end, they always fall. Think of it—always.

—Mahatma Gandhi (October 2, 1869)

THE PLUMB LINE OF TRUTH[93]

How can the soul born into the sign of the scales achieve balance and equanimity in a world characterized more by turbulence than by peace? How can he separate truth from error when the culture into which he is born cultivates illusion? And why are Librans the most vulnerable of all the signs to betrayal? The Libran Hero-to-be must align himself with the plumb line of truth within his heart of hearts and not be moved, not for gale or storm, not for wealth or want, nor for love of friend or fear of the enemy.

Libra is the second sign of *the Air Triplicity* (Gemini, Libra and Aquarius) and one of the four Cardinal-Power signs (Aries/Libra, Cancer/Capricorn). In Libra is released the *power* of Wisdom (Air) to exercise right judgment. Libran souls are challenged to access and develop the heart's wisdom that they be able to separate reality from unreality and truth from error.

On the Astrological Wheel, Libra lies at 180 degrees on the cusp of the Seventh House, midway around the circle and opposite Aries at zero degrees on the cusp of the First House. This line divides the astrological wheel into two halves, called hemispheres. Aries represents *me* while Libra represents *me and you*. Any planets in the First House color the personality. Planets in the Seventh House tell about marriage, partnership and relationships with others in general. The Sun (I Am principle) is exalted in Aries. In Libra, the Sun is in its fall. While Arians tend to see life from their own perspective and need to become more aware of others' sensibilities and perceptions, Librans naturally gravitate toward forming

---

[93] Plumb line: A cord weighted with lead that is used in building to check that vertical structures are level. It is used symbolically to refer to the divine standard of truth and right action.

[94] In Genesis, the Serpent or Fallen Angel beguiles Eve, who allows herself to be tempted due to her desire to be thought wise, to partake of the Tree of Good and Evil—that is, to enter into a consciousness of Duality. Once she does so, she can no longer abide in Eden, the Higher Realm, where all is One. Adam is not duped, but elects to be cast out with Eve rather than be alone in Paradise.

meaningful partnerships—they tend to see *me* in terms of *we*.

In Aries, we choose to be who we are—men created in the image of the Creator—or to embody the serpent's lie; in Libra, we meet the consequences of that decision.[94] When in Aries, we identify with who we are not, creating a persona called by poets and mystics by various names: *the mask, the carnal mind, the false ego, or the imposter*—in Libra we will be stripped of the unreality we have embraced. Librans find mirrors in the close relationships they form, which they use— albeit subconsciously—as a means to separate the real from the unreal within themselves.

The soul born with the Sun in Libra can become so wrapped up in the lives of other people that he loses his sense of self. When this occurs, an emotional or mental imbalance, like feeling overwhelmed or even momentarily confused, causes him to retreat into his spiritual and psychological center. Or perhaps some event will trigger him to withdraw, so that he might reset his priorities and bring back order within his world. By choosing vocations bringing them into close and meaningful contact with people on a daily basis, some Librans fulfill their desire to be intimately involved with others without becoming enmeshed in their lives. At the end of the workday, they benefit by closing the door.

THE WELL-BALANCED LIBRAN PERSONALITY

Of all the twelve Zodiacal signs, Libra is the only one whose symbol is an object rather than an animal or man. The Scales have been used from ancient times as an instrument for determining the worth of gold and other precious stones and gems by their weight. The Scales are also spoken of symbolically, especially as an expression of judgment, such as, "he was weighed in the balance and found wanting."

We enter Libra at the time of the Autumnal Equinox, when night and day are of equal length. The Libran Scales symbolize this perfect balance, often apparent in the physique and personality of those born with the Sun in this sign. Both male and female Librans typically display strong characteristics of both genders. Even the most feminine of Libran women will portray some defining masculine trait such as a strong and outspoken mind, while the Libran man often is soft spoken with an engaging graciousness and social refinement.

Venus rules Libra. Born under the influence of the planet of love and beauty, Librans tend to be sociable with a marked genial demeanor. And yet there is something impersonal (Air) about the Libran personality. Librans typically are very personal in their involvement with others while being simultaneously objective, independent and somewhat detached. Moreover, Saturn, which denotes responsibility and a sense of duty to fulfill one's dharma (obligation to life), is strong in this sign. Its serious cast is notable in the appearance and lifestyle of most Libran personalities.

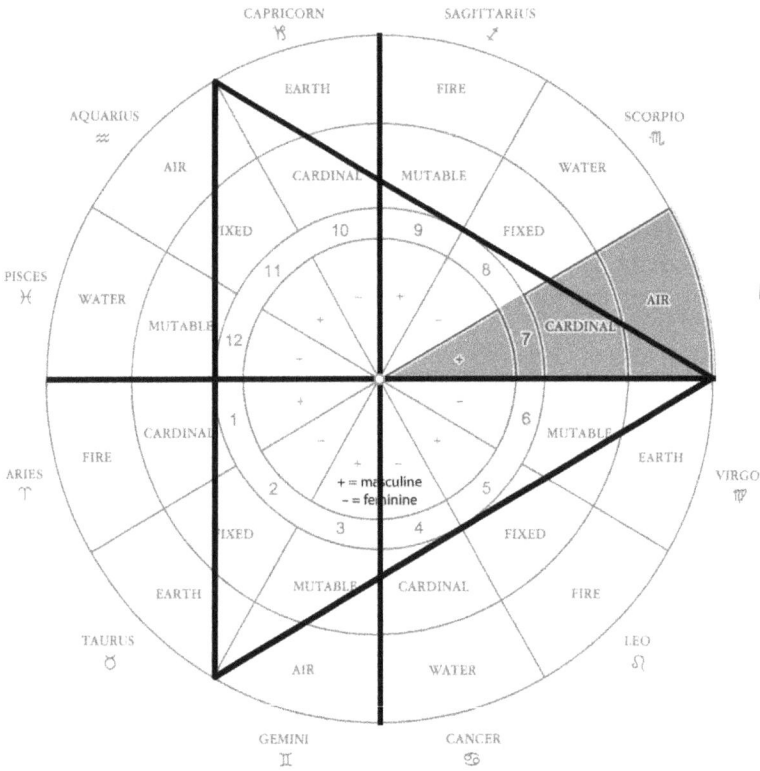

Libra:
7th House
Cardinal-
Power Cross
Air Element

Harmony and balance are at the heart of the Kabbalistic Tree of Life. For example, love, manifesting in the form of generosity, by *Hesed*, a sephirah on the right-hand column of love, is a positive virtue, but too much generosity can deplete one's funds and potentially weaken others, such as happens in spoiling a child. Judgment, associated with *Gevurah* (opposite *Hesed*) on the left-hand column, adjusts love's excesses and is based on the need for resolutions and discernment in human affairs. But if not balanced and harmonized by love and mercy, judgment can be too severe. *Tiferet*, the sephirah on the middle column blends and harmonizes the energies of *Gevurah* and *Hesed*. Compassion (*Tiferet*) urges us to take into account factors we may have ignored in placing judgment upon others or ourselves. Likewise, we may desire to give and forgive, but as is sometimes true in the case of a child, a balanced discipline may be the most merciful and loving response.

Gevurah (Judgment) ♂ — **Hesed** (Mercy) ♃ — **Tiferet** (Beauty) ☉

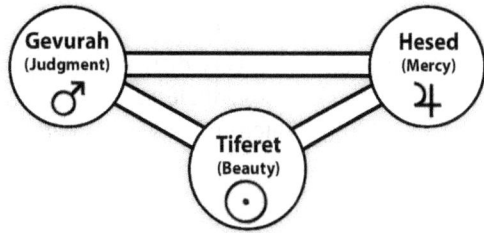

Kabbalah Triad—Tiferet (compassion) harmonizes the energies of Gevurah (judgment) and Hesed (love).

In his book, *Practical Kabbalah*, Rabbi Laibl Wolf illustrates an exercise in *Tiferet*:

> *Bring to mind someone you admonished recently. It might have been a family member or someone in the workplace, or possibly a friend. As you do, you will momentarily sense the fires of Gevurah. But immediately move back into your center— the pleasant warmth of Tiferet. Find a plausible reason for that person's misbehavior or mismanagement. Allow that reason to settle upon your heart. While you focus on that person in your mind, see yourself projecting your warmth as waves of compassion. Allow the warmth of compassion to subdue the egocentric hurt you feel. See the person experiencing your compassionate warmth. Allow a smile to arise on that person's face. Allow yourself an inner smile as well.*

Rabbi Wolf asks us to see the comforting yet powerful presence of the Angel Michael (*Hesed*) and of the Angel Gabriel (*Gevurah*) present during our meditations.

The same principle of finding balance and maintaining harmony between different energies holds true in astrological interpretation. Trine aspects, for example, are seen as indicating good fortune, positive karmic return, talents and gifts the individual can easily develop. But trines weaken when these gifts are taken for granted. Similarly, the more challenging astrology can limit and feel burdensome, but when approached with great determination it becomes the point of greatest power and achievement. People we admire rarely have "easy" charts, but a combination of very difficult configurations usually balanced by positive positions. The key, nevertheless, is in the determination to gain one's victory over one's astrology, which reflects one's karma, and in essence, is the victory over one's self!

LIBRA & THE KIDNEYS

Libra rules the kidneys and the renal system. Simply put, the kidneys are the body's major filters. By removing toxic waste and excess water through the urine, the kidneys maintain balance within the body.

Obstructions within the kidneys lead to imbalance, even as karmic records and states can manifest in kidney disorders. Especially when transiting outer planets aspect the Sun in Libra, acute or chronic kidney problems may manifest. Natives of this sign can grasp the opportunity to heal not only the outer obvious manifestation, but also the inner cause as well.

A Los Angeles-based psychiatrist once related the following true story. Although I do not know the client's birthdate, the story illustrates how karmic and psychological states register within the physical body. Sybil was 24 years old, intelligent, educated and attractive. She came from a well-to-do Jewish family and, having recently obtained her degree in fashion design, was looking forward to establishing her own business. In the midst of this positive setting, she developed a kidney disease. She now had to face the shocking news that her kidneys needed to be removed and that she would have to undergo dialysis treatment for the rest of her life. Understandably, Sybil was distraught and angry. What had she done to deserve such misfortune? She agreed to the psychiatrist's suggestion that he help her come to peace with her diagnosis through guided meditation. As she entered a deep meditative state, Sybil relaxed. A soft light shone over her face. She began to relate her vision in which she saw herself as a young woman standing at a well, drawing water in some ancient place. A man close to her age came up to her, parched with thirst, and asked her for a drink. She looked at him and in anger dropped her two ceramic jugs, which fell to the ground cracking into pieces. As the water ran out, she looked upon this man's face. He radiated love and compassion. Sybil realized this man was Jesus and that her kidneys represented the jugs of water.

Although Sybil knew a long road awaited her, she felt peace and gratitude, love and joy for this opportunity to balance her accounts. Sybil now was ready for her next step. All medical procedures went well and she was able to launch her career. Making time each year to give talks around the country to people of all ages undergoing dialysis, she has inspired many with her story and infused them with hope.

In the Aquarian Age, the Libran soul can help maintain healthy kidneys through right diet and exercise and through the Aquarian Science of Sound and Invocation to transmute past records, making room for new opportunities!

THE RHYTHM OF THE GAME & THE RHYTHM OF LIFE

Time magazine's article on American actor Will Smith, born September 25, 1968, reads like a classic description of an amicable yet no-nonsense Libran man: "What we always sense about the Wise Guy is that he's essentially a Sweet Guy, eager to learn, eager to please, eager to be heroically helpful and romantically obliging."[95]

The article goes on to describe Smith as a hard working actor with a definitive strategy for success, an integrated man who puts principles and family first. Similarly, we see in Libran actor Matt Damon (October 8, 1970), that charmingly *powerful* Libran smile and good looks (Venus), an intelligently genuine manner, but the signature "this is the way I want it done" Libran backbone. Damon is passionately dedicated to his philanthropic work, most notably his effort to awaken attention to the global water crisis.[96]

Check out Robert Redford's film, *The Legend of Bagger Vance,* starring Will Smith and Matt Damon, and you will see the Libra-ness in these two men beautifully matched in their respective roles. Smith

Libran Actors *Matt Damon* & *Will Smith*

plays Bagger Vance, a Christ-like figure or Angel in disguise who appears on the scene as a humble, and as it turns out, a mysteriously sagacious black man. Damon plays Captain Junnuh, a down-and-out former golf champion who's stuck in a ten-year slump, a reaction to the horrors he witnessed in WWI. Bagger comes on the scene, asking Junnah if he might be his caddy for an upcoming golf tournament. During this initial encounter between the two men, Bagger tells Junnah:

---

[95] See www.Content.Time.com.
[96] Damon founded the H_2O Africa Foundation, which merged with WaterPartners to create www.Waters.org in 2009.

"A man's grip on his club is just like his grip on his life…the rhythm of the game is just like the rhythm of life."

On an online interview,[97] Smith made this comment about the game of golf:

> *What's great about golf is that it is the most difficult thing you will ever do in your life. It's that shot you chase for the rest of your life - that one piece of greatness, that one piece of perfection, that excellence. There is no other sport that's like that.*

The Legend of Bagger Vance is a great movie for Librans learning what it takes to focus and to win. Replace the word *swing* with *balance* for a Libra formula for getting back in the game! In Bagger's advice to Junnuh: "…the trick is to find your swing…you've lost you're swing, we've got to go find it."

Where is the perfect swing? Bagger explains that it's "somewhere in the harmony of all there is, there was, all there will be…" and that "there's a perfect shot out there for each and every one of us, what we've got to do is get ourselves out of its way…" In a decisive moment in the game, he instructs Junnuh to seek "the place where everything that is becomes one. How to find that place? Bagger tells him, "You've got to seek that place with your soul, Junnuh."

THE IRON LADY WITH THE VELVET GLOVE

Margaret Thatcher, born October 13, 1925, exemplifies the influential, elegantly cordial yet unmistakably powerful Libran woman. One of the 20th century's most dominant political figures, Thatcher became the first female Prime Minister of the United Kingdom. Tastefully dressed to the tee and demurely feminine, she said of herself, "What Britain needs is an Iron Lady." She once told Members of Parliament, "I was born under the sign of Libra—it follows that I am well-balanced."

Lessons in balance appear repeatedly in the Libran soul's life as he keeps practicing and fine-tuning his ability to be—as the well-known Yogi, Paramahansa Yogananda teaches, "calmly active and actively calm." When in life an emotion, thought, situation, stance or reaction is imbalanced, the sensitive Libran feels an uncomfortable sensation within his heart that he would be wise not to ignore. In time, he comes to know that maintaining balance is the key to his victory.

---

[97] See www.Hollywood.com/static/the-legend-of-bagger-vance-will-smith-interview.

INTENSE GENTILITY

While Mars-ruled Arians are obviously argumentative, Librans generally give the impression of being agreeable when in fact they are mounting a convincing, and in their minds, irrefutable case. It has been said, step on a Libran's toes and you will be told (politely, of course) everything you have done wrong since you first met! Positively speaking, if you find yourself in a disagreement with a Libran, and have a bit of Air in your own make-up, you can agree to disagree for the sake of enlightenment! The Sun in Libra person typically enjoys intellectual discussion as long as it's spirited and civilized! When your Libran friend exclaims, "Ah, now I get it," not only have you reached a friendly accord, but in the Libran's eyes, at least, you've also spent a most enjoyable time together. On the other hand, since Librans tend to take the truth they perceive as self-evident, they can become visibly piqued when challenged. They need not accept other points of view, but they do gain by learning to truly listen to what another person is trying to communicate to them. Not only are they more likely to remain balanced and composed, but also their own message will receive a more receptive audience when the exchange is mutually respectful.

Despite their attractive and cooperative spirit, make no mistake about it—Librans like to be in charge! They need to watch out that they not arouse resistance by assuming unwarranted responsibility for others, telling them how they should act and what they should do. Most Librans tend to be socially active, strong-willed and self-directed, but can be temporarily swayed and their confidence shaken by an exaggerated preoccupation with the happiness of others and/or a desire for approval.

STRIPPING THE LIE

Lovers of peace, Librans nevertheless must muster the courage to tell the truth even if in so doing they risk rocking the boat, being reprimanded or losing popularity. Surprisingly, in this sign representing reality, the liar has had a field day! In Libra we find the lie manifesting in myriad forms of dishonesty, from the lie of omission and so-called white lies, to downright conscious trickery, calculated intrigue, and malicious treachery.[98]

Because that which is real is true, during Libran cycles we learn the danger of misrepresenting ourselves to another. The Libran who is so surfeited in pain or so blinded by selfishness as to chronically lie can actually come to believe the lies he has woven, despite the most obvious evidence to the contrary and the

---

[98] Lying by omission is lying by either omitting certain facts or by failing to correct a misconception.

timely advice of loved ones. Such a one is in a state of denial. One day he will receive the initiation called *The Stripping*! During this harrowing experience the light of truth exposes the lie. Bereft of his mask, the one so mercifully stripped of illusion experiences a sense of nakedness, of vulnerability and often of shame. Moreover, the experience is often a public one. Hard as the stripping may be, humiliation and a cold glass of water can save the soul! In reality, the light of truth and that of love are one and the same.

LIBRAN LESSONS IN CHILDHOOD

In his autobiography, *The Story of My Experiments with Truth,* Mohandas K. Gandhi, known worldwide as *the Mahatma*, relates a lesson he learned in childhood that served him the rest of his life. Gandhi was born on October 2, 1869, in Porbandar, India. His account of an event that took place when he was in High School is illustrative of how the Libran young person, hurt by being falsely accused, can nonetheless benefit from the experience.

Mohandas was excessively shy, but also very conscientious during his youth, especially because he knew that any dishonesty on his part would hurt the people he loved most. One day he was late arriving to his high school's Saturday afternoon physical education activities. When asked to justify his tardiness (he was usually punctual), he explained truthfully that he had left his home and walked straight to school, but that he did not have a watch and so had lost track of the time. The schoolmaster did not believe him and imposed upon him a small fine. Gandhi writes: "I was convicted of lying! That deeply pained me. How was I to prove my innocence? I cried in deep anguish." But Mohandas learned an important lesson he would never forget: he realized that "an honest man must be meticulous in all his ways." He adds, "This was the first and last instance of my carelessness at school."

Libran children benefit when taught from an early age that truth brings its own reward. Being heart people and doers of the Word, their natural gifts of diplomacy and kindness need to be given plenty of room for expression. Many of these children, like the young Mohandas Gandhi, hold very definite notions about what is right and what is wrong. At the same time, they must be encouraged to dare to say 'no' when necessary and taught not to compromise truth to avoid getting into trouble, to buy a moment's peace or a playmate's friendship. Some Libran children will lie, not so much out of fear, but rather due to their deep desire to make people happy!

THE SCALES OF JUSTICE

Like Capricorn, Libra is a sign of judgment. While Saturn rules Capricorn, the planet of "accounts are due" is exalted in the Sign of the Scales. Statues and images of "Lady Justice," or the "Goddess of Justice," usually depict her holding the Scales of Justice in one hand and a sword, symbolizing the division of light from darkness, in the other. Oftentimes she is blindfolded symbolizing that justice must not be based on outer vision, for things are not always what they seem. Nor must justice be swayed by subjective prejudices through whose lens reason is distorted.

Most Librans have an innate sense of fairness and impartiality, an inner attunement with the Law written not only upon slabs of clay and pages of books, but also confirmed upon the very heart itself. They will defend the underdog, stand on principle, and are unlikely to allow a perceived injustice to stand undefended. Some Librans actually do pursue a career in law. But for most people born under this influence, thoughtful deliberation leading to right choice and just decision is simply a way of life!

WHEN CONFLICT UPSETS THE SCALES

Astrological tradition calls Libra the sign of open enemies—those who openly oppose us, such as in a direct confrontation or lawsuit. Natives of the Scales typically wince at, and if at all possible avoid and even retreat from conflict. The frequencies of discord jar their nervous system and threaten their mental equilibrium. Disharmony can be physically and psychically uncomfortable, if not unbearable for natives of this sign. Notwithstanding, conflict can be purposeful. However uncomfortable, conflict tests the durability of any union and marks the need for change, often becoming the means toward some greater good in the seeking of resolution. When opposed, Libran souls often strengthen in character in response to the opportunity to put the tenets of their faith into practice. Not only lawyers and mediators, but also peacemakers, tacticians, medical and legal advocates and public relations people often have pronounced planetary placements in Libra.

Because they focus less on themselves and more on others, persons born with the Sun in Libra typically seek ways to help others solve their problems. In actuality, being an Air sign, they don't *feel* as much as they perceive, unless the Water element—(Cancer, Scorpio and Pisces)—is strongly present elsewhere in the chart. Intellectually oriented, insightful and capable of being impartial yet understanding, they often make excellent counselors.

Librans instinctively realize that there are two sides to every story. Life teaches them to reserve judgment until they have heard from all parties concerned. They are known to consider fairly both sides of any given issue and are often called upon to act in some capacity as mediator between opposing sides. Many Librans excel at the art of compromise; grasping the matter from the other person's viewpoint helps them to meet him halfway. A truce is called, peace abounds, the agitated heart is calm—balance!

Nonetheless, when compromise signifies a betrayal of principle, the Libran soul is challenged to summon the courage to stand his ground even if he must withstand the havoc that ensues when the applecart is overturned. When he compromises what he knows is right in order to buy the peace, the relief he feels is short-lived. Either his conscience plagues him or the ignored problem later erupts causing a greater discord than it would have had it been addressed sooner. Experience teaches him (although some Librans take longer than others to grasp the lesson) that he must never betray his inner truth nor mislead another.

Yet when natives of the Scales determine to hold the line, their stern sense of right and wrong may smack of intolerance and an inappropriately judgmental approach. When should the Libran parent discipline his child, gaining his respect and helping him forge character and when should he be lovingly forbearing? When must he allow his children to find their own way, even if in so doing, their errors cause them pain? The best choices in these and in other close relationship scenarios can be difficult to fathom. But even before the Libran soul understands why, he can intuit the answer by tuning into his heart's wisdom.

LIBRA IN THE ARTS

Courtesy, good manners and elegance frame the Libran mindset well. Most Librans feel at home in lovely surroundings and shun vulgarity. Even Libran babies will respond to flowers, color and other touches of beauty and harmony in their surroundings. Born under Venus' rays, many Librans are naturally attracted to and may excel in one or more of the fine arts, especially when given the opportunity to develop their talent from an early age.

Along with outer observation, a study of Venus, as well as the Sun, in the Libra person's natal chart reveals the nature of their talent and abilities in the arts. For example, in Welsh singer and actress Catherine Zeta-Jones' (September 25, 1969) natal chart, Venus is trine Mars; this beautiful (strong Venus) Libran actress has taken on many daring action roles (Mars). In the famous Italian Opera Singer, Luciano Pavarotti's natal chart, the Sun is in Libra (October 12, 1935); Leo (entertainment) is the rising sign while Venus is emphasized by being in the First House in trine aspect (positive, indicative of potential talent) to Uranus in Taurus (voice).

Well-known author, playwright and humorist, Oscar Wilde, was born in Dublin (October 16, 1854). In Wilde's natal chart, Venus is strong in Libra and in trine (positive) to Saturn (often a career indicator) in Gemini (literature). His famous play,

Oscar Wilde (1854–1900)

Apex Saturn T-Square

Apex Moon T-Square

Apex Neptune
Minor Grand Trine

Neptune-based
Kite

Grand Earth
Trine

Sun/Saturn
Trine

Oscar Wilde
Oct 16, 1854
Dublin , IRE
03:00:00 AM LMT
ZONE: +00:00
006W15'00"
53N20'00"

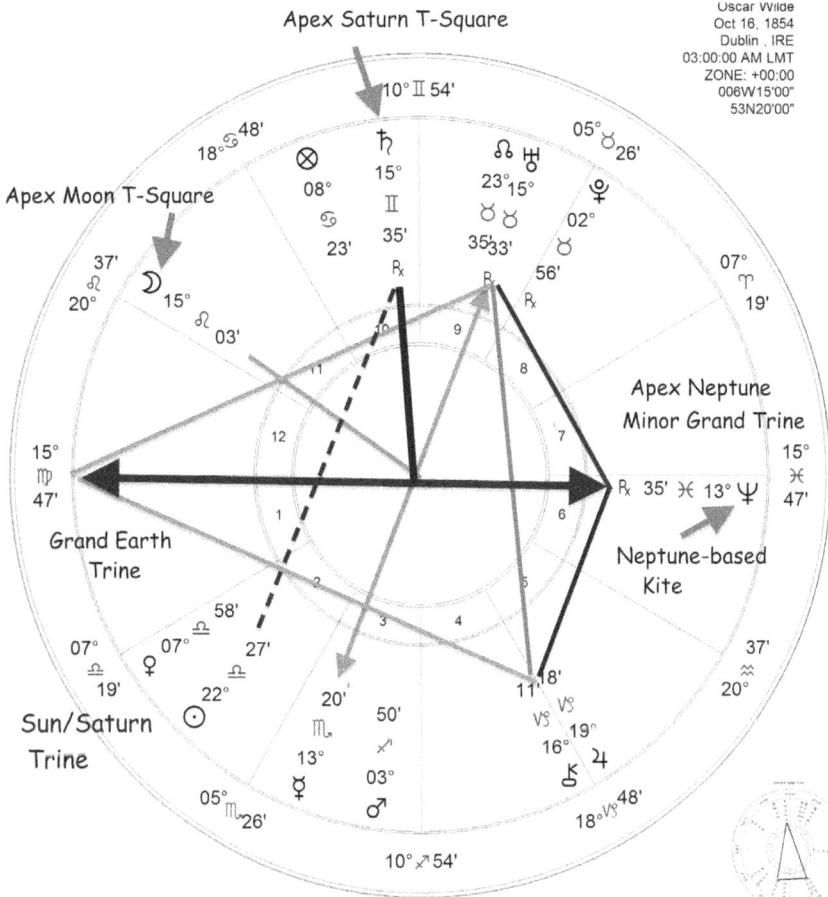

[99] Mercury in incisive Scorpio rules Wilde's Ascendant in Virgo (writing). It also stimulates (multiple aspects) a Grand Earth Trine: (Virgo Rising trine Chiron and Jupiter in Capricorn, trine Uranus in Taurus). Saturn, which rules Capricorn, is strongly placed in Wilde's Tenth House (of career) trine both Venus and the Sun and sextile the Moon, forming a Minor Grand Trine. Here we see Wilde's considerable talent, his academic excellence, intelligence, and brilliance as a writer, the acclaim and prosperity he earned, and the positive aspects of his relationship with his parents and with English society. Neptune in Pisces is the midpoint planet of a second Minor Grand Trine. It also ties into one of four Yods active at the time of Wilde's birth. He felt out of step with the Victorian values of his day, whose hypocrisy he so artfully exposed. Wilde was a leader in the new- Aesthetic Movement that emphasized the portrayal of love in art and literature—expressed also in- Wilde's life—freed from the bonds of social mores. He did not, perhaps, realistically assess how far he could get away with his tendency to shock and challenge others by flaunting social codes and expectations (shown in a Moon-based Fixed-Love T-square involving an opposition between Uranus and Mercury). Moreover, Saturn in Gemini (schism) is square Neptune (confusion) in Pisces.

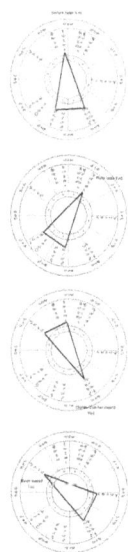

135

The Importance of Being Earnest, still popular on stages and in film today, could be a humorous primer for Librans on the folly of dishonesty.[99]

Although married with two children, Wilde led a double (gay) life. He became embroiled in an intrigue (Libra) that ended in poverty, imprisonment, and exile. In 1895, he was accused of "gross indecency" and sentenced to two years of hard labor. Oscar Wilde died on November 30, 1900, scorned by society. Today he is lauded as one of England's finest writers.

But Wilde's life was triumphant. Librans must separate truth from error, reality from unreality, within their hearts. One of Wilde's first requests from prison was for books, among them, the Bible, a good biography of St. Francis of Assisi, and all of Dante's literature. During those two years of confinement, Wilde found truth (as happened to St. Francis when he was a prisoner of war), and salvation in Christ. In *de Profundis*, we sense in Wilde's writing a spiritual maturity lacking in his earlier work:

> *The moment of repentance is the moment of initiation... It is the means by which one alters one's past. The Greeks thought that impossible. They often say in their gnomic aphorisms "Even the Gods cannot alter the past." Christ showed that the commonest sinner could do it. That it was the one thing he could do. Christ, had he been asked, would have said—I feel quite certain about it —that the moment the prodigal son fell on his knees and wept he really made his having wasted his substance with harlots, and then kept swine and hungered for the husks they ate, beautiful and holy incidents in his life. It is difficult for most people to grasp the idea. I dare say one has to go to prison to understand it. If so, it may be worthwhile going to prison.*

THE MARRIAGE SIGN

Libra rules marriage, a union of opposites, and other close partnerships as well. Most Librans feel compelled to find their other half. Or perhaps their other half finds them! Marriage, in fact, is the testing ground of the Libran heart. Rarely will a native of this sign go through life single. The purpose of marriage is that through love, the greatest force in the universe, each one may help the other to carry his karmic load, to bring forth children, support one another in manifesting his or her dharma or life's work and ideally, do more good together than one could possibly do alone. No other relationship is more crucial to happiness and success. But marriage and close ties purge the heart, often through sorrow and pain. Intimacy provides a mirror of parts of self we would otherwise never see or whose existence we might deny. Love will expose all unlike itself. No other known force is more transforming in its effect.

THE SEARCH FOR THE OTHER HALF

An astrological analysis of the Sun and Venus, particularly in the natal chart, reveals many details about the whys and wherefores, the timing and the lessons to be learned in the Libra person's life through intimate relationships. American film actor, *Mickey Rooney*, born September 23, 1920, separated from his eighth wife in 2012! His chart tells of his impulsive love nature, the intensity of his search, the testing of his soul, and the many lessons of love in his life. Near the end of his life and contentedly single, he could meditate upon the many trans-formative changes he had experienced in his search to find the right one![100]

[100] In Mickey Rooney's natal chart his Libra Sun is quincunx (adjustment) Uranus (impulsive) in Pisces, opposed Chiron in Aries (Fourth House of the family) and square Pluto (intense soul testing) in the Eighth House (sex, money, death, and regeneration)—a very in-tense Pluto-based Cardinal T-square. The Pluto/Sun square can be tough, but transformative. Note that Chiron's ruler, Mars, is in Sagittarius (in the First House) trine Neptune in Leo, great for theatre, but adds drama and illusion, impatience and restlessness in love!

The saying, "God is a jealous god," originating in Exodus, is actually a reminder that wherever we place our attention is where our energy goes. To get overly involved with another person to the point of distraction is to have become idolatrous, to have made of a human being a god. When the person born with the Sun in Libra loses himself or parts of himself by being overly involved in the life of another—an idolatrous mindset—some event or loss will shake the relationship up or take that person from him, mercifully bringing him back to the reality of his first love.

On the other hand, sometimes people born in Libra will skirt close relationships to avoid reopening an old wound; they opt to be alone rather than risk broken heartedness, the betrayal of trust and the loss of love. As the Sufi poet Rumi, himself a Libran (born September 30, 1205, Gregorian), poignantly wrote: "The cure for pain is in the pain." The wounded Libran must go through the healing process of forgiving himself and the one whose love is lost. He must search within himself, discovering the true nature of love within his own heart and soul, that he might, when the cycle appears, open his heart and love anew. In forgiving life and embracing his pain, he will know a deeper love than he ever thought possible.

LET US TRAVEL TOGETHER[101]

The world was blessed by the unusually harmonious marriage of Libran artist, Theosophist, writer and peacemaker, Nicholas Roerich, to the writer and fellow Theosophist, Helena Roerich. Nicholas Roerich was born in St. Petersburg, Russia on October 9, 1874. Although they did not spend time together during their childhoods, Helena, an Aquarian, was born in the same town four months later. Although Helena's relatives opposed the union, they married in 1901. Very much in love with one another and submitting all aspects of their lives to higher occult principles, they successfully raised two sons, traveled extensively in search of the greater Wisdom, supported one another in many ways, and together founded The Agni Yoga Society.[102]

"Together we overcame obstacles," wrote Nicholas Roerich about his marriage in the latter part of his life, "and obstacles turned into opportunities. I dedicated my books, *To Helena, my wife, my druginya, fellow traveler, inspirer.* In Petersburg, in Scandinavia, in England, in America, and in all Asia we worked, we studied, we broadened our consciousness."*[103]*

In his articles devoted to his wife, Nicholas Roerich wrote:

> *Justice, love for the laboring, and constant search for the truth transform the whole life round a young and strong spirit. And the entire home, the entire family - everything is built according to these blessed principles. All difficulties and all dangers are overcome under the same unconquerable guidance.*

The Roerich's son, Svetoslav, wrote how the atmosphere of love and mutual understanding between his parents impacted his life:

> Both in my father and mother there was the unique balance and harmony of two perfectly synchronized beings that realized the great ideal of life and lived the chosen path as a perfect example of dedication and fulfillment. Their radiant image always remains my greatest inspiration, my great source of happiness.[104]

Nicholas and Helena Roerich's example of two souls united in love, mutually supportive of one another on the spiritual path and in their service to humanity, is the way of the future. As Librans realize and remember who they are in reality and why they are here, they will more likely attract their divine complement with whom they will fulfill their divine destiny and be an example to mankind of marriage in the Aquarian Age.

PEACE IN THE EYE OF THE HURRICANE

Betrayal! The very word sends shudders through the heart! Libra is the sign of reality and in the relative sense, of unreality. In practical terms, natives of this sign do well when they learn to trust no man, not even themselves—for all are clothed in the imperfect karmic state—but at the same time look for the highest good in all! The breaking of trust is by no means a given in this sign but, perhaps due to personal or even planetary karma, Librans seem to be particularly susceptible to infidelity, both as the betrayer and the betrayed. Who is to say if any one treachery is more painful than another, but the compromising of trust between

---

[101] From *New Era Community* (1926): "Wayfarer, friend, let us travel together. Night is near, wild beasts are about, and our campfire may go out. But if we agree to share the night watch, we can conserve our forces. Tomorrow our path will be long and we may become exhausted. Let us walk together. We shall have joy and festivity. I shall sing for you the song your mother, wife and sister sang. You will relate for me your father's story about a hero and his achievements. Let our path be one. Be careful not to step upon a scorpion, and warn me about any vipers. Remember, we must arrive at a certain mountain village. Traveler, be my friend."

[102] Agni Yoga, "affirms the existence of the Hierarchy of Light and the center of the Heart as the link with the Hierarchy and with the far-off worlds. Though not systematized in an ordinary sense, Agni Yoga is a Teaching that helps the discerning student to discover moral and spiritual guideposts by which to learn to govern his or her life and thus contribute to the Common Good. For this reason Agni Yoga has been called a "living ethic." See AgniYoga.org/ay_info.html.

[103] *Druginya* is a Russian word meaning "female friend."

[104] These notes are taken from an article called, "She Who Inspired," about Helena Roerich. See www.Found-HelenaRoerich.ru/eng/inspir/.

those who have vowed to remain faithful is a wound not easily healed. One Libran man, upon discovering that his beloved wife, after over 20 years of marriage, was involved in an affair, called his devastating experience "a crucifixion of the heart." Even so, dark and forgotten secrets may be so hidden within the heart that one no longer notices the weight he has carried for so long. A broken heart, for a time at least, is an open heart, whose secrets once revealed can be accessed and the heart healed. In the end, are not all human loves the tilling of the garden of the heart for the lover of one's soul?

Sonya, an October Libran, was experiencing the excruciating pain of a broken heart—her husband of many years had suddenly left her and she was bereft. Her 20-year-old daughter, an Aries, approached her mother. "Mom, I cannot bear seeing you pine away for Dad like this," she boldly stated. "Love has not disappeared from your life. We need you. Come out of your room. Love has simply been rearranged! Besides, haven't you always said that Librans must abide in the eye of the hurricane?" Comforted by her daughter's love and strengthened by her wisdom, Sonya paused and reflected—as Librans are wont to do—and concluded, "that makes sense." She not only resolved to forgive her husband, but she also vowed to herself that she would pray for him for a certain period of time. In so doing she discovered an inner peace unknown to her before. When Libran souls anchor their resolve firmly within their hearts, they emanate a particular calming strength; no longer tossed and turned by emotional waves and mental agitation, they become once more the Master of their ship.

In Aries, the soul must control the fire of the Sun, his powerfully ebullient energy, and in so doing learn patience—in Libra, patience becomes steadfastness and the ability to endure. The true Libran will endure the transformative pangs of pain with great strength of character. It is a choice, a soul testing demanding resolution that comes, one way or another, to almost all people born into this sign.

Energy does not disappear—it has to go somewhere. Pain ignored too long can calcify and manifest as physical disease. So even though traumatic experiences can be jolting to the Libran in love, they can also be liberating. When grief has purified the heart, pain turns into bliss. After all, he who has loved and lost, for all his suffering, has drunk of the cup of life more than he who has not dared to love at all. Through love's many trials and great joys, the Libran heart matures.

THE CHOICE TO TAKE A STAND

If need be, or if conviction stirs his soul, the courageous Sun in Libra person will determine to fight the good fight inside or outside the courtroom, even if he finds himself alone. Standing up for what is right is a test of character, an opportunity for love to be victorious in the Libran soul's life. During this date with destiny, the Libran soul often comes face to face with his own Goliath. While the ultimate battle still awaits him, such a moment may prove to be a major turning point in his life.

Mohandas K. Gandhi became the spiritual and political leader of the Indian Independence Movement. At the time of his birth India had been under British rule for almost 200 years. Nothing in his childhood past suggested the future awaiting him. In fact, Gandhi, educated in London as a barrister, (a Libra profession) was failing miserably when he grasped the opportunity to take part in an Indian lawsuit in Transvaal, South Africa. He was 24 years old. Leaving his wife and children back in India, Gandhi promised to call for them once he was settled.

Not all Librans are born to become a symbol unto a generation or the key to their nation's salvation, but almost all know times when a circumstance challenges them to make a vital choice. Librans will typically face on numerous occasions the choice of compromising to buy the peace or to withstand the storm that a greater peace might prevail. This testing of the soul and the life lessons it brings may all lead up to one, perhaps totally unexpected, and life changing decision.

The Libra person at the crossroads may not yet realize the gravity of the situation, but the direction his life will take from that moment on may depend upon his election. A week after Gandhi arrived in South Africa, a single event aroused within this shy man the fire of justice that was to propel him into his fated role as Mahatma, the Great Soul. For Ghandi was destined to help India win a war, not with guns, but through *Satyagraha*, called non-cooperation by the West, but actually a Sanskrit word meaning "truth and firmness."

Destiny's stage was set on a cold wintry night. Despite having a first class ticket, Gandhi was thrown off the train he was traveling on by a South African constable. Indians in South Africa at the time were considered little more than lackeys. Here is a description in Gandhi's own words of how that night changed the course of his life:

> *The train steamed away leaving me shivering in the cold. I entered the dark waiting room. There was a white man in the room. I was afraid of him. What was my duty; I asked myself. Should I go back to India, or should I go forward, with God as my helper and face whatever was in store for me? I decided to stay and suffer. My active non-violence began from that day.*

LIBRA LESSONS ON THE SPIRITUAL PATH

The Libran Aspirant on the path to spiritual wholeness begins, as do all new students, by sorting out the Real from the Unreal. He studies *the Law*, the spiritual standard by which he can measure *right action*. He begins to seriously question and comes to see as false and illusory much of what he has been previously taught and accepted as reality. So much is new and unfamiliar, and yet he is not one to blindly believe. He typically puts any doubts he may entertain on the shelf for a time while he confirms the veracity of new ideas through his own experience. Once he accepts a spiritual tenet as truth, he will faithfully steer his course by its compass. And so, the Libran seeker of truth gradually puts on the Real Man while taking off the old. Like Nicholas Roerich, whose spiritual teaching was that of a practical path, he determines to be in the world while remaining true to spiritual principles. He practices becoming a man of integrity and sound judgment.

THE BALANCED HEART

Life tests the Libran seeker of reality repeatedly and in many ways, so that he might gain greater mastery over the Heart chakra. Through prayer, meditation and dynamic decree (focused affirmations), he is able to transmute blocks and correct imbalances within the spiritual and physical heart. The representation of the three Astrological Crosses (Cardinal-Power, Fixed-Love and Mutable-Wisdom) within the natal chart corresponds to the balance or imbalance of these qualities within the Threefold Flame ablaze within the Heart chakra.[105]

The Aspirant may be stronger in one aspect than in another or, conversely, deficient in one area while another is complete. He may, for example, be powerful and strong, but if he lacks love and wisdom, he is likely to be a tyrant. For the Libran Aspirant, being in his heart is not enough; if he would achieve a sense of equilibrium in both his outer material life and within his inner spiritual being, the flame within his heart must be balanced.

Now, reason is one of the Libran Aspirant's best gifts, but reason can also be his nemesis. He relies upon reason to *see, to understand and to determine* viable and just solutions. By and by, it happens that even the most intelligent native of the Scales finds himself in a quandary—his head reasons one way and quite intelligently, while his heart prompts him to act otherwise without any assuring logical explanation. He feels stumped and procrastinates—not like the Taurean lost in contemplation, nor like the Gemini beset by duality, but simply because he sees equally the opposing points of view. He may sense a trap, but cannot put his finger on it. Aware that his judgment is being put to the test, he naturally wants to choose the best course, but typically, cannot find his way out of reason's maddening comparisons. He can spend all his energy, become mentally exhausted, and still be weighing one choice against the other with neither winning out.

---

[105] See www.TSL.org/2010/11/the-threefold-flame-of-the-heart/-

Although Venus rules Libra *exoterically*, Uranus (planet of revelation through the Higher Mind) rules Libra *esoterically*. When accessing a given question, the Libran Aspirant naturally does his homework, gets his facts, and lays them out before himself. But ultimately, the Libran seeker finds the answer not in reason, but through intuition, which requires the meeting of the balanced heart with the Higher Mind. He must be willing to stretch his mind outside the box of "2 plus 2 always equals 4." After all, what is right for one situation or person at a certain stage of development may not be right for another at a different point of self-awareness. The Libran Aspirant may intuitively perceive the truth without being able to prove to himself, let alone to another, as to why it is so. The lawyer in him looks for the argument. He wisely resists going on gut feelings alone—he knows emotions can be misleading. He asks, "What, [LORD], would you have me do?" And so, he discovers an intuitive confirmation—*he just knows!* After X number of occasions of daring to follow his intuitive perception, he learns to trust this "inner man of the heart," whose wisdom he can now access at will. When his heart is balanced, when he remains poised and unmoved, the Libran soul discovers that he intuitively knows the way—not by reason but by vibration!

MEETING THE ENEMY

Libra is the sign of outer enemies; the Libran seeker may find he becomes trapped in round after lamentable round of conflict or argumentation. Nicholas Roerich wrote this about one's enemies: "Yet enemies, urging us to indefatigable activity, also forge for us the armor of heroic achievement." The enemy (or the nature of the conflict, which may repeat itself in different scenarios with different persons playing the adversary) may be useful in exposing to the Aspirant that the only true enemy he needs to be concerned with is the enemy within! When he goes after his own weakness and darkness, studying his psychology and astrology, praying and decreeing faithfully, and applying himself diligently to the path, he will not easily be trapped into forgetting who he is. When he is true to himself, no one can deceive him!

Gandhi adopted a position that he knew could not fail him. He saw the enemy, not as the British per se, but rather as the error in their thinking. Despite being opposed, and even imprisoned on several occasions for years at a time, he harbored no resentment. Astutely leading the nation into an unknown future, Gandhi wanted England to serve as a political ally and not as a foe after India gained her independence. The Mahatma often found himself in the midst of volatile situations. His rule of thumb for any Libran on the path was, especially when weighing one's options, "Don't listen to friends when the Friend inside you says, do this."

More than ever before, the Aspirant of the Scales discovers that he cannot always please others and remain true to his own conscience. Standing in the eye of the hurricane and being unmoved takes on a higher, more urgent meaning now, as does having the courage to say no, and even good-bye, if necessary. This can be difficult. It takes practice, faith and a strong heart. Rarely does the Libran Aspirant regret leaving behind what he no longer could carry in good faith.

THE DARK NIGHT OF THE SOUL

Although the path of Love is one of joy and ultimately of bliss, it is marked by deep purgative and transmutative pain for love exposes and consumes within the Aspirant all negative momentums and lesser desires than his longing to be one with God. The 16th century Carmelite monk, mystic and saint, St. John of the Cross, called this period the Dark Night of the Soul. He wrote about it in exquisite detail:

> *For the same fire of love, which afterwards is united with the soul and glorifies it, is that which aforetime assailed it in order to purge it; even as the fire that penetrates the log of wood is the same that first attacked and wounded it with its flame, cleansing and stripping it of its accidents of ugliness, until, by means of its heat, it had prepared it to such a degree that it could enter it and transform it into itself.[106]*

The Dark Night is hardly comprehensible to those who have not experienced it. Written of in the Book of Job, in the lives and words of the saints and of poets, it is the dark before the dawn. We can understand the Dark Night as being essentially a Libran initiation; on the Power Cross, Libra occupies the position of the action of the Holy Spirit.[107]

This Holy Spirit—described in Isaiah[108] as the spirit of the [LORD] and in the Hindu Trinity as the equivalent of Shiva, known as The Destroyer is the *Power of Divine Love*, a frequency unknown to this world, capable of transmuting

---

[106] *The Dark Night of the Soul,* by Saint John of the Cross, chapter ten, stanza one.
[107] See Elizabeth Clare Prophet on the Threefold Flame at www.YouTube.com/watch?v=S1dkn0jX9eI
[108] Isaiah 11:2, "And the spirit of the [LORD] shall rest upon him, the spirit of wisdom and understanding, the spirit of counsel and might, the spirit of knowledge and of the fear of the [LORD]."
[109] The third representation of God in the Hindu Triumvirate, Shiva is the destroyer of the ego and of ignorance and ultimately of the cosmos itself. Shiva is also the Restorer. Shiva destroys the old, dissolving all that keeps us in a consciousness of separateness from our inherent divine reality.
[110] "The Roerichs were Theosophists, studying the ageless wisdom of East and West in depth and working inwardly with great spiritual Masters, called, "The Hierarchy of Light." *Nicholas and Helena Roerich, the Spiritual Journey of Two Great Artists and Peacemakers,* by Ruth A. Drayer.

imperfections, freeing men from the effects of negative karma and raising them to their divine estate.[109]

In Libra, also, we see the denial of the Holy Spirit when the soul gives entrance to *the liar and the lie*. As the action of divine love's fire intensifies within in his heart, the Aspirant feels a burning sensation. Mystics describe this experience as a deep and searing passion, that strips, purges, exposes and consumes all vestiges of unreality. The seeker of Enlightenment passes through a time when he feels engulfed in darkness. In submitting to love's fire, he must have stored within his heart and chakras sufficient light to withstand the ordeal. Only by passing through this Trial by Fire can he emerge purified, ready to receive—indeed, to merge—with the Beloved.

ADVOCATE FOR THE AGE OF LOVE

When asked what his favorite motto was, Nicholas Roerich, at age twenty-five answered: "Forward and no looking back!" Although he lived in the final century of the Piscean Age, his present was the future for others. Roerich felt strongly about his role in heralding a New Era (the Aquarian Age), a time when an enlightened humanity would work alongside the Hierarchy of Light in order to usher in a culture of Beauty and Universal Brotherhood.[110]

At last, the Libran Hero has fought the good fight and won. His heart purified, and his mind one with his Divine Presence, becomes a messenger, as Roerich was called, of beauty, justice and peace, the standard bearer for a culture of love whose heights the world has not known, even in past Golden Ages.

He is the advocate, the messenger, and the bridge—awakening others to their divine nature as a defender of truth and the One Reality!

6.

Aquarius

Symbol.......***The Water Bearer***

Born....................Jan. 20 ~ Feb. 18

Archetype............... *The Alchemist*

Key Phrase........................***I Love***
Element............................. **Air**
Cross...................... **Fixed-Love**
House....................... **Eleventh:**
    Friendships, group associations, diplomacy,
    goals & aspirations, inventions & technology

Rulers................. **Uranus & Saturn**
Esoteric Ruler..................... **Jupiter**
Polarity............................. **Leo**
Chakra....................Seat-of-the-Soul
Anatomy.............Shins, calves & ankles,
    Achilles' heel, circulatory system

Spiritual Qualities.........**Freedom, brotherly love,
tolerance, invention & technology, utopian
consciousness, open-mindedness, social
& political reform, spiritual surrender**

Vulnerable to.......... *Mental conceit, licentiousness,
stubbornness, hatred & dislike, irritability, eccentricity,
aloofness, emotional unavailability, rebellion & anarchy*

Must Acquire........ **Compassion, soul-sensitivity,
distinction between freedom & license,
true revolution & chaos, trust**

Abraham Lincoln • Francis Bacon • Oprah Winfrey • Thomas Edison • Thomas More

THE SUN IN AQUARIUS

Am I not destroying my enemies
when I make friends of them?

—Abraham Lincoln (February 12, 1809)

ARCHETYPE OF THE AQUARIAN-AGE MAN & WOMAN

The Age of Aquarius is destined to be an era of universal freedom and brotherly good will, a time when outer differences no longer separate, but rather enhance the common chord of Love, binding souls to one another and each one to his own Higher Reality. During this 2000-year-plus cycle, mankind is intended to evolve from a Sun centered, egocentric consciousness to a galactic, supercon-scious awareness. This dissonant planet at war must evolve into a world of great diversity vibrating like a beauteous chord of many strings, sounding individually, yet finely tuned in One harmonious *AUM*. The Aquarian Hero is the archetype of the true man of the New Era. An alchemist of the highest order, he is brilliant, in-ventive, freedom loving and universally compassionate. He is both friend and brother to the many, a wayshower for people of all Sun Signs who would seek to be free from the divisive dogmas of ages past.

Aquarius is the sign of Alchemy, the science of precipitation. In olden times, the legendary alchemists would employ secret formulas to change base metals into gold. Although a natural penchant for accessing and manipulating en-ergy and vibration is certainly characteristic of souls born into this sign, the greater Alchemy that the individual Aquarian soul may seek to achieve is that of the spir-itual transformation of his own self, his destiny and his world—from base instincts to golden precepts.

THE WATER BEARER

Aquarius' symbol, the Water Bearer, depicts a man pouring out an inex-haustible stream of water from an urn in his left hand. The man represents hu-manity. The waters of life, the free flow of spiritual energy into the world of men, represent the purification and the awakening unto Love of a world and its people. Aquarius' waves also symbolize the freedom and the multiplication of creative possibility that result from accessing energy in new ways by invention and tech-nological advances, so much a stamp of the Aquarian personality and the Aquarian Age.

In Kabbalistic Astrology, Aquarius relates to the month Shevat, whose meaning is that of Unification. When we speak of Universal Brotherhood in

Aquarius, we envision a communion of souls in which love is no longer blocked by those discords that pit one man against another. When we envision Aquarius' rushing waters cascading like a Niagara Falls of love and light, we sense the enlightened consciousness of man, freed from a sense of separation from God.

THE SENSE OF THE AQUARIAN CONTRADICTION

Despite being generally friendly fellows, there's something peculiarly individualistic, even quirky, about Aquarians. They seem to march to a different drumbeat; their strangely futuristic ideas can appear odd and out of place. Aquarians traditionally have been labeled "eccentric," "idiosyncratic," and sometimes downright "weird"! Those who may impress you with a polished exterior reveal their Aquarian *freedom-to-be-me* stamp upon closer inspection. Visions of Utopia come so readily to the minds of so many souls born with the Sun in Aquarius as to make them perceive themselves to be out-of-sync with the world as they find it. Now that the winds of Aquarius are blowing throughout the planet, Aquarians increasingly appear to be the example and less the exception to the norm, making it more fascinating, rather than uncomfortable, to engage them.

A certain contradiction exists within the Aquarian temperament that makes sense. Of all the signs, Aquarians are the most individualistic and at the same time, the most humanitarian. Their minds are open to new possibilities (Air sign) and yet they are notorious for stubbornly holding on to their point of view (Fixed Cross). Outwardly, they appear admirably collected, but underneath the calm exterior they can be high-strung and anxious. They are the friendliest, and yet, the most impersonal of all the signs. They gravitate toward groups, but will typically disappear in the midst of a crowd into their own space.

The planetary rulership of Aquarius reflects this paradoxical nature of those born under its influence. Both Saturn and Uranus govern Aquarius. Saturnian currents have the strength of slow but steady movement. Uranian lightning-like bolts knock us off our feet! Saturnian energy consolidates and preserves and thus, is related to tradition and the stability of the Law. Uranian energy shatters and upsets and thus, is related to innovation, revolution and unexpected change. Understanding and reason are Saturnian and grow with time, while the high-frequency energy of revelation is Uranian in nature. Saturn admonishes, "Be patient!" Uranus exclaims, "Out with the old!"

Some Aquarian types are more Uranian. Typically *atypical*, you can count on them to be anything but normal. Especially in the more immature stages of their development they seem to thrive on upsetting the status quo. They tend to have a political bent, especially for throwing out the old order. They typically spearhead social reform and change, often of a radical nature. The Saturnian type is also magnetized to getting involved in larger community policymaking, but he is quieter, a tad more reserved, and perhaps a bit too self-conscious. Somewhat

Aquarius:
11th House
Fixed-
Love Cross
Air Element

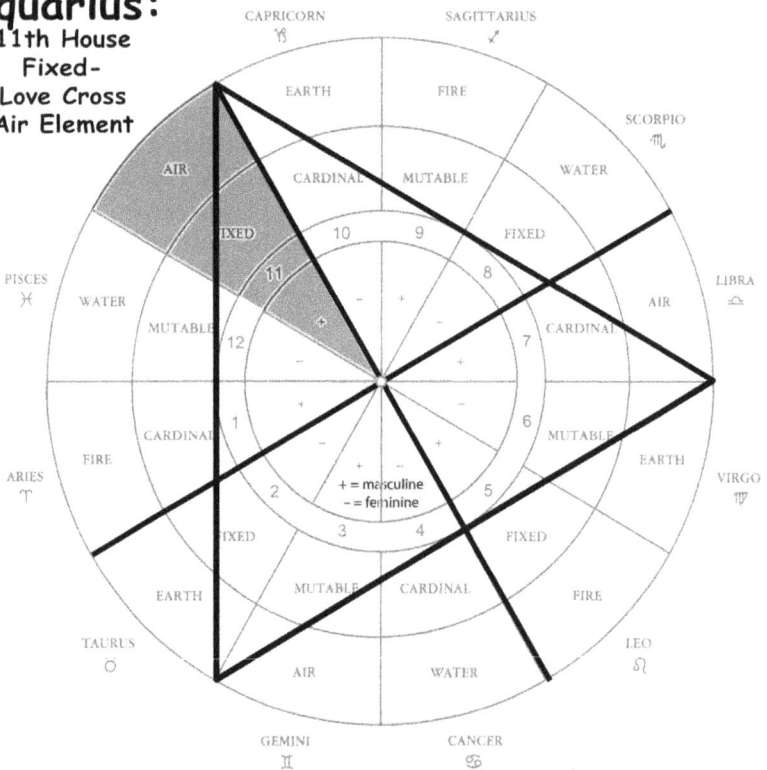

withdrawn, often taciturn, he typically lives in his head, in a world of abstract thoughts and notions.

Will is such an Aquarian. He projects a protective wall, making him outwardly unapproachable, but if he allows you access into his world, you'll soon discover that there's more to him than meets the eye. Like his Uranian counterpart, he's immersed in astrology, audiovisual work and high tech. A silent inventor, a secret alchemist and Shakespeare enthusiast (all Aquarian activities), he enjoys setting up his home with the latest alternative-energy system. Although he insists that he prefers to work behind the scenes, Will's strong social conscience, coupled with his ability to communicate clearly formulated and ingenious proposals, has thrust him repeatedly into policymaking positions within his community.

Most often, Aquarian personalities show a mixture of Saturnian and Uranian traits, describing their temperament, while others evolve as they mature, depending somewhat upon other variables acting in their lives as well as the cycle in which they find themselves.

DISCIPLINE, THE KEY TO FREEDOM

Aquarius is the sign of freedom. Aquarians sometimes confuse license with liberty. Contrary as they may be, the coupling of Saturn and Uranus in this sign, each in right measure and relationship to one another, energetically creates the perfect equation. Bottom line: *there is no freedom (Uranus) without responsibility (Saturn)*. Exercising free will recklessly actually imprisons the soul in a karmic equation—the more a person assumes the liberty to act without conscience, the more likely he is to err; hence, fate (karmic return), like a guard, necessarily constricts the chaos of his world.

An experiential understanding of the relationship between freedom (Uranus) and discipline (Saturn) begins in childhood. The Aquarian child needs plenty of room to move and to foster his innate sense of independence. But he also needs to learn to cooperate, which does not always come easily to him. He especially benefits when he learns as a child that when he chooses to break the rules (Uranus), he will reap the consequences (Saturn) that are best related to the action at hand. Hopefully, the rules are fair and the consequences balanced in type and severity. The point is not to punish, but rather to offer him exercises in using freedom responsibly. As he receives greater privileges and is capable of handling increasing levels of responsibility, the Aquarian young person comes to understand that in order to be free (Uranus), a person needs to be self-disciplined (Saturn) so that no outer force needs to come down upon him. Saturn—as the chart reveals challenges and positive momentums—may appear in the guise of a parent for the child, a teacher for the Aspirant, the government in relation to its citizens or simply the Aquarian soul's returning karma.

A certain inborn intolerance for limited thinking characterizes the Aquarian personality. If a habit, condition, social norm, relationship, etc. inhibits his ability to love and to create, his natural impulse (Uranus) is—get rid of it! However, a tension within him warns against throwing the baby out with the bathwater. Although the Aquarian man desires freedom for all, he discovers that the key to genuine freedom and the awakening of divine potential within himself is that his soul, which is not permanent, be bound (Saturn) to the spirit of light within him, which is immortal.

THE AQUARIAN FRIEND TO ALL

Gemini (an Air sign on the Wisdom Cross) governs brothers, Libra (an Air sign on the Power Cross) rules marriage and important partnerships, and Aquarius (an Air sign on the Love Cross) rules friends. Friendship, in some cultures, is even more meaningful than marriage.

When Abraham Lincoln, born February 12, 1809, became President of a nation on the brink of a long, drawn-out and bloody Civil War, he was surrounded by rivals who openly defied his election and his command. Rather than ousting those that opposed him, he drew his rivals close to him by granting them positions in his Cabinet. Lincoln was a friend to all, but few who knew him understood him. His Aquarian consciousness was far ahead of the times in which he played such a vital role.

Aquarian entertainer and talk-show host, Oprah Winfrey (January 29, 1954), rose from abject poverty and a troubled youth to become one of the most esteemed and wealthiest women in America. Oprah won hearts throughout the nation and gave the world a public example of the Aquarian friend-to-all consciousness by her ability to connect, uplift, and bring out in the best in people around the world.

The true Aquarian feels equally at home with heads of state and the man on the street, relating to one and all at a soul level. Like Lincoln, Oprah has remained accessible and genuine throughout her career, nor has she become corrupted by fame or fortune. As she once said, "Although I am grateful for the blessings of wealth, it hasn't changed who I am. My feet are still on the ground. I'm just wearing better shoes."

Life will test the Aquarian soul, especially during his youth, in choosing well the causes he espouses and the company he keeps. Friendship and camaraderie mean a lot to the Aquarian. Among his friends are likely to be a great variety of persons from all walks of life. Once the Water Bearer forges a friendship, his loyalty tends to be unwavering. Although his friends epitomize the Aquarian open-mindedness and universality of spirit, he will walk away from any relationship that imposes restrictions upon his liberty. When he does break off a friendship, he will do so decisively and permanently.

AQUARIAN LESSONS IN LOVE

Aquarius is the sign of divine love. If the Aquarian person desires more love, he needs to consciously let go of some measure of fear, for it is true that, "perfect love casteth out fear, because fear hath torment."[111]

It sounds simple enough—despite the complexities of karmic circumstance, *more love* is always the solution to any Aquarian conflict. And here is where the *no pain, no gain* truism comes in. For the Aquarian soul to be able to give and receive love freely, he must recognize and consciously release emotional and mental attitudes that block the flow of understanding and forgiveness.

Aquarians almost inevitably experience hatred. Hatred is love energy convoluted due to fear. Love in Aquarians can be so intense that it exposes all that is less than love in another, often provoking anger and hatred. Moreover, the Aquarian visionary threatens those who fear change. This is when the Aquarian soul must remain true to himself, even if this means standing alone, which is often the case. If he gives in to the opposition, going against his own conscience, he inevitably regrets his weakness as events play themselves out.

But almost all Aquarians deal with residues of hatred within themselves as well. Most won't admit to entertaining such nasty feelings, but chronic irritation and "mild dislike" are less obvious forms of love perverted. Such emotional stances are symptomatic of the soul attempting to insulate itself from pain by creating barriers between itself and others. The Aquarian soul who fears to be hurt tends to switch frequencies, withdrawing into his own space and becoming, even if physically present, emotionally unavailable. This habit of refusing to engage is perhaps more common in Aquarian men and is maddening to the women in their lives (who tend to be more emotionally communicative), causing all manner of misunderstandings and hard feelings.

Aquarians can be stuck in their heads (Air sign) and strangely cut off from their feeling world, depending on reason to get them by. Somewhere along the way they will seek, consciously or perhaps unconsciously, that relationship, situation or training that will help them tune in to and explore their feelings. Often a fear of intimacy, of getting too close, of being submerged in waves of turbulent emotions whose meaning eludes them, keeps them safely, or so it seems, insulated from the world's and their own potential madness.

Hope, a bright and clever young Aquarian physician from Sydney, Australia is distinguished by heightened intuition and an incisive, analytical mind. Hope's father, whom she adored, brought her up to be self-reliant, honest, ethical

---

[111]1 John 4:18

and rational. Hope felt even as a young girl that she had to be strong. Although he was a friendly man with au upbeat sense of humor, her father's strict moral code lacked warmth and compassion. Although Aquarians tend to be open-minded and avant-garde, they can—like all the Fixed Signs (Taurus & Scorpio and Leo & Aquarius)—become fixated on their point of view. Born with her Sun in Aquarius square Saturn (Father) in Scorpio, Hope adamantly refuses, like her Father, to forgive other seemingly less reliable souls. For Hope, what was done was done; he who had lost her trust had lost it forever. These and other tough attitudes keep her set on her path, but at the same time, out of touch with the love she so yearns to know. Hope tends to attract persons and situations that upset her universe, bring out her tears and help open her heart! Although she braves considerable heartache along the way, in these intimate relationships she has uncovered an inner resistance to grieve and a refusal to forgive.

I cannot tell you the end of Hope's story, for it is still in progress. But for Hope and all Aquarian souls, born on the Fixed-Love Cross, the only way to have more love is to face their fears and dissolve the barriers they have constructed to keep love out! An astrological session often can pinpoint the nature of the problem and its solution. Therapy often helps, as does music. The invocation of the Holy Spirit through the Aquarian Science of Invocation accelerates the transmutation of karmic records and habits.

Love does not always make sense, nor is forgiveness a guarantee against being hurt anew. But forgiveness frees the soul from a torturous burden and releases to God the one who erred. Only by willingness to forgive can love flourish within the Aquarian heart!

FREEDOM TO LOVE—HEALING THE SOUL OF PAIN

Aquarius relates to the Seat-of-the-Soul chakra. Here the soul accesses the frequency of love as freedom. Like Leos, who polarize with Aquarians and who also are associated with this chakra, the soul in Aquarius who chooses to be more sensitive and communicative must make the effort to dissolve hardness of heart and its corresponding wall around his soul. As he does so he will face the fear behind any antisocial habits and attitudes he may harbor. He then must replace these negative momentums with positive expressions of his intent. If, however he chooses to ignore the problem, he not only risks being alone, but also having that unresolved toxicity emerge one day as disease within his physical body. And because the soul desires healing more than temporal happiness, the Aquarian in search of love will face his demons time and time again in the relationships he magnetizes to himself, until, of course, he resolves to be done with hiding from love!

Natives of this sign seeking inner and outer wholeness discover that the process of connecting with, guiding and parenting their own soul, called the Inner

Child, can be a wondrous adventure, which, like any exploration, occurs in stages and over time. Keeping their mind's eye on the flame within the heart and upon their own Divine Presence and focusing upon the divine within others, Aquarians can refine their soul's senses, heighten their intuition, deepen compassion and enhance their personal communion with God.

What is the difference between the hard-hearted, insensitive Aquarian and the Aquarian who has transcended the foibles common to so much of mankind? The key can be seen in the merciful or the unmerciful heart—in the compassionate and humble consciousness of the true humanitarian—versus the mental conceit and know-it-all stance of the Aquarian who has closed his heart.

Although Aquarians are generally not closed to the idea of partnership and marriage, children and family, they are reluctant, and sometimes may refuse to give up their independent lifestyle. They tend to insist on paddling their own canoe their own way and on their own schedules. They can be extremely stubborn and will resist those who would impose change upon them. As a rule, they are not homemakers, and being free-spirited do not easily tolerate being confined to routine. Because of the vein of zany gusto running through even the more sedate Aquarian, they can make interesting companions providing their partner accepts that a certain eccentricity comes with the package.

While often sincere, honest and loyal companions, Aquarians can be emotionally indifferent to a fault. Being "airy" by nature, they would benefit from acquiring some of the warm and personal style of their Leo opposite. On the other hand, a naturally philosophical nature, a love of truth, and a predisposition for objective analysis helps the more emotional of Aquarians to work out and transcend their disturbing feelings.

In dealing with conflict, inevitable in close relationships, the Aquarian soul has an opportunity to choose to love more rather than withdrawing into his own space or calling it quits. Aquarians typically have a way with words and tend to be intellectually analytical. At a certain point, their intelligence gets in the way! A useful rule of thumb for any Aquarian is, "As soon as you get opinionated, assume that you're wrong no matter how right you feel you are!" The rightness of attunement with love far outweighs the rightness of any temporary difference of opinion.

REVOLUTIONARIES OR ANARCHISTS?

Aquarians are born politicians and often become the instigators of change. Lovers of freedom and diplomats, they characteristically employ wise counsel and peaceful methods to bring people together in order to promulgate necessary change. Nonetheless, when consensus seems impossible, the Aquarian temperament will seek other avenues to promote reform. Aquarians have responded to the calling to herald revolutions and stir up socio-political uprisings.

Whether history sees them as national heroes or as outlawed anarchists depends much upon the point of view, the time in history, the role they play, and the perceptions of their contemporaries.

Many Aquarians are called to serve the cause of freedom in some wise. Revolutionaries by nature, they still need to practice great discernment. For just as there are revolutions that liberate, other revolutions masquerading under the banner of freedom actually take the law into their own hands; their destructive agenda is fueled by a dark and selfish purpose.

THE AQUARIAN INVENTOR & VISIONARY

The Aquarian mindset is avant-garde and strangely ahead of its time, which makes for a certain solitude. In truth, the Aquarian type perceives consciously what is still dormant within the collective unconscious, as if the future imprinted itself upon his present even as a recollection of a forgotten past. It is curious that today's miracles and flights of fancy are tomorrow's realities, taught to children in grade school!

Jules Verne (February 8, 1828), the prolific French writer and pioneer of the science-fiction genre, was an Aquarian whose entertaining tales awoke men's imaginations to awe-inspiring possibilities. Best known for the classic novels, *Journey to the Center of the Earth* (1864), *Twenty Thousand Leagues Under the Sea* (1870), and *Around the World in Eighty Days* (1873), Verne described air and underwater travel long before submarines and airplanes were invented.

Jules Verne's "The Albatross," fictional propeller-sustained airship as depicted in his novel, *"Robur the Conqueror"*

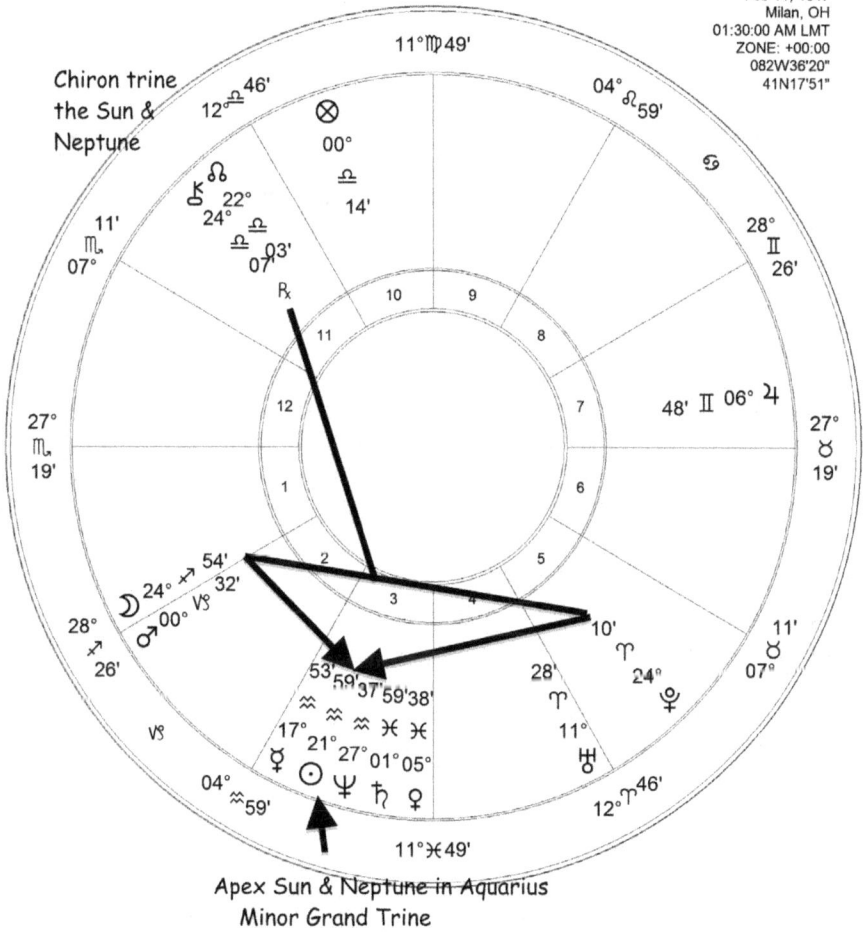

Thomas Alva Edison
Feb 11, 1847
Milan, OH
01:30:00 AM LMT
ZONE: +00:00
082W36'20"
41N17'51"

Chiron trine the Sun & Neptune

Apex Sun & Neptune in Aquarius
Minor Grand Trine

Thomas Alva Edison, born February 11, 1847, epitomizes the Aquarian genius that revolutionizes life through brilliant (Uranus) inventions. Edison is known as the inventor of the phonograph—imagine the world's excitement in seeing for the first time a machine that could record sound! He also developed the telegraph and the alkaline battery. Characteristic of many Aquarians, Edison was eccentric, independent in thought and lifestyle (Uranus), futuristic in his ideas, but he was also a *practical* (Saturn) inventor. In the process of making the phonograph, he also developed records to play, equipment to record the records, and equipment to manufacture them. In short, he created the recording industry!

In 1891, Edison demonstrated a motion picture device, which "does for the eye what the phonograph does for the ear." He began to commercially produce "movies" two years later. While Edison did not invent the light bulb (others had

157

experimented with forms of electricity), he improved upon an older idea and came up with a practical, reliable and long-lasting source of electricity. He invented the incandescent light bulb and everything necessary to make electrical lighting practical, safe and economical. Edison's Aquarius Sun and Neptune were trine Chiron (futuristic inventions from an ancient past). As the apex planets of a Minor Grand Trine involving the Moon in prophetic Sagittarius conjoined Mars in industrious Capricorn, trine Pluto in Aries (pioneering new inventions), the Sun and Neptune (invention) became the focus of his visionary genius. Note that Saturn and Venus in Pisces (concern for humanity) were sextile his Mars—he worked hard to make his dreams (Neptune) come true. Although he held more than 1,000 patents during his life, not all of Edison's ideas panned out. He once said, "I have not failed. I've just found 10,000 ways that do not work!"

Aquarians tend to follow their own star! Most value independence over money. When Verne's father cut him off financially because he was not pursuing his law degree in Paris as planned, Verne supported himself by selling his stories, and in so doing, got his career off the ground. Staying true to himself paid off— he ended up becoming a very wealthy man and the third most translated author in the world.

Edison had only a few months of formal schooling. At age seven, his first and only classroom teacher found the independent boy to be "addled" and difficult. His mother pulled him out of school and taught him basic reading and arithmetic at home. Self-educated, an independent thinker, and a self-made entrepreneur, Edison became a successful businessman and cultural icon. He continued to seek ways to learn and to do things better his entire life.

SAVING THE UNION

Aquarius is the sign of Brotherhood and of Unity. The American Civil War was a conflict that pitted brother against brother—figuratively and literally. Lincoln's passion was above all to preserve the Union, conceived in Liberty as a brotherhood of free men. That he won the Presidency—a self-made and self-educated man born in humble circumstances—is itself a testimony to economic freedom and opportunity in this nation and to the Aquarian spirit of pursuing a dream until it is realized. (Aquarius in traditional Astrology is called the Sign of Hopes and Wishes.)

Was Lincoln eccentric? His wife, Mary Todd, was often frustrated by his wild hair and odd habits. When Lincoln knew he was to give a speech, for example, he would write down the thoughts that came to him (Uranian revelations), stuff them in his top hat, and then throw the pieces on the kitchen table when he got home!

Those Aquarians who open our minds to new possibilities may be celebrated, but they are too rarely understood, often poorly compensated for their genius, if at all, and even maligned or conspired against for their bold stand! When the Aquarian Visionary proclaims truth that others are unable and perhaps unwilling to embrace, some will cling to his side, but others will hate and scheme against him. Lincoln suffered from dark spells and periods of *melancholy*, the 19th century word for depression. No wonder, in addition to the loss of his two sons, the war took more lives and lasted longer than Lincoln or anyone had thought possible. Thousands of lives depended upon his leadership and were affected by his decisions. The point of great strength in Lincoln's chart, his Mercury conjoined Pluto in Pisces, helped him keep his faith and sanity throughout this terrible war; however, it was also a point of great soul testing. Lincoln's chart was activated the very day he took office and coincided with the beginning of the Civil War— a date with destiny.[112] (See Lincoln's chart and note on the following page.)

The Civil War was causing great losses on both sides. While the country was divided on their sentiments regarding slavery and on the right course to take when the Southern States seceded in 1860–1861, few, if anyone at all, shared Lincoln's vision of saving the Union and of freeing the land from slavery. His second son, William Wallace Lincoln, died at age 11 of illness, while Lincoln was still President. And the extent of Mary Todd Lincoln's burden of physical and mental illness is still debated today.

What sustained him was a deep sense of destiny, of being ordained to fulfill a vital mission. In his Annual Message to Congress, on December 1, 1862, one month before signing The Emancipation Proclamation to end slavery, Lincoln's meaning was disquieting but clear:

> *The dogmas of the quiet past,* [Saturn] *are inadequate to the stormy present. The occasion is piled high with difficulty, and we must rise—with the occasion. As our case is* new [Uranus]*, so we must think anew and act anew* [Uranus]*. We must disenthrall ourselves, and then we shall save our country* [Saturn and Uranus]*... We hold the power, and bear the responsibility. In giving freedom to the slave, we assure freedom to the free—honorable alike in what we give, and what we preserve. We shall nobly save, or meanly lose, the last best hope of Earth. Other means may succeed; this could not fail. The way is plain, peaceful, generous, just—a way, which if followed, the world will forever applaud, and God must forever bless.*

And while the true Aquarian may be moved to give his life for his brethren, he is often seen as a troublemaker. His stand for truth is typically met with much opposition.

As Lincoln took office for his second term, the Civil War was coming to a close. Once again, on March 4, 1865, the President addressed the nation with an Aquarian message of love almost incomprehensible to most men. Even as he

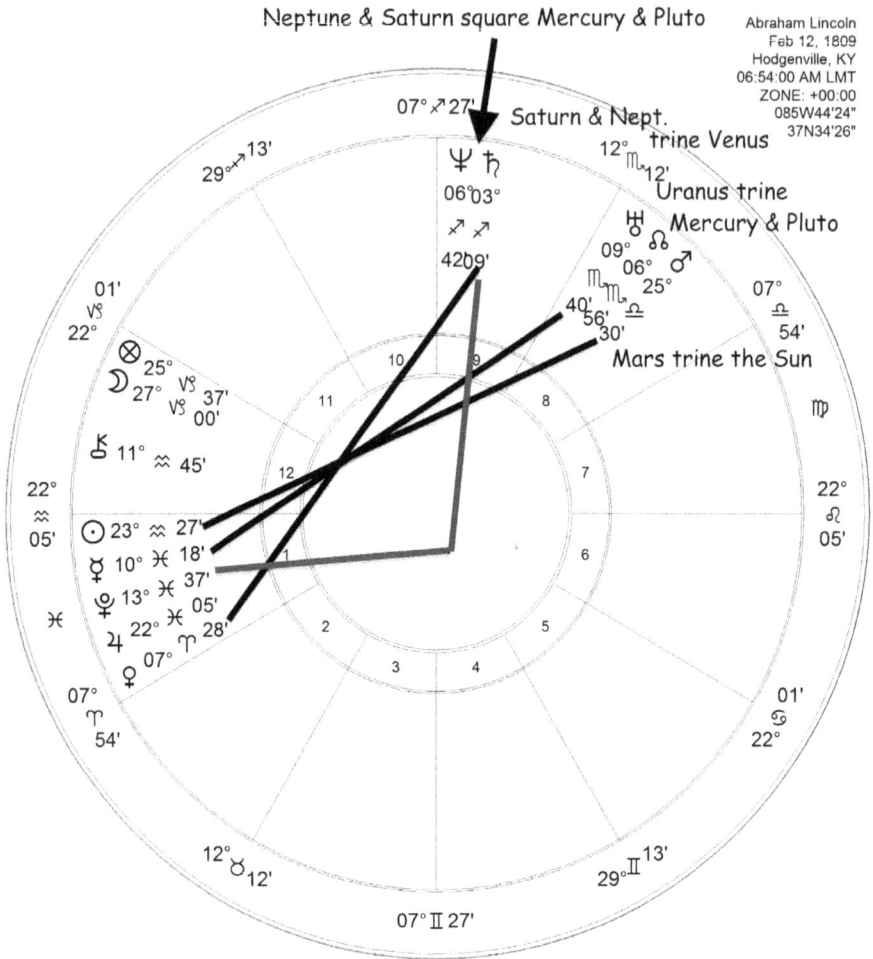

Neptune & Saturn square Mercury & Pluto

Abraham Lincoln
Feb 12, 1809
Hodgenville, KY
06:54:00 AM LMT
ZONE: +00:00
085W44'24"
37N34'26"

[112] Although he is described as being somewhat socially awkward, Lincoln loved people (Sun in Aquarius). He held high hopes for humanity. His Sun was in trine to Mars (action planet), in Libra, his natal Venus was trine Saturn, the signature of Lincoln as a brilliant, common sense lawyer. Mercury (mind) was conjoined Pluto in Pisces and in the First House, if his time of birth is accurate. He was capable of extraordinary kindness and compassion; he was poetic and spiritual in nature. Moreover, this sensitive coupling was trine Uranus, which rules Aquarius and is exalted in Scorpio (his love of freedom, vision for the nation, and determination to fulfill what he felt was his God-given mission). But with Mercury and Pluto square Saturn and Neptune in Sagittarius, it is no wonder, especially under the trying circumstances he faced, that he fell into periods of melancholy. The day Lincoln took office, on March 4, 1861, transiting Saturn in Virgo turned the square into a T-square on the Wisdom-Mutable Cross that would last throughout much of the Civil War. Only a soul of great spiritual attainment and sponsorship could sustain such pressure and keep his faith intact.

spoke, conspirators were plotting to take his life.[113]

Both sides, the President said, had sought to avert war. Both prayed to the same God for triumph. However, in the end neither was guiltless of the suffering placed upon the "the bondsman's two hundred and fifty years of unrequited toil." Lincoln prayed that the war would soon come to an end and that the nation would be healed, noting that, "as was said three thousand years ago, so still it must be said: The judgments of the Lord are true and righteous altogether." [114]

Lincoln concluded his address with these oft-quoted words:

With malice toward none; with charity for all; with firmness in the right, as God gives us to see the right, let us strive on to finish the work we are in; to bind up the nation's wounds; to care for him who shall have borne the battle, and for his widow and his orphan—to do all which may achieve and cherish a just and lasting peace among ourselves, and with all nations.[115]

GROUP DYNAMICS IN AQUARIUS

Aquarius, its ruling planet Uranus, and the Eleventh House rule groups and organizations. (Co-ruler Saturn tells about the groups' structure and goals). Aquarians attract groups. Aspects to the Sun, Uranus and Saturn plus the sign on the Eleventh House cusp and any planets therein tell much about the type of group in which the individual is likely to become involved, plus the nature of his role within it. Characteristically at the center of a circle of friends or followers, the Aquarian personality somehow stands apart. The Aquarian-age team model, so prevalent in business today, suits natives of this sign. They prefer egalitarian structures to the hierarchical boss/manager/employee model that went out with the Piscean Age.

Aquarians typically look out for the interests of the group with which they identify. Nevertheless, like their Leo counterpart, they will seek to somehow retain their individuality and freedom of movement within the group. The test comes when the direction that the group is taking and what Aquarians want for themselves somehow clash. Acquiescing does not come easily to the Aquarian Sun person. He may disassociate himself from the group and seek another affiliation, but more often the higher choice, the way to harmony is through spiritual

---

[113] John Wilkes Booth shot President Abraham Lincoln at a play at Ford's Theater in Washington, D.C. For a detailed account, see www.History.com/this-day-in-history/lincoln-shot.

[114] Psalms 19:9

[115] See Lincoln's full second inaugural address, delivered March 4,1865, at www.Bartleby.com/124/pres32.html.

Illustration from Thomas More's Utopia
Woodcut depicting More's fictitious island,
frontispiece from the 1st Edition (1516)

surrender. When the individual Aquarian is asked to give up something personal for the good of the group he passes a test in love. When a family goes through difficult times, for example, the Aquarian may need some private time and space to survive the ordeal, but should avoid shutting down emotionally. When we roll up our sleeves, grateful for the opportunity, we discover that there is no problem that love cannot resolve!

AQUARIAN MEN OF DESTINY

Two Aquarians whose example continues to inspire those who would dare to be different today were the English chancellor, lawyer and author, Thomas More (February 7, 1478),[116] and the English scientist, alchemist, philosopher, author, and statesman, Sir Francis Bacon (January 22, 1561).[117]

Both of these men led extraordinary lives; both sought divine guidance and took a stand in the midst of human folly and political corruption. And both left classic works describing a future world, an ideal society where the good of God would be reflected in the world of men.

Bacon is believed by many to be the real author of the Shakespearean plays. Even as Leo relates to entertainment, Aquarius relates to drama. As the clandestine Shakespeare, we see in Bacon's work, beyond the subtle wit, the inventive language (adding many thousands of words to the English language) and the classic drama. Experiencing the plays actually carries a soul through the process of change that is true-to-life; for indeed, "all the world's a stage" with a cast of characters, conflict, a climax, denouement, and resolution.

---

[116] Thomas More was born February 7, 1478 (Julian; February 16, Gregorian)
[117] Francis Bacon was born January 22, 1561 (Julian; February 1, Gregorian)

Bacon's *New Atlantis* is often compared with Thomas More's *Utopia*. A man of incomparable genius, Bacon was a major figure in the Renaissance's "scientific revolution." In *New Atlantis*, Bacon described a future society in which scientific advances (Uranus) would free men from drudgery, allowing for a lifestyle of happiness and prosperity. He described inventions akin to today's telephone, submarine, airplane, and more.

An Aquarian par excellence, Bacon's foresight into the future was framed by dim remembrances of a time past. Like Plato, Bacon evoked images of the lost continent of Atlantis. Some say that the misuse of science, both exoteric and occult, caused Atlantis' demise! The greater part of New Atlantis is dedicated to moral and spiritual safeguards necessary to prevent an idolatrous materialism. A solemn warning for today's time!

From the cover of Sir Francis Bacon's New Atlantis, engraving from an early edition of Bacon's unfinished utopian novel (published in 1627)

AQUARIUS & THE SPIRITUAL PATH

What happens when the Aquarian soul enters into a resolution of conscious self-transformation? Whether he is converted on the spot or comes into his path gradually, the Aquarian soul is destined to be a living manifestation of divine love. His opportunities for growth may come through encounters with friends or perhaps with an organization with which he strongly identifies. Along life's way, he will come to access hidden stores of charity as well as surprising levels of irritation. Whatever lessons in love his soul needs, he can expect to receive them—it is his Aquarian destiny.

Trust, like loyalty, is also an Aquarian issue. Does the Aquarian Aspirant trust that God will provide for all of his needs? Does he trust his spiritual teacher? If he tends to be mistrustful, he may have to study his psychology, going back to the time when he was a child, resolving any fears possibly stemming from forgotten early traumas. Uranian and Plutonian transits to the Moon and Sun, while upsetting in that they tend to stir up hidden emotions, are particularly useful in revealing to the Aspirant infantile emotional responses no longer appropriate to the present.

Even so, such events are usually only the tip of the karmic iceberg. Now an adult on the path of self-mastery, the Aquarian seeker can purge himself of doubt and misgivings by fervently invoking the transforming fires of love. Endowed with the Presence of pure love, he thus comes to trust first and foremost himself—his Real Self! And then, filled with the joy of spirit, he must summon the courage to take the leap of faith!

Spiritual surrender is a major test of love in Aquarius. For the individual Aquarian, the issue of personal independence is often an irksome one. He cherishes his freedom, but enjoys companionship. Marriage involves commitment, as does being part of a family or an organization—there is no way around it! Surrender does not mean giving in as in defeat, rather it means letting go. Whatever the situation may be, when the Aquarian Aspirant releases the entire matter to a higher Power, he trusts Life will give him back what he needs. Once he has surrendered the problem, the Aquarian Aspirant no longer has a reason to be agitated. Now he must wait and listen for the solution and right course of action.

For some Aquarian Aspirants the harder tests come in recognizing and relinquishing mental conceit. This can be tough because the attitude itself—a kind of crystallized pride—convinces him he's got it right. He thinks he's right, he knows he's right, but by and by he realizes the wisdom of listening and learning from others.

THE COURAGE TO STAND ALONE

While the Aquarian on the path often is tolerant of many conditions outside the norm, once he commits himself to an idea or principle, his mind sets upon it like a steel trap! The core of the controversy in which Thomas More found himself pitted against King Henry VIII revolved around the conflicting powers of Church and State. When the Pope refused to allow King Henry VIII a divorce so that he could marry Anne Boleyn, Henry declared himself, "The Supreme Head of the Church in England," thereby instating his own church laws so as to sanctify his marriage to Anne. Thomas More resigned his position as Chancellor of England to remove himself from the heat of the controversy. In Aquarian nonattachment, he adapted to his income being severely reduced.

More did not openly oppose the King, but he did refuse to sign the Act of Succession, passed in March of 1534, which required More and others to sign an oath acknowledging Henry and Anne as legitimate heirs to the throne. More was well aware of what he stood to lose by his refusal, but to support the edict would mean going against his conscience in the matter.

Certainly those who loved Thomas More, especially his wife Lady Alice and his beloved daughter Margaret, grieved at his tragic fate. Their arguments of persuasion that he return to them and be less unbending tore at his heart. Was he being stubborn, inflexible, and opinionated? Indeed, Aquarians have been known to be all of the above, and more. Yet, what distinguishes Thomas More is that he stood by his convictions even though not one person agreed with him, nor dared to take his side at the time. More was, above all, true to his conscience, come what may!

While the case may be less dramatic and the stakes less extreme, Aquarian souls homeward bound should watch out for those tests of integrity when what is expected or asked of them clashes with their best interests. Are they prepared to be true to their soul regardless of how great the temptation to be popular may be, how scary and disheartening the risk of being mocked and ostracized, how alluring the shine of material gain?

How can the Aquarian Aspirant tell if he is blinded by selfishness, the pride of mental conceit, and a veiled sense of superiority, or if he is defending the highest truth? As he advances on the path back to God, the danger of confusing one state for another increases. Sometimes, the only way to know the difference between delusional pride and self-evident truth, between the right and the wrong path, is by assessing the vibration. He may elect to spend a period of purification in fasting and prayer in preparation for such encounters.

Because Aquarius is a Fixed Sign, there will be times and cycles, relationships and initiations, in which the Aquarian Aspirant would best simply hold on with all his might, and other times when he best let go, even if doing so is difficult. When to let go and when to hold on? The Aquarian Aspirant must cultivate attunement, a faculty of the soul bound to the Higher Mind through the Heart.

RIGHT ASPIRATION & THE SEAT-OF-THE-SOUL CHAKRA

The second point of Gautama Buddha's Eightfold path, called *Right Aspiration, Right Thought and Right Resolve,* relates to the Seat-of-the-Soul chakra.[118]

In that this chakra relates to the Leo-Aquarius polarity, Aspirants on the way with their Sun in these signs can ask themselves, "Are my desires God's desires for me? Are my aspirations such that lead to greater love and the freedom of my soul at last?"

All the Signs on the Fixed-Love Cross (Taurus and Scorpio and Leo and Aquarius) relate to *Attitude,* the quality we give to the Will on the Fixed-Love

---

[118] See the last page of *The Sun in Taurus* to read more about the Buddha's Eightfold path.

Cross. Love correlates with emotion and desire; directing *Will* is motivation. Spiritual seekers born into any of these four astrological signs must meet the test of Will versus desire. As they attain greater self-control and mastery, they become teachers to others who would follow in their footsteps.

And so, the Aquarian Aspirant must ask himself, "What is my motivation?" Motivation comes from desire, but also from thought. Clear understanding, only possible in the peaceful mind, can quiet or purposefully direct desire. Right motivation and right attitude give birth to right aspiration, which manifests in right action—action that is harmonious with spirit and indicative of the soul that is free. What is the right attitude for the soul in Aquarius? Gautama teaches that *right attitude* is the desire to be non-attached to temporal gain and circumstance and to be free from hate and ignorance. He who has *right attitude* is free of all greed and selfishness. His major aspiration, to which all lesser desires must submit, is to serve life and be the instrument of compassion. In the Summit Lighthouse's teaching about the relationship between the soul and right aspiration, we read: "The soul's aspiration must be centered in God—in having right thought, right contemplation upon the law of God and the right resolve to accomplish her mission in life."

Although the soul's urge to be free is associated with Aquarius and with the Seat-of-the-Soul chakra, when misinterpreted and misapplied, this energy is interpreted to mean, "I can do whatever I want to do." Such a willful attitude naturally is not freedom but licentiousness and such a soul is hardly free. Since he cannot control himself, he is controlled by his karma. Only by attaining what Tibetan Buddhists describe as successive stages of spiritual Awakening (becoming free from ignorance and the bondage of the passions), can the Aquarian Aspirant hope to transcend his former state. Uranus and Saturn, Aquarius' co-rulers, provide an important key: the soul who is free (Uranus) from karmic limitation is self-disciplined and accepts the rightful restraints of the law (Saturn).

Our understanding becomes more meaningful when we meditate upon the polarity between the chakras; the Seat-of-the-Soul chakra polarizes with the Third Eye chakra, the place of vision. As it is written: "Without vision, the people perish.[119]

CLEARING THE SEAT-OF-THE-SOUL & THIRD-EYE CHAKRAS

But hatred (misuse of love) blocks the Third Eye even as it tortures the soul itself. So when, through right thought, aspiration and the transmutative action of the violet flame, we transmute vibrations of hatred, the Third Eye spins and we see what was obscured before.

All comes back to love. But how can the Aquarius Aspirant practice being more loving? Gratitude, love's joy in Leo, Aquarius' polarity, is indeed the

Great Attitude. Recognizing that we have brought all our problems upon ourselves, and being grateful for the Spirit that beats our hearts, let us see all fortune that comes our way as opportunity.

The Seat-of-the-Soul chakra is associated with the *violet transmuting flame*, which accelerates the transmutation of negative karmic records, essential for true soul freedom, and which is therefore a tremendous dispensation for the Aquarian who would dissolve the barriers surrounding the soul and encrusted around the spiritual and physical heart.[120]

Moreover, by invoking the violet flame with great love and devotion the Aquarian devotee clears the way for his soul to make its way from the Seat-of-the-Soul chakra, through the tumultuous records of the Solar Plexus chakra en route to the Heart chakra, his spiritual center. As he advances on his path, attaining greater mastery, he will be directed by his Divine Presence to the Secret Chamber of the Heart. Only the disciplined one knows true soul freedom, freedom in the heart and upper chakras, and freedom to love with all one's heart, mind and soul! The violet flame unlocks the incredible creative genius of the soul, bringing down gifts unknown from his own spiritual Presence with which he will fulfill his reason for being while blessing all mankind.

The Aquarian Aspirant's attunement is compromised when he gives way to lesser choices. So, in this wise, there is only one choice, one way. To decide otherwise is to be stuck in the downward spiral of karmic consequences—what one sows, one must reap. The same that is true for the individual is true for the nation and for a planet—in order to transcend the karmic cage we must come up higher!

INNER SENSE

In following the dictates of his conscience, Thomas More lost his position as Chancellor, was imprisoned in the Tower of London and, after a mock trial, was beheaded. While so many around him vied for positions of power or succumbed to save their lives, More guided his life by the edicts of his faith. Thomas More's last words on the scaffold summed up his life, "I die the King's good servant but God's first." Pope Leo XIII beatified Thomas More on December 29, 1886. Pope Pius XI canonized More on May 19, 1935, and Pope John Paul II named Saint Thomas More the Patron Saint of Statesmen and Politicians in 2000.

He who would be transformed in Aquarius must one day be willing to stand alone in vision and on principle. Bacon was denied his right to the throne, More was executed, and Lincoln was assassinated; yet history has exalted all three men.

---

[119] Proverbs 29:18
[120] See final chapter, *The Aquarian Science of Invocation.*

More was less concerned with the saving of his neck than with the salvation of his soul. Bacon (when denied the throne he deserved as the legitimate son of Queen Elizabeth) changed the world that he could not rule through brilliant statesmanship and the penning of Shakespeare's works and more. Lincoln understood he was playing a vital role in the forging of the course of history.

Although men and groups of people have risked their lives to be free, few know freedom's true meaning. Freedom is, in fact, the highest expression of divine love. After all, of all things living, only man is endowed with free will. The soul that is free does not throw care or caution to the wind, but rather strives (Saturn) to be free (Uranus) from the bonds of fate (Saturn). The Aquarian Hero sets the pace for the New Age that bears his name.

He is the Universal Brother. The water that he bears is that of Compassion and the return to a walk with God not known since Eden. No longer innocent, he has developed "inner sense." Draped in the light of the Christos, the exemplar of love, the Aquarian Hero is the wayshower in the New Age when the Word made manifest in the One proclaimed is destined to manifest in the many.

~ Part Two ~
The SUN in the WATER & EARTH Signs
Feminine

Capricorn:
10th House
Cardinal-
Power Cross
Earth Element

Scorpio:
8th House
Fixed-
Love Cross
Water Element

Pisces:
12th House
Mutable-
Wisdom Cross
Water Element

Virgo:
6th House
Mutable-
Wisdom Cross
Earth Element

Taurus:
2nd House
Fixed-
Love Cross
Earth Element

Cancer:
4th House
Cardinal-
Power Cross
Water Element

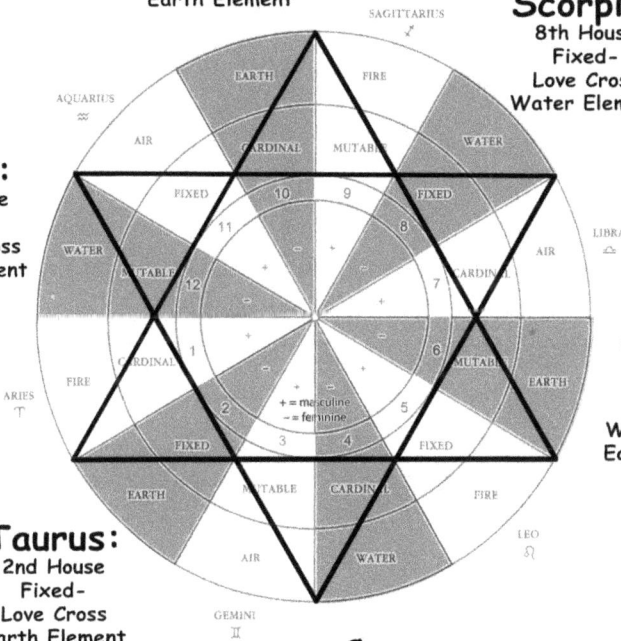

7.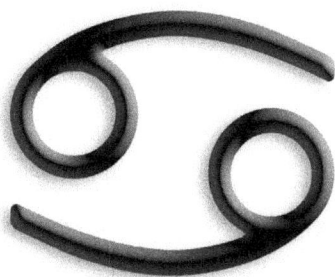

Cancer

Symbol	***The Crab***
Born	June 21 ~ July 22
Archetype	*The Mother*
Key Phrase	*I Feel*
Element	**Water**
Cross	**Cardinal-Power**
House	**Fourth:**

Home & family, food, shelter & personal property, psychological & ancestral roots, later years, subconscious & unconscious minds

Ruler	**Moon**
Esoteric Ruler	**Neptune**
Polarity	**Capricorn**
Chakra	Base-of-the-Spine
Anatomy	Stomach, chest, mammary glands, the pancreas, peristalsis

Spiritual Qualities **...Harmony & peace, abundance, lawful raising of Kundalini, self-discipline, expression of Divine Mother's love**

Vulnerable to ...... *Self-pity, human sympathy, emotonal discord, fear & possessiveness, self-justification, self-indulgence, Indecision, over-personalizing*

Must Acquire ..... **Inner peace, self-assurance, self-discipline, integration with feminine energies, objectivity, oneness with the Father (Spirit)**

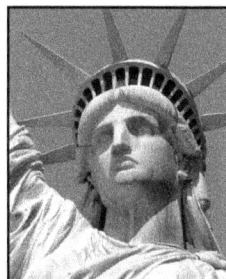

Dalai Lama • Ann Landers • Princess Diana • Nelson Mandela • United States of America

THE SUN IN CANCER

I learned that courage was not the absence of fear,
but the triumph over it. The brave man is not he
who does not feel afraid, but he who conquers that fear.

—Nelson Mandela, July 18, 1918

RAISING THE LIGHT IN CANCER

The Cancer Hero at the dawn of the Aquarian Age shows the way to a prosperous economy, to the building, development and governing of thriving communities characterized by harmonious and loving families. He may be on a rescue mission, requiring much sacrifice, endurance, courage and love—whether his destiny be primarily related to one particular soul he is called upon to succor, his family and/or his community, his nation or the entire world. He shows by his example, the possibility, indeed, the destiny of millions of souls during the Aquarian Age, to rise in the ritual of the Ascension at the end of this or a future embodiment.

Astrologers recognize each sign on the Cardinal Power Cross (Aries, Cancer, Libra and Capricorn) as a gateway to one of the Four Quadrants, corresponding to Fire, Water, Air and Earth, respectively. The areas represented by this Cross—oneself, home & family, important partnerships and marriage, and career—form the physical bracing of the astrological chart and speak of the basic areas of life where we gain our mastery over time and space, the staging of our self-development, our ties and our achievements. In *Transformational Astrology*, this cross is also designated as *The Cross of Right Identification*—an understanding of its coordinates helps us come into right relationship with ourselves, with our God, and with one another. For example, the vertical bar represented by Cancer and Capricorn reminds us, "to keep our eye on the Presence," focused on God, that we not be distracted or deceived by temporal realities. The horizontal bar tells of who we think we are (Aries) and the partnerships we attract (Libra), the dy-

---

[121] In resolving our psychology, we almost inevitably must examine our childhood roots. Planets in the Fourth House and their aspects, the placement of the ruler of the sign on the Fourth House cusp, as well as the Moon, reveal dynamics of our childhood not always readily understood. Note that although the Fourth House is the natural house of Cancer, and as such, describes the home and family life, the exact moment of birth determines the sign found on the Fourth House cusp. Persons born with a Pisces Ascendant, for example, will in most cases have Gemini there. Their homes, typically full of books, are likely to be places where much conversation and study take place.

namics of which very much depend upon our sense of our relationship with God. Acknowledging that true self-transformation requires "being in the world but not of the it"—a balance of strength and receptivity. Calling the light down into daily affairs, raising mundane matters up, until Earth truly reflects its Heavenly Source! He that would be the Hero in Cancer takes responsibility over the riddle he was born to resolve: How can he be successful both secularly and spiritually?

YESOD—HARMONIZING HEAVEN & EARTH

The Kabbalistic Tree of Life offers a clue! The person who is one with God can change the world! In Kabbalah, such a one is called *Tzadik*.

Cancer and the Moon are related to the sephirah, *Yesod*, on the Tree of Life's central pillar between the sephirah *Malkuth* (Earth) and *Tiferet* (Higher Awareness), *Yesod* represents the principle harmonizing Heaven and Earth. For example, the study of Torah is an outer activity meant to open the flow of heaven into the mind and soul of man, that during his earthly journey he never lose the way. The *Tzadik* is associated with *Yesod*. His path is not that of a hermit who shuts himself off from the world. He shows his faith by his works, thereby, in honor and joy, bringing a taste of heaven to earth!

Joseph of the Coat of Many Colors (in Genesis) saved his brothers and family from starvation during the Seven Years Drought, thereby saving the entire Hebraic lineage. He is an example of the *Tzadik*, the Righteous One. Through trial and temptation, Joseph kept the bond, the covenant, between man and God, He was trustworthy to be endowed with worldly power and not be corrupted. He was a humble man. This is the principle of divine harmony we see in Cancer. Harmony is the commitment of Heaven and the promise of man, a beauteous chord, the music of love. Without harmony, in our daily lives, and in the Cosmos itself, the universe collapses!

The keeping of the Covenant, represented in *Yesod*, is identified as the foundation of the Tree of Life, of the man himself. The *Tzadik* represents the spiritual foundation of the world. Cancer and the Fourth House represent the foundation of the entire chart. Cancer is the sign of the mother, of home and family, of our roots and origins. As is true in a physical house, the strength or fragility of the entire structure depends upon how well the foundation has been laid.[121]

Kabbalistic tradition teaches that there is always at least one *Tzadik* alive in the world. In the Age of Aquarius, many may take up this calling!

CANCER, WATER & THE BASE-OF-THE-SPINE CHAKRA

A Water sign, Cancer represents the flowing currents of life, health, happiness, and abundance. Water in Cancer nourishes, heals, and delights, and when

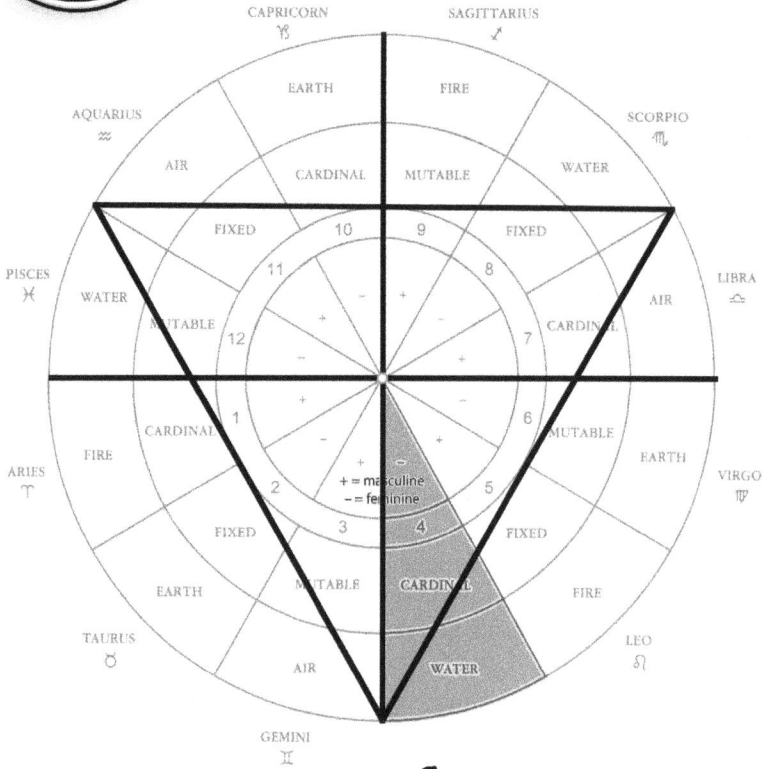

Cancer:
4th House
Cardinal-
Power Cross
Water Element

rightly harnessed, becomes a vital source of tremendous energy. Cancer rules the Base-of-the-Spine chakra. The movement of Spirit in the Base chakra causes its energies to rise, nourishing and spinning all the other chakras and expanding consciousness as it does. The Base chakra is related to the sexual organs and to procreation. (The seed and the egg are related to the Seat-of-the-Soul chakra.)

Cancer also brings disease, death and devastation to those who misuse the light of life anchored in the Base chakra, esoterically referred to as the sacred fire, through the following: self-pity (the woe is me consciousness); self-justification (making wrong seem right through twisted reasoning); forming emotional attachments that deplete rather than energize; the exploitation and waste of natural resources; giving sway to emotional tantrums and outbursts and otherwise disrupting life's natural rhythm and harmony. The disease Cancer is named after the sign, a manifestation of untransmuted reservoirs of hatred, especially self-hatred. On a larger scale, we see the accumulation of toxic wastes resulting from the abuse of the earth's natural resources. Additionally, water relates to memory so in the Water signs (Cancer, Scorpio and Pisces) we meet the need to release and transmute past records. Water has the healing power to comfort us and heal our wounds.

Internationally renowned self-help author, Louise Hay, points out the connection between Cancer and deep or secret hurt and grief and suggests the following affirmations to assist in healing Cancer, the disease: "I lovingly forgive and release all of the past. I choose to fill my life with joy. I love and approve of myself."

Eastern mystical traditions speak of the desecration of the sacred fire through the premature or inappropriate arousal of the sexual energies (the Kundalini). Desecration means the violation of that which is holy or sacred. We see this rampant today in pornography, child abuse, prostitution, careless sex and the wanton spreading of sexual diseases, in drug and alcohol addiction and in the misuse of science and natural resources, and in war itself.

Visualize, then, Cancer as a luminous fount of many colors, anchored at the bottom, the Nadir, of the astrological chart.[122]

See her waters rise in perfect symmetry, in rainbow rays, nourishing and splashing every other point on the wheel. Understand, then, that the key to self-transformation for the soul born in Cancer at the dawn of the Aquarian Age is the conscious and harmonious raising of this *mother light of life*, the disciplined control and harmonious direction of powerful emotions and desires. This is also the key to victory in every other sign of the Zodiac!

---

[122] The Nadir is also called the I.C. (*Imum Coeli*), Latin for "bottom of the sky."

"Mother of the World," painted by Nicholas Roerich, is often referred to as "Veiled Isis" or the "Cosmic Mother."

THE WOMB OF CREATION

The powerful energy, so pronounced when the Sun makes its annual transit through Cancer, is the defining spirit of the Aquarian Age, that divine, cosmic, feminine energy called by Hebrews, the *Shekinah,* by Hindus the light of *Shakti.* According to the classic of esoteric literature, *A Dweller on Two Planets,* by Phylos the Thibetan, in old Atlantean times, this energy was also known as the *Night Side of Nature.*

The Ancient Mayans recognized the mother light as a cosmic force when they spoke of the Mother Goddess *Ixchel*, and correctly identified the Galactic Center, which they called "The Womb of Creation." Mystics of many faiths pray to the Cosmic Virgin, seeking her intercession in their lives. This essence, called by so many names and personified in differing degrees in souls born in Cancer, is the manifestation of God as Mother. More specifically, it is the spirit of the Mother adoring the Father and likewise receiving and manifesting the Father's Love. From this cosmic tryst, this figure-eight flow, the Matter Cosmos is born!

THE ANCIENT ABANDONMENT OF THE MOTHER

In Cancer, the soul faces a most primordial and universal fear. It is the fear of abandonment, the fear that as a helpless child, he will be left to fend for himself, or be placed in the hands of those who might harm him, or simply the fear of losing the Mother's comforting warmth. Oddly, it appears that it is *we* who have abandoned the Mother as she agonized at the inevitable results of her children's free-will choices! Tales so ancient that their scripts are buried under the sea and in the deepest recesses of memory offer glimpses of a time when we, as a culture, lived within the Mother's loving embrace.

Remembrances of the Ancient Motherland of Lemuria echo in legends and oral history passed down in many diverse cultures throughout the world. (The ancient legends, once deciphered, recount how a people's ingratitude forced the Cosmic Mother to retreat to higher dimensions, appearing only occasionally over the millennia to those whose intense love and purity magnetized her Presence.) How eagerly we run to hear stories that evoke the mist-like images of past ages of beauty and peace flourishing within the ineffable Presence of the Cosmic Mother.

THE RETURN OF THE MOTHER IN AQUARIUS

In the Aquarian Age, the Divine Mother is destined to reappear among men, if we would have her and if we lovingly accept her disciplines and change our self-centered habits. And yet the soul in Cancer, while longing to run into his Mother's arms, will more likely retreat (like the crab, Cancer's symbol) into his shell for fear of the Mother's chastisements. But only the Mother can teach the soul how to raise up the light within his being—and raise it he must. The day arrives, and indeed has come, when the crab has outgrown his shell. He leaves his home and for a time has no shell. He is now vulnerable to being eaten, not only by other creatures, but also by other crabs. There is no other way.

The tremendous technological advancements of recent years are, in fact, expressions of the Mother energy in the Age of Aquarius, the sign of science and innovation. Aquarius is also the sign of divine love and brotherhood. Will we, the children of the Mother, use technology to free ourselves from drudgery and stress, to come into a greater union of brotherhood and love, more freely exploring our spiritual journey? Or will we partake of the gifts of the Mother without devotion and gratitude for their source and thus become prey to a mechanized materialism?

"COME, I WILL SHOW YOU HOW!"

Our mother is the most personal presence in our life. A dynamo of energy, she loves, she chides, she forgives, she teaches and disciplines, she feeds our bodies and our souls, she heals us and comforts us, and sometimes she pleads to the Father on our behalf. And so, Cancers can be identified by their most personal touch. Most tend to be up and doing and quite naturally directing the show—nourishing, organizing, protecting, and providing for those they love and oftentimes for strangers, setting up a home, or perhaps a community or a company—consoling, comforting and joyously delighting others through an irresistibly warm sense of humor. Their engaging personal manner and their characteristically strong yet soft look seem to communicate: "What do you need? I can help you. Come, I will show you how!"

Cancers are often exceptionally capable, organized, friendly, and humorous. (Unless emotionally distraught, in which case, they typically drop their affairs, live in disorder and withdraw for a time). They are concerned and helpful, kind by nature and, more often than not, financially astute. Most Cancers like being in charge; at the very least, they insist on being able to freely exercise choice on a daily basis. Natives of this sign are drawn to professions and positions where they can care for others and handle a multiplicity of responsibilities. You may find them as managers, nurses, cooks, in the hospitality industry, in spa and salon work, in positions of public service, in real estate and construction, and in customer relations. However, being stuck behind a desk with mounds of paperwork is definitely *not* a typical Cancer career!

THE POWER IN BEING POSITIVE

Experience proves and wisdom teaches that we are never subject to temptation or thrust into an ordeal without having within us the wherewithal to avoid the trap and pass the test.[123]

When the Cancer individual feels unfulfilled or powerless, he can study the situation, roll up his sleeves, and come up with a dynamic plan of action that he implements to the best of his ability. Better still, recognizing that he need not struggle, he can make the most of a difficult circumstance, resolving to maintain his inner peace and harmony. Then again, he may come to recognize that what often begins as an apparent tragedy or loss may turn out to be a blessing in disguise. But oftentimes, the Cancer person who feels helpless and unable to make changes resorts to complaining and a negative mindset, which may become habitual even when outer circumstances have improved.

Cancers typically find themselves repeatedly caught in stressful circumstances in which the urge to retreat within their shell feels overwhelmingly strong. Perhaps they must contend with some trying physical condition, economic stress, or fear of failure when much is expected of them. Perhaps their challenge is related primarily to being endowed with too much sensitivity and an overactive imagination. They benefit by seeing such challenges as opportunities, testing their determination to stand, face and conquer. In facing their fears, they overcome them. In determining to be disciplined and to turn handicaps into incentives for growth, they thrive.

MADIBA — GIVING ALL FOR ONE'S PEOPLE

Choosing to put on a happy face and be positive is a winning strategy for the Cancer soul. When he determines to keep on keeping on, regardless of the fears parading before him, the overwhelming odds, the seeming impossibility of

---

[123] Letter from Paul to the Corinthians: *There hath no temptation taken you but such as man can bear: but God is faithful, who will not suffer you to be tempted above that ye are able; but will with the temptation make also the way of escape, that ye may be able to endure it.* 1 Corinthians 10:13

what he wants to accomplish, he discovers stores of courage that he never knew he had.

Freedom fighter Nelson Mandela was born *Rolihlahla,* a Xhosa tribal term meaning "troublemaker," on July 18th, 1918 in Transkei, South Africa. In later years he became known by his clan name, *Madiba.*

In 1964, he was given a sentence of life imprisonment for his stand against the repressive apartheid government, but was freed after 27 years. During his long years in prison he was known as a teacher to his co-inmates, and a father to his jailers. He became president of South Africa on May 9th, 1994, after South Africa held its first multi-racial elections. A courageous and compassionate leader, Mandela once said:

> *I am fundamentally an optimist. Whether that comes from nature or nurture, I cannot say. Part of being optimistic is keeping one's head pointed toward the sun, one's feet moving forward. There were many dark moments when my faith in humanity was sorely tested, but I would not and could not give myself up to despair. That way lays defeat and death.*

How much is too much? This is the mother (Cancer) in the man whose sacrifice for her children knows no bounds. Mandela once said, "Real leaders must be ready to sacrifice all for the freedom of their people."

SAFE AT HOME BASE

Cancers like to feel secure. Their well-being depends upon feeling emotionally grounded and economically secure. Even the socially shy Cancer child is often outgoing when he feels safe at home base. All children, and especially Cancer children, blossom when spending their days in a home and school environment that is lovely, full of harmonious sounds, colors and smells, with chairs, tools, and things that are child-friendly.

Many Cancers take well to traveling as long as the essentials of life are taken care of and in order. This true story tells of how a Cancer woman and her restless Gemini husband struck a bargain that kept them both happy. He was a high-ranking official in the Army, her work was primarily that of caring for their home and four children. The Army moved them every 2 ½ years—ouch! The Crab frowned and snapped every time she had to pack up her home, uproot her children and leave, bound for wherever was to be their new place of residence. He lovingly and patiently assured her that all would be well. (Patience and affection are musts when relating to a Cancer.) Then, they would arrive at their new destination and she saw another *beautiful* and spacious home awaiting her mother's touch. This arrangement worked for many years until he retired.

WHERE IS LOVE?

When the Cancer soul suffers from the absence of the Mother's love and orderliness, when Crabs refuse or know not how to let go of fears and phobias, disturbing psychological symptoms may manifest, such as: a disorderly environment, a lack of funds and necessities, emotional turbulence, sloppiness, eating disorders, sexual promiscuity, a lack of self-discipline. In extreme adult female cases, these children of the Mother may actually tie their tubes due to fear of being unable to raise children properly.

Other telling symptoms of the fear of abandonment are vacillation and indecision. Evelyn, an intelligent and attractive Cancer woman in her late thirties, seems to have it made. Having inherited a small fortune, she travels the world, doing basically whatever she pleases. Yet, whether the matter is as small as buying a plane ticket or as large as choosing her next career move, she plagues herself needlessly — no matter what decision she makes, it's always the wrong one in her mind! If she chooses white, she later reasons, "I should have picked black," but when she then decides to choose black, she will conclude, "I should have stuck with the white!" To rid herself of such a maddening condition, Evelyn needs to come to terms with and resolve her infantile anger at having been brought up by nannies while her wealthy parents spent their time developing and managing the family business.

Tom Hanks and Meg Ryan
in the 1998 movie, "You've Got Mail"

So, here's a practical and fun, once you get the hang of it, Cancer exercise in decision-making. The setting is New York City at noon (or some other bustling metropolis) when everyone is pouring out of the buildings going to lunch. Head for a Starbucks (frankly, any deli will do). Get in line and get ready to make several on-the-spot decisions. As Joe Fox, the character played by Cancer Tom Hanks in *You've Got Mail,* explains in his e-mail chat with Kathleen Kelly (played by Scorpio Meg Ryan):

---

[124] Check out this fun movie and take note of Tom Hanks' friendly, nice-guy, no worries, I'll-take-care-of-you (mother energy) Cancer smile and soft eyes, contrasting with Meg Ryan's Scorpio stare, implying, "What? You're kidding!"

> *The whole purpose of places like Starbucks is for people with no decision-making ability... to make six decisions just to buy one cup of coffee. Short, tall, light, dark, café, decaf, low-fact, non-fat, etc. So people... can, for only $2.95, get not just a cup of coffee but an absolutely defining sense of self: Tall, Decaf, Cappuccino!*[124]

Seriously, when Cancer souls find simple decisions practically impossible to make it can be a exasperating condition in which they often, understandably, feel despair. The surface problem is indicative of a deeper issue that can be healed. The Cancer soul so determined to turn this problem around must summon the courage to go after the fear causing the block responsible for his disconnect from his own Higher Self. He can support his resolve by using positive affirmations and a simple mantra, such as, *I and my Father are one!* Remembering the dynamics of the Cancer/Capricorn polarity on *The Cross of Right Identification*, he re-establishes his relationship to the Father-Mother God and to his own divine reality.

WHY CANCERS TAKE THINGS SO PERSONALLY

Others born in signs of less sensitive dispositions find it hard to understand why their Cancer friends are so touchy. Water sign people (Cancers, Scorpios and Pisceans) are by nature emotional. Mastering the emotions is challenging. The key phrase of the soul born under the influence of Cancer is "I feel," to which we might add, "all the currents swirling around me—all the time!" Sensitivity is a definite Cancer asset; as long as he learns to depersonalize energy; that is, not take upon himself all the energies he feels around him. Such objective reasoning must be acquired, but it rarely comes naturally to the Cancer soul.

Many Cancer children find it hard to accept correction, even from a loving parent or teacher. They tend to react defensively, and sometime angrily. Cancers involved in intimate relationships upset love's harmony when they lash out at their partner for imagined slights. On the job, their natural resourcefulness and can-do spirit make them a valuable asset to almost any team, but an overly emotional temperament, unless curbed, puts a damper on the reputation and desirability of these otherwise enterprising and valuable team players.

One mother of a Cancer teenager solved her communication problem with her son in an effective manner. She first consciously eliminated "shoulds, woulds and why didn't yous?" from her speech. Assuming a respectful tone of voice, she tried to communicate more compassionately. The problem improved but remained. The mother finally was able to resolve the problem by saying to her son, "I am not blaming you. You may *feel* that I am blaming you, and I understand that, but it's simply not so. When you want to withdraw, I suggest you try taking a deep breath and telling yourself, "My mother loves me. She is not blaming me, but trying to help me!"

Judging that one is being blamed as well as laying blame upon others (rather than objective analysis helpful to resolve problems), is a manifestation of feeling impotent on the Cancer/Capricorn polarity (Capricorns condemn themselves and others) and is, in many cases, symptomatic of unresolved childhood (or past life) traumas.

DO YOU LOVE ME?

Truly, the Achilles heel for many Cancers involved in intimate relationships is a gnawing sense of insecurity. A Cancer romance can be wonderful. Cancers in love are thoughtful, affectionate, active and effusive. They enjoy life, love and good food with gusto and have an intuitive sense of beauty and love for family. The powerful mother energy in Cancers of both sexes inclines them to be highly defensive and protective of their loved ones, giving their all to provide for their families. The Cancer home is usually a place of warmth and comfort. The list goes on and on—but...! Cancers, beware of doing for others what they can do for themselves. Avoid *the smothering mother syndrome*! Moreover, the fear of being hurt or abandoned, expressed in constant demands for outward reassurance of being loved, weakens the bond and throws an insidious apprehension into even the best match.

Especially when Cancers have been hurt before, they typically resist engaging in a new relationship and so may lose out. Love is a risk—Cancers who become overly controlling or possessive of their partners to protect themselves from fear can sabotage the relationship. Natives of this sign will therefore benefit by working on their psychology (Astrology offers many vital clues) to help them get to the core of their trepidations, empowering them to take a chance and be ready for love once again when romance comes their way. Often, the problem is quite simple, but the self-protective mechanisms that were built to insulate them can be complex. Ultimately, the Cancer soul cannot find outside of himself what he must access from within.

MASTERING THE MOON

To be born under the influence of Cancer is to be ruled by the Moon. The Moon represents the feeling world and the subconscious mind. The reference of the woman "with the Moon under her feet," spoken of in Revelation 12:1, represents the mastery of the emotions. Especially, the Cancer soul must learn to manage his emotions. He must master the constantly changing lunar tides, lest the emotional sea engulf him.

To live in ignorance is tough, no matter what sign heralded at birth. But to be unaware in Cancer is to be tossed about by the changing lunar tides—one moment happy, the other sad, one moment enthusiastic, the other disappointed or curiously disinterested. Imagine a child born on an island. His life, and later his livelihood, will depend upon his ability to master the waters of the emotions.

For Cancers, the keys, without which peace is impossible, are practicing mindfulness, cultivating an optimistic outlook, objective self-awareness, and self-discipline as a means to lawfully control the emotions. In addition, to be successful, the Cancer person must garner a momentum of harmony and practice decisiveness.

Are you involved in a relationship with a Cancer? Whatever the nature of the tie, dealing with these Moon-ruled emotional individuals can be challenging, less so perhaps for a Scorpio or Pisces who can better go with the Cancer flow. How to deal with their Moon moodiness? One minute they're hot, another they're cold. It is simply part of the Cancer package. First, try not to take it personally, thereby showing them how to do the same—unless, of course, the Cancer person has gained some degree of emotional mastery. When the Sun transits through Cancer (from June 21st to July 22nd), people of all signs find themselves more emotional and reactive than usual. We can be more compassionate toward our Cancer friends who many times can teach us all how to be emotionally sensitive, intimately caring and yet serenely at peace!

THE CANCER CHILD

Cancer children are moved by strong, constantly changing emotional currents. Learning how to achieve and sustain inner peace and harmony by mastering the emotions can be a lifelong task for Cancers, very much influenced by childhood experiences within the family environment. Parents and teachers, especially those weak in the water element in their own charts, may find it challenging to be patient with the temperamental Cancer child. Anger and severity from elders can scar this sensitive child's sensibilities and are best avoided at all costs.

The Cancer child must learn that doing things because "I feel like it" is not necessarily the best choice—in fact, it rarely is! As he matures, becoming more disciplined and composed, he experiences the joy and satisfaction in doing what is right, even when he doesn't feel like doing it. By developing a sense of duty, his correct choices become more purposeful and he gains self-confidence, despite the pull of emotional energies and mood changes that threaten to derail his happiness.

Most Cancer children are loving, affectionate and kind. Little crabs do, however, become crabby. Sometimes, when they feel hurt or out of sorts, they are snappish. Like the crab, with a hard shell but soft inside, the Cancer child may hide in his room and sulk, or enter a world of his own making, if his feelings have been hurt or to escape a harsh environment. Water is reflective; beautiful colors and soothing music help him tune in to the reservoir of peace and creativity within his soul. Even young Cancer children enjoy meditation.

The parents' attunement to the Cancer child, their understanding of the daily astrological forecast, and right diet at home, help them direct this child toward acquiring the necessary self-discipline to ride the waves of changing moods and emotions. This child typically needs guidance and guidelines; sulking, brooding, feeling sorry for oneself, justifying wrong behavior and all manner of self-indulgence are squalls best to be avoided! Parents to the Cancer child are advised to reassure their son or daughter that he or she is loved, while never assenting to whining![125]

Canadian psychologist and educator, Gordon Neufeld, talks about the importance of helping the child "find his tears." By releasing his pent up feelings, especially in situations that seem without remedy, he not only feels relieved, but also discovers that the moment of futility passes. In the end all is well. The idea is not to somehow ignore nor block out changing energy patterns, but rather to gain mastery in riding the waves—it can be done!

Since Cancer is the sign of the Mother, Cancer children of both sexes respond readily to being needed and instinctively seek to care for others. Like a capable mother, they often abound in common sense practical solutions and remedies to life's many cares. The older Cancer child looks to help mom care for younger brothers and sisters. When the child is old enough to share responsibility for a pet's care, a little friend is often the way to bring out and help refine his caring instincts.

Cancer signifies our roots and heritage, our home and shelter. The crab carries his house on his back! Cancer children benefit from receiving much love and reassurance during their early years. When parents are separated, divorced, constantly arguing or somehow unable to reliably fulfill their parental duties, as often happens, for example, in the alcoholic household and in homes in which both parents work full time, the Cancer child typically tries to take over, assuming responsibilities not rightfully his own to help keep the family intact.

Of all the signs, Cancer is the most family-oriented. The healthy tree must have strong roots, and herein lies the fundamental determining factor between the Cancer child who grows up to sustain and nurture others as a self-sufficient individual and the neglected Cancer child, fearful of rejection or punishment, that later hungers for security as a clinging vine (or smothering protector) in adult relationships. Childhood impressions may last for life!

---

[125] The barometer for the Cancer child's emotional forecast (and younger children of all signs) can be seen in reading the Moon's daily position (its meaning and aspects to the child's natal and progressed astrology) and by awareness of exact aspects made by the progressed Moon.

Although little Crabs often delight in sharing with others, they may fear to let go of possessions or friends. Life will teach him the difference between tenacity and possessiveness. Parents are advised to gently encourage self-reliance in their Cancer child who may tend to hold unto Mommy's apron strings.

The Mother's loving protective energy is strongest in Cancer women, but is also evident in Cancer men and boys. Although Cancer boys can be endearing and sweet, and oftentimes protective of their families, mothers should discourage them from becoming "mama's boys." Their loyalty to mom and home can find many modes of positive expression, such as in-home repair and cooking, helping to care for younger siblings, and in exercising their innate problem-solving abilities. This close bond to the mother and family characteristic in the most manly of Cancer men has a marked influence, for better or worse, upon their lives in general and especially upon their adult relationships with women.

Regardless of birth sign, there will be times when a man ties into the feminine aspect of his being and expresses himself as mother. The great prophet Moses acted much like a mother defending her children before the judgment of the Father when pleading to God that the dispensing of His impersonal law not be so severe upon the children of Israel. Jesus sounded much like a mother grieving the direction her children had taken when he compared himself to a mother hen: "O Jerusalem, Jerusalem, how often would I have gathered thy children together as a hen doth gather her brood under her wings and ye would not!" (Matthew 23:37)

We also perceive the mother in Patrick Henry's passionate cry, "Give me liberty or give me death!" This is reminiscent of the sacrificial love a mother has for her own, seen here as that of a patriot ready to give his life, if need be, for his homeland (Cancer).

DEAR ANN & DEAR ABBY

In a classic sense, the father tells us what we must do, while the mother teaches us how to do it. Cancer is the "how-to sign" — its natives tend to be practical, resourceful and imaginative. The famous columnist, Ann Landers, along with her twin sister, Abigail Van Buren, became household names for over 50 years through their newspaper advice columns syndicated around the country.

Ann and Abby were both born on July 4th, 1918. They offered caring but no-nonsense solutions to almost every query under the sun and were especially sought after for their how-to advice on relationships and family life. In response to one concerned parent with a child showing signs of entitlement, Ann once wrote:

What the vast majority of American children need is to
stop being pampered, stop being indulged, stop being chauf-

feured, stop being catered to. In the final analysis, it is not what you do for your children but what you have taught them to do for themselves that will make them successful human beings.

THE WAY TO A CANCER'S HEART

Cancer relates to the stomach and to nutrition. Most Cancers love to cook and they almost all love to eat! Many are drawn professionally to some aspect of the food industry. But a large belly, even on a young Cancer child may indicate an unhealthy tendency to store, rather than to correctly process, their pain—to hold in secrets that torture the psyche rather than to seek resolution.

The Cancer individual must guard against using food for comfort, an unhealthy practice of hiding away worries in fat cells. As such a one determines and begins to lose weight, he must be ready to deal with memories of fear that surface into the mind and feelings as fat is burned off and toxins released. And so it goes for any of us when we determine to become lighter—even when the weight we shed is not physical, but the density of emotional baggage or an egocentric temperament.

LET GO, LITTLE CRAB!

Cancers have trouble letting go—of people, of things, of hopes and desires, and of memories. Cancers are known for their remarkable memory, a definite plus, except when they refuse to move on! They can get stuck in the past, forever reopening wounds that need to be cauterized and healed, once and for all. Normally protective and loving, natives of this sign must avoid the tendency to be possessive, domineering, or oppressively caring, as in the "smothering mother syndrome" describing the Cancer person whose constant care, even when well intended, can suffocate. An excessive attention on another's needs is usually indicative of a deep-seated insecurity that needs to be addressed and healed. If the underlying issue is ignored, it can sabotage an otherwise healthy relationship, or attract abusive partners or dysfunctional relationships, which serve to bring the Cancer persons' insecurities to the surface over and over again.

"Let go, little crab," one mother would lovingly admonish her Cancer daughter, imitating the crab's grabbing claws. Ah, but how to let go of what must be released and yet hold on and never give up on hope and right desire! Tenacity and persistence are the markings of positive self-esteem, the means to self-fulfillment. They are a joy to behold in the well-raised Cancer child!

FOOD AS COMFORT OR AS PUNISHMENT

Cancer relates to the stomach; Cancers need to avoid creating food disorders and addictions. Some Cancers feel so abandoned that they deny themselves necessary nourishment in sadness or perhaps in anger against parents and/or spouses. However, it is more common for Cancers to over-eat emotionally, seeking solace from food, a habit that can be self-destructive and self-defeating. Excess fat, which is so harmful to physical well-being, can actually feel comforting on a certain level. When the Cancer individual determines to lose weight and begins to burn off unnecessary fat, fears come tumbling to the surface. This is when yoga, physical exercise and powerful spoken affirmations can make all the difference! A bulging waistline often means that painful memories are stuffed rather than processed.

IRRESISTIBLY VULNERABLE

Of all the 12 signs of the Zodiac, Cancer Sun Signs are among the easiest to identify. Just look into their eyes — so sweet, so sensitive, so caring, so strong and yet so vulnerable. You sense the mother's bountiful and very personal energy, even in men. You sense the mother's pain and longing. And you smile, for their eyes reach out to you, lightening the load with sweet humor. Check out actor Nelson Eddy, born June 29, 1901. True, he had Mercury and Venus in Cancer too, but that's just icing on the cake!

Nelson Eddy & Jeanette MacDonald.
Caring and protective, actor Nelson Eddy holds on to his twin flame, the love of his life.

PRINCESS DIANA—20TH CENTURY MOTHER ICON

Lady Diana, Princess of Wales, was born Diana Spencer on July 1st, 1961, to an aristocratic English family. Striking out on her own at age 17, she tried her hand at different vocations, but nothing took off. Diana was born for a much larger role, as can be seen in her natal chart. Along with Mother Teresa, who was Diana's close friend, she became an iconic symbol of the Mother for the

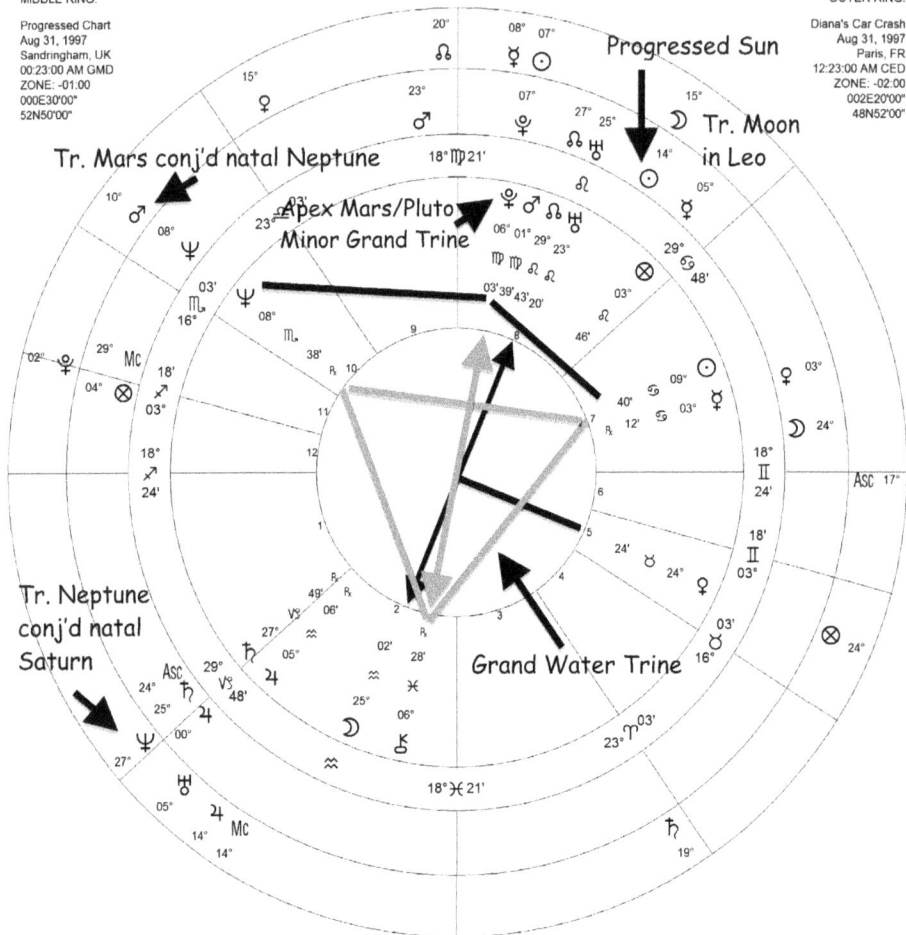

MIDDLE RING:

Progressed Chart
Aug 31, 1997
Sandringham, UK
00:23:00 AM GMD
ZONE: -01:00
000E30'00"
52N50'00"

OUTER RING:

Diana's Car Crash
Aug 31, 1997
Paris, FR
12:23:00 AM CED
ZONE: -02:00
002E20'00"
48N52'00"

Progressed Sun

Tr. Mars conj'd natal Neptune

Tr. Moon in Leo

Apex Mars/Pluto Minor Grand Trine

Tr. Neptune conj'd natal Saturn

Grand Water Trine

Progressed Chart

Pl	Geo Lon	R	Decl
☽	24° ♊ 48'		+18° 39'
☉	14° ♍ 12'		+16° 34'
☿	05° ♌ 49'		+20° 05'
♀	03° ♋ 45'		+21° 41'
♂	23° ♍ 39'		+03° 10'
♃	00° ♍ 39'	R	- 20° 38'
♄	25° ♑ 13'	R	- 21° 16'
♅	25° ♌ 23'		+13° 43'
♆	08° ♏ 37'		- 12° 42'
♇	07° ♍ 02'		+20° 33'
☊	27° ♌ 48'		+12° 14'
Mc	29° ♏ 11'		- 19° 59'
Asc	24° ♑ 09'		- 21° 17'

INNER CHART:

	Geo Lon	R	Decl
☽	25° ♒ 02'		- 12° 55'
☉	09° ♋ 40'		+23° 05'
☿	03° ♋ 12'	R	+18° 41'
♀	24° ♋ 24'		+15° 59'
♂	01° ♍ 39'		+11° 55'
♃	05° ♒ 06'	R	- 19° 32'
♄	27° ♑ 49'	R	- 20° 44'
♅	23° ♌ 20'		+14° 25'
♆	08° ♏ 38'	R	- 12° 40'
♇	06° ♍ 03'		+21° 01'
☊	29° ♌ 43'		+11° 34'
Mc	23° ♎ 03'		- 08° 58'
Asc	18° ♐ 24'		- 22° 56'

Princess Diana
Jul 01, 1961
Sandringham, UK
07:45:00 PM GMD
ZONE: -01:00
000E30'00"
52N50'00"

Geocentric
Tropical
Placidus Houses

THE THREE MAGI
p.o. 81. Emigrant, Mt.
(406)333-4804

Diana's Car Crash

Pl	Geo Lon	R	Decl
☽	15° ♌ 06'		+13° 25'
☉	07° ♍ 34'		+08° 44'
☿	08° ♍ 47'	R	+04° 27'
♀	15° ♌ 46'		- 06° 09'
♂	10° ♏ 28'		- 15° 43'
♃	14° ♒ 22'	R	- 17° 28'
♄	19° ♈ 39'	R	+05° 12'
♅	05° ♒ 30'	R	- 19° 31'
♆	27° ♑ 35'	R	- 20° 15'
♇	02° ♐ 55'		- 08° 36'
☊	20° ♍ 15'		+03° 52'
Mc	14° ♌ 46'		- 16° 24'
Asc	17° ♊ 08'		+22° 49'

entire world. (Mother Teresa was a Virgo. Virgo is the Mother Sign in the Earth element). One billion viewers tuned in to watch Diana's marriage to Prince Charles on July 29, 1981. Billions of viewers worldwide mourned her untimely death in a car accident on August 31, 1997. Or was her death really an accident? Some think her death was orchestrated. (British investigators in 2006 concurred with a 1999 French investigation that concluded the crash was caused by the inebriated chauffer who was speeding and lost control of the car.) Certainly, the deck was stacked! Curiously, Mother Teresa died a week later, on September 5, 1997.

Diana fit in well enough to become a princess, not without some misgiving on the part of the Royal Family, and she was beautiful and dignified in her new role. But with her Moon in Aquarius and Uranus (Aquarius' ruler) in Leo (self-expression) square her Venus, Diana was not about to be consigned to a stuffy role. Diana's royal status allowed her to fulfill the idealistic hope and karmic accounts of her natal Chiron—that planetoid so indicative of a destiny that is not perceived, but written in the stars—which was in dreamy reconcile-with-the-past Pisces, part of a Grand Water Trine. Diana won over hearts worldwide and became an idealized image of modern womanhood for many young women. But her Chiron (which always figures strongly in intimate relationships) was opposite Mars and Pluto in Virgo—Diana was tormented by the stormy turbulence of her unhappy marriage. The world loved Diana. The public forgave her for her indiscretions and lack of good judgment—a giving in to her impulsive Uranian side. Perhaps the stress she bore was just too much. Nonetheless, she never faltered in her humanitarian efforts.[126]

---

[126] That fateful day, transiting Neptune was exactly conjoined natal Saturn in Capricorn in Diana's chart, a fateful combination—especially considering that transiting Mars in Scorpio exactly conjoined her natal Neptune. Mars/Neptune aspects certainly can point to subterfuge, but I have also seen this combination of Mars (action) and Neptune (negligence) in tragic accidents where passengers did not wear their seatbelts. We note that her natal Neptune (in the Tenth House of power) was trine her Sun in the Seventh House (of marriage), and trine Chiron in Pisces. This fortuitous combination tells in part of Diana's mystique and of her rise to power and fame through marriage. But Scorpio's rulers, Pluto and Mars, were conjoined in her natal chart. While this intense coupling formed the apex of a fortuitous Minor Grand Trine, Mars opposed Diana's Moon in "I-will-to-do-it-my-way" Aquarius. This astrological signature portrays what endeared her to us but made her such a nuisance for the palace. The same opposition speaks of her aloneness. Although a mother figure to so many, she was suicidal and tormented within herself. On August 31, 1997, the transiting Moon in Leo conjoined Diana's progressed Sun and natal Uranus in her Eighth House (death, endings), adding the final touch to this volatile astrology, portending sudden, unexpected death—not necessarily fated—but certainly the stage was set.

LIBERTY & THE CULTURE OF THE DIVINE MOTHER

The United States of America was conceived on July 4th, 1776, as a government "of the people, by the people, and for the people," with the Sun at 13 degrees Cancer propitiously conjoined the Fixed Star Sirius, the brightest visible star.[127]

Did the Founding Fathers secretly enlist the help of astrology to choose the date for launching the revolution (through the signing of the Declaration of Independence) destined to represent the Flame of Freedom to the world? Or did destiny's hand choose this auspicious moment?

The statue representing Mother Liberty in New York Harbor symbolizes what this nation has represented for people throughout the globe. Inscripted at her base, reminiscent of a Cancer mother's heart, are the words, *Give me your tired, your poor, your huddled masses yearning to breathe free, the wretched refuse of your teeming shore.*

America's destiny, since her inception in 1776, has been to bring the Culture of the Divine Mother to the planet, clearing the way for the many wonders prophesied for the Aquarian Age, the Age of Freedom. The challenge before the nation, and now before all of Earth's people, is considerable, especially for those born while the Sun transits through Cancer during this phase of history, as the Divine Mother is stepping through the veil. In these early stages, all that is anti-mother individually and globally is awakened. The role of women, in relationship to men and family, indeed in shaping the structure of the family itself, is necessarily being transformed. This is so that the Earth will be prepared to receive souls of higher intelligence and spiritual attainment who are meant to incarnate now. We, as individuals and a people, are being shaken to our very roots—the roots of an ages-long density of consciousness from which we are finally being aroused.

Because the United States is a Cancer country, the attributes and challenges of this sign apply to every one of her citizens. Consider the vision, bravery, accord and the will-to-win that was necessary for the signing of the Declaration of Independence. Americans have paid dearly for indecisiveness, misuse of natural resources, the manipulation of the economy, disharmony between the people and their representatives, and a tendency to mother those who would perhaps do better if left to stand on their own two feet.

---

[127] Forty times brighter than the Sun, esoterically related to God Government, and known as the God Star, the energy of Sirius is related to the destiny of the United States.

CANCER & THE SPIRITUAL PATH

The Cancer Aspirant brings to the path a particularly sensitive attunement to beauty, an intuitive grasp of truth, an empathetic personality, a joy in service, and gifts of proactive self-enterprise—all wrapped around a can-do spirit! He begins by consciously sorting out the real from the unreal within himself and his surroundings—a task that will often require a spiritual guide or teacher. In declaring his independence from unconscious living, he essentially is deciding first and foremost to act rather than react. As he grows in experience and self-awareness, he realizes that if he were to follow every emotional impulse, he would end up taking some serious detours, potentially placing himself in precarious situations.

If the Cancer seeker is reticent, perhaps smarting from bruises of past encounters, or depleted of energy of light due to unwise habits—if he has dabbled in psychic phenomenon, was embroiled in dysfunctional relationships, or if he has unresolved problems relating to his parents (especially with his mother), then working on his psychology and cleaning out his inner and outer home will be required for any real spiritual advancement.

The Cancer Aspirant must be willing to be purged, pummeled, guided and at times left entirely alone. A sound diet, exercise on a daily basis, and a good night's sleep help keep his "chi energy" in balance, a safeguard against becoming susceptible to feeling sorry for himself, complaining that he is being picked on, or grumbling about the rigors of the path. Instead, let him be up and doing! Sometimes, his major gauge of progress is his ability to capitalize upon the lessons he learns from his mistakes and failures. If he opts to feel down on himself, precious time will be lost!

A young Cancer teenager, normally quite sensitive to criticism, once said of her fastidious voice teacher who seemed to correct her with every breath, "She sees me on stage. She is tweaking and perfecting me. She knows what it takes to make it big!" If the Cancer Aspirant reacts to the teacher or guru in a childish, rebellious, or angry manner, he can be almost certain that the relationship is exposing aspects of his psychology tied into some problem with a parental figure in this, or even in another, lifetime. When the Cancer Aspirant loves the Teacher and is grateful that he has been accepted as a student (or disciple), he will know that the many corrections he receives are an expression of the highest love.

MIND OVER MATTER

The path is not easy. The climb to the top requires an intense fervor to succeed against all odds! Desire is a powerful force, more so for those engaging in prayer and spiritual meditation. Essential to the Cancer Aspirant's progress is his ability to use his mind to fan his fervor and devotion while controlling his tendency to be emotionally reactive. Buddhism teaches that all *dukkha* (suffering) comes from *inordinate* desire. His Holiness, the 14th Dalai Lama, a Cancer, born July 6th, 1935, teaches us how to use the mind to remain unmoved by emotional currents. His teachings are of great worth to anyone searching for truth, but especially for the Cancer Aspirant intent upon governing his stars:

> *A great rock is not disturbed by the wind. The mind of a wise man is not disturbed by either honor or abuse.*

Noting that we tend to get easily offended by childishly insignificant matters, whereas we tend to not take the important matters of long-term importance so seriously, the Dalai Lama again remarks:

> *The fundamental philosophical principle of Buddhism is that all our suffering comes about as a result of an undisciplined mind, and this untamed mind itself comes about because of ignorance and negative emotions. For the Buddhist practitioner, then, negative emotions are always the true enemy, a factor that has to be overcome and eliminated. Since these negative emotions are states of mind, the method or technique for overcoming them must be developed from within. There is no alternative. They cannot be removed by some external technique, like a surgical operation.*

A young monk from Nepal once commented that communicating with the Dalai Lama was sometimes hard to do. Why? Because he laughs so much! The Cancer Hero is marked by a special quality of joy, which is, in fact, the manifestation of the rising of the mother light, accomplished through daily disciplines and transformations until the growing light fills the entire aura.

COMPASSION VERSUS PITY

By and by, the Cancer Aspirant encounters experiences meant to teach him the difference between true compassion, which is always positive and proactive, and that of pity, which has an insipid vibration like stagnant water breeding disease rather than sustaining life. Feeling sorry for others or even for oneself brings one's energy down. Sharing another's depression rarely results in constructive gain. Truly, such a sentiment more often than not is but the flipside of anger, based on a sense of injustice and upon ignorance of the merciful nature of opportunity. Cancers may unwittingly fall into this trap through their desire to serve and help others.

On the contrary, to be compassionate is to love unconditionally. It is to assess another's needs accurately and to help that one in right measure, not only with their circumstances, but also in terms of their soul. The compassionate Cancer sees any problem or dilemma as an opportunity to practice problem solving!

LOSING THE WAY THROUGH SELF-JUSTIFICATION

One dangerous trap that is rarely seen for what it is and that tests the resolve of the Cancer Aspirant is self-justification—the temptation to make a wrong into a right, with reasoning such as, "Well, I know I shouldn't lie, but a little white lie will get me out of a lot of trouble and it won't hurt anyone." One lie, in this case, can open a Pandora's box and lead to a sequence of decisions and events that culminate in finding oneself far adrift from home. The Cancer Aspirant, perhaps months later, asks himself, "How did I get here?" He barely recalls the choices that pulled him out to sea. Cancers on the path back home will certainly encounter situations testing their ability to choose the right, despite the inconvenience!

One of the first requirements of the path is for the Aspirant to maintain his peace, acting rather than reacting. As he progresses, he gains greater self-mastery in this respect. The Cancer Aspirant's sensitivity increases manifold; he is not less, but rather, more sensitive, but he learns to maintain his attention always upon his Divine Presence. Through prayer, meditation and the dynamic decrees, he succeeds in raising the Kundalini, the Ascension Fires, from the Base to the Crown. He becomes increasingly more self-disciplined and less reactive. Esoterically, Cancer is ruled by Neptune, whose higher emanations few have been able to perceive. Connected with the light of his Presence, his prayers are a walking meditation, a constant communication with God. For the soul in Cancer, holding the vision necessary to attain his goal, versus being an indulgent dreamer, is often simply a matter of holding to a higher vibration!

THE CANCER HERO

The Cancer Aspirant becomes the Hero through self-discipline and loving service to humanity, through fearless compassion and joy, and by remaining resolute to pass every test. He has successfully integrated heart, head and hand. So strongly anchored is he in his divine reality that no outer force can rile his emotions or sense of purpose, now safely under his control. He can now be trusted to safely harness the Mother energy lodged in the Base chakra and to raise a fount of potentially creative energy and abundance!

8. ♏ Scorpio

Symbol . . . . **The Scorpion, the Phoenix, the Eagle**

Born . . . . Oct. 23 ~ Nov. 21

Archetype . . . . *The Warrior*

Key Phrase . . . .*I Regenerate*

Element . . . .**Water**

Cross . . . . **Fixed-Love**

House . . . . **Eighth:**
Sex, death, joint finances, financial support, trusts & inheritances, real estate, surgery, research, mysteries & the occult, unconscious anger

Rulers . . . . **Pluto & Mars**

Esoteric Ruler . . . . **Mars**

Polarity . . . . **Taurus**

Chakra . . . . .Third Eye

Anatomy . . . . .Sex organs, prostate, bowels, blood, nose

Spiritual Qualities . . . .**Selflessness, fearlessness, purification, regeneration & transformation, creative vision, persistence, kindness, wealth**

Vulnerable to . . . . Selfishness, narcissism, fear & paranoia, compulsiveness, hypersensitivity, misuse of sex, over-self-concern & jealousy, cruelty

Must Acquire . . . .**Forgiveness, selflessness, transmutation & resolution of past, clear seeing, release from pain, compassion, kind-heartedness**

Theodore Roosevelt • Gen. George Patton • Julia Roberts • John Adams • Fanny Brice

THE SUN IN SCORPIO

Great achievement is usually born of great sacrifice
and is never the result of selfishness.

—Napoleon Hill, October 26, 1883

THE GODDESS KUNDALINI

Scorpio is the most potent sign of the Zodiac. But Scorpio is also the most potentially destructive of the twelve. The Scorpio experience is that of "regeneration." Webster defines "regenerated" as: 1) formed or created again; 2) spiritually reborn or converted; 3) restored to a better, higher, or more worthy state. To be transformed into men and women of a New Era, we must necessarily all pass through Scorpio's purgative process. He that would be the Hero in Scorpio at this time of evolutionary transformation is destined to demonstrate this process to others, whether his circle of influence be great or small. Perhaps no sign requires more stamina, more guts, more love!

The soul, when born in Scorpio, inherits a most direct access to what has been called the Goddess Kundalini, the sacred fire, Shakti, the *Shekinah*—the light of the Divine Mother—and by some, simply, the life force. The creative potential of Scorpio is truly awesome, but this Zodiacal package comes with a serious warning—the deliberate or even unintentional misuse of Scorpio energy can be deadly! No wonder so many Scorpios have that telltale serious demeanor! Like a child with a box of matches, it is best for those uninitiated into the mysteries of the Mother to resist the temptation to tamper with her fire.

What does it take for regeneration to take place? First of all, it requires something degenerate, that is, something, or someone, or a state of consciousness that has fallen from a higher unto a lower or denser and undesirable state. Secondly, and integral to the process, is an agent capable of acting upon the degenerate element in such a way as to restore its native purity. Thirdly, and most importantly, in the case of human beings, is a conscious recognition on the part of he that would be purified of the need for change and a willingness to submit to that process.

THE SCORPION, THE PHOENIX & THE EAGLE

Scorpio is represented not by one symbol, like the other eleven signs of the Zodiac, but by three—the Scorpio experience is encrypted in the saga of the ***Scorpion that becomes the Phoenix that becomes the Eagle***. The Scorpion, with its potentially lethal sting, associated even from ancient times with death and

temptation, symbolizes the dangerously low condition into which man, created in the image of God, has fallen through his own free will. The Scorpion, then, represents the degenerate or fallen state.

According to some traditions, the Phoenix, also known as the firebird, lives for 300 years, while other cultures grant the mythical bird a lifespan of 500 and even 1300 years. According to Jewish folklore, the Phoenix was the only creature not to leave Eden with Adam, an allusion to its native purity and unworldly nature. When its long life is coming to a close, legend has it, the Phoenix builds itself a nest of cinnamon and myrrh. Once settled within the nest, flames engulf both the bird and the nest, which are consequently reduced to ashes. Out of the ashes emerges a new young Phoenix, destined to live as long as did the parent bird. Significantly, only one firebird at a time is said to exist in the world. Self-perpetuating without a mate, the firebird appears to be immortal!

The Phoenix, then, represents the possibility and means of regeneration, the birth of the new man out of the ashes of the former self, and the middle phase of transformative change. The impurities the soul has accumulated over lifetimes (the Scorpion substance) must be purged and purified. The agent of alteration is fire, spiritual fire, and more specifically, the sacred-fire energy of divine love. Submitting to love's purging fires is painful, and so it is said that if one claims he loves and knows not pain, it is not love!

Now, the majestic Eagle—extraordinary for its acute vision, magnificent wingspan, and its fierce and dignified visage—is the bird that soars closest to the Sun. The Eagle represents the triumph of the spirit of man when aligned with God. Only then does man gain his ultimate freedom—in the Ascension—from the eons-long enslavement to his self-created karmic condition.

Biblical allusions (there are 33 in all) use the Eagle as a symbol for strength, swiftness, renewal, deliverance and redemption:[128]

---

[128] The Eagle is cited in the Bible as a symbol of renewal. At a certain point in their long lives, eagles pass through a time of retreat in which they molt their old feathers, old claws and even their beaks, growing new ones.

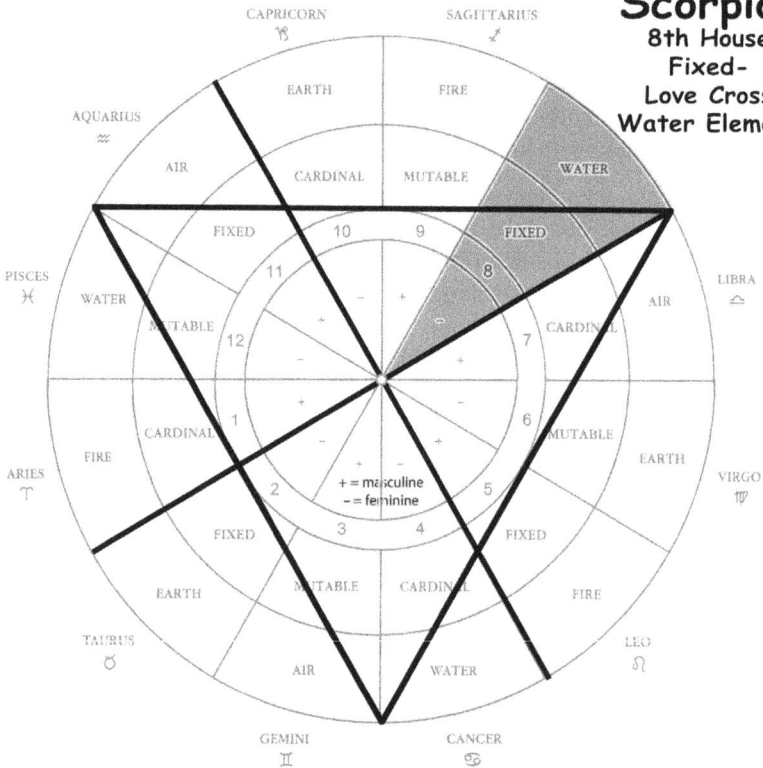

Scorpio:
8th House
Fixed-
Love Cross
Water Element

And Moses went up unto God, and the [LORD] called unto him out of the mountain, saying, "Thus shalt thou say to the house of Jacob, and tell the children of Israel, 'Ye have seen what I did unto the Egyptians, and how I bare you on eagles' wings, and brought you unto Myself. Exodus 19:3-4

But they that wait upon the [LORD] shall renew [their] strength; they shall mount up with wings as eagles; they shall run, and not be weary; [and] they shall walk, and not faint. Isaiah 40:31

And to the woman were given two wings of a great eagle, that she might fly into the wilderness, into her place, where she is nourished for a time, and times, and half a time, from the face of the serpent. Revelation 12:14[129]

Many Native American nations honor the eagle, thought to be a "medicine bird" endowed with supernatural powers, for the eagle flies close to the heaven where the Great Spirit dwells! During *The Eagle Dance*, participants don eagle feathers, considered to be sacred, especially those of the Golden and the Bald Eagle, and call upon the Eagle as an intermediary between heaven and earth. Among the Cherokees, it is tradition for a brave to gift his bride an eagle feather as a symbol of their life-long union (the equivalent of a wedding band).

Metaphysical movements and esoteric teachings speak of *the Flying Eagle* in reference to Sanat Kumara, spoken of in the Bible as *The Ancient of Days,* who came to earth from Venus eons ago accompanied by 144,000 souls to

---

[129] Other mentions of the eagle in Revelation: "And the first living creature was like a lion, and the second beast like a calf, and the third beast had a face as a man, and the fourth beast was like a flying eagle." Revelation 4:7 Also: "And I saw, and I heard a single eagle (not "angel," as in the English version) flying in mid-heaven, saying with a mighty voice, Woe, woe, woe, to those that dwell upon the Earth by reason of the remaining voices of the trumpet of the three angels who are about to sound!" Revelation 8:13

save this planet from certain destruction. Sanat Kumara is said to occupy the office of *The Eagle* as the mother, demonstrating the path of *Selflessness.*[130]

This remarkable bird is emblazoned upon the flags and standards of diverse cities and nations. In 1789, the Founding Fathers officially adopted the Bald Eagle as the national symbol of the emerging United States, and so it has remained to this day.

AMAZING GRACE

Scorpios run the gamut—from the lowest of the low, who are so selfish, even cruel in their self-seeking, their lives so degraded as to have given the sign a bad name on this planet while on the other end of the spectrum, we find Scorpio souls who are selfless, pure in mind and in spirit, and one-pointedly dedicated in their service to God and to mankind. All Scorpios emit a strong magnetism, which those of other signs often find to be intimidating. The *Scorpion* type entices, seduces and manipulates others while those of higher consciousness exercise the most kind and yet impartial and incisive judgment. One thing is certain: there is nothing wishy-washy or irresolute about natives of this sign!

Some Scorpios go through all three stages of transformative change in one lifetime; they feel as if they have lived several lives in one and their life stories often are sagas of amazing grace. Other Scorpios remain stuck in the hellish grips of the Scorpion death energy, and still others, the majority seeking self-realization at this time, work out the equation of being symbolized by the Phoenix—for years, if not for lifetimes, the matter resting not so much upon fate, regardless of how heavy karma might be, but rather upon will. With the path available to all ready to make the commitment to their higher reality, and the teaching of how to accelerate progress while transmuting lifetimes of karma by employing the Aquarian Science of Invocation and the violet flame, many courageous souls born into this sign of such great promise will mount as Eagles in this Age!

Scorpio is the Eighth Sign of the Zodiac. In the number eight (8), we see symbolized the notion of the figure-eight flow between that which is above with that which is below, the secret of wealth, health, love and all manner of abundance! Now, Libra is the Seventh Sign: at 180 degrees on the astrological wheel, Libra is the gateway to the upper hemisphere of the chart. In noting that more ex-

---

[130] Sanat Kumara is also associated with Cancer, the sign of the Mother. At www.SanatKumara.com we read: "References to Sanat Kumara are found throughout the world. References to Shamballa are found in Eastern texts and traditions in geographical proximity to the Gobi Desert. References to the 144,000 are found in the Bible as well as in Native American tradition." See also: www.SummitUniversityPress.com/ books_spirituality/opening_seventh_seal.htm.

tremes of character are found in Scorpio than in any other sign, and that Scorpios seem to evolve either as the evil type or the good, prominent nineteenth-century astrologer Alan Leo, in *Astrology for All*, conjectured:

> *Scorpio marks the higher octave, after the balance (of Libra) has been turned. It would seem as though the worst products of Scorpio were failures from the preceding seven signs, whereas the strongly individualized types would be those who had succeeded in learning the mystery of this sign. The sting of the Scorpio must be extracted before upward progress through the following signs can be accomplished.*

PURGE & PURIFY

Metamorphic change is virtually inevitable for those born under Scorpio's piercing rays. While other signs offer means toward transcendence that are relatively gentle, in comparison, Scorpios know life as a series of continually intense, purgative transformations leading to a major transfiguration or spiritual rebirth. Note that in all stages of major change for the soul in Scorpio, the death of one state of being is the birth of another. The Scorpio experience captures the truism that endings are at once beginnings and that something must die so something else may live. Even the lowly Scorpion eats through its mother's stomach at birth and she dies.

While Scorpio represents death and dying, this so-called death is understood as part of life. All is transformed; nothing is ever really lost. Within the man still lives somewhere the child he used to be. Likewise, the soul continues its journey after the transition called death.

The Scorpio experience of self-transformation and hope for rebirth may require first "touching bottom." Alcoholics Anonymous explains that in the case of people with addictions (of any kind) things oftentimes have to get a lot worse before they get better. The main symptom of any addiction is, in fact, denial of the problem! Only by almost tasting death (the sting of the Scorpion) does the addict finally admit that he has a life-threatening problem that he is powerless to overcome. With this realization, the soul then cries out for help—a great turning point, the beginning of the re-birth experience! We all harbor unrealities. The story of the Scorpion, the Phoenix, and the Eagle represents the inevitable fork in the road waiting for every one of us; if we are to become eagles, free and soaring high, we will have to leave our comfort zone, reach for the light and wrestle with the shadow!

The danger in Scorpio is the slow death and self-destruction of the soul caused by becoming trapped in the death consciousness, symbolized by the Scorpion. Natives of this intense Sign almost unknowingly can become wrapped up in themselves and their own pleasures. During the Scorpio Sun cycle, we all tend to be more concerned than usual with personal matters. The Greek myth of Narcissus, who fell so much in love with his own reflection in a pond that he literally pined away, staring at himself, warns against the dangers of self-love and of becoming self-absorbed. Self-idolatry is essentially a twisted Scorpio-like mindset; narcissism, the misuse of the Third Eye chakra, is a Scorpio disorder.

When light is misused, it spawns and multiplies conditions of darkness, disease, degeneration and death, rather than spreading love, peace and freedom. Misqualified light emits a certain false potency and sheen. The soul in Scorpio must come to recognize this counterfeit emanation so that he will not be snared by it or caught off guard, neither by the hypnotic pull of subliminal seduction, nor by the titillating stimulation of worldly glamour, nor by the magnetism of false teachings, gurus and prophets. All that glitters is not gold!

DEALING WITH THE SHADOW-SELF

Scorpio is governed primarily by Pluto (known as the ruler of the underworld) and secondarily by Mars. The underworld is the realm of the unconscious mind and of seething, buried desires. The unconscious is the repository of forgotten memories and long-lost talents, but also of pain so great that the soul, in order to survive, blocks the conscious recall of it. Pluto is pronounced in the charts and personalities of most Scorpios as well as persons of any sign having Pluto conjoined the Ascendant or in hard aspect to the natal Sun.

In astrological analysis, Pluto represents the shadow aspect of self, sometimes called *the Dweller-on-the-Threshold,* because this conglomerate of consciousness abides at the threshold of the subconscious and conscious mind. Of course, everyone has Pluto somewhere in his or her natal chart, but Scorpio individuals deal with the Dweller more directly than most.

Astrologer Donna Cunningham's book, *Healing Pluto Problems,* is a must-read-reference for identifying and healing the intense obsessions marked by Pluto in the natal chart. Positive Plutonians, as Cunningham points out, spend their lives healing, transforming and transmuting blocks within themselves and those around them. However, the negative Plutonian type tends to be guarded, withdrawn and secretive, rigid and afraid to allow others to get too close. Cunningham points out that Plutonians have the gift, if they will access it, of finding methods to deal with and transmute painful events in their past. She offers tools for healing the Plutonian problems we all face (such as jealousy) that are so dramatically present in these souls—and in many Scorpio individuals. I have found that those who persist in love, embracing their pain and at the same time surrendering their loss, beam mercy, a quality of love only known to those who have fought the good fight and won.

Physical and also psychic toxicity caused by holding on to that which needs to be released is a major danger in Scorpio. The degenerative contents within the unconscious, if left alone and allowed to fester, eventually emerge in the physical body as disease—or perhaps one day, like a dormant volcano they may suddenly become active and explode (tripped off by a Mars or Uranian transit). Such eruptions are upsetting, but a healthier alternative to chronic illness.

Medical Astrologer Eileen Nauman points out that one of the worst problems that Scorpios face is constipation. I would note that constipation correlates with the tendency to stuff, rather than process, pain. As Nauman points out, the accumulation of toxins in the system that occurs in constipation can have serious consequences if not addressed. Nauman calls the colon, ruled by Scorpio, the body's sewer. Scorpio rules sewers, drainages, and the body's processes and organs whose function it is to eliminate and cleanse. (Libra, however, rules the kidneys.)

Interestingly, Scorpio Sun types (or Ascendants) may be magnetized to some kind of work underground or a vocation dealing with the removal of poisons or detoxification.

Scorpios oftentimes deny that anything is wrong; "I am fine," they stoically insist, when in fact, they may be seething with anger. Physical inflammations (Mars), so common among Scorpios, may be outer manifestations of holding on to anger or of ignoring psychological or physical imbalances.

Eagles-to-be delve beyond the surface; they are the Zodiac's natural detectives, characteristically perceiving that which eludes those of less penetrating vision. Scorpios have a natural inclination toward resolving mysteries. Many are attracted to occult studies. When the Scorpio individual gets to the cause and core of an inner and outer imbalance, life-changing transformation results.

So, processing pain, dealing with life as it comes, calling forth the love to see the good in all things and circumstance, empowered by the Presence and running to meet the Dweller daily with joy, maintaining elasticity and flow—such is the way of the Scorpio-Hero-to-be.

THE SCORPIO WARRIOR

Mars rules the armed forces and artillery, whereas Pluto rules wars and warriors. Many Scorpios find their niche in police and detective work or in active military service. George S. Patton, born November 11, 1885, distinguished himself as a commander in WWI and as a leading American general in WWII. Patton was suited for the military; in fact, he claimed to have been Hannibal in a past life. (On one campaign, he reflected that he had brought elephants over the pass that he now was covering with tanks.) Patton had definitive Scorpio characteristics. He was fearless, an excellent strategist, indefatigable, incisive, and no-nonsense. He was energized, rather than stymied, by obstacles.

In Patton's chart, Scorpio's ruler, Pluto, was in Gemini (speech) in an auspicious trine to Jupiter and Uranus, denoting Patton's strategic vision, his acute intuition, and spiritual depth. Scorpio's co-ruler, Mars, was in Virgo, the sign of the general. But Patton's natal Pluto opposed Mercury (communication) in at times exaggeratedly frank Sagittarius, and both were square Mars (aggression), forming a challenging Apex-Mars Mutable-Wisdom T-square.

Patton's outspoken manner and often callous speech became his Achilles' heel. And although his men revered and looked up to him for his uncompromising leadership, his too-harsh manner was perceived as tyrannical, which caused his reputation to suffer.

PASSIONATE & INTENSE

Scorpios have a reputation for being intense. But, are *all* Scorpios intense? Just about! But how much so, and for how long? To answer that question, and bearing in mind that intensity can be either a positive attribute or a negative danger, and of an acute or chronic duration, we need to consider these three major factors integral to the Scorpio equation: 1) Scorpio is a Water sign; 2) Scorpio is a Fixed-Love sign—in astrological lingo, we would say that Scorpio is a Water sign on the Fixed-Love Cross; 3) Scorpio is related primarily to the Third Eye chakra and secondarily to the Base chakra.

Being a Water sign, souls born in Scorpio are emotional, and being a Fixed Sign, they feel intensely—deeply, passionately, poignantly, persuasively, and forcefully. In some cases or during some moments, when feelings are tinged with negativity they may consequently behave obsessively, compulsively, possessively, jealously, and perfidiously! Balance is the key to integrity, regardless of birth sign, but to be unbalanced in Scorpio can be particularly perilous. Skewed emotions can possess the Scorpio soul in a most gripping fashion. Moreover, the fixed nature of the sign makes it harder for the individual Scorpio to unburden himself from such states that possess the mind and torture a soul that is too focused upon itself.

Those Scorpios who are capable of tying into the sign's higher vibrations are remarkably intuitive and psychically sensitive. Highly focused in the Third Eye, some show evidence of real genius even at an early age, but their learning style, perhaps very visual and graphic, or musical, may be mistaken as a disability! Some Scorpio personalities are uncommonly compassionate, generous and thoughtful. They espouse high ideals and can be unflinchingly loyal. They'll defend or care for a friend in need to the end. However, they do not tolerate repetition of error or weakness in others very well. Enough is enough! Once they resolve to end a relationship, there is no talking them out of it!

Mars rules knives, swords and blades—the cutting edge. A cut-the-frills approach sometimes manifests as an attraction to sharp instruments. Scorpios may be attracted to some vocation, like that of a surgeon, requiring a steady hand and precise incision. Many hairdressers and tailors have the Sun in Scorpio.

Scorpios express their love of excellence in the thoroughness, efficiency and precision of their work. Nevertheless, in their search for perfection they tend to be too hard on others and even harder on themselves. Their natural drive to excel can devolve into extremism based on pride. Almost all Scorpios are prone to extremes. Many see things in black and white, this way or that way, with no in-betweens—a characteristic especially pronounced during the teenage years. The Scorpio *Tikkun,* a Hebrew word meaning "correction," is to seek and attain balance in all the sephirot, in all the chakras. In their intense striving to be secularly or even spiritually successful, Scorpios can stay balanced and avoid becoming trapped in a web of selfishness by seeking the perfection of the compassionate heart first and foremost. As is true for people born in Taurus (Scorpio's polarity), natives of this sign must seek the Middle Way, but that way is rarely apparent and, once known, may not seem appealing.

THE ART OF MANAGING SUPER-SENSITIVITY

The soul in Scorpio typically bears an auric intensity with a telltale piercing and steady gaze. Even though many Scorpios are typically secretive, their charged, magnetic presence gives them away. Some natives of this sign actually mimic in their facial structure the aquiline nose and intimidating stare of the eagle! Under the Scorpio person's characteristically quiet or cool demeanor, and even beneath an occasionally feigned passivity, often lies a whirlpool of churning emotional energy.

Although Scorpio sensitivity is a gift, it takes much mastery to be so sensitive and yet not to over-personalize other people's energies. Being hypersensitive can be uncomfortable. Some Scorpios are particularly touchy. People may feel intimidated or uncomfortable in their presence—sensing that saying or doing the wrong thing might light their fuse or hurt their feelings. Paranoia is a Scorpio-related problem.

Transformational Astrology recognizes the paradox inherent within each sign. Included in this concept, borrowed from Kabbalah, is the notion that all paradoxes can be reconciled. Of all Signs, the Scorpio Paradox is perhaps the most challenging; how to be intensely passionate, sexually magnetic, pulsing with powerful desires and yet surrendering all to God, remaining pure in heart and soul, in seeing and in intention? How to be so aware of the darker side, and yet, not allow it to overtake the goodness of one's true nature? How to enjoy wealth and be selfless and honorable, a just steward of the mother's light? A friend, a Scorpio physician, never ceases to astound me by her ability to treat the most far-gone cases and yet see the person as whole! Her vision, I believe, accounts for much of her success. In Scorpio, the problem and the solution are intrinsically bound: where love is crucified, love must be redeemed.

THE HIDDEN WORLD OF THE SCORPIO CHILD

Another challenge confronting souls born in Scorpio is that they typically perceive vibrations that are out of the range of the majority of people. It is as if they actually pick up on another person's shadow self (subconscious negative karma and traits). Often, however, they read into what they perceive to an exaggerated degree, causing them to come to erroneous conclusions. Scorpios should avoid negative and judgmental thinking, which can easily cause them to slip into a state of distrust, suspicion and self-sabotage. However, innately equipped with deep vision, the ability to perceive even subtle vibrations and penetrating intelligence, Scorpios often make terrific detectives, researchers, physicians and psychiatrists!

The problem, common to Scorpios, is assuming erroneously that others have equally sharp senses. The trouble begins, especially for the Scorpio child, when there is no one to explain to him the meaning of what he feels, which can be terribly frightening. He hardly knows how to explain it, so he remains quiet. For some, silence is a survival mechanism during childhood.

How can the concerned parent or teacher be aware of the Scorpio child's needs when he keeps his feelings to himself? This, plus a native tendency toward secrecy, may lead to painful misunderstandings.

Often the Scorpio child best reveals his inner world through artistic or musical expression. It is as if music speaks to his soul on a deep level unreachable through words. Some Scorpio youth blossom behind the camera. Their natural tendency to observe life quietly helps them see compositions that elude others of lesser vision, sensitivity and inner stillness.

Scorpio teenagers especially need an adult, parent or mentor whom they can trust in sharing their feelings—especially those who have experienced rejection as a young child (such as when parents separate or divorce). Some Scorpio teens experience peer rejection during adolescence as overwhelmingly painful.

If the Scorpio youngster doesn't communicate his needs, it often happens that no one knows how to help him and, if no one helps him, he's apt to erroneously conclude that no one cares. Young Scorpio children are especially sensitive to discord in the home. One five-year-old never spoke of explosive problems at home but would curl up in a catatonic roll in the classroom.

A supportive and loving family environment can make all the difference for youngsters of this sign. Miles is a young Scorpio child who delights in seeing the elementals (nature spirits). Mom encourages Miles's exploration, and has helped him make wonderfully crafted elemental houses for his nature friends. While few know of Miles's secret, he happily opens his heart to his mother. If she had mocked or reprimanded him, or dismissed his admissions as fanciful, Miles would more than likely have retreated deep within himself.

TAPPING THE SCORPIO ADOLESCENT'S POTENTIAL

Teenage Scorpios especially benefit from being challenged mentally and physically. When Venus is highlighted in the young Scorpio's natal chart, his sensitivity, willingness to practice long hours, and to work hard may incline him toward one of the arts. Scorpio youths so engaged find a healthy outlet for their powerful emotions; they often can tap into their creative resources and avoid becoming seriously sidetracked.

Felipe, a young Scorpio man who grew up on a ranch out west, found his niche in studying *Parelli Horsenality*, a "Horse Whisperer" approach, in which the trainer learns how to understand each horse's innate characteristics, individual temperament, and unique personality. *Horsenality* teaches specific gentle approaches for bringing out the best in each horse. Felipe's love of animals and his quietly intuitive nature were great assets for this work. Felipe is a strong, nice-looking and intelligent young man who was as a child extremely shy and self-conscious. Besides the joy he experiences working with the horses, the constructive channeling of his Scorpio striving and willingness to take on challenges has helped to build his self-confidence.

Scorpio teens can be unduly hard upon themselves; teenage brain's egocentricity coupled with the Scorpio tendency to see what is wrong makes for a merciless combination. One 7th grade Scorpio girl burst out crying before every test because the stress was too great! What if she failed? This particular girl did not receive pressure from home. Her parents continually sought ways to boost her self-esteem and help her relax, but until she was in her twenties, the tendency remained. Never mind that her lowest grade was 94 percent!

The Scorpio teenager who has experienced rejection as a child (such as an alcoholic parent, the death of a parent or a parent abandoning the home) may carry deep-seated wounds others do not see. Establishing trust and keeping open and honest communication with Scorpio youngsters is so important; otherwise they tend to shut out access to their inner world. Some Scorpio young people are exceptionally strong. Others do not tolerate the cruel mocking so common among youth today.

HANK

Hank's story may not be typical, but his case was so unexpected, I feel I must speak about him, if only to prevent tragedies such as his from happening elsewhere. Hank's crisis occurred when he was sixteen years old. He fell in love, spending every extra moment with his girlfriend. After three months, however, she broke off the relationship—she wanted to see other guys. I believe the rejection stirred up Hank's unresolved feelings about having been rejected by his biological father, a one-night stand whose name his mother could not remember. No one saw it coming until it was too late! Hank hung himself from a tree in the back yard. Evidence suggests he thought he would make it and meant to draw attention to himself; apparently he had viewed such a scenario in a movie. I strongly recommend all parents of teenage kids to be aware of the signs of self-destructive and suicidal tendencies, but especially parents of Scorpio adolescents. And, if parents can be sensitively alert but not unduly alarmed, I advise they take note especially when transits to or from Pluto enter any child's astrological picture.[131]

"BULL-MOOSE HEADEDNESS"

The Scorpio's staying power is impressive. Once natives of this sign resolve to take a given track, they will finish the course, come hell or high water, for better or worse. In so doing, they display exceptional valor or intractable stubbornness—and at times a greater or lesser combination of the two! However, even when objective analysis would suggest a wiser path, the Scorpio may not be dissuaded from his committed-upon plan. He may feel too overwhelmed by desire or perhaps too proud to change his course.

Biographer Roscoe wrote of Theodore Roosevelt, born October 27, 1858, "He had an irremovable block of stubbornness in whatever cause he thought right." Roosevelt's physical stamina and sheer fearlessness were remarkable. Once, while delivering a speech, he let the audience know that, although a would-be assassin had lodged a bullet in his chest—he held up his speech with the bullet holes in it—he said, "It takes more than that to kill a Bull Moose!" and, "I have altogether too many important things to think of to feel any concern over my own death."

TRANSMUTING SEX ENERGY

Scorpio-born author, Napoleon Hill (October 26, 1883), spent 20 years of his life studying the secrets of success. He once said, "When your desires are strong enough, you will appear to possess superhuman powers to achieve." Hill wrote extensively on how to harness the power of the sexual energy (the Kundalini) as a means to success. Those who squander it, or keep it dammed up, he discovered, rarely make the grade.

Scorpios emit a strong sexual magnetism, rivaled only perhaps by Leo. The commerce or interchange involved in both sex and money are Scorpio-

---

[131] I recommend reading, *Wanting to Live: Overcoming the Seduction of Suicide*, by Neroli Duffy, MD and clinical psychologist, Dr. Marilyn Barrick.

ruled—areas in which souls born into this sign will be tried and tested! The strength of desire in this sign is not to be underestimated. Seen spiritually, money is considered to be the sacred fire crystallized in physical form. In Scorpio come up issues of control and of the multiplication of investments; banks, insurance companies, stocks, bonds, securities, and the like are all ruled by Scorpio. As in personal relations, where sex is in-

Andrew Carnegie and Napoleon Hill—In 1908, the world's wealthiest man, Andrew Carnegie, commissioned Napoleon Hill to interview 500 successful people. Hill's mission was to discover and publish a formula for success that the average person could duplicate. He researched for more than 20 years. His 1937 book, *Think and Grow Rich*, has sold over 30 million copies.

volved and in commerce, Scorpios grapple with the questions of who gets what, when, and in what measure. When the Scorpio person (or anyone) spills his light in excessive or self-absorbed sex, the life energy is siphoned from him. He becomes will-less and open to negative energies, or obsessed with desire. When he is overly controlling, love cannot flow. The same is true in the accumulation, the saving of, and the right distribution of wealth.

In the eleventh chapter of, *Think and Grow Rich,* "The Mystery of Sex Transmutation," Hill notes that men (and women), when driven by sexual desire, develop "keenness of imagination, courage, will-power, persistence and creative ability unknown to them at other times," and that the desire for sexual contact is so strong and impelling that men freely run the risk of life and reputation to indulge it." Hill points out that sexual emotion can be transmuted, that is, changed into another form of energy. When harnessed and redirected along other lines, this same motivating force retains its positive qualities of drive and imagination and may then be used for bringing forth great works of art and literature and accomplishment in any profession, which gives rise to the accumulation of riches. Hill equates the sex energy with the *fight* in man and in woman.

SACRED SEX

Kabbalah teaches that sex is sacred; the holy union between man and wife commemorates the meeting of the feminine and masculine energies in all of Cosmos as symbolized on The Tree of Life. Without sex, there would be no continuance of the human race.

In *The Way of Splendor, Jewish Mysticism and Modern Psychology,* Edward Hoffmann expounds upon the idea that for the Kabbalist, sexuality has always been viewed as a basic quality of the universe—the primary masculine and feminine energies seen as underlying every aspect of Creation:

> *These twin forces, opposite but complimentary, appear in the tiniest blade of grass to the furthest galaxies of space. The better we are able to penetrate the nature of the mysterious union—in all its diverse manifestations—the more we will grasp about the highest realms that surround us and consequently our innermost makeup as well.*

Noting that a strong sexual current surges openly through the *Zohar*, the basic text of esoteric Judaism, Hoffman continues to show that in mystic Judaism, in the Gnostic Teachings (and indeed, in esoteric thought) God the Father has a female counterpart, just as we are divided into two sexes.

The Book of Splendor (The Zohar) tersely declares, "The King without the Matrona is no king, nor is he great, nor highly praised." Hence, only when the two are united—depicted in explicit sexual terms—does harmony truly govern the universe.

Attitudes manifest on the Fixed-Love Cross. The problem lies not in sex itself, but in wrong thinking and selfishness resulting in an imbalanced attitude.

INTENSE & SUBDUED SCORPIO MAGNETISM

Natives of this sign are particularly striking in their expression, exuding a highly magnetic if subdued magnetic presence (in contrast to magnetic Leo radiance) with an engaging if somewhat to-the-point sense of humor. An analysis of the position and aspects in the natal chart made by the Sun in Scorpio, as well as the aspects made by Pluto and Mars, Scorpio's rulers, fills in the picture.

Actress *Fanny Brice* was born in New York City on October 29, 1891. Known for her exaggerated, theatrical Yiddish accent and zany parodies, Brice gained fame as a comedian and as a radio and film entertainer. The day she was born, Mars in Libra was trine (positive) Pluto and Neptune (entertainment), both in Gemini (radio). Pluto and Neptune were both exactly square (challenges) Jupiter in Pisces (self-deprecating humor).

Grace Kelly was born on November 12, 1929, in Philadelphia. Her Mars, also in Scorpio, was trine her Pluto in Cancer and her Moon in Pisces, a powerfully emotive combination (Grand Water Trine). Kelly gained some fame in film, but became a real star when she married Prince Rainier III of Monaco in 1956, becoming a princess overnight. Her stunning Scorpio beauty was softened by the wistful quality of her Pisces Moon trine her Sun, and by her Venus in elegant Libra, conjoined her Scorpio Ascendant.

Julia Roberts is, at the time of this writing, the highest-paid actress in the world. (She earned 25 million for her role in 2003's *Mona Lisa Smile* alone!) She was born October 28, 1967, in Atlanta, Georgia.

Grace Kelly (1929–1982)

Two Minor Grand Trines and a Saturn based Finger of God mark Roberts' talent and tremendous creativity, energy and drive. Her Scorpio Sun in the Fourth House is a very private, family-oriented position—despite her high public profile, Roberts has managed to keep her family life relatively out of the news. What is it like to work on set with Julia Roberts? Actor Tom Hanks, who has worked with Roberts as co-star and director, called her a "formidable force," adding that, "She raises your game—she's got the spirit of life that brings everybody up and makes them do their best work." (See note for Julia Roberts' chart below and her chart on the page following.)[132]

---

[132] Julia Roberts' Mars, strongly placed in productive Capricorn in her Sixth House (of employment), trines her natal Jupiter (opportunity) *in let's-get-to-work* Virgo, which is conjoined her Moon in the later degrees of magnetic Leo (entertainment) in her Second House (of income). Her Sun (me) in Scorpio sextiles (creativity) both Mars and the Moon, the apex point of a Minor Grand Trine. Also note that Saturn (career), in self-motivated Aries, is the only major planet in the upper hemisphere of the chart, placed in the Ninth House (of philosophy, many of her films have a message). This career point squares Mars (she works hard), but is also the base of a Finger of God (Yod), quincunx Jupiter sextile the Sun, which becomes the handle into which the creative energies of the Minor Grand Trine are naturally directed. The planetoid Chiron (destiny), in the later degrees of Pisces, is also in the Ninth House, trine Roberts' Cancer (the mother), Ascendant. Also note that Roberts' Pluto, which rules Scorpio, conjoins Uranus and Venus in the Third House (of communication), sextile her Cancer Ascendant and her natal Neptune in Scorpio, which are trine one another—a second Minor Grand Trine!

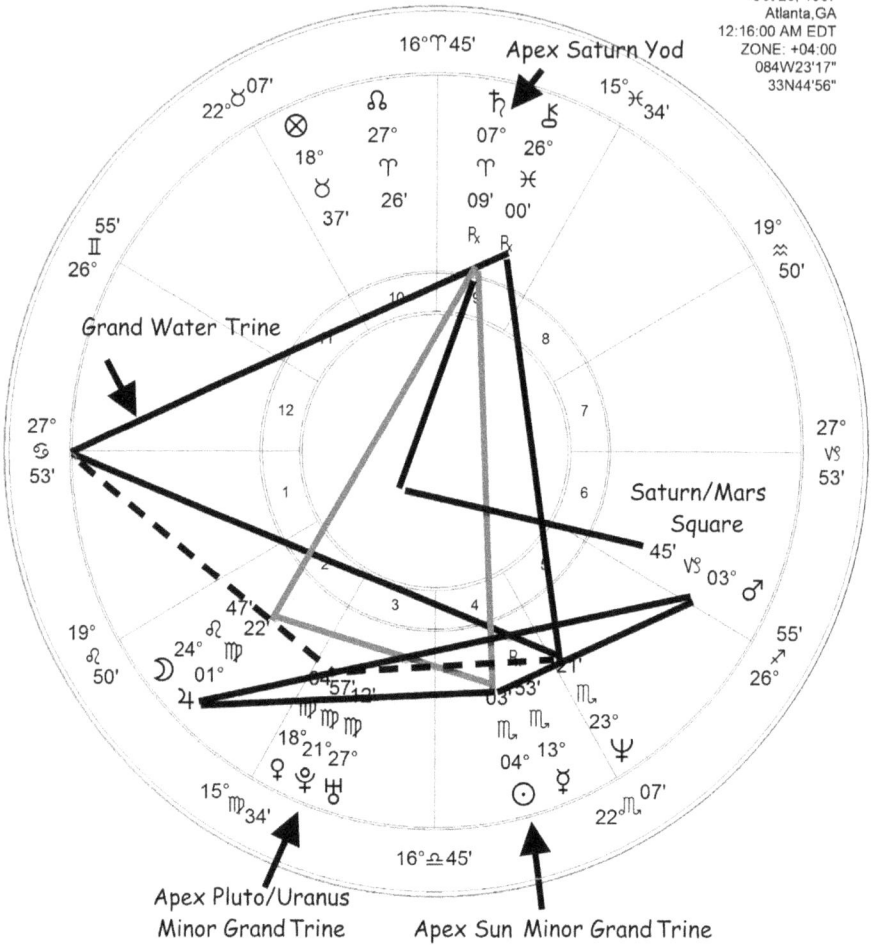

Julia Roberts
Oct 28, 1967
Atlanta, GA
12:16:00 AM EDT
ZONE: +04:00
084W23'17"
33N44'56"

"WHEN HE IS WOUNDED, I BLEED"

Abigail Adams was born November 11, 1744 (Julian; November 22, Gregorian), in Weymouth, Massachusetts. The Sun was at 30-degrees Scorpio, which is the same as 00 degrees Sagittarius—she was born on the cusp of Scorpio and Sagittarius. Pluto in Scorpio was exactly conjoined Mercury. Adams was a woman of indomitable strength, courage and fortitude. She was capable of tremendous sacrifice, and was deeply passionate in her convictions and in the expression of her love for her husband, John Adams, who also was a Scorpio. Joseph Ellis, in his Pulitzer Prize winning book, *Founding Brothers*, names Abigail Adams as one of the eight prominent political leaders in early America, alongside John Adams, George Washington, Benjamin Franklin, Thomas Jefferson, and others. It is almost unimaginable to consider Abigail without John or John without his wife's constant love and her political wisdom and insight upon which he depended throughout their life together. Between them, John and Abigail are known to have written at least 1,100 letters now archived and considered to be national treasures.

John Adam's birth date was October 19, 1735 (Julian; October 30, Gregorian, according to the *Massachusetts Historical Society*). Scorpio suns suited this couple born to a challenging destiny—the fomenting and winning of a revolution of independence and the guidance of a new nation during its first years. During this tense and exciting time, the Adamses played an essential role in the outplaying of events. They loved each other intensely, personally, tenderly, and selflessly. Through it all, they put love of country before their personal desires— a winning Scorpio formula for any couple. Where attention goes, there goes energy.

Perhaps the Adamses needed that Scorpio inner strength to help them weather the tremendous sacrifice required of them—the years of separation while she managed the farm, the finances, and the education of their four children—including John Quincy who would become America's sixth president. While John debated at the Continental Congress and was abroad on various diplomatic missions, Abigail nursed their children through raging epidemics. She sheltered them from the often explosive and anger-filled situations surrounding them. The postwar years were full of trials of their own: Abigail's beloved son, Charles, died an alcoholic, their daughter, Nabby, died of cancer after a painful battle, while Abigail supported John in helping the young nation get off its feet.

John, always the visionary, was incredibly instrumental in determining the future of the USA, but he was not popular. He characteristically stuck to his guns with Scorpio single-mindedness, often going against popular sentiment. Acting in the role of the nation's second President, he managed to keep the United States out of France's revolution, although Thomas Jefferson and many Francophiles put considerable pressure on him to give way. As is true of many Scorpio men, he was passionate and intense, somewhat paranoid, and struggled with extreme mood swings. Tender and generously loving with his family, he seemed cold and aloof to most outsiders. His no-nonsense approach was much balanced by Abigail's practical understanding of human nature. Her love kept him going.[133]

Abigail Adams' is often cited as America's first feminist. She applied her Scorpio vision and Sagittarian sense of the future to extend the revolutionary cause to include that of woman's rights. She wrote to John:

---

[133] See www.PresidentialHam.com/u-s-presidents/john-adams-with-ham/.

> *If particular care and attention is not paid to the ladies,*
> *we are determined to foment a rebellion, and will not hold our-*
> *selves bound by any laws in which we have no voice, or repre-*
> *sentation.*[134]

For his part, John's letters to Abigail, besides being full of all kinds of details and insights into the daily goings-on at the Continental Congress, and later abroad. They also reveal a tender and loving side of this man who gave his life for his nation. His advice to Abigail on how the children must be educated rings true today. On October 29th, 1775, John wrote:

> *It should be your care, therefore, and mine, to elevate*
> *the minds of our children and exalt their courage; to accelerate*
> *and animate their industry and activity; to excite in them an ha-*
> *bitual contempt of meanness, abhorrence of injustice and inhu-*
> *manity, and an ambition to excel in every capacity, faculty, and*
> *virtue. If we suffer their minds to grovel and creep in infancy,*
> *they will grovel all their lives. But their bodies must be hard-*
> *ened, as well as their souls exalted. Without strength and activity*
> *and vigor of body, the brightest mental excellencies will be*
> *eclipsed and obscured.*

SELFISHNESS—THE NAME OF THE BEAST

While the Beast we meet in Scorpio takes on many forms and pseudo-nyms, its core name and identity is SELFISHNESS. Selfishness blinds and it is often only when we grow in selflessness that we realize how selfish we have been. At the heart of the matter is a throbbing drive to love and to be loved. In the mix is fear—fear of the loss of love, fear of the loss of the object of one's desire, fear of being alone. All fear is anti-love—for love has no fear. Fear pervades the Scorpion consciousness. Only love, divine love, can transform this shroud of death into life.

SCORPIO'S CHOICES ALONG THE HERO'S PATH

Eagles-in-training must learn to conquer the passions and effectively and selflessly manage powerful emotions and compelling desires. In so doing, they develop the power of their will, and it is through willpower that they ultimately triumph.

One of the first steps the Scorpio Aspirant takes when committed to the

---

[134] Excerpt from a letter written to John Adams on March 31, 1776

path of self-realization is to break any indulgent, pleasure-seeking habits. For many, this is easier said than done. The passions blind, the tests become subtler, and the line separating right from wrong temporarily appears blurred. Perhaps the Scorpio Aspirant is successful in many areas of his life except for one secret corner of self-indulgence. This hole must be sealed lest it becomes the opening to the abyss! How to accomplish the turning around of a habit that may have been in-grained for lifetimes?" The key lies in examining the motive.

The moment the Scorpio Aspirant acknowledges that he must examine the motive behind his actions, he is on the way to becoming the Scorpio Hero. Moreover, it is far better to purify motive consciously than inevitably have one's motive exposed and purged. The Scorpio Aspirant asks himself, "Am I acting selflessly or am I thinking mostly myself and of how to manipulate others to ac-commodate my desires?"

The spiritual Aspirant, born under Scorpio's rays, may find himself en-meshed in circumstances exposing inordinate attachment to desire within himself, hardness of heart, an unwillingness to listen to others or to take advice, behavior that is controlling, stubborn or manipulative. He may wrestle with overwhelm-ingly strong sexual desires. Or perhaps he finds himself on the other side of the fence, dealing with this obsessive state of consciousness within another. Power struggles arising over sex and money can become all consuming.

Some Scorpios awaken to the path after having fallen to the lowly estate of the Scorpion. Of course, not all come to the door of transformation so burdened, but there is something to say about the soul who, having reached the fork in the road where one must consciously choose Life over death, chooses aright.

Another's path might entail a great mission, perhaps involving the amass-ing of great amounts of money and influence; his challenge is to be in the world and yet to not allow himself to be corrupted. After all—*Sic transit gloria mundi.* *(The glory of this world passeth away.)*

Of mayor importance is the overcoming of denial and then the sorting out of the real from the unreal, which can only occur when the Scorpio soul is willing to surrender measures of secrecy and not perpetuate unreality at conscious, subconscious or unconscious levels. At a certain point, he realizes that the perfection he seeks is impossible to obtain in the human sense of things. He must instead pursue a perfection of the heart.

Many of the tests of the scorpion must be passed before entering Eagle-hood. Once in the final stages, as the Phoenix rises and Eagle ascends, the pain of a world groaning in travail around him can feel crushing. The antidote to Scor-pio's ultra-sensitivity and the unguent to his wounds, as well as his strongest pos-itive attribute, is compassion, a most profound and encompassing aspect of kindness in which one identifies with and seeks to assuage the burden of another.

FORGIVE & FORGET

Whatever the life circumstance, the Scorpio Aspirant will, at some point, meet compelling temptation and the necessity for spiritual surrender. The most essential spiritual attribute for the Scorpio Aspirant, without which spiritual surrender is virtually impossible, is forgiveness—without it, he can only go so far. This includes forgiveness of others and of self. Scorpios possess phenomenal memories. All the Water signs (Cancer, Scorpio, Pisces) bring lessons in transmuting and learning from the past. While Scorpios may forgive, they often refuse to forget. But forget they must, in the sense of letting go of and transmuting pain that otherwise will haunt them. The Scorpio Aspirant can learn how to use prayer, mantras, and meditation to transmute memories. He can work on his astrology and his psychology to heal underlying fears that he finds difficult to release.

In some cases, what must be forgiven is great indeed, but in healing his pain, in determining to forgive even the seemingly unforgiveable, the Scorpio Aspirant frees himself from negative attachment to the injurer and frees that person as well. God alone is the judge and only the Great Law can dispense justice, balanced with mercy. As long as he refuses to forgive, he is choosing to make another responsible for his happiness—a lamentable state!

Scorpio is the doorway to unconscious anger. This applies to Scorpio sun signs or anyone passing through an initiation under Scorpio. In this sign, the initiate embraces his pain, his awareness of his attachment to earthly things, and his vulnerability to temptation. He holds on with all his might to his faith in God. In this process, he is apt to uncover hidden pockets of unconscious anger. Few, if any, are free of it.

Scorpios struggle to let go of desire, even when that desire is hurtful. Although the Scorpio Aspirant recognizes his past misuse of light, he must forgive and not condemn himself for past errors. Rather, in releasing the cause and core of erroneous thinking and perception, he must leap into a consciousness of the miraculous. The pain of illumination (self-exposure) can be very great, but this pain is the result of the the the meeting of light and darkness. Truly, at the other side of heartbreak is bliss.

PURIFYING THE INNER EYE

Once having gained a measure of self-discipline and freedom from self-deception, the Scorpio Aspirant must hold the vision of perfection, love, and beauty. The development of the Third-Eye chakra as the center of spiritual vision is vital for finding and perfecting what the Buddha called "right livelihood," for making right choices and for recognizing the twin flame (divine partner, or soul mate). The Third-Eye becomes purified in stages over time. Working with excellence sharpens the eye's inner senses.

The key to Selflessness and the purification of the inner eye is found in consistent prayer, in the mastery of the emotions, and in continual service. In the earlier stages, the Aspirant chooses consciously to give and to receive selflessly, but at a certain point, service and sacrifice are the tempo of his life. In emptying the self, he is filled with light of the Higher Self. In putting his eye on things of the spirit, he is rewarded with higher vision.

Although the Scorpio Aspirant may be acutely aware of others' shortcomings and of the need to purge impurities within himself, let him practice placing and maintaining his inner eye on his own Divine Presence. Let him practice seeing the true self within others, even as he greets them along the way. In emptying the self, he is filled with the Higher Self. In focusing his eye on things of the spirit, he is rewarded with higher vision. To be at peace in this world that is still in the death throes of a failing civilization, and while in the midst of the birth pangs of the new era, there is no other solution.

THE INITIATION OF THE FLYING EAGLE

Scorpios meet in a most intense way, the ultimate test of *Will versus Desire*. As the Scorpio Aspirant advances on the path, intense and compelling desire and acute sensitivity increase many times over. But this longing must be surrendered and channeled to a greater good. For love to be the victor in Scorpio, selfish attitude must be replaced by selflessness and conditional, possessive love replaced by unconditional love that seeks not to control nor to possess, but to be naught else than itself. But the blindness caused by over attention on self, causes the Scorpio soul to be unaware that he is selfish until he becomes less selfish. Only through loving unconditionally can the selfish Scorpion be transformed, earning the Ascension, symbolized by the Flying Eagle![135]

Once his vision is purified, the Hero in Scorpio may lawfully dip into the light of the Divine Mother anchored in the Base chakra, now rising up to nourish all of the chakras, and which he now may wield for the raising up of others and for bringing into the physical plane realizations destined to catapult the race into a better tomorrow. The Hero in Scorpio will open the inner sight of a people to manifest what few can even yet imagine!

---

[135] *The Opening of the Seventh Seal,* by Summit University Press. See also www.SanatKumara.org.

9.

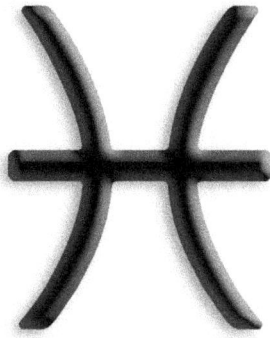

Pisces

Symbol . . . . ***The Fishes***

Born . . . . Feb. 19 ~ March 19

Archetype . . . ***The Dreamer, The Mystic***

Key Phrase . . . . ***I Heal***

Element . . . . **Water**

Cross . . . . **Mutable-Wisdom**

House . . . . **Twelfth:**
Endings, the past, hidden enemies, service, retreats, inner strengths & weaknesses, imagination, creativity in the arts

Ruler . . . . **Neptune & Jupiter**

Esoteric Ruler . . . .**Pluto**

Polarity . . . .**Virgo**

Chakra . . . . Solar Plexus

Anatomy . . . . .Feet, lymphatic system

Spiritual Qualities . . . . **Self-mastery, faith & joy, givingness, self-sacrifice, imagination, compassion, idealism**

Vulnerable to . . . . . *Doubt & fear, depression, confusion, escapism, negative psychic energies, guilt*

Must Acquire . . . . **True spirituality, sense of mission & vision, peace with the past, boundaries**

Steve Jobs • Albert Einstein • Sharon Stone • Josh Groban • Charlotte Church

THE SUN IN PISCES

I will send a Prophet to you,
A Deliverer of the nations,
Who shall guide you and shall teach you,
Who shall toil and suffer with you.
If you listen to his counsels,
You will multiply and prosper;
If his warnings pass unheeded,
You will fade away and perish!

The Song of Hiawatha,
—Henry Wadsworth Longfellow
(February 27, 1807)

THE PEACE THAT PASSES UNDERSTANDING

At the dawn of the Aquarian Age, the Piscean Hero, a compassionate man of unbreakable Faith, ensouls the serene and joyous presence of one who lives among men and yet walks and talks with Masters and angels. Firmly established and secure with his identity in the physical world, he is at once attuned with the supernatural dimension of being. He may appear in many guises — teacher, minister, healer, scientist, musician or poet supreme. Whether his mission is a public one or behind the scenes, he emanates a comforting presence of irrepressible and immutable peace — that force spoken of long ago that passes understanding, transforming all who believe and come into contact with it.[136]

THE HEALING POWER OF FAITH

Faith is power. This was one of the underlying themes of the Piscean Age, launched with the dramatic coming, crucifixion, resurrection and ascension of Jesus the Christ birthing the revolution in spiritual thought and practice, later to be known as Christianity. Consider the miracles recorded in the New Testament: the blind man whose sight Jesus restored, the cripple who took up his bed and walked at the Master's command, the woman who was ill for some 30 years, but was instantly healed when she touched the hem of Jesus' garment. How were they

---

[136] "And the peace of God, which passeth all understanding, shall keep your hearts and minds through Christ Jesus." Philippians 4:7

healed? The Piscean Master would say over and over again, *The Father worketh in me and I work,* and *Your faith hath made you whole.*

Pisces is the sign of self-mastery through Faith. Each Piscean receives a karmic package of circumstances and conditions unique unto himself, but regardless of the staging of life and the relative severity or ease of his circumstances, the Piscean soul is challenged to overcome fear and doubt through the power of faith. Essentially, the Piscean personality is optimistic. He believes in blessings in disguise and has faith that all will be well. But his sensitive perception of the weight of the world, with all its woes and sorrows, can be physically and psychically taxing. The Piscean Paradox is plainly seen—because he must conquer fear, he typically faces some trauma or belief that would belie his faith and that threaten to push him over the edge. But he never receives a test he cannot pass! As the old Kabbalist would say, "If it were easy, it would not be to the glory of God!"

THE DOUBTING-THOMAS SYNDROME

One common manifestation of fear that can infiltrate the mind in Pisces is the intellectual reasoning of the doubting Thomas who insists that whatever cannot be proven has no validity. Such reasoning quickly accelerates into argumentation and an angry insistence on being right, exposing the presence of pride—the root of all doubt and fear. Pisceans caught in the "Doubting Thomas Syndrome" can become quite inflamed and will defend their point of view regardless of how irrational their line of reasoning may be. While natives of this sign tend to feel justified in their disbelief, from an astrological viewpoint, such doubt and questioning in Pisces most often reveals, as with the original apostle, a lack of faith.

Doubting Thomas—Was the apostle simply testing the spirits, as Jesus had instructed the disciples to do? How can a Piscean tell the difference between doubt and discernment? (1874, by F. Alexandre Bida)

When Thomas heard of Jesus' resurrection, he insisted, "Except I see in

Pisces:
12th House
Mutable-
Wisdom Cross
Water Element

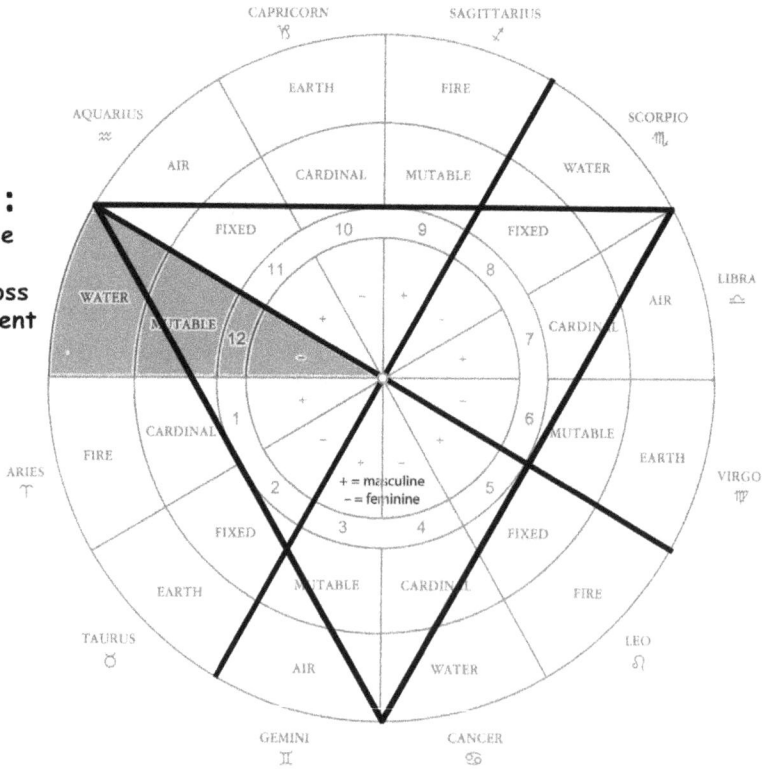

his hands the print of the nails, and put my finger into the print of the nails, and thrust my hand into his side, I will not believe."[137]

Admonishing Thomas to, "be not faithless, but believing," Jesus, nonetheless, allowed Thomas to touch his wounds, saying, "Blessed are they that have not seen, and yet have believed."[138]

We can understand Thomas' caution. The times were tense. The miracle of the Resurrection was unparalleled. In addition, the Master had taught his disciples to beware of wolves in sheep's clothing and to test the spirits. In admonishing Thomas, Jesus was not teaching that we should blindly accept whatever we see or hear. But when the heart is developed, faith is not a risk, but a positive affirmation of an inner knowing. As one of the inner circle, Thomas should have been able to confirm the Master's presence by vibration!

And so, while Pisceans benefit by adopting an objective stance and by knowing the laws, human and divine, they also are advised to consciously develop their soul faculties, which, when free of misgivings and disbelief, prove to be remarkably accurate.

ZEN FISHES—TRANSCENDING DUALITY

The Piscean symbol is that of two fish bound together and yet swimming in separate directions. Most natives of this sign recognize on some level that to not be caught in the schism caused by duality—by definition, the state or quality of being twofold, of having two, often opposite parts within a single whole—requires an almost Zen approach to life in which apparent contradictions make sense. All the Mutable-Wisdom signs (Gemini, Sagittarius, Virgo, and Pisces) wrestle with the question of duality:

> *How can man, being made in the image of God and therefore born with the promise of everlasting life, reconcile that he is, at the same time, clothed in flesh and blood and subject to the limitations of mortality?*

Individual Pisceans meet this dichotomy over and over again during the course of their life. Their ability to "be in the world but not of the world," varies according to the soul's present state of awareness, somewhat upon the person's age and maturity, as well as the nature of current cycles of world and personal astrology.

---

[137] John 20:25
[138] John 20:27-29

TAKING RESPONSIBILITY FOR THE CHOICE

Life is full of uncertainties and the Piscean person is prone to worry. But he can choose whether to embrace faith and walk with his head held high or to be overwhelmed by trepidation and bowed down by discouragement. Awareness of the choice is empowering. To choose fear, even by default, is to become its servant!

The day that the soul in Pisces realizes that regardless of trials and tribulations, he can maintain peace of mind and inner joy, he begins the transformational process. Even so, he must affirm his positive stance many times over, for while the Piscean soul may determine to stay upbeat in all things, when the going gets tough and his faith is put to the test, the sun may not peek through the clouds until the very last moment!

WATER IN A GLASS—PERSONAL BOUNDARIES

In Pisces, emotion (Water) and mind (Mutable-Wisdom Cross) meet, manifesting as a particular sensitivity, an ability to perceive deeply, intuitively, and empathetically. Pisceans place themselves so readily into another's shoes. They care. They understand. And they often fail to comprehend why most other people on the planet were simply not born with the same ability! Pisceans have a connection, more conscious in some than in others, with an inner knowing—a dipping into soul senses still dormant in the majority of people on earth, except when triggered, possibly, in moments of awe or trauma.

But, as we shall see, feelings play tricks on the Piscean mind and vice versa. Some Pisceans are so psychically sensitive that they actually feel another's pain as if it were their own. Moreover, Pisceans are prone to personalize (Water) the energy they pick up, and so, they typically will, almost always erroneously, conclude that some action of theirs caused the problem.

Unless they learn to strengthen and protect their auric forcefield, Pisceans tend to become psychic sponges. This extreme impressionability, this interplay between the mind and the Solar-Plexus chakra, agitates the nervous system (examples would be the butterflies common to stage fright, fainting from fear, or feeling chills up and down the spine). Such disturbing sensations can be felt at the cellular level and may cause psychological, even physical damage if not checked. One of the best ways for Pisceans to stay positive and to avoid depression is to periodically shake off and detoxify themselves of negative, stagnant energy. Dynamic affirmations through the Aquarian Science of Invocation, soothing music, regular exercise, massage, and/or mindfulness—all are healing tools for Piscean souls.

How can Pisceans manage being so sensitive and at the same time be objective? It seems like a necessary contradiction. Keeping their minds free of troublesome thoughts and images for many Pisceans requires real mental discipline, but it can be done. Many will say they do not so much think, but rather that ideas just come to them. Nonetheless, they can learn to develop a naturally perceptive awareness while filtering out bogus messages.

Vacillating mindsets, as in: "Yes, but what if _____ happens?" are quicksand to the Piscean soul. One Pisces man credited his mother's insistence that, "no blaming, no shaming, and no *what-if-ing* allowed!" during his childhood as a major influence, helping him to respond to life's difficulties with faith and optimism.

Not only in interpersonal relations, but also in monetary transactions, and in so many areas of life, the Piscean person must determine and communicate his personal boundaries. After all, water poured into a glass (bound by its container) is more purposeful than water spilled on the table. Therefore, Pisceans more easily maintain their composure and peace when they know and communicate clearly and appropriately that, "This is what I tolerate; this is where I draw the line. This is what I am willing to give; this is what I am expecting to receive back."

FEARLESS COMPASSION

Because they enjoy ministering to life, Pisceans typically attract people with problems. Good listeners, they also enjoy counseling and are often sought out for their wisdom and comforting presence. They have a soft spot for the underdog. Many Pisceans experience the greatest joy when helping others and feel the most trying grief when those that they wish to see healed refuse to be helped.

The native of the Fishes needs to develop discernment. He benefits by determining who he will help, whose energy he is willing to take on, when and in what manner. He must learn the difference between human sympathy and fearless compassion. Sympathy, a type of attraction often characterized by pity, actually weakens both giver and receiver, In contrast, fearless compassion is an expression of true love, giving only what is helpful and lawful in any given situation. The Piscean individual may soothe, counsel, share in another's pain and lend a helping hand. But even when he desires to selflessly serve another's needs, experience will teach him that in the long run it is far better to help another help himself.

Moreover, while holding the vision for the soul's overcoming is a Piscean gift, natives of this sign are advised to evaluate another's current state realistically. Especially the Pisces child must be protected from "venturing where angels would fear to tread." Teenagers and young Piscean adults benefit by understanding the problems inherent in being unequally yoked, i.e., the dangers of associating intimately with people suffering from addictions and other psychological imbalances. Even so, inexperience in managing their natural and blossoming sense of empathy and compassion, often compounded by a typical adolescent rebellion against their parents' guidance, sets them up to learn the hard way why saying *no* is sometimes the most loving response of all.

Pisceans are naturally motivated to give. They love to serve. Most natives of this sign thrive when doing volunteer work. Young Pisceans may find fulfillment when participating in some sort of community service. Knowing that their contribution counts is a reward, in and of itself. Such self-satisfying service often makes it less likely that they will inappropriately offer help elsewhere.

Many Pisceans are attracted to one of the healing professions, such as psychology, astrology, or medicine, or some form of work in which their intuitive ability is a great asset, yet in which their training teaches them how to emotionally separate themselves from their patients or clients. The Piscean physician, for example, helps a patient heal. His soul feels satisfied. The session ends and is reciprocated when the patient pays for his services. The circle is complete. There is no need to get overly enmeshed (as Pisceans without boundaries are wont to do) or inappropriately involved in the patient's life.

WHEN DEBTS ARE DUE

Pisces is the 12th and last sign of the Zodiac. So, Pisces is a sign of endings, of wrapping things up, of resolving the past, accessing its rewards and assuaging its wounds. When the soul reincarnates in Pisces, he is in an embodiment in which he must tie up past cycles. No longer is he afforded the luxury of living off credit—his debts must be paid! While he sojourns through this sign, the burden of past karma can feel exceptionally heavy. Nevertheless, the conscious resolution to pay one's debts, otherwise known as repentance, is the beginning of the way back home. Moreover, the good fruits of the past, in many cases considerable, lighten the load, blessing the soul who, in turn, radiates his uplifted spirit to encourage and assist others in their travails. In truth, the Piscean soul is typically most generous in nature. He is quick to take upon himself another's burden. Who can say how much of the burden is his own, how much is another's, and how much is a percentage of the planetary weight he has accepted to bear?

RESOLVING KARMIC TIES

The karma-balancing aspect of this sign may bring into the Piscean's life persons to whom he owes some karmic debt, or vice versa. This may entail economic support, training or education, the bringing forth of children, helping someone heal from addiction—the scenarios are many. While these relationships are challenged when faced with lifetimes-long conflicts, the Piscean soul intuits that all is in right order and accepts his role graciously. Such a relationship, then, need not become one of co-dependency, but rather of spiritual fulfillment.

When the karma is balanced and the debt paid, a lifting occurs that may be signified by an outer transit, such as Uranus or even Saturn or Pluto finishing a cycle over the natal Sun. In such cases, the nature of the relationship may suddenly (with Uranus) or gradually (with Saturn) change. Perhaps the couple in question will find that they have truly grown to love one another during their years of association, and so their lives together take a positive turn. Sometimes, however, the initial attraction that brought them together suddenly disappears and the Piscean will desire to end the union or will drift away.

But, Pisceans beware! Sometimes what may feel like a date with destiny is, in fact, an opportunity to walk the other way, to resist reacting to someone or to a scenario in the same way as one has for lifetimes! Karma blinds, so this is a chance to use discernment, determination, objectivity, and spiritual attunement.

HEAVEN ON EARTH: PISCEANS IN THE ARTS

Pisces is ruled primarily by Neptune and secondarily by Jupiter—an inspirational combination. Neptune rules dreamers and dreaming and is our antenna to the unseen worlds. Jupiter's rays impart a love of travel, adventure, and a natural bent toward religious and philosophical exploration. Most Pisceans feel a psychic connection; for some it will be a simple sixth sense, for others a faculty for prophesy. Many Pisceans can be identified by an otherworldly, faraway look in their eyes. The combined influence of Jupiter and Neptune provides natives of this sign with a natural ability to tune into and respond to higher frequencies. Their creative capacity for image making is pronounced. Many souls born in this sign are blessed with fertile imaginations and transcendent intuition.

Among the many notable Pisceans who have made their mark in the arts, elevating the spirit and bringing a taste of heaven to earth are: Michelangelo (March 6, 1475, Julian; March 15, Gregorian), Renaissance artist and sculptor; George Frideric Handel (February 23, 1685, Julian; March 05, Gregorian), whose *Messiah* continues to thrill audiences today; Enrico Caruso (February 25, 1873), the great operatic tenor; Howard Pyle (March 5, 1853), illustrator and author whose imaginative, classic tales, such as of King Arthur and his knights, were written so vividly that it appears he was there; Tamaki Miura (Feb 22, 1884), Japanese opera singer famous for her role as Cio-Cio San, the geisha wife, in Puccini's opera, *Madama Butterfly*; and finally, Josh Groban (February 27, 1981), the American singer and songwriter who, along with the Welsh soprano, Charlotte Church (February 21, 1986), is another Piscean singer who is said to have the voice of an angel.

DEEP-SEA DIVING

In meeting his past and contemplating his future, the soul in Pisces knows times of great hope and promise, as well as moments of sorrow so deep as to be almost unfathomable. That he not be swept away by dreams so grand and visions so elevating that he neglects his everyday responsibilities, nor overwhelmed by the specter of fear looming at the doorway, the soul in Pisces must work on maintaining his equanimity and inner peace. Yielding to the death-like energies of depression can trap him in a murky swamp, *the Piscean bog*, from which it is hard to emerge! Likewise, giving in to the temptation to escape rather than resolve life's problems—through the use of alcohol, for example—can cause the soul to drift far off course.

Pisces and Neptune rule alcohol, alcoholism and alcoholic beverages. For many persons with their Sun or their Moon in Pisces or with Neptune in close aspect to the Sun, Moon, Mars or Ascendant, drinking proves to be their number one nemesis! While some alcoholics initially choose to drink as a coping device, others are simply looking for spiritual answers in the wrong places.

Getting sidetracked by psychic enthrallment can be an even more alluring and potentially dangerous trap! Those Pisceans who get involved in séances and the like may be curious, but more often, they are desperately looking for connection with the Neptunian "unseen worlds," such as those who would contact a deceased loved one. One woman in her early twenties was lured into a "session" while searching for spiritual teachings. It took her over twenty years to return from what she called "a psychic nightmare."

Mystical traditions warn against attempting "to take heaven by force," that is, trying to force one's way into higher dimensions through using mind-altering drugs. Drugs in general, including prescription drugs, also come under Pisces' and Neptune's domain. To safely open his consciousness to the higher worlds, the soul needs a solid foundation in this world. Indeed, the deeper a man delves into other realms, as in deep sea diving (a favorite Piscean activity) the trickier the mirages become.

Beautiful music, art, meditation, and the disciplined use of prayer and dynamic decrees in accordance with the various disciplines and rigors of a spiritual path are the means to safely ascend Jacob's Ladder.

Learning to discern both good and evil takes effort, attunement and much practice. These sensitive souls are advised to "test the waters" and to shun places where they know evil dwells, since they pick up negative energies almost imperceptibly.

WALKING UPON THE WATERS

Water represents the emotional pull of the subconscious and unconscious mind, a realm of thought and feeling swirling beneath the surface of conscious awareness. There also is found what esoterically is referred to as the memory body, containing wonderful remembrances, the wisdom of the ages, and even the memory of things not yet seen, as well as memories of pain, death, loss of life and love—the soul's Pandora's box.

Great saints and avatars such as Jesus, and *Kuan Yin, the Goddess of Mercy* in the East, are often depicted walking upon the water, sometimes referred to mystically as the astral sea.[139]

Their bodies are literally lifted up in light. He that would be Hero in Pisces must determine to do likewise. He can learn to manage his sensitivity and to seal his aura in light, even as he summons the

Kuan Yin is honored in Asia as the patroness of fishermen and is often shown crossing the sea seated or standing on a lotus or with her feet on the head of a dragon. (This image is said to have been captured miraculously on film by someone taking a picture of the clouds from an airplane window.)

---

[139] *The astral plane* refers to a frequency of time and space corresponding with the (less than physical) body of *emotional energies* in man and the collective unconscious of the race. Although potentially a fount of tremendous creativity, the astral plane has been muddied by impure human thought and feeling. Therefore, the term "astral" is also used in a negative context, to refer to what is impure or psychic.

courage to resolve his past, to be positive in the present, and hopeful of wonderful possibilities in the future.

Pisceans often are drawn to spend time near or on the sea, perhaps for a season, perhaps for many years. For some, the physical challenge of being sea-worthy is a fitting metaphor for mastering their own changing emotions.

FORGIVE NOT ONCE, BUT MANY TIMES[140]

While guilt is not exclusive to Pisces, it essentially is a Neptunian, Pis-cean and Twelfth House problem. To awaken and come to grips with error, and the way our actions have hurt others, is initially painful, but is a vital step toward self-correction. The dark and oppressive energy of guilt, akin in its vibratory pat-tern to condemnation, would erode faith by insinuating to the mind that the soul is unworthy to receive grace and forgiveness.

The soul born in Pisces must summon the courage to defy these energies of the night! Furthermore, once the soul confesses to having erred, it is time to learn from the lesson, to heal whatever can be repaired, and move on! Although Piscean souls may fervently desire to be free of such self-torture, they often labor long to erase the self-incriminating images from the films of their minds.

Even as the revolving of guilt is a Piscean problem, its antidote—the offering of the balm of forgiveness in kindness and love—is a Piscean virtue. For-giveness allows the soul to transmute the errors of the past and be free. Pisceans experience great joy in the forgiving of self and others. To withhold forgiveness is to risk not only being tied to another (or to one's own past memories) by bonds of negativity, but also to eventually experience such psychological toxicity as dis-ease within the physical body. Oftentimes, great healing follows the soul's reso-lution to truly let go of past hurts. Forgiveness is the pinnacle of fearless compassion!

THE PISCEAN CHILD

Some Piscean children are very jovial while others have a marked quiet side; still others may be introverted and shy. Most little dreamers are naturally spiritually inclined; many are musical or artistic. The Piscean child who seems slow or reticent may actually be struggling against fear of failure. The introverted child may feel bombarded with psychic energy and will seek to withdraw from

---

[140] "Then came Peter to him, and said, *[LORD], how oft shall my brother sin against me, and I forgive him? Until seven times?* Jesus saith unto him, *I say not unto thee, Not until seven times but, until seventy-times-seven.*" Matthew 18:21-22

harm's way or to hide in his room where he feels safe. Nevertheless, these sensitive children often are quite talented and bright.

Piscean young people of all ages pick up energy unknowingly, absorbing almost by osmosis, the atmosphere around them, copying others' behavior patterns, body language and even their tone of voice. The Piscean child's changeable moods may actually be a subconsciously taken reading of the family or school atmosphere. (When they apply such soul sensitively consciously, such as when acting in the school play, what was a detriment turns into an asset!)

Sometimes Piscean children empathize so much with someone else's burden that tears flow freely. The Piscean child's sense of individuality may be unclear due to his identification with the suffering of others. Teach him always to affirm his self-worth. He suffers the pangs of rejection when less sensitive souls fail to show appreciation for his services, do not return his friendship, or are cruel to one another or to animals!

The tendency to feel guilty and to take the blame is especially pronounced in the Piscean youngster. All children place themselves at the center of their universe, and therefore tend to assume they're to blame for circumstances actually out of their control, like when Mommy and Daddy argue. This tendency is even more pronounced in the Piscean child who so readily absorbs other people's energies that he sometimes confuses another's emotions for his own. If the Piscean child's burden of assumed culpability goes undetected or unresolved during childhood, it will almost inevitably spill into adult life.

Many Piscean children appear to be dreamy. Perhaps they are reaching for higher worlds. They benefit when introduced to the more transcendent dimensions of being through art, music and religion, while at the same time keeping their feet squarely planted on the ground.

Piscean children typically take to the water like fishes. One Piscean teenager told me that the physical experience of diving in the waves helps boost her courage and directly deal with seemingly overwhelming problems and fears. The Piscean, when Neptune is pronounced in his chart, may be adept at putting on a mask to suit the occasion or his whims. Intuition, imagination, and a love of fantasy may lead to a career in art, dance, or writing. Parents must have fine attunement to rightly discern when the Piscean child's pathos is real, and when he is putting on crocodile tears intentionally or even unintentionally!

Most Piscean children can be taught compassion from an early age as well as spiritual techniques that help them learn how to hold on to their light while screening out negative energy. Parents and teachers who are positive, non-condemnatory, and who help the Piscean child develop his natural gifts, while celebrating his personal journey, impart tools that help the child build his self-confidence for a lifetime.

WISE AS SERPENTS, HARMLESS AS DOVES

The dominant influence of Jupiter, called the harbinger of good tidings, explains why most Pisceans sense a protective influence in their lives, despite the hardships they may encounter. Once the outer man resolves to live a life of faith, he has set the wheels of inner peace in motion. His thinking may or may not be framed by religious or spiritual tenets. Perhaps he simply determines to adopt a genuinely positive mental outlook. Such a stance does not necessarily mean that the Piscean person has consciously willed to govern his stars; that is, to be the captain of his destiny, but the adoption of such a mindset makes it less likely that his stars (fate or karma) will govern him.

The balanced Piscean soul who expects the best, and yet prepares for the worst, is free of anxiety and capable of expressing true compassion to his fellow man. Adopting a hopeful stance, without also reckoning with the human condition, can make him vulnerable to deception. When a gullible Piscean's trusting nature causes him to fall into the trap of another's malintent, he is apt to feel devastated, as if stripped of innocence. The all too typical Piscean reaction to the foibles of human nature is to then expect to be disappointed.

Edgar Cayce
(1877–1945)

Such a shield against bad news shrouds the soul. Let him heed Jesus' admonishment to his disciples as he sent them out to the four corners of the world: *Behold, I send you forth as sheep in the midst of wolves: be ye therefore wise as serpents, and harmless as doves.*[141]

TO SLEEP, PERCHANCE TO DREAM[142]

Neptune, Pisces and the Twelfth House rule sleep, dreams and dreamers. Pisceans often can be identified by that wistful, *somewhere-over-the-rainbow* look. Dreamers can be visionaries, artists, geniuses or healers. Without dreams, where is hope for better times? Ah, but dreamers can be lost in illusion. The line separating one state from another is not always clear!

Piscean born Edgar Cayce (March 18, 1877), earned the title, "The Sleeping Prophet." Cayce possessed an extraordinary psychic gift that gained him great fame and with which he was able to help thousands of people. His chart was Pisces-packed—Mercury and Saturn in Pisces were in the Seventh House (of others), while his Venus and Sun were in the Eighth House (of mysteries and the occult), a classic astrological signature for an interpreter of others' dreams.[143]

During the forty-three years of Cayce's adult life, he would lie down and

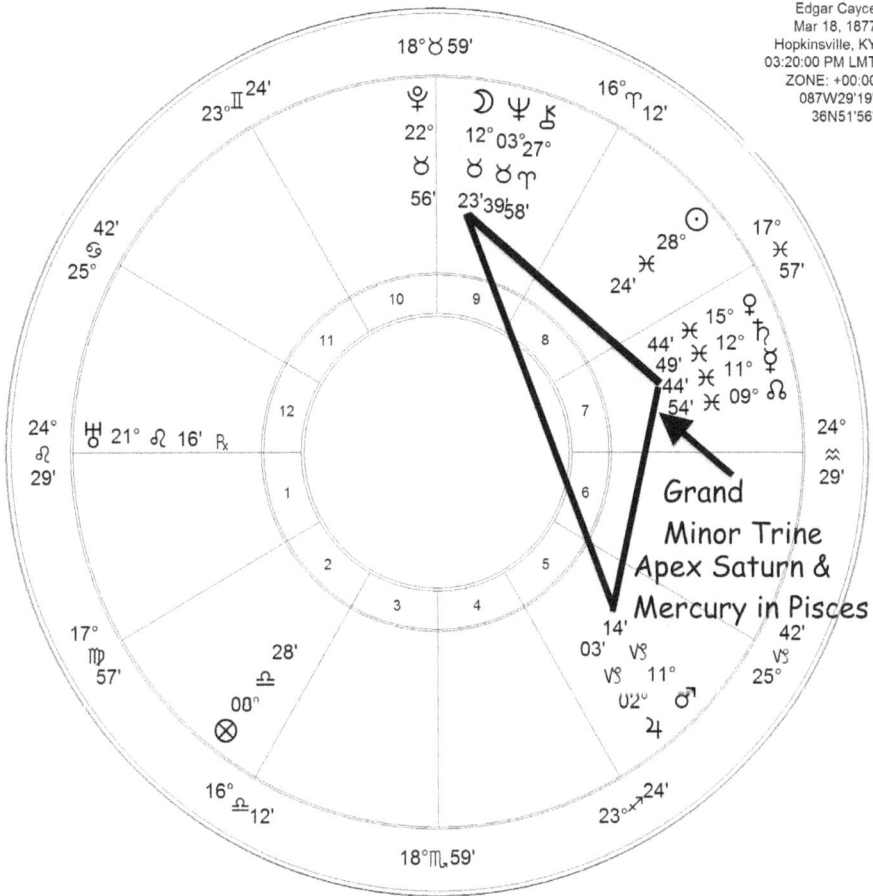

Edgar Cayce
Mar 18, 1877
Hopkinsville, KY
03:20:00 PM LMT
ZONE: +00:00
087W29'19"
36N51'56"

Grand
Minor Trine
Apex Saturn &
Mercury in Pisces

---

[141] Matthew 10:16

[142] "To sleep, perchance to dream; Aye, there's the rub. For in that sleep of death, what dreams may come." *Hamlet, Act 3, Scene 1,* Shakespeare

[143] In Cayce's natal chart, the Sun in Pisces—the Sun is the ruler of the chart due to his Leo Ascendant—signifies his extrasensory perception. Pisces' ruler, Neptune (psychic) conjoined the Moon (subconscious) in Taurus, indicates Cayce's deep listening skills. Both planets trine (positive) Mars, powerfully placed in Capricorn, which is conjoined Jupiter (Pisces' co-ruler in the Fifth House of entertainment and self-expression). All these planets sextile (creativity) Cayce's Mercury, Saturn, and Venus, in Pisces, forming a Minor Grand Trine. Seven planets in Cayce's natal chart form part of this auspicious configuration!

[144] Cayce began his work when he was healed of laryngitis through work with a hypnotist; however, hypnotism should be considered as another Piscean/Neptunian pitfall—not recommended, as it opens one's subconscious to the manipulations of another's suggestions.

enter into a self-induced sleep state. Somehow, in that out-of-body state, he was able to respond with uncanny accuracy and in a normal voice to questions received from many parts of the globe. Cayce became recognized as a medical clairvoyant.[144]

Interestingly, during Neptune's long sojourn in Pisces (February 2012 to February 2026), a cycle still not completed at the time of this writing, intuitive medicine is becoming increasingly more mainstream.

The temptation to escape the harsh realities of life and the allure of a quick ticket to higher planes of consciousness is particularly strong in Neptune-ruled Pisceans. Teen-agers are especially vulnerable to being attracted to addictive substances. They need to know the dangers of trying to open up their awareness of the higher worlds without the proper preparation and a solid foundation. Even young Pisceans, guided by a parent or teacher, can learn spiritual techniques and teachings with which they can raise consciousness safely, step-by-step.

HEAD IN THE SKY, FEET *OFF* THE GROUND

The part of the body ruled by Pisces is the feet. People with their Sun or other positions in Pisces may be attracted to some work related to the feet, such as reflexology or podiatry. If they suffer injuries to the feet, they are most likely dealing with Piscean karma. And it is their feet that most Pisceans need to practice keeping on the ground! Piscean Suns don't seem totally here — and they're not! Being exceptionally attuned to the higher spheres, as well as the lower spheres, can be a gift when understood, and frightening when not. Who's to say that the voices little Piscean children claim to hear or the ethereal images they describe are unreal, when they may simply be out of the view of most people. Regardless, life on Earth operates within a narrow spectrum for most of us. A brilliant Piscean surgeon's intuition never failed him in the operating room, but he was notorious for fumbling through his pockets and asking the nurses, "Where are my car keys?"

Such is the price of Piscean genius, or shall we say, the challenge of tuning into higher dimensions while functioning in this denser and more material world. Take a look at Albert Einstein's picture. Einstein was born Mar 14, 1879. His Theory of Relativity revolutionized physics. The faraway look in his eyes and his disheveled hair seem to say, "I'm much too busy thinking about the cosmos to bother with mundane details!"

The Piscean Suns who master anchoring their intuitive sense and mystical nature in the here and now sense the trends and enjoy financial prosperity, often using film, TV, or the latest technology to get their message across.

Steve Jobs (February 24, 1955), founder of Apple Computer, Inc., created and launched Macintosh computers, iPods, iPhones, and iPads, helping the world to tune in to their own intuitive sense. He once said:

Don't let the noise of others' opinions drown out your own inner voice. And most important, have the courage to follow your heart and intuition. They somehow already know what you truly want to become. Everything else is secondary.

The Piscean temperament seeks times and places in which to get away, quiet the senses, and recharge. (Steve Jobs would periodically go to spiritual retreats and practiced Zen Buddhist meditation, which he said helped him to concentrate.) Of all the signs, the Piscean is the most attracted to a secluded, religious life. Yet the times require, more than ever before, that we live a spiritual life while still making our way in the material world. Many Pisceans find their search for balance and inner peace aided by activities such as yoga, Pilates, meditation, reading, dancing, swimming, listening to or playing music, or walking in the woods. Pisceans can help stabilize and strengthen their auras and stay grounded by maintaining a balanced diet and an active lifestyle.

A MIDLIFE TURNING POINT

At age 43, actress, film producer, and fashion model, Sharon Stone, born on March 10, 1958, experienced an unexpected event that almost took her life, but which, in fact, became a turning point for embracing what became her true destiny—that of bringing relief from suffering to a troubled world. In Pisces, the sign of miracles, it sometimes happens that a great trauma creates the setting for great faith and the inner strength to overcome—turning adversity into a blessing in disguise.

In the fall of 2001, Stone suddenly was gripped with such a painful headache that she had to be rushed to the emergency room. In an interview with *AARP Magazine*, Stone describes her situation upon emerging from a nine-day coma: "By then, I had bled into my spinal column, brain and facial cavity at a steady pace. My brain was pushed forward into my face. I had lost 18 percent of my body mass." Grateful to have survived this near-fatal encounter, Stone left the hospital partially paralyzed. She could not hear out of her left ear and her left leg was numb. She suffered short- and long-term memory loss. Stone, who had been voted the most beautiful woman in the world, after being released from the hospital, felt ugly. Would she ever act again? She would spend the next eight months in bed. More troubles followed. Her marriage to *San Francisco Chronicle* executive editor, Phil Bronstein, fell apart and ended. Two years later, she lost shared custody of her oldest son. The future looked bleak.

We have all experienced moments of seeming futility, when all seems lost. It is not that such times are reserved for Pisceans alone, but natives of this sign oftentimes are destined to show others how to walk upon the waters even during the stormiest night! (Others, especially those with key planets in the Twelfth House, such as Eduardo García, a Leo with his natal Sun in the Twelfth

House, experience this also. Read about Eduardo in the Sun in Leo chapter.)

A positive mindset, a core belief that God has a plan and that all will be well, is essential for all of us, but especially for the sensitive and idealistic Piscean soul. Pisceans are prone to deny or run from their pain. But knowing that they have a choice to either succumb or conquer is empowering! When Piscean souls opt to numb their senses or blur their problems, with a drink, drugs, excessive sex, junk food, etc., they find themselves trapped in a place from which it is difficult to emerge.

When born with the Sun in Pisces, or when Neptune, Pisces' ruler, forms difficult aspects in the natal or progressed chart (or by transit, such as when transiting Neptune squares natal Neptune during the mid-life years, as was indeed the case for Stone) anyone may find themselves challenged by adversity and confusion. During the mid-life years, circumstances often conspire to wash away former beliefs and ambitions, replacing them with new currents of thought that create fundamental life changes. For a time, we may feel in the mist of this crisis, as the ground we once stood upon seems swept away and our new foundation is not yet apparent.

Pisces and Neptune often challenge the soul to access the higher energies of spirituality, love and imagination, transforming crisis into the opportunity for balancing karma through service and sacrifice. After her stroke, Stone realized how precious is every moment of life. She determined to get back on track. The way out of what may feel like a dark tunnel is simple—help oneself by helping others, heal one's pain by assuaging that of others.

This is precisely what Sharon Stone did. She plunged herself into the priorities of her life, which, she states, are being the mother to her three children, serving as a global humanitarian and activist, and lastly, her acting. She converted to Tibetan Buddhism—the tenants of her faith gave her the mindfulness and emotional detachment she needed to make peace with her situation and move on. A friend's prayer, says Stone, captures her spirit: "Thank you, God, for everything you gave me. And thank you more for everything you took!"

Noting that, "once you've had your life burn down, it takes time to be a phoenix," Stone did make a full recovery. She closes her interview with this grateful reflection: "What was an endless and desperate plea has become an endless, peaceful walk. I am so free, so blessed. I have the most gorgeous children."

WHEN THE DREAMER BECOMES THE MYSTIC

Pisceans on the path are in their element, on a journey of self-mastery and transfiguration. Many of the challenges they receive as their souls are tested, pruned and disciplined are similar to those they received in earlier years—ridding the mind of doubt fear and guilt, maintaining a positive mindset, setting boundaries, resolving the past and moving on, and so forth—but the stakes have changed. The Piscean Aspirant's emotional sensitivity is even more pronounced than before, yet his practiced reaction is that of one who believes in his heart and soul *that all things work together for good for those who love God.*[145]

The Piscean Aspirant embraces his karma, claims his ultimate victory, and knows God to be the giver, the receiver and the gift of grace itself. He seeks the lesson in every experience and encounter.

Even after the Piscean Sun person has determined to win the race, until fear is vanquished for good, he must guard against seeking some easy way out. His resolve to keep on keeping on will be put to the test many a time!

Somewhat dependent upon the tenor of the entire chart, the Piscean Aspirant may live in his head to the neglect of his physical body. But by staying physically healthy, which includes getting sufficient exercise and recreation, he tunes his inner instrument, helps stabilize his emotions, and is more able to stay anchored in the here and now. After all, the line between mysticism and madness is a thin one!

WHY WORRY WHEN YOU CAN PRAY?

In cleaning out his psychological closet and looking at his past, the Piscean Aspirant may be susceptible to self-condemnation more than ever, for as his love increases, he comes to sincerely regret his past moments of spiritual blindness and folly. Nonetheless, he realizes that depression and non-self-forgiveness come from pride and these, too, he surrenders as he humbly and joyously accepts God's grace. Sometimes, forgiveness is hard because the soul has not passed through the grieving process. Grieving can be an expression of great compassion and inner joy, of acceptance in ultimate good but recognition of pain, not only in response to trauma, loss and heartbreak, but also to be able to sustain hope and thanksgiving when all around oneself seems lost. But care must be taken, lest one drown in his tears! Let grieving be a clearance and not a murky puddle! I have found homeopathy to be of tremendous value in assuaging a broken heart.[146]

Faith's handmaid is holy prayer. At the dawn of Aquarius, the lost chord of the Science of Invocation is being restored to accelerate the transformational process. He invokes light from higher spheres in order to quicken the purification

---

[145] "And we know that all things work together for good to them that love God, to them who are the called according to his purpose." Romans 8:28

[146] *Aurum*, homeopathic gold, is used to help transmute old, even past life, records. *Ignatia* is often recommended for sudden grief. See your homeopathic counselor, as each case is different.

[147] Philippians 4:6-7

of the memory, restore the divine memory in the outer consciousness, guard the aura against extraneous influences, and to maintain a continual fount of inner peace. As Edgar Cayce used to say, "Why worry when you can pray?"[147]

There is no situation that prayer, rightly employed with a sincere and humble heart, will not resolve! To deny our need for prayer is to risk forgetting who we are, from whence we came, and where we are headed.

PERFECT LOVE

Lecturer and author Helen Collier, who created *The Science of Success Seminars,* was born March 13, 1927, with the Sun, Mercury, Jupiter and Uranus all in Pisces. Helen once shared with her audience that she had struggled for many years with Piscean fear. In speaking about how she was able to overcome this condition, Helen said, "You know, it is not faith alone that will vanquish fear, but love."

In her seminar, entitled, *Self-Esteem of the Soul,* Helen identifies fear— alarm, dismay, dread, horror, anxiety, fright, terror, and worry—as the number- one enemy of the soul. When the soul is able to view its circumstances calmly, Helen teaches, it opens the flow to receiving greater strength and wisdom.

Fear and love are like oil and water. If the Piscean Aspirant would be perfected in love, he must identify, resolve, and transmute his fear.[148]

This transformation does not happen all at once. Who could withstand it? Rather, it comes in measured increments and preferably under the guidance of a spiritual teacher.

I asked Helen what advice she could offer Pisceans, from her experience. She shared with me a story about Napoleon Hill who pioneered the concept of having a positive mental attitude to obtain success. "You know, many people came to Napoleon Hill to be mentored by him; they wanted to become his students. He asked them if they believed in a higher power. If they said no, he refused to work with them. He said there is nothing I can offer you. I cannot work with you if you don't believe in something higher, because that is where your help is going to come from." Helen added, "If you don't believe that, right up front, you are miss- ing the main ingredient."

PEACE, BE STILL![149]

Gaining control over his emotions is a major test for most spiritual aspi- rants of this sign, sometimes lasting for many years. The Piscean devotee's goal is to be an instrument of a Greater Light. He must recognize that this is not a pos- sibility when he allows his forcefield to be disrupted by emotional outbursts that disrupt his peace and agitate those around him. Recurring problems with depression or with anger—perhaps he is known for a short fuse—may be tolerable in the more worldly man, but in the Piscean Aspirant, they must go. When circumstances occur, or when people provoke him, he comes to recognize these as setups, testing his ability to hold his inner peace. If he desires greater light, he needs to be confident that he will not be tempted to misuse or spill this light by being caught off guard. Moreover, all the Mutable Signs are particularly vulnerable to negative mental projections. These, too, can be blown away with the command, "Peace be still!"

The Piscean Hero-in-the-Making is aided in knowing himself through his practice of mindfulness—the daily, gentle observance of oneself, one's habits, attitudes, mindsets and emotional reactions—as a means of removing those elements of his psychology that may block or delay his progress on the path. Some tendencies actually stem from other lifetimes and cannot always be ascertained through normal psychological analysis. Daily use of the power of prayer and other spiritual disciplines help him in replacing negative momentums with positive ones.

Pisces and its polarity, Virgo, are associated with the Solar Plexus chakra, sometimes called the Place of the Sun. Located above the naval, this is where people feel gut reactions and where emotions initially register. This is the place where the Piscean Aspirant must attain mastery over the emotions by maintaining harmonious flow and peace in the water element. In Pisces, the Solar Plexus relates to the Mother energy in water, while the Throat chakra relates to the Father energy in Air. In prayer and powerful invocation, these two energies merge within the Aspirant, causing the Kundalini energy at the Base-of-the-Spine to rise.[150]

While Virgos are prone to anxiety, Pisceans tend to worry. For his prayers to be effective, the Piscean Aspirant must surrender his fears; he must have faith that all will work out, remembering that every problem has a solution and as it is written that, *All things work together for good to them that love God, to them who are the called according to his purpose.*[151]

He must silence guilt that would hound him and disrupt his serenity. Even in the midst of situations that seem overwhelming or those smaller, yet disturbing, happenstances that can easily catch one off guard.

---

[148] "There is no fear in love; but perfect love casteth out fear: because fear hath torment. He that feareth is not made perfect in love." 1 John 4:18

[149] "And he arose, and rebuked the wind, and said unto the sea, *peace, be still.* And the wind ceased and there was a great calm." Mark 4:39, Matthew 8:23-27

[150] See *Intermediate Studies of the Human Aura*, Djwal Kul (1976, The Summit Lighthouse)

[151] Romans 8:28

The Piscean Aspirant practices using his mind to still his feelings and to control his tongue. He cannot afford to make the common slip-ups of saying things that he later regrets. In meditation, he may visualize a pond that is free of agitation, not a ripple disturbing the crystal-clear reflection, upon which sits a water lily and its pad. Yoga and some of the martial arts may help him tune into his core and access the tremendous creative potential and strength in the Solar-Plexus and Throat chakras, while staying grounded. As he gains control and equanimity, he also becomes masterful in lending the word of wise counsel, of inspiration, solace and forgiveness.

IMPERTURBABLE INNER PEACE

Yogananda, who brought the path of Kriya Yoga to the United States, taught the importance of mediation. Through the practice of daily meditation, the Piscean Aspirant learns to release all sense of struggle as he becomes more adept in maintaining inner calmness. In the spirit of true compassion, he forgives those who (in most cases ignorantly) would shatter his peace, remaining unmoved by constantly changing outer circumstances and energies. In *Inner Peace,* Yogananda writes:

> *A lump of sand cannot withstand the erosive effect of the ocean's waves; an individual who lacks imperturbable inner peace cannot remain tranquil during mental conflict. But as a diamond remains unchanged, no matter how many waves swirl around it, so also a peace-crystallized individual remains radiantly serene when trials beset him from all sides. Out of the changeful waters of life, let us salvage through meditation the diamond of unchangeable soul-consciousness, which sparkles with everlasting joy of Spirit.*

"FOR WITH JOY YOU SHALL GO OUT..."

In Kabbalistic Astrology, Pisces is associated with the month of *Adar*. A Hebraic saying goes, "When Adar begins, joy enters." In Kabbalistic Astrology, both Sagittarius and Pisces are times of great celebration. During *Kislev* (see the Sun in Sagittarius), Jews celebrate Chanukah, the Festival of Lights, a time of re-membering the victory of light over darkness — faith, courage and miracles in the midst of troubles. On the 14th day of the Hebrew month of *Adar*, Jews celebrate *Purim*, often called *The Celebration of Deliverance*. A joyous holiday, Purim com-memorates God's salvation of the Jews from the wicked Haman, through the courage and faith of Queen Esther, her cousin Mordecai, and the prophet Daniel (as recorded in *The Book of Esther*).

The special combination of Neptune and Jupiter in Pisces (and in Sagit-tarius) relate to the special quality of *Joy*. A basic Kabbalistic teaching is that without joy, the light of God cannot sit upon one. At a Chassidic service, Torah study, or meal, the Rabbi may suddenly burst out in song and all join in. This is because the founder of the Chassidic movement (pronounced *Hassidic*), the Rabbi Israel Baal Shem Tov (1698–1760) taught that the ability to be joyous, by discerning the good within every experience, is considered by Chassidim as a biblical command! Baal Shem Tov opposed the "fire and brimstone" method popular with *maggid* (teachers) in his day.

Life was hard enough! Better to bring hope, inspiration and happiness than severity and punishment! The Rabbi taught that when one lives in perpetual joy his heart is in tune with God's heart. Tradition had spoken of joy in studying the sacred scripture, but the Baal Shem Tov proclaimed the importance of infusing every action and thought with joy, that even mundane activity such as eating and walking, is a service to God. The Rabbi's famous adage, "with joy you shall go out," has been interpreted as, "when you are joyous, your afflictions will leave you!"

Let the Piscean seeker of peace replace then, the *habit* of constant worry and anxiety with the practice of perpetual joy!

GREATER WORKS SHALL YOU DO[152]

Even for souls of great spiritual attainment, the danger always exists of becoming overly surfeited in materialism or of becoming confused with the disparity between eternal verities and everyday life. The Piscean Hero remains mindful to not be so disenchanted with the temporal world as to attempt to escape from it. Nor is he afraid, but he rather welcomes the challenge that his extraordinary awareness of higher dimensions inevitably sets into motion.

As he progresses on the path, the Piscean Aspirant reaches a point where he can give without ceasing, for he has developed a highly attuned discernment. Being mindful, he is sensitive to others and their problems without unlawfully taking on their energy or assuming responsibility for burdens that are not his own. In the earlier stages, the Piscean Aspirant is cautioned against psychic phenomena, which can easily suck him into a lower track, an imitation of spirituality that traps his energy and brings him down. As he develops greater self-mastery, he may, however, actually possess highly developed extrasensory senses, the principal one being a precise intuition. He ministers unto life. Above all, he radiates joy, truly the signature of the one who has learned to walk fearlessly upon the waters of the astral sea.

---

[152] "Verily, verily, I say unto you, He that believeth on me, the works that I do shall he do also and greater works than these shall he do, because I go unto my Father." John 14:12

The uplifting sounds and exulting lyrics of Handel's *Hallelujah Chorus* capture the victory of the Piscean Hero's victory over death and hell (mortality and all negative karma), proclaiming jubilantly that the kingdom (the consciousness) of this world is indeed become the kingdom (the consciousness) of Heaven! This joy of love's triumph is not a trumpet blown at some final day, but a reality the Piscean Aspirant who has become the Hero may know even as he finishes his course on earth. In order that the wonders of the Aquarian Age appear in the one and in the many, the simple key given in Pisces must be understood — as the Piscean Master taught, "Look not here, nor there, for the kingdom of God is within you!"[153]

---

[153] Luke 17:21

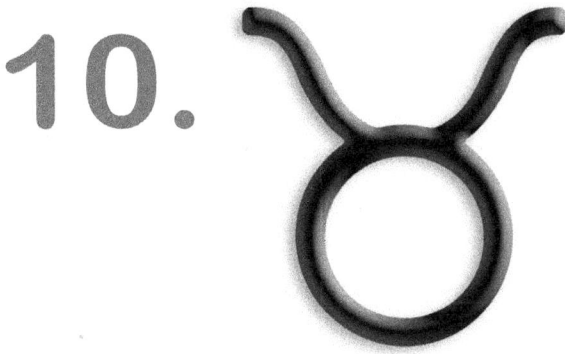

10. ♉

Taurus

Symbol	**The Bull**
Born	April 20 ~ May 20
Archetype	*The Buddha*
Key Phrase	*I Build*
Element	**Earth**
Cross	**Fixed-Love**
House	**Second:**

Personal income & debt, moral, spiritual
& material resources, personal values, sense
of self-worth, gains & losses, possessions

Ruler	**Venus**
Esoteric Ruler	**Vulcan**
Polarity	**Scorpio**
Chakra	Third Eye
Anatomy	Throat, vocal cords, tonsils, thyroid gland, ears & hearing

Spiritual Qualities .... **Dominion over the earth, right desire, inner sight & hearing, non-attachment, obedience to divine law, service to life, imperturbability, buddhic peace**

Vulnerable to .... *Rebelliousness & disobedience, inordinate desire, stubbornness & mental density, materialism, insecurity*

Must Acquire .... **Attunement, self-worth, flexibility, right stewardship, receptive mindset**

Gautama Buddha • Johannes Brahms • Eva Perón • Irving Berlin • Shirley Temple

THE SUN IN TAURUS

And God blessed them, and God said unto them,
Be fruitful, and multiply, and replenish the earth,
and subdue it: And have dominion over the fish of the sea,
and over the fowl of the air, and over every living thing
that moveth upon the earth.

—Genesis 1:28

THE STEWARD OF THE LIGHT

The inner eye of the Hero, with the Sun in Taurus at the dawn of the Aquarian Age, is open. He senses the feminine manifestation of spirit throughout the mater universe. He knows himself to be the just steward, the husbandman, and the guardian of this mother light. In turn, he is blessed with wealth and abundance, beauty and comfort, and all that he needs to fulfill his life's calling. He sees, he creates, he builds—and then, he lets go of it all. Firmly tethered to his own divine reality, he is non-attached to temporal goods and luxuries. In this most physical of all the signs, the Taurean Hero's wonder is like that of the child in awe of the wind on his face, a raindrop shining on a leaf, the sound of rushing waters, or the symphony of stars lighting up the night. Life, for him, with all its marvels and complexities, is simple in its essence. He is peaceful, steadfast, patient and forbearing. He appears as a wise and patient teacher, fierce before the forces of darkness, and yet kindly compassionate toward those still bound by their karma and blinded by selfish desire.

HEAR & UNDERSTAND[154]

The soul in Taurus asks the question, "What should I do?" The Astrologer queries, "Why don't you know? Pray." The Taurean replies, "I have prayed, but do not receive an answer." The Astrologer concludes, "What good is it that God answers you when you do not hear the answer? Pray that your inner hearing be restored to you. Then you will hear and in hearing, you will know." In Taurus we must listen, but the karmic consequence of having ignored the voice of conscience is that our inner hearing becomes atrophied.

---

[154] "For this people's heart is waxed gross, and their ears are dull of hearing, and their eyes they have closed; lest at any time they should see with their eyes and hear with their ears, and should understand with their heart, and should be converted, and I should heal them." Matthew 13:15

OBEDIENCE—ANSWERING LOVE'S CALL

In Taurus, the soul meets his momentums, created and reinforced over many lifetimes, both of loving obedience to the higher Will and those of rebelliousness and defiance of the Inner Law. The word "obedience" comes from the Latin root, *obedere*, meaning *to hear*. When we ask someone to obey us, we are asking him or her to listen to us. The Taurean Hero-to-Be wills to be *obedient* to the inner voice, the voice of conscience, sounding within his soul and written upon his heart. In so doing, he resolves to hear and to answer love's call.

To choose *not* to hear is to choose to ignore. Such willful and defiant *ignore*-ance invariably results in the clouding of the Third-Eye chakra leading to a state of mental density or dullness. Moreover, to choose to hear the voice of conscience is to choose *not* to listen to the intimations of the lesser or carnal mind, for to hearken to one is to ignore the other, and vice-versa. Taurus, in fact, is often the culprit in the charts of those prone to hearing problems. People tend to think of obedience as a punishment or some sort of enforced behavior, but actually, when the soul in Taurus heeds the voice of conscience, he is being true to himself.

It is not enough to hear—Taureans must learn to listen carefully. The planetary din is so great, the noise of daily life so deafening, that even the most advanced of Taurean souls are challenged to separate out the one voice among the many!

Another manifestation of the karma of not listening common to Taureans (whether personal or planetary) is being or *feeling* ignored. The native of this sign experiences, in lesser or greater measure—whether for years or during certain times in his life—that his opinion is being scoffed at or that his way of life, his values and beliefs, are condemned, ridiculed, or seen as worthless.

One Taurean man was adopted by a loving family after spending the first eight years of his life in a crowded orphanage. He spent the next 40 and more years coming to terms with, and finally putting behind him, the deeply buried, but powerful, memory of crying out as a little babe while the busy attendants passed him by. María, born toward the end of April, worked hard, raised her family, and experienced her loved ones' outright rejection of her person when she stepped out of a limited and oppressive lifestyle to fulfill her passion to be an artist (a Taurean vocation). María realized how she had bent over backwards to love and make others happy. She expected that she would in turn be validated and loved. When she finally broke through (transiting Uranus conjoined the Ascendant) from years of feeling repressed and controlled by others, she had to be patient and painstakingly pick up the broken pieces of her life and put them back together again. To follow her passion, she had to make a difficult decision—a daunting task requiring much faith, forgiveness and self-affirmation. María kept

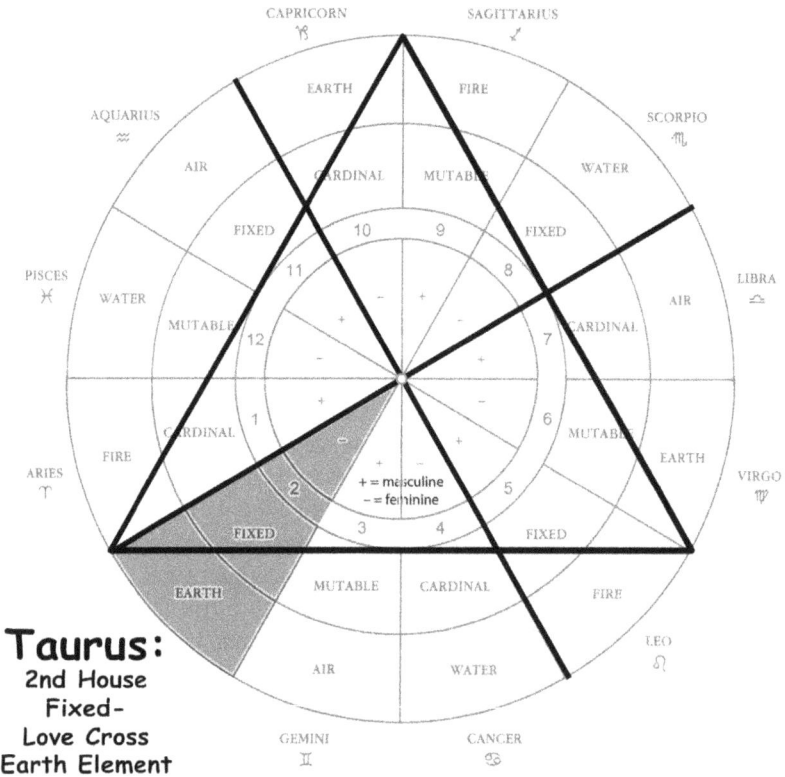

Taurus:
2nd House
Fixed-
Love Cross
Earth Element

on keeping on. She never regretted having taken such a courageous leap of faith!

The Taurean who elects to be free, to reach for his star, and to walk the higher way finds that the air gets rarefied—and his true friends become fewer the more he advances on his journey. To be awake is to be an anomaly when living among those still deep in slumber!

THE INNER MAP

All souls come into existence with a life plan, which they have at inner levels prior to entering the birth canal. The soul knows where he has been and what he must become. He grasps the purpose and meaning of the life into which he is about to embark. And then, once more, he is covered in the veils of time, space, and forgetfulness. He that would be Hero in Taurus must uncover and come into alignment with that inner map, esoterically referred to as *the blueprint of being,* in order that he might find and fulfill his *sacred labor*, his life's unique and special work.

Aries is the sign of choosing which *me* I want to be—my real self or my human ego and it precedes Taurus on the Zodiac wheel. He who in Aries has allowed his heart to be tinged with pride and arrogance cannot in Taurus perceive the way, being blinded by desire. Yet to know and to wholeheartedly embrace his destiny, the soul born with the Sun in Taurus must necessarily come to understand who he really is—and who he is *not*. Who would think that so apparently simple an assignment would prove to be so arduous?

TAURUS, THE BULL

Taurus' symbol is the Bull. Like the bull, most Taureans are slow to anger, but when they are roused, the fury they unleash is terrible and intense! Moreover, desire is stronger in Taurus than in any other sign. As witnessed in a bullfight, the bull instinctively charges after the red cape of desire and in so doing meets his end. But in India, carved on ancient *stelae,* the Bull has his Third Eye open, signifying the illumination that occurs when the animal nature is subdued.[155]

The Bull is stubborn. For all their many differences, what Taureans have in common, the trademark that distinguishes them from other signs, is an intractable stubbornness. The Taurus Sun person is likely, in different measures and intensity, to manifest tenacity, determination, persistence, and undaunted striving. Once his mind is made up to commit himself, whether to another, or to a job, a cause, or even to a personal resolution, the true Taurean is unshakable, reliable

---

[155] *Stela* (plural, *stelae*) is an archaeological term for an upright stone slab or column typically bearing a commemorative inscription or relief design.

and trustworthy. He is able to endure many trials in order that he meet his goals and carry out his promises. Indeed, many souls of this sign are known to be hard working, resolute, patient, and often long-suffering.

Naturally, such noble virtues turn sour when applied to dubious causes. And so, in Taurus we also find unreasonableness and obstinacy, inflexible attitudes, and/or a stubborn refusal to budge or to change bad habits. As the saying goes, "He's stubborn as a (Taurean) bull!"

The tale of the boy Krishna wrestling with the demon-possessed bull tells the story symbolically—the stubborn, willful, animal nature must be tamed to make room for higher consciousness. In the story, the demon possessing the bull is enraged by Krishna challenging him. This describes the backlash that he who would be saved will face from the forces from without and from within that have enslaved him for eons and are not easily subdued. Krishna's companions, lacking his mastery, were not so brave![156]

THE OX THAT SERVES

Another symbol for Taurus is the Ox. In Hinduism, the ox is a symbol of wealth, strength, plenty, selfless giving, and a rich life.[157]

Chinese Astrology describes people born in the Year of the Ox as hard-working, steadfast, and persistent—all character traits associated with Taurus in western Astrology. In esoteric Astrology, the ox is typically depicted pulling a plow and represents Taurus as the patient burden-bearer. True, there is the selfish type of Taurean, trapped in the grip of unrelenting desires or habitual self-indulgence, and sense gratification, but the more evolved native of this Earth/Love sign is kind and gentle, dependable and constant, down-to-earth and ready to lend a helping hand.

Once engaged, Taureans tend to be conscientious and industrious. Among them are found indomitable workers capable of carrying a tremendous load of responsibility. They never seem to tire. Loyal to the end, often at the price of considerable personal sacrifice, they sometimes struggle to let go and move on. If

---

[156] Aristasura, the fearsome bull-demon entered the little village of Vrindavan, confident of overpowering Krishna to fulfill his master Kamsa's wish. His demonic appearance and wild fury scared off the common people of Vrindavan. With his violent grunt and giant horns he shattered the dam and flooded everything around. But Krishna took him by his horns and flung him over. The earth trembled as they fought till Krishna swung him violently in the air and shattered his horns bringing an end to the bull demon. See www.en.wikipedia.org/ wiki/Little_Krishna.

[157] The cow is associated more with Cancer. Both Cancer and Taurus relate to abundance and the economy.

they leave, they reason, who can possibly fill their shoes? Due to the intense quality of the sign, Taureans can become workaholics, but they can find balance by scheduling recreation, rest and exercise into their day.

Taureans do need to be careful lest they become stuck or even complacent. Procrastination, born of fear, or simply of habit, can be fatal to success. Some Taureans, at moments, or perhaps during a particular chapter of their life, could be described by the old saying, "Don't move until an elephant steps on your toes!" Especially in our quick-paced society, the Sun-in-Taurus type may appear to be out of step or abnormally slow, even to himself. Nevertheless, once they arrive at a conclusion, whether truly enlightened or erroneous, they are apt to stick to it.[158]

Astrologers typically advise spouses of Taureans to reason with their partners while they are still in the contemplative stage. Once the typical Taurean makes up his or her mind, there's no changing it!

THE CALF—SYMBOL OF CHRIST CRUCIFIED

In Christian mysticism, Taurus is represented by the Calf, symbol of the Christ and the Christ Consciousness in the Earth element. The Calf is one of the four figures on the mystical cross, spoken of in the vision of John the Beloved in Revelations.[159]

Astrologically, the four symbols are related to the Fixed Love-Cross, named by the Astrologer Isabel Hickey as the Cross of Serpent-Wisdom Energy (the Kundalini). This cross reveals the manifestation of divine love in each of the four Elements: Fire (Spirit/Leo, The Lion), Air (Mind/Aquarius, the Man), Water (Emotion/Scorpio, the Flying Eagle) and Earth (Physical/Taurus, the Calf). The sacrifice of the calf, a common ritual among the early Israelites, and symbolized in the persecution of Jesus, shows the crucifixion of the Christ in the world. The Taurean Initiate's path is one of loving and selfless service. Non-attached to the praise or persecution of the world, he comes as a teacher of the ancient mandate to take dominion over the Earth. He is an example of the integration of the inner and the outer man.

DARE TO LOVE

Often the root of the Taurean soul's entrenched and obdurate attitudes and compulsive attachments lies in the soul's response to some past trauma or

---

[158] This is especially true when the Moon, Venus, or Mars are in Taurus, Cancer or Pisces. If Fire is strongly emphasized in the natal chart and/or the Cardinal-Power Cross, the native's general demeanor will be modified accordingly.

[159] "And the first beast *was* like a lion, and the second beast like a calf, and the third beast had a face as a man, and the fourth beast *was* like a flying eagle." Revelations 4:7

loss. Rather than working through his pain, he tries to protect himself from it. But when he anesthetizes himself from pain, he effectively shuts down his capacity to give and to receive love. Moreover, he may not only fear losing once again, but also he may be angry at the Universe for handing him such a fate! His fixed stare reveals that he is energetically choosing to ignore. A common gesture, a way to pick out the recalcitrant Taurean in a crowd, is that he crosses his arms over his chest. People tend to shout at him, as if he were hard of hearing, but actually nothing will move him except his own resolve to overcome his fears and to dare to love.

EPICURES OF THE ZODIAC

Several signs are associated with food and the digestive process. Taurus governs certain aspects of agriculture as well as farming, marketing, food preparation, and food sales. A signature sign for chefs, Taurus relates to appetite as well as to the various vocations related to the culinary arts. The most sensual of all the astrological signs, Taureans need to guard against satiating themselves to excess. Known for good taste in food, drink and clothes, they run the gamut from epicures to gluttons. Moreover, imbalance in Taurus often manifests in the form of obsessive compulsions, eating disorders, and other fixated, emotional habit patterns that can be difficult to break. Note that Taurus rules the thyroid gland. Taureans who find it hard to shed excess pounds are advised to check out their levels for this gland that regulates metabolism. In order to heal the cause and core of the affliction, let them explore and resolve any repressed pain that they may be holding on to and refusing to face.

WORK

Taureans excel at almost any occupation they put their mind to. Whatever their chosen field of expertise, they are characteristically reliable and thorough. However, those who indulge in drugs, too much food, drink, or sex, will lose their drive and become indolent and laid back. Many Taureans seem blessed with a proverbial green thumb. In the garden, or simply in life, much flourishes under their direction. Many natives of this sign work with the land, some directly, while others thrive in professions such as surveying, designing homes, or planning building codes. Taureans whose work is primarily mental, typically seek balance in some physical pastime; mountain climbing, gardening, ceramics, building, tiling, making jewelry, weaving, sculpting, carpentry, cooking, and even golf, a few of many activities that combine the vision of the mind with the dexterity of the hands.

Ruled by Venus, planet of love and beauty, and being endowed with so much physical vigor, Taureans are known to be excellent masseurs/masseuses, personal fitness trainers, ballet dancers, hands-on beauty consultants, and the like. The martial arts, being both spiritually and physically demanding, have great appeal to many natives of this sign. One young Taurus woman traveled to India after graduating college. She launched her spiritual journey by becoming a master yoga teacher after taking several retreats with the Dalai Lama.

Many Taureans excel in retail sales. Looking for a bargain? Shop with a Taurus. They have an eye for finding the best quality at the best price that is unrivalled by any other sign!

Apart from the nature of their particular line of service, Taureans often have lessons to learn related to money management. Some actually have careers in finance. Many, however, elect to work at a given job simply to have enough income to fulfill their financial obligations, thus allowing them the freedom to pursue their passion and true life's calling on the side.

TAUREANS IN THE ARTS

Taureans typically seek beauty in physical objects, in fine clothing and jewelry, in the creative arts, and in the preparation and partaking of good food. Moreover, Taurus rules the throat, and many Taureans have made their mark as composers, musicians or singers.

Shirley Temple receiving the first Academy Juvenile Award from Walt Disney in 1935, at 6 years old.

Among the long list of Taurean entertainers shines forth the child actress, Shirley Temple, born April 23, 1928. This bright Taurean child's many endearing film performances brought hope and joy to Depression Era America. Her films are still treasured by children today. By the time she was 5, the child actress was financially supporting her family and had saved Fox Studios from bankruptcy! Taureans almost inevitably grapple with money matters. In her autobiography, *Child Star*, Shirley writes of how she came to forgive her father, George Temple, a bank teller, for mismanaging and losing the bulk of her fortunes.[160]

---

[160] *Child Star, An Autobiography*, by Shirley Temple Black (McGraw-Hill, 1988)

Zubin Mehta, born April 29, 1936, into a musical Parsi family in Bombay (now Mumbai), has earned international acclaim as one of the world's greatest conductors. While Mehta's achievements are truly remarkable, the following description of the conductor could fit many other, less recognized but hard-working natives of this sign:

> *Once Zubin Mehta sets his mind on a goal, his dedication, determination, and commitment are extraordinary. Mehta pursues his ambitions tenaciously and will stubbornly refuse to give up, let go, or be influenced in any way. Like Aesop's tortoise, Zubin labors patiently and steadfastly until he achieves what he wants—or until it is clear beyond a shadow of a doubt that all is lost. He is a reliable, consistent and productive worker, and he often shoulders more of the workload than his co-workers, usually without complaint... Getting started is more difficult. Zubin Mehta has a lazy, comfort-loving side and there is often a good deal of inertia for him to overcome before Mehta gets going, but once he gets a momentum going his energy level is strong and steady.[161]*

The soothingly calm characteristics of the Taurean demeanor are captured beautifully in the lullabies of Johannes Brahms (May 7, 1833), as well as by actor and singer, Bing Crosby (May 03, 1903), in the sultry yet powerful voice of singer and actress Barbra Streisand (April 24, 1942), and in the slow gait and soft-spoken drawl of actor James Stewart (May 20, 1908). Then there's the Broadway stage, choreographer, singer, musician and actor, Fred Astaire (May 10, 1899). Astaire's first performance was at age four and a half. He retired at age 70. His smooth, apparently effortless style onstage was the result of his eye for perfection and meticulous behind-the-scenes work in preparation for each act.

THE MELODY LINGERS ON![162]

Irving Berlin is considered to be one of the greatest and most beloved of all American songwriters. He was born May 11, 1888, in or around the city of Mogilyov, Belarus. His father was a Jewish cantor.[163]

When Irving was only five years old, his parents smuggled themselves

---

[161] See www.TopSynergy.com.

[162] Irving Berlin quote: "The song has ended, but the melody lingers on!"

[163] In Judaism, a cantor, also known as a *chazzan* or *hazzan*, is the person who leads the congregation in prayer. Cantors play an important role in Jewish religious life because music is an important part of Jewish prayer services.

and their eight children out of Russia to escape the pogroms.[164]

In his early twenties, he worked as a singing waiter in different restaurants. He published his first song in 1907. The rest of this prolific artist's career is history. Berlin wrote more than 900 songs, 9 musicals plus he composed the scores to 18 movies!

Many of Berlin's songs, spanning his 60-year career, have stood the test of time, including, "White Christmas," "There's No Business Like Show Business," and "God Bless America." Venus-ruled Taurus creates a strong focus for the arts, for music and for making money. Berlin roused his fellow Americans' patriotic love through song. "God Bless America" was so popular, it threatened to replace the national anthem!

He made more money than any other American songwriter, donating generously to multiple charities and causes. Berlin raised millions of dollars for the Boy and Girl Scouts of America by assigning to them copyrights to "God Bless America." His destiny was stamped upon his chart! Consider that Taurus rules singing and money. Half the planets in Berlin's natal chart are in Taurus, all in the Eleventh House of Community![165] (See Irving Berlin's natal chart on the next page; notes are below.)

---

[164] In the late 19th and early 20th century, Jews in Russia were victims of widespread pogroms. *Pogrom* is a Russian word designating an attack, accompanied by destruction, looting of property, murder, and rape, perpetrated by one section of the population against another.

[165] Because differences exist as to whether Irving Berlin was born in Mogilyov or Tyumen, the house position could shift slightly. His Venus might be in the Tenth House of career. Venus (Taurus' ruler) leads the Taurean stellium at 4 degrees; the Sun, Mercury, Moon, and Neptune are all conjoined in Taurus. Note that Venus is square Saturn in Leo (entertainment), a position that, in and of itself, can show hardship. There was plenty of it in Berlin's early life in Belarus, and then as the family struggled in New York, but squares denote mastery for those who can rise to the occasion.

Saturn represents his hard work and technical skill, and Venus his inspiration and love of beauty, intrinsic to any art form. Saturn in Leo and Jupiter in Sagittarius form an inspiring Fire Trine.

The Saturn/Jupiter trine helps to steady Jupiter in Sagittarius (foreign lands) in the Fifth House of entertainment, opposing Pluto in the Eleventh House in Gemini (writing), which otherwise could have manifested as an unmanageable expansion of activity.

Berlin's chart gains dynamism—his reaching out to others through song, his many charitable projects—through Mars and Uranus conjoined in Libra (Cardinal-Power sign), ruled by Venus (in melodic Taurus), trine his Pluto in Gemini.

As a young man, Berlin looked for ways to help support the family (Taurus), and with only a few years of formal education, thought to join his gift of singing (from his father) and reach out to people's sentiments (Taurus, Libra, Venus) through song.

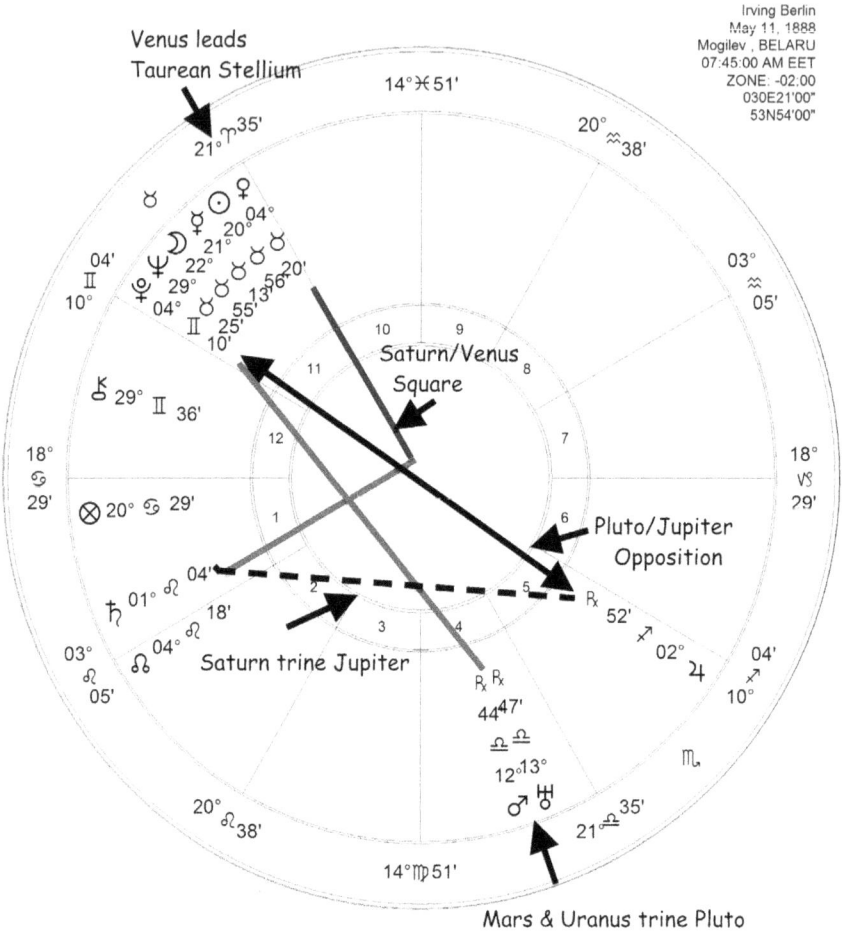

Venus leads
Taurean Stellium

14°♓51'

Irving Berlin
May 11, 1888
Mogilev , BELARU
07:45:00 AM EET
ZONE: -02:00
030E21'00"
53N54'00"

20°
♒38'

21°♈35'

04'
♊
10°

04°
♅
04°

☿ ☉ ♀
20°
♃ 21°
22°
☽ 29°
♆
♂ ♂
♂ 56°20'
♂ 13°
♊ 55'
25'
10'

03°
♒
05'

Saturn/Venus
Square

10   9
8

☄ 29° ♊ 36'

12

11

7

18°
♋
29'

⊗ 20° ♋ 29'

1

6

Pluto/Jupiter
Opposition

18°
♑
29'

♄
01°
04°

04'
♌
18'
♌

2

5

℞
52'

3   4

Saturn trine Jupiter

℞ ℞
44°47'

02°
♐
♃

04'
♐
10°

03°
♌
05'

♎ ♎
12°13°

♏

20°
♌38'

♂ ♅
21°♎35'

14°♍51'

Mars & Uranus trine Pluto

FAIR LADY, SAVING THE WORLD'S CHILDREN

Considered one of the top female film stars of all time, Audrey Hepburn, was born in Brussels, Belgium, on May 4th, 1929. She gained fame for her role in movies that became classics, such as, *Breakfast at Tiffany's* and *My Fair Lady*. Taurus has to do with economic well-being, with food, and with scarcity.

During the German occupation of the Netherlands in WWII, Audrey and her mother faced near starvation. Although Hepburn gained both fame and fortune in film, the experience remained with her always. She became a philanthropist. Her greatest passion was her work on behalf of children throughout the world. A

Audrey Hepburn lived the philosophy of putting others before herself. In her work with Unicef, visiting countries in Africa and South Asia even during the last months of her life.

UNICEF Goodwill Ambassador, Hepburn traveled to twenty countries. Visiting heads of states throughout the world, she raised consciousness about the plight of the world's children in need, many of whom struggle just to survive. In speaking about her work with children's charities, Hepburn said, "I speak for those children who cannot speak for themselves, children who have absolutely nothing but their courage and their smiles, their wits and their dreams."[166]

Taurus deals with values. We talk about the value of an object or a position, but we also can define those values, the underlying beliefs that we hold dear and that guide our lives. During the resistance to the Nazis, when Hepburn was still quite young, she courageously delivered messages to the Allies, hiding them in her shoes. She is credited with having said this inspirational quote: *Nothing is impossible—the word itself says, "I'm possible!"*

Since Taurus is the *I Have* sign, many Taureans hold on to things and to people way beyond their usefulness. At the extreme end of the spectrum is the tendency to hoard, both a Taurean and a Cancerian disorder. Hepburn, however, brings the concept of having and caring for others to another level of love and active doing: *People, even more than things, have to be restored, renewed, revived, reclaimed, and redeemed. Never throw out anyone.*[167]

---

[166] In 1994, the *Audrey Hepburn Children's Fund*, a non-profit organization, was created in New York to continue Audrey's international appeals on behalf of ill-treated and suffering children around the world.

[167] Both quotes are from www.Values.com/inspirational-quotes.

THE MONEY SIGN

In the Earth Triad, Taurus relates to income, Virgo to employment, and Capricorn to career. In addition, Taurus polarizes with Scorpio. Together, Taurus and Scorpio are the money signs. Taurus relates to *my* money, *my* belongings, *my* space, etc., as opposed to Scorpio, which governs *our* money—the money, possessions, and space that *we* share, and the ways in which *we* invest and form financial commitments, such as with taxes, banking, insurance policies, pensions, inheritances, and the like. Taurus governs banks, bankers, stockholders, brokers, financiers, tellers and cashiers.

Venus and Taurus govern the economy—not just dollars and cents, but the economy of energy, the right use of resources, in any given activity. We can, for instance, consider the economy of speech. Idle chatter is as wasteful as is the careless spending of money. Interestingly, money is often the number-one source of conflict in marriage. It's often less a matter of how much, but rather about how it is spent and who controls it!

Taurus relates to the Second Astrological House; in an adult's chart, the Second House tells of a person's income and also of his values; in the child's chart, his possessions and attitudes about them. Man, knowing who he is and in right relationship to the Father-Mother God in Aries, is directed to take command over the earth and all thereon.

Being Earth oriented, the Taurean is concerned with physical security. Nevertheless, he must beware lest he become too attached to some person, place, position, or possession. The Sun-in-Taurus individual must build, create, accumulate, and then he must let go, for he is but the administrator of his wealth, not the source. His money is not meant to be hoarded, but exchanged. In many religious traditions, would-be disciples are tested by being asked to give up their worldly goods.

Money, in and of itself, is not seen as evil, but rather it is the all-too human attachment to money, and to "the things of this world;" it is the tendency to seek power to control others through money, the propensity for greed and the fear of loss that plagues not only those who have, but also those who have not. It is the distraction from the inner life that is common to those involved in mercenary activities. And yet, in the highest of esoteric traditions, money is but a crystallized form of spiritual energy in the physical plane—the very essence of the Divine Mother manifest as an exchange unit and symbol of sharing and interchange.

SEX & MONEY—RIDING THE BULL OF DESIRE

The powerful presence of the mother energy concentrated in Earth endows Taureans with strong sexual magnetism and powerful desires. In astrological analysis, both sex and money, mediums of exchange, are ruled by the Taurus/Scorpio polarity. The creative potential in these signs is tremendous, but cravings are so compelling that Taureans and Scorpios easily become selfish, using people to meet their needs or to satisfy their desires. If they would seek to control their desires with their mind and channel this potency toward a positive end, they must resolve to be selfless, considerate, and compassionate to all. Even with the best of intentions, however, they often do not even realize how intense they are, or how selfishly motivated, until they become less so and their inner eye is cleared. Taureans trying to ride the demon-possessed bull, as did Krishna, would be wise to practice common sense and courtesy and to learn and respect the Inner Law—even a law as simple and obvious as the Golden Rule.

Napoleon Hill, author of *Think and Grow Rich,* points out that relatively few individuals are wealthy before age 40 because they waste their greatest creative resource when they seek continual sexual satisfaction. Hill explains: "When harnessed, and redirected along other lines, [the sex drive] maintains all of its attributes of keenness of imagination, courage, etc., which may be used as powerful creative forces in literature, art, or in any other profession or calling, including, of course, the accumulation of riches."

FREEDOM FROM FEAR

All Taureans, in varying degrees and in one form or another, will wrestle with their attachment to compulsive urges and compelling desires. All know the fear of insecurity and are guided by their longing to enjoy emotional and material well-being. Naturally, so do we all. But the major life lesson for the person born with the Sun in Taurus likely revolves around letting go and letting life flow.

An astrological axiom states, "What we fear to lose, in Taurus, we will lose." The magnetic pull of the Earth causes some natives of this sign to become inordinately attached to their wealth and possessions, which in their minds, often include their spouses and children! Two Taurean women, both born on the same day, but at different hours, shared a similar astrology. One had the Sun in the Second House of income, while the other was born with the Sun in the Seventh House of marriage. One struggled with overcoming her fear of poverty, even though she had inherited a considerable fortune. The other, frightened that she might lose her spouse, was jealous, possessive and controlling. One went bankrupt and the other's heart was broken when her husband, unable to gain her trust and quell her fears, finally divorced her. Life, in its mercy, frees us from fear by taking from us the person or thing whose potential loss torments us. On the other hand, it is also said, "When there is loss in Taurus, something is taken that something else might appear!"

ARGENTINA'S SPIRITUAL LEADER

María Eva de Peron, affectionately known to the Argentine people as Evita, was born May 07, 1919, in Los Toldos, a province outside of Buenos Aires. Born into humble circumstances, she would rise to become South America's first truly powerful woman and Argentina's *Spiritual Leader of the Nation,* a title officially bestowed upon her by the Argentine Congress a few weeks before her death (from cervical cancer) in 1952.

In Evita's natal chart, the Sun in Taurus was conjoined Mars, sextile Jupiter, endowing her with an intense and relentless (Fixed Cross) drive (Mars) to strive (Taurus/Mars), to become

Offical portrait of **Juan Domingo Perón** and **María Eva Duarte de Perón**, known popularly as Evita. The painting was finished in 1948. Among the presidential portraits, it is the only case in which a president appears smiling, and furthermore, accompanied by his First Lady.

what she needed to be (Sun) in order to accomplish her dreams (Jupiter). The stamp of a destiny entwined with that of the Argentine people was written in the stars: Jupiter conjoined Pluto was trine Uranus in Pisces on that May 7th. It was also conjoined Argentina's Venus in Cancer and trine her Jupiter in Scorpio—this Argentine generation would live to see tremendous change in their nation![168]

Evita's story is well known. By the time she was a year old, her father, Juan Duarte, a well-to-do rancher and a married man, returned to his legal wife, abandoning Eva's mother along with Eva and her four older siblings, leaving them in poverty having to fend for themselves—a common, if censored, occurrence in the Argentina of that day. Evita grew up in Junní, a small town, but at age 15 she took off to find her future as an aspiring actress in Buenos Aires. While Evita was somewhat frail in appearance in her younger days (she knew the pangs of hunger and want) she was tough in spirit. The Taurus Sun/Mars conjunction squared (challenges) her Moon conjoined Saturn (need to overcome fear and meet restrictions with patience) in bold and theatrical Leo. The way was strewn with obstacles but she was determined (accessing power in the square) to succeed. Evita's dogged Taurean persistence paid off. By her mid-twenties she was making enough money to support herself and even to send money home to her mother and siblings.

All of Eva's early life was to bring her to a moment, one she called *mi día maravillosa (my marvelous day)* when her life and that of Coronel Juan Perón would coincide—on January 22, 1944. By then, she had gained enough recognition (mostly on radio but also in film) to be asked to attend a charity event Juan Perón was sponsoring in which local stars would help to raise money for the many victims of a devastating San Juan earthquake that had occurred a week earlier. Transiting Saturn (fate) was conjoined Evita's natal Venus (love and money). Transiting Uranus (revolution, awakening) in Gemini was opposed Argentina's natal Uranus in Sagittarius and square Evita's Uranus in Pisces. Juan Peron's chart was also activated that day.[169] (See the Tri-Wheel on the following page.)

The time for change had come. It was indeed a date with destiny—for Evita and Juan Peron, and also for Argentina! Eva and Juan would marry less than a year afterwards (October 22, 1945). When they met, Juan Perón was Minister of Labor. He would soon be President of the nation. Together, he and Evita would become a formidable force, taking Argentina into her future!

Evita would say that as Eva, she fulfilled the expected role of the wife of the Argentine President whose work was "simple and agreeable," but as Evita, her heart and soul belonged to the people (*el pueblo*) who deposited in their leader "all their faith, hope and love." Even before he became Argentina's President, Juan Perón had championed reform for the poor, the workers, the people—*los descamisados* (literally, *those without a shirt*). She became the personal presence, the tireless worker, the beautiful, tender and personal contact with them as she received them one by one and visited them in their homes, schools and factories. Evita had excellent political and organizational abilities and she was a powerful and persuasive speaker—her natal Saturn in Leo was strengthened through its sextile to Venus (endurance, beauty) and trine to Mercury (communication).

---

[168] Argentina declared her independence officially on July 09, 1816.

[169] Juan Perón was born October 08, 1895. On January 22, 1944, transiting Uranus in Gemini activated Perón's natal Moon/Pluto/Neptune conjunction in Gemini, trine his natal Sun and Mars in Libra. (Note that both he and Eva were born with Sun/Mars conjunctions ruled by Venus, as this planet rules both Taurus and Libra.).

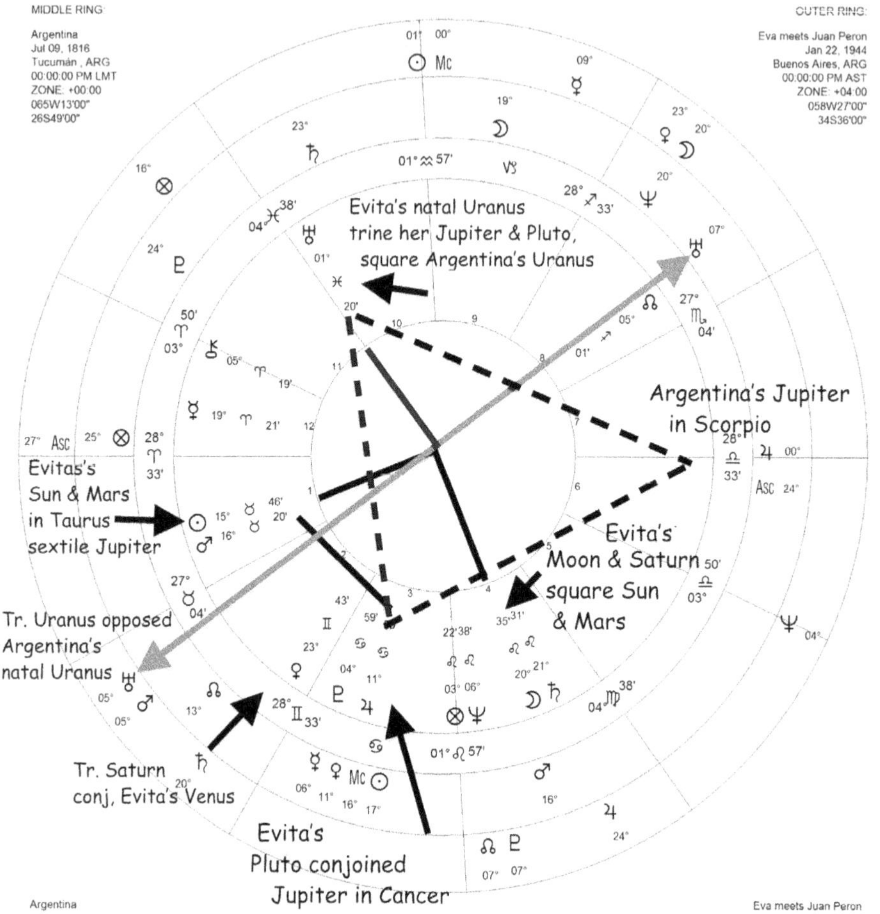
MIDDLE RING:
Argentina
Jul 09, 1816
Tucumán, ARG
00:00:00 PM LMT
ZONE: +00:00
065W13'00"
26S49'00"
OUTER RING:
Eva meets Juan Peron
Jan 22, 1944
Buenos Aires, ARG
00:00:00 PM AST
ZONE: +04:00
058W27'00"
34S36'00"
Evita's natal Uranus
trine her Jupiter & Pluto,
square Argentina's Uranus
Argentina's Jupiter
in Scorpio
Evitas's
Sun & Mars
in Taurus
sextile Jupiter
Evita's
Moon & Saturn
square Sun
& Mars
Tr. Uranus opposed
Argentina's
natal Uranus
Tr. Saturn
conj, Evita's Venus
Evita's
Pluto conjoined
Jupiter in Cancer

Argentina

Pl	Geo Lon	℞	Decl.
☽	19°♑10'		- 24° 58'
☉	17°♋14'		+22° 21'
☿	06°♋33'	℞	+18° 35'
♀	11°♋06'		+23° 25'
♂	16°♌56'		+16° 55'
♃	00°♏28'		- 10° 32'
♄	23°♒04'	℞	- 15° 02'
♅	07°♐54'	℞	- 21° 36'
♆	20°♐02'	℞	- 21° 42'
♇	24°♓08'	℞	- 16° 46'
☊	13°♊44'		+22° 28'
Mc	16°♋07'		+22° 29'
Asc	24°♎02'		- 09° 20'

☽	20°♌35'		+09° 47'
☉	15°♉46'		+16° 34'
☿	19°♈21'		+04° 44'
♀	23°♊43'		+25° 15'
♂	16°♉20'		+16° 41'
♃	11°♋55'		+23° 09'
♄	21°♌31'		+15° 42'
♅	01°♓20'		- 11° 42'
♆	06°♌38'		+18° 33'
♇	04°♋59'		+19° 23'
☊	05°♐01'		- 21° 09'
Mc	01°♒57'		- 19° 44'
Asc	28°♈33'		+10° 58'

INNER CHART:

Eva Peron
May 07, 1919
Buenos Aires, ARG
05:14:00 AM AST
ZONE: +04:00
058W27'00"
34S36'00"

Geocentric
Tropical
Placidus Houses

THE THREE MAGI
p.o. 81 Emigrant, Mt
(406)333-4804

Eva meets Juan Peron

Pl	Geo Lon	℞	Decl.
☽	20°♐48'		- 19° 19'
☉	01°♒31'		- 19° 50'
☿	09°♑07'		- 20° 38'
♀	23°♐22'		- 21° 40'
♂	05°♊48'		+23° 55'
♃	24°♌38'	℞	+14° 17'
♄	20°♊27'	℞	+21° 48'
♅	05°♊01'	℞	+21° 03'
♆	04°♎10'	℞	- 00° 22'
♇	07°♌44'	℞	+23° 44'
☊	07°♌02'		+18° 31'
Mc	00°♒15'		- 20° 06'
Asc	27°♈05'		+10° 26'

Taureans characteristically work hard to better not only their welfare but also that of others. Evita worked around the clock, using her position as First Lady to help the children and youth, single mothers, and the aged—none in need were ignored! While the masses loved her, the oligarchy (the two percent in power) hated her and feared the changes to their luxurious lifestyle that they knew would inevitably result from a more democratic society.

Evita is recognized as a courageous woman whose example and fight for social justice helped win Argentine women the right to vote while paving the way for future generations. Her brand of feminism—natal Venus (women) trine Uranus (revolutionary)—captured the heart of the Latin American woman, for she felt that a woman did best when united with a man worthy of her trust. In her own life, Evita spoke of accessing an inner strength and intuition she felt was particular to women. She saw herself as a bridge, bringing the people closer to their Juan Perón, their leader, and he to them. In her autobiography, *La Razón de mi Vida*, she reasoned that if women had for so long created beautiful homes for their families, why should they not earn the right to, along with men, create a better humanity?

When Evita's death was announced over the radio, the nation braced itself for a period of mourning that lasted for weeks. Evita Perón's short but eventful life had taken on an heroic significance for her people, lighting the way for them and strengthening their resolve to triumph!

THE TAUREAN CHILD

Taurean children are generally willing to listen to others, take cues, and then reflect and build upon that information. Like the calf, they are characteristically gentle, grounded and, for the most part, kind. But the bull can be stubborn indeed! Once the Taurean child digs in his heels, to try to force him to comply is to invite a power struggle. Wise parents and teachers avoid locking horns with the Taurean youngster. The more they push, the more he will resist—somehow knowing that the adult will tire and give sway before he does. His ability to resist, block out, and refuse to move is nothing short of phenomenal! If the parent also happens to be a Taurus, he can provide the child with a good role model by putting into practice Taurean patience and forbearance. Certainly, it is far better to go around the back door and enter through love, helping this child learn how to free himself from such obstinate moments when he feels stuck, rather than confronting him head-on.

Kindness, even when in the form of loving discipline, is the key. When the little bull is ready, usually in a moment or two, his fixed attitude is likely to disappear with a smile, or perhaps with a tear. Now he is receptive to receiving instruction and any necessary correction. Hopefully, as he grows, he'll recognize the signs and will choose to communicate his needs in a more positive manner. The wise parent will guide the Taurean son or daughter to rightfully employ this concentrated energy. Like the proverbial tortoise who won the race, such a persistent child in adult life may not necessarily outrun his opponents, but he is likely to outlast them!

The rulership of Venus inclines the Taurean personality, like the Libran, also ruled by the planet of love and beauty, to want to please others. The child must learn to discern when it's right to help without placating and when it's best to walk away. Perhaps he's attached to his wants and desires and mostly wants to please himself! Does he tend to be a "yes man," agreeing so all are happy, when his intentions are clearly determined to do otherwise? Such dishonesty needs to be gently but firmly discouraged. The Taurean adult who has been spoiled in childhood may be hard-pressed to garner the discipline necessary to fulfill his obligations.

Earth sign children need proper materials and assignments to get to work. The Taurean child is both practical and purposeful. He may start with blocks in the sandbox and later go on to bigger things, but his theme is always, "I build." Taurean children are highly sensorial; they love to explore all the five senses. Trips to the seashore, through the forest, and to other places full of sounds, sights, and wonderful textures, captivate the young Taurean child. Give this child his own vegetable patch and child-sized tools and he is likely to be happily occupied all summer long.

Parents and teachers who take the time to instill a healthy work ethic in the Taurean child, whether through some child-appropriate work, through musical training, or another field of endeavor, will endow him with a gift that will benefit him for life. Stubbornness, as tenacity, persistence and determination, may be the bedrock of the Taurean child's future success, which he develops in childhood through challenging tasks and projects that interest him and that bring out his natural steadfastness!

Born gourmets, Taurean children typically have strong opinions about what they will and will not eat. Above all, the Taurean child seeks comfort and security in material things. If he overeats, he may actually be seeking comfort through his food. He needs good eating habits. Taurean children that are overindulged by their parents can become indolent in the lap of luxury, possibly leading to obesity.

Young Taurean children typically identify with their things, holding on to old slippers and habits way beyond their usefulness. He may not easily share his belongings. They may represent security to him. The Taurean child may try to "possess" his friends. He likes to rule the roost and may want to be the boss around the house. But he is affectionate and more willing to obey, in progressive stages, when he respects his parents and they respect him.

Even baby Taureans will respond readily to a lovely voice, the sound of rippling water, or a soothing lullaby. As he matures, the Taurean youth is likely to develop his natural love for fine and beautiful things in the clothes he or she selects. Unless other aspects in the chart indicate otherwise, little Taureans may not respond well to change when it is unexpected or unannounced. If he becomes rigid and not willing to budge, he may be saying, "I'm scared." Therefore, parents of Taurean children are advised to prepare their child ahead of time for changes in the family agenda.

KAVANNAH

Kavannah is a Hebrew word that can best be understood to mean, "right attitude, intention, or direction of the heart." Without Kavannah, true learning is not possible. In *Transformational Astrology*, attitudes relate primarily to the Fixed-Love Cross (Taurus, Scorpio, Leo, and Aquarius). According to Kabbalistic Astrology, the greatest gift of love from God to man is the gift of Free Will. Made in the image of God, man has the right to determine which way he will go. On the Tree of Life are three pillars: Will on the feminine pillar can manifest as *will-less-ness*: "I don't feel like it; let someone else do the job!" On the masculine pillar, man is sometimes seen to be willful, demanding his own way. But on the middle pillar, he humbly wills to be God-taught.

When he has Kavannah, when will, guided by the heart's wisdom and right intent, is stronger in him than is desire, the Taurean soul is ready to take the next step up into higher consciousness.

BECOMING THE BUDDHA

The Greatest of Taurean Heroes was born in May during the Full Moon, over 500 years before the birth of Jesus Christ.[170]

Born Prince Siddhartha, upon receiving enlightenment, he became known as Gautama the Buddha. While Gautama is recognized as the founder of Buddhism, the title Buddha is used in mystical traditions to refer to any soul who has achieved complete enlightenment.

At Siddhartha's birth, a learned Brahmin revealed to his father, King Suddhodana, that his son would grow up to be either a Universal Monarch or a great Sage who would free the world from ignorance. Determined that his son become the heir to the throne, and not wanting to lose him, the King raised Siddhartha in an idyllic palace environment, taking great precautions to afford the kind prince every luxury and shielding him as much as possible from human pain and misery. King Suddhodana, thus for a time, prevented Siddhartha's innate compassionate nature from being aroused. Nevertheless, upon attaining manhood, the prince left the palace and for the first time witnessed sickness, old age, and death. From that moment on, Siddhartha found no peace in the pleasures of palace life. In *Foundations of Buddhism*, Helena Roerich writes, "His heart continued to respond to each human sorrow and his mind, perceiving the transitoriness of all that existed, knew no rest. He roamed through the worlds of his palace like a lion stung by

---

[170] Siddhartha Gautama is thought to have been born in 583 BCE in or near what is now known as Nepal.

some poisoned dart, and in pain he groaned, 'The world is full of darkness and ignorance; there is no one who knows how to cure the ills of existence!'"

For the Taurean who seeks to know what to do and how to find his dharma, his divine calling, it is good to begin as Siddhartha did—with a question. When the question is answered, another likely will appear. This way, confusion is replaced by a moving meditation, inner turmoil quieted by the peaceful assurance that the answer, in time, will appear. Siddhartha's question was, "Why is there suffering in the world?" At age 29, the time of his first Saturn Return, Siddhartha abandoned the palace, leaving behind him the joys of family and youth.[171]

He did not lightly go against the wishes and counsel of his father the King, nor was he indifferent to the fears of Yashodhara, his beautiful wife, who had dreamt of his imminent departure. The story relates that a celestial messenger, a higher authority than the King, appeared to Siddhartha confirming his inner knowing that the time for him to leave and seek the truth had arrived.

In the story of Siddhartha's quest, he let go not once, but over and over again. And so it is in the life of the Aspirant born in Taurus. According to his evolution, his particular temperament, and his zeal, he will continually practice, as did Prince Siddhartha, letting go of one thing or state of being to make room for higher possibilities.

Letting go can be difficult for the Taurean Aspirant, especially during the earlier phases of his path as he is called to relinquish this habit or that worldly possession—whatever the weight may be that is no longer lawful for him to carry. Inevitably, he must surrender his resistance to carrying out divine purpose. Note that giving up one's way for God's way may (or may *not*) mean letting go of a relationship, or job, or a practiced discipline or lifestyle (such as asceticism). In time, the Taurean seeker of truth comes to realize that nothing he once had that seemed so valuable does he now want. In the process of becoming increasingly non-attached, his very soul comes more into alignment with his true identity and purpose.

The young prince adopted the life of an ascetic, stripping himself of his princely attire, cutting his hair and eating barely enough to stay alive. Even so, the Taurean seeker of truth must determine to get out of the grip of harmful habits and to sever the magnetic pull of old momentums. Let him recall that the way to say "no!" to one desire is to replace it with another, higher one. This takes courage, faith and tenacity. To refuse to meet the challenge is to become a prisoner of the thing or person that one fears to lose. The key, of course, is that one can only be detached to the degree that he feels attached to God, to the degree that he trusts that God will provide, and indeed already has, for all of his needs.

---

[171] The Saturn Return occurs when transiting Saturn returns to the exact position it had at birth, a cycle taking anywhere from twenty-eight-and-a-half to thirty years.

After six years of self-denial, Siddhartha realized that he was no more illumined than when he lived in the palace. He realized it was time to abandon this approach and find a better one. Taureans are like that, although they do not necessarily begin that way. Sometimes they get stuck in some habit, state of self-imposed limitation, or attachment fueled by fear. But the relatively integrated Taurean tries one approach to a problem and if it doesn't work, he's apt to discard it and try another. Taureans, after all, are Earth sign people, who naturally look for what works!

Siddhartha ended the period of asceticism and left the forest. He received nourishment at the hands of the Gopi girls (young, unmarried, cow herd girls) and sought what came to be known as the Middle Way, a practical application of spiritual truth captured in the popular saying, "To be in the world but not of the world." The Taurean person often tends toward extremes; nevertheless, experience will teach him, as it did Siddhartha, that the best way is the middle way!

Multiple temptations of Mara (the Evil One) and his army failed to prevent *Siddhartha* from attaining Enlightenment under the Boddhi Tree.

Siddhartha then sat in meditation beneath the Bodhi Tree. He determined to remain so seated until he received illumination. Despite the multiple temptations of the demon, *Mara,* he declared, *Vajra!* His hand touched the ground in what Buddhists call the Earth-touching mudra, which action translates to declaring, "I have a right to be doing what I am doing!"

The Taurean Aspirant must recognize and affirm his inner worthiness. In so doing, he would do well to prepare to face, as did Siddhartha, the temptations of Maya (illusion), the terrors of the night, his own subconscious fears and trepidations, the challenges of inclement weather, the lure of loved ones or sirens wooing him away from his calling, and the demons that would frighten him from his resolve. In such moments, he will feel strengthened by calling upon the spirit of Gautama Buddha, claiming his space, and proclaiming with resolute trust in divine purpose, *Vajra!*

Many souls born with the Sun in Taurus are endowed with a Buddhic-like nature whether they know it or not! Being naturally contemplative, they ponder and meditate before acting. However, the Buddha pictured sitting so quietly under the Bodhi Tree is not idle, but in intense, active meditation upon the inner fire. But who today can take off a month or two for a personal vision quest? Those who must be up and doing must practice meditation in motion: pose your question, keep your mind upon the light within your heart, see the Buddha sitting in a lotus upon the crown chakra and, as you go about your day, listen!

After meditating beneath the Bodhi Tree for forty days and forty nights, Siddhartha became enlightened. He understood the cause of suffering to be attachment to desire. Now Gautama the Buddha, he spent the rest of his life teaching so that others might become awakened. His wife, Yashodhara, and his foster mother (his maternal aunt, Mahapajapati Gotami), became his first female disciples.[172]

THE WAY

Compassion is said to be the gateway to the Buddhic nature. Indeed, compassion is the keynote of the New Age. He that would be Hero in Taurus at the dawn of the Aquarian Age must also rise to the position of Teacher, as did Gautama of old. He must, in essence, become a master of love, defying and overcoming within himself the very temptation that beset Adam and Eve, the twin flames of Eden. The density of the typical, untransmuted Taurean consciousness simply will not make it through the Aquarian Gate!

Love provides the motivational force driving the will. The force of intense emotion and passion becomes even stronger for the Taurean once on the path. The Taurean seeker must purify the Third-Eye chakra. He must keep his eye steadfastly focused on his goal, that his attention not strays from meditation upon the inner light. Through self-discipline and the intensification of the fire of love within his soul, the mother light rises and the Third-Eye chakra spins, transmuting

---

[172] Gautama was Siddhartha's family name; Buddha means *awakened one*.

the negative substance of lifetimes. The Taurean Aspirant's sight becomes clearer. He begins to gradually come into alignment with his divine calling.

One native of this sign, who since his early youth sought the spiritual path, would often feel an inclination to leave all and go to some faraway place. He hearkened to and acted upon what he felt was an inner prompting, but when he got there he realized he was mistaken. In addition to clearing his inner sight and hearing, the Taurean Aspirant must acquire the gift of discernment—the ability to tell one voice from another. Life will teach him, in response to his call, to recognize the attitudes that block his inner understanding. He will have to be patient; while some are awakened by lightning-bolt shocks, the path of the Taurean, more often than not, is more gradual.

As he progresses, the testing of the Aspirant becomes more and more subtle. Experience will teach him, but he must be able to rightly interpret the happenings in his life. As his perspective shifts, so will his outlook. Seeing what he did not see before—realizing how others have suffered as a result of his selfishness and non-caring—is painful. Grasping loss when the clock cannot be turned back, regretting bitterly his past actions, he must summon the courage to embrace his pain, practice forgiveness, and move on. He must resist the temptation to take the easy way out. Rather, he must hold on with all of his might, somehow sensing when to build, stone-by-stone, with diligence and persistence, and when to let go and walk away, even from what he has spent much time creating. Taureans must beware of temptation at the dividing of the way, where many have taken the left-handed path to use occult powers for their own aggrandizement. He must concentrate his mind on the Inner Light, as did Gautama, for truly there is a time when to leave (the palace) would be to lose all, but also when to stay would be to miss the opportunity of a lifetime.

The Buddhists speak of a state called mindfulness, observing oneself as an actor in one's own play. The seeker, when mindful, is not emotionally detached, but rather aware and watchful, and therefore, more cognizant of his choices. The Taurean Aspirant would do well to adopt mindfulness. Knowing the map of astrology also helps foresee the coming tides. As long as he remains mindful of where he is headed, he need not be discouraged by apparent setbacks.

Taureans who aspire to be free need not be Buddhists to grasp **Gautama's Noble Eightfold Path**, also known as the path of the Middle Way, the means to enlightenment and the antidote to inordinate desire, the cause of all suffering. As you read the eight "right" ways, below, remember *Kavannah,* or right attitude—right action depends upon the intention and direction of the balanced heart:

1) <u>Right View/True Understanding</u>. Recognizing the transitory nature of life, understanding *dukkha* or suffering as a part of life.

2) <u>Right Aspiration</u>. Striving for what is lawful and beneficial, not

only to oneself, but also for others as well.

3) <u>Right Speech</u>. Avoiding gossip, vulgarity, lying and all other forms of harmful or abusive speech. As wrote the ancient Psalmist, "Let the words of my mouth, and the meditation of my heart, be acceptable in thy sight, O [LORD], my strength, and my redeemer."[173]

4) <u>Right Action/Conduct</u>. Avoiding violent behavior; assuring one's works are motivated by selfless compassion.

5) <u>Right Livelihood</u>. Shunning work that requires slaughter, such as that of a Butcher; choosing and fulfilling a sacred labor (dharma) that uplifts others.

6) <u>Right Mental Attitude and Effort</u>. Avoiding negative thoughts and selfish actions; aiming always for the highest good.

7) <u>Right Mindfulness</u>. Maintaining pure thoughts that the mind of man becomes a chalice for higher intelligence.

8) <u>Right Concentration</u>. Practicing meditation, which opens access to the Third-Eye chakra and leads to the highest degree of enlightened understanding.

The Taurean Hero at the dawn of the Aquarian Age is a servant of love. He embodies the spirit of true Compassion. His mind freed from delusions, he is one with Universal Truth and hence enjoys true peace and happiness. Having experienced spiritual awakening, he goes forth, as Gautama did, to guide those still seeking the way that leads to freedom from suffering.

---

[173] Psalms 19:14

11. ♍ Virgo

Symbol	***The Maiden***
Born	Aug. 23 ~ Sept. 22
Archetype	*The Teacher*
Key Phrase	*I Serve*
Element	**Earth**
Cross	**Mutable-Wisdom**
House	**Sixth:**

Health & healing, employees, co-workers & servants, diet & habits, pets, fashion

Ruler	**Mercury**
Esoteric Ruler	**Moon**
Polarity	**Pisces**
Chakra	Solar Plexus
Anatomy	Intestines, spleen, digestion, autonomic nervous system

Spiritual Qualities ... **Purity, forgiveness, excellence in work & service, justice, constancy, attention to detail, balancing of karmic debts**

Vulnerable to ...... *Anxiety & fear, emotional agitation & frustration, criticism, sense of injustice, workaholic, over-attention to detail*

Must Acquire .....**Patience & forbearance, serenity, positivity & faith, joy in service, the larger picture**

Mother Teresa • Colin Firth • Maria Montessori • Sophia Loren • Itzhak Perlman

THE SUN IN VIRGO

Work is only a means to put love into action.

—Mother Teresa (August 26, 1910)

TERRA, THE MOTHER IN THE EARTH

The M-symbol in Virgo's glyph represents the energy of God as Mother. Also called Terra, the Mother (*mater* in Latin) in the Earth element teaches her children abiding in the material universe the "how-to" of the Father (*pater*), Spirit. And so, the Virgo Hero at the dawn of the Aquarian Age comes as the bearer of the Mother's wisdom, applied practically, as in education, in diet and healing, in science, agriculture and technology, in literature, music and the arts, in fashion and beauty, and in many other fields, as well as in the rhythm and demands of everyday life. We see in the Virgo Hero (of both sexes) the Mother's love of excellence, the meticulous quality of her care, her diligence down to the last detail, her remarkable patience and perceptive understanding and her prudence and mastery in managing money and whatever resources are at hand. Like the Mother, the Virgo Hero draws from unseen founts of energy. Seemingly tireless, he works until the job is done and the victory won—often in spite of overwhelming odds and obstacles. And because Aquarius is the Age of the return to mankind of the Mother, the feminine ray, the possibilities abounding for souls born in Virgo are greater than ever before in recorded history!

THE MAIDEN—PURITY, JUSTICE & THE HARVEST

The only Sign whose symbol is that of a woman, Virgo has received many titles over the millennia, all aspects of the Divine Mother's purity and love. Sometimes called "The Maiden," the name of the many-starred constellation associated with Virgo in Hebrew is *Bethulah*, meaning "a virgin," in Arabic, *Adarah*, the pure virgin, and in Greek, *Parthenos*, "the maid of virgin pureness," a reference to the goddess, Pallas Athena.

The Greeks associated Astrea, daughter of Jupiter and Themis, the Goddess of Justice, as one of Virgo's 110 stars. Legend tells us that Astrea ruled mankind when beings of such great attainment as to be called gods lived among men on Earth. As so often happens, the teacher and the Teachings were rejected by great numbers of embodied souls, forcing Astrea (the representative of the Divine Mother) to withdraw to the Heaven world. Legend states that she was the last to walk among men before joining her fellows in the stars, her uplifted scales of justice stretching to the next constellation, Libra.

The ancient Egyptians saw Virgo as Isis, "the enthroned Queen," the wife of Osiris, and called her *Apollia* meaning "ears of corn" and "the seed." The Romans associated Virgo with *Justa*, again the Goddess of Justice. The historian, Professor E. Raymond Capt, notes in his book, *The Glory of the Stars*, that Virgo in a prophetic sense represented, "the Virgin, the Daughter of Zion," which is a reference to the nation of Israel, comprised of all the 12 Tribes.[174]

The website, LiveKabbalah.org teaches that the root of the word בתולה (Betula, or Virgo) is בתואל (Betuel) meaning the daughter (בתו) the House (ביתו) of God (El אל).

The Virgo virgin symbolizes light's pure estate before it has been adulterated in its descent into lower or denser levels of manifestation. Virgo men and women express the purity of the feminine ray in that they tend to be sensible and industrious, discerning and thoughtful, particular in tastes and preferences, refreshingly reliable and naturally modest. Both Virgo men and women endear themselves to others through their thoughtful, gentle nature. Insistent upon cleanliness and order, their thorough approach is apparent in every aspect of their lives.

Nonetheless, Virgos, when out of balance, whether for a moment or for years, may behave strangely opposite to their true nature. They may be fussy and nitpicking, anxious and impatient, slovenly and promiscuous, incensed with a sense of injustice, emotionally explosive, idle, unreliable or ceaselessly critical; they skew their innate intelligence to justify their aberrations. Of course, as much as any Sign represents virtue, it can also represent vice, each one according to its nature. In almost every instance, an outer aberration points to an inner wound.

PERFECTING THE IMPERFECTABLE

Perfection implies finishing, and nothing is ever finished in time and space, but is rather constantly evolving. A perfect moment becomes a bead in a sequence of moments, but never a finality in and of itself! However, because they naturally perceive the order inherent in all creation, Virgos are perfectionists by nature. Regardless of whether their attention is upon mundane activities, such as formulating the family budget, or upon more transcendental work, like composing magnificent arias or analyzing star systems, the Virgo Sun person is ever busy perfecting the imperfectable.

Virgos hold very definite ideas about the way things need to be. They intuitively sense what's wrong. In their work and in their interactions with others, they insist upon precision, accuracy, and fidelity to original purpose and design.

Famed conductor and composer, Leonard Bernstein (August 25th, 1918), conveyed the Virgo striving to mirror divine order when he said:

---

[174] Isaiah 27:2

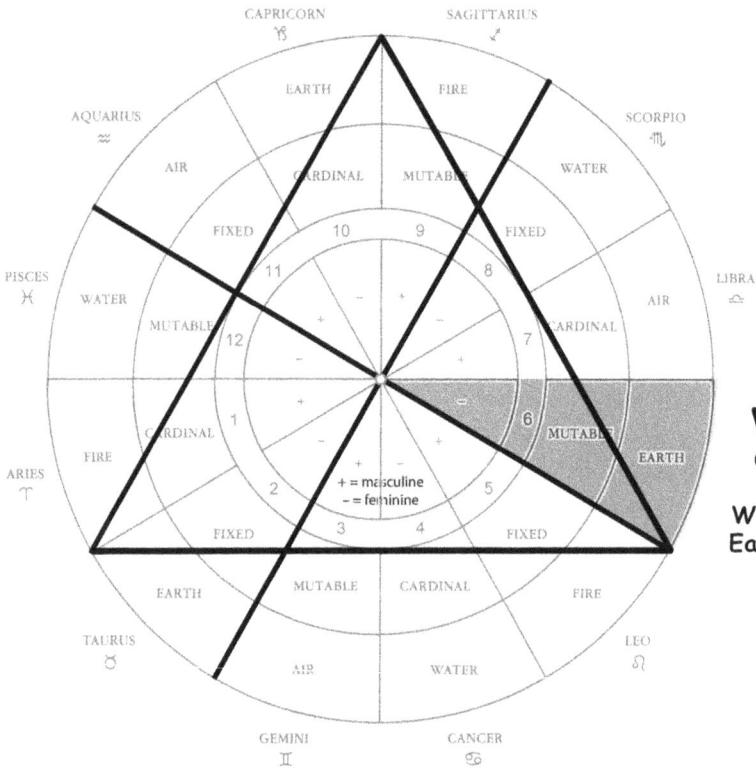

Virgo:
6th House
Mutable-
Wisdom Cross
Earth Element

The key to the mystery of a great artist is that, for reasons unknown, he will give away his energies and his life just to make sure that one note follows another and leaves us with the feeling that something is right in the world.

This Virgoan discriminating faculty works wonders in editing, refining, fixing, dissecting, prescribing, cleaning, and in so many activities devoted to improving things and/or finding and correcting error. Virgos characteristically engage in occupations requiring a discerning intelligence capable of handling much detail and diversity, e.g., medical and pharmaceutical positions, teaching, writing and research, web design and computer repair, engineering, mechanics, and the like. They are the tweakers—always perfecting, refining, and adding the final touches to a given work. Especially equipped in analyzing and assessing the feasibility of any given endeavor, they are valuable assets to almost any team—nothing escapes their attention. Certainly, attention to detail is an attribute of the Divine Mother. Nonetheless, Virgos do need to guard against micro-managing!

As Virgo is the second of the *Earth Triplicity* (Taurus, Virgo and Capricorn), it may be said that right behavior and their accompanying mindsets delineated in Taurus get very particular in Virgo, every potential action having its requirements. Virgo days are typically framed by rules, rituals, itemized agendas, lists, and other such tools designed to create order and manage time efficiently. Exacting as they may be, Virgos are not actually rigid. They seek, albeit subconsciously, remembrances of the divine matrix in all things. The Virgo soul reasons that it is far better to observe and to take a daily inventory of one's habits than to be bound by them. To keep the way is to have peace; to ignore the steps along the way is to be lost in a labyrinth of error.

NEVER MIND—THINKING WITH THE HEART

These perceptive souls tend to be critical of others and critical of themselves, a fault they do not easily see nor accept as such, since they feel justified in pointing out where someone else falls short and how they can do things better—for their own good, of course! The Virgo native may have the best of intentions—his advice may be timely and his observations insightful—yet few people welcome unasked-for advice, much less having their flaws pointed out! One accomplished, generous and intelligent Virgo husband almost lost the love of his beautiful young wife due to his constant pruning of her person. Bottom line? Criticism wrecks popularity and kills romance. As Jesus taught so long ago, *And why beholdest thou the mote that is in thy brother's eye, but considerest not the beam that is in thine own eye?*[175]

[175] Matthew 7:3

Even so, Virgos can be hardest on themselves. Excessive self-criticism can stop a Virgo person right in his tracks. In his mind, he is simply never good enough!

Constant correction, then, can put a damper on almost any close relationship, except by mutual agreement, as in that of a guru and disciple, a mentor and trainee. A Virgo piano and voice teacher pointed out every minor note missed, every breath held too long, the position of the chin, the placement of the tongue, the attention of the mind, any tension in the shoulders, and so on and so forth. Not all of this master musician's students stayed with her, but those who did loved her and welcomed her miniscule refining of their performance. Indeed, some among them reached great heights. Although the action be the same, clearly there is a difference between the nagging Virgo who confuses the journey of another soul with his own, and the detailed observations of a master teacher engaged to awaken and develop potential within the student—perhaps it is the underlying loving intent, or the lack thereof, that makes the difference.

It takes much experience and quite some mastery for the Virgo native to see what is out of place, and yet not be unduly affected by it, to discern when to intervene and when to best let be. In advising Virgos to be less critical and more loving, Astrologer Isabel Hickey explains, "Venus, the love principle, is unhappy in an area where the lower mind operates. We relate to others through the heart, never through the head." We recognize this fact subconsciously, Hickey adds, when we say "Never mind."[176]

A TIME TO REAP[177]

Illustrations of the Virgo Maiden are most commonly depicted with a sheaf of wheat in her left hand and a sprig of corn behind her right ear. The corn and the wheat are symbols of the autumn harvest, the time for reaping the fruit sown in Taurus (first Earth sign) in springtime. And so, we understand the harvest as a kind of karmic accounting in Virgo—the separating of the chaff from the wheat, the good deeds, habits and mindsets from the injurious ones—preceding Libra's evaluation of the evidence, Scorpio's exposure of that which has been hidden, the deliberation of the courts in Sagittarius and the judgment handed down in Capricorn at the end of the year.

Indeed, karma tends to return with tremendous intensity and rapidity during Virgo cycles. Souls born in purity's sign wrestle with intense karmic records

---

[176] From *Astrology, A Cosmic Science,* by Isabel M. Hickey, 1981 (originally published in 1970)
[177] "A time to be born, and a time to die; a time to plant, and a time to pluck up that which is planted." Ecclesiastes 3:2

and experience the pain of deep-seated emotions as well as the anguish of unfulfilled desires. At the same time, they are blessed by the harvest of talents developed over many lifetimes. Of course, any individual, regardless of birth sign, incarnates for the purpose of balancing karma. However, Virgo and its polar opposite Pisces represent the soul's opportunity to understand and account for the consequences of past actions more than any other polarity in the Zodiac. Natives born into these two signs typically experience not only the weight of their own karmic burden, but also that of the planet's as a whole.

The karmic return of the rejection of the Divine Mother, an ancient story buried so deeply within the collective unconscious as to be forgotten, increases as the Aquarian Age advances. We see the absence of reverence for the feminine ray in the misuse of sexual energies (esoterically referred to as the sacred fire), in the refusal to forgive, in the wide-scale ignorance of the Mother's wisdom, and the scoffing at her disciplines, even in the misapplication of technological devices and advances, all of which are truly gifts of the Mother. It is indeed a travesty when the Mother's gifts are used in a way that is devoid of love and misapplied to mechanize rather than to enhance life, or in the selfish negligence of children, even babes aborning in the womb.

TESHUVA—REPENTANCE

The law of the return of karma is inexorable and impersonal. Nevertheless, the Earth Mother also represents Mercy in the form of Opportunity. The emphasis in Virgo need not be on the wrongness of mankind's error and consequent fall from the realms of perfect harmony, but rather on the soul's opportunity in time and space to reclaim what has been lost.

The Kabbalists associate Virgo with the month *Elul*, a period of *Teshuva*, or repentance, in preparation for the holy days of Yom Kippur, a time of purification and atonement. Looking more deeply into the meaning of the days associated with Virgo, *Live Kabbalah* notes:

> *The days of Elul are known as days of Teshuva (repentance), from the word LaShuv (לשוב to return (returning to ourselves, our truth, our real inner connection). Rabbi Nachman from Breslov says that the Hebrew word, Tikun (תיקון correction) has the same letters of Tinok (תינוק a baby). Meaning that a person, who corrects himself by removing separation and disconnection from his soul, returns to his initial state, like when he was a baby, sort of restarting all systems, and this is the purpose of these forty days—losing our suffering, pain and distorted self and returning to our real selves. This is the purpose of creation and the secret of the journey of the Month of Elul.*

To redeem also means *to buy out*, hence the concept that Jesus the Christ, who is associated with Pisces and the Piscean Age, paid the price (he took upon himself the karma of the world) *to buy mankind the opportunity* to be made whole. To be redeemed, then, is to be purified, unshackled and freed of burden.[178] Virgo brings the manual, a step-by-step mapping out of the way.

MIND OVER MATTER, SPIRIT OVER MIND

Mercury, the planet representing the thinking process, the Word, and all manner of communication, rules Virgo. Mercury also rules Gemini, another Sign on the Mutable-Wisdom Cross. The difference between Virgo and Gemini is that Virgo is an Earth sign, whereas Gemini is an Air sign. Natives of both signs are busy sharing and disseminating knowledge. But Geminis characteristically enjoy learning for learning's sake, while learning without a practical purpose is meaningless for most Virgos.

An astrological adage states that a Virgo can, "make a purse out of a sow's ear." Inquisitive, observant, efficient and resourceful, they are forever searching for ways to get the job done, fix the problem, repair the rent in the garment, show or teach another how to do whatever better! Virgos learn quickly. Their ability to retain information is impressive—like the Virgo waitress who remembers six people's different orders with all their particulars, often without needing to write it all down. But Virgos are also prone to being highly impressionable, picking up others' thoughts, and even picking up thoughts hanging in the atmosphere and confusing them as their own.

Virgos are not easily stymied by challenging situations. Relying on deductive reasoning and logic, they are expert at analyzing the problem and determining what steps must be taken to remedy almost any situation. However, they inevitably find themselves, at some time or another, thrust into circumstances that will not yield to even their best analysis. While such times may evoke feelings of frustration, fear and anger, the experience most often helps them get out of their lower minds, forcing them to take a leap of faith. Even as idealistic Pisceans benefit by employing Virgo's practical reasoning to test the waters of their dreams, Virgos sometimes are challenged to think less and believe more—a mindset more characteristic of their Piscean complement!

Noting that people born under Virgo's influence are forever using their minds to better control matter, Astrologers Sakoian and Acker write, "Virgos have to learn that although the body must serve the mind, ultimately the mind must serve the spirit."[179]

---

[178] Psalms 130:7-8; Luke 2:38; Acts 20:28; Galatians 3:13 and 4:5
[179] *The Astrologer's Handbook,* by Frances Sakoian and Louis S. Acker

THE INDEFATIGABLE WORKER

Leonard Bernstein offers the following formula for success, showing that Virgos work well under duress: "To achieve great things, two things are needed: a plan, and not quite enough time."

Above all else, the inner destiny of the soul in Virgo is to serve. Virgo rules employment, employees, and co-workers. His very soul, the expression on his face, the receptive and loving nature of his spirit, and his kind words communicate, "I am here to help you." Conscientious and dedicated workers, many Virgos will work after hours if need be and go the extra mile without being asked to do so.

Natives of this sign typically feel devastated when their efforts are rejected. Whether the cause be traced to events in this or in other lifetimes, circumstances conspire to help these souls overcome their fear of rejection by finding inner peace. Many among them are gentle souls and their anger is not always apparent. A Virgo who is apparently apathetic, unemployed, or who chooses to employ himself in dubious services may have accepted at some level that his services are neither wanted nor good enough.

Leonard Bernstein was asked to make his conducting debut with the New York Philharmonic Orchestra on November 14, 1943, as a last minute substitute for German-born Bruno Walter. The performance was broadcast throughout the nation. The following day, *The New York Times* gave Bernstein front-page coverage, celebrating him as the first American to conduct the Philharmonic. He was 25 years old.

IF AT FIRST YOU DON'T SUCCEED...

Virgo rules the intestines and the digestion. Virgos typically are prone to a host of digestive disorders—the cause: anxiety. The means to end such suffering is to stop worrying and relax! If only it were so easy! Actually, it is.

On the required reading list for Virgos is, *Don't Sweat the Small Stuff and It's All Small Stuff!* by American psychologist, Dr. Richard Carlson. Essentially adapting a Buddhist teaching to make sense to the Western mind, Dr. Carlson shows that it is not so much what happens to us, but rather how we react that determines our peace of mind. Dale Carnegie, one of the first and best of the self-improvement authors, offers this simple but effective formula to avoid falling into excessive preoccupation: "Be content to do the best you can!"

The Virgo person who gets caught up in pursuing perfection can be mercilessly exacting of others and even more so of himself. While he enjoys fixing and repairing, researching and understanding, he characteristically entertains a subconscious sense of, "If I don't succeed, I am worthless; if I make a mistake, I will be rejected." Moreover, each time he fixes one problem, obtains a long sought-after object or completes a given project, another one appears. If he comes to perceive life in general as a series of challenges that sharpen his will, he often proves to be the best of problem solvers. But he needs to beware not to create a habit of continual dissatisfaction and frustration. Clearly, with such a mindset, he can never win because something is always wrong.

Once the Virgo Sun person allows negative thoughts to fill his mind and psyche, they tend to revolve over and over again with nagging persistence. Such constant inner scolding can be tortuous to the soul; the inner noise itself can be exhausting. For some Virgos, a tendency to focus on what's wrong gets out of proportion; no unwanted freckle escapes their razor-sharp eye. The Virgo child benefits by learning from an early age that he can choose whether to see the cup as half full instead of half empty!

The Virgo soul finds peace of mind when he discovers the joy of the journey, the great lessons learned from mistakes and even from failure. Even as Virgos delight in a job well done, they may come to celebrate the opportunity to try and try again! Virgos will naturally discard one way of doing things if it doesn't work and pick up another—whatever it takes to get the job done! Persistence and patience pay off in the end. Nonetheless, Virgos are challenged to discern when to let go of a project—or even a relationship—and move on.

"TRUST YOUR ABILITY!"[180]

When the famed Israeli violinist and conductor, Itzhak Perlman (August 31, 1945), was but three years old, he told his parents that he wanted to learn the violin. He was turned down from Tel Aviv's Shulamit Conservatory on the grounds that he was simply too small to hold the violin. Showing his trademark spirit, "it is the artist's task to find our how much music he can still make with what he has left," even then, little Itzhak taught himself to play on a toy fiddle. Hardly a year later he contracted polio that left both of his legs paralyzed. Many thought the future for this talented child had been tragically derailed; nevertheless,

---

[180] Itzhak Perlman quote

he persevered. At age 10, Itzhak did enter Shulamit where he successfully gave his first recital. At 13, he transferred to the Juilliard School of Music in New York City on scholarship. He made his debut at Carnegie Hall in 1963, and won the prestigious Leventritt Memorial Competition prize in 1964, which effectively launched his brilliant professional career at 19 years of age. Considered to be the pre-eminent classical violinist of his time, Itzhak Perlman has played on virtually every major stage around the world.

When the going gets tough, the Sun in Virgo person can easily slip into the negativity of complaint and depression. Or, like Perlman, he can choose to smile at the wonder of it all, meet adversity with optimism and faith, thereby discovering resources within that were previously unknown.

Was Perlman's polio meant to be an inescapable karmic return? Perhaps. But then again, like the blind man that Jesus healed, the condition might be there to teach the world a lesson, to make this Earth a better place, and to increase the soul's grit and determination. We cannot know—in the last analysis, it doesn't matter. We are stirred and inspired by those among us who go far beyond ordinary expectations. We pay even closer attention when such individuals reach great heights despite severe handicaps. Their choice to be positive and to persevere, despite their limitations, encourages us to embrace our destiny and outstrip our fate as decreed in the stars.

FOUNTAIN OF YOUTH

Most Virgos pay detailed attention to their appearance. Fields such as aesthetics, fashion and cosmetology naturally appeal to them. But some among them are forever primping, teasing their hair, changing their outfits and, when they can afford it, submitting to plastic surgery to alter their features and skin color. Good is just never good enough!

Virgo actress Sophia Loren's elegance and beauty did not fade with age. (She was born on September 20, 1934.) So, what is this captivating Italian star's secret? "Beauty is how you feel inside," she insisted, "and it reflects in your eyes. It is not something physical." She also stated, "There is a fountain of youth: it is your mind, your talents, the creativity you bring to your life and to the lives of people you love. When you learn to tap into this source, you will truly have defeated age."

THE TEACHERS

Motivated to teach and to be taught, Virgos often make excellent teachers, whether by trade or simply by nature. Pulling from a variety of sources, they excel at breaking down a subject into its component parts and skillfully presenting it in an interesting, accurate and digestible format. Like the Earth Mother, the

Virgo teacher diligently creates and maintains order and patiently repeats the necessary instruction while searching for and finding interesting ways to present lessons and to impart greater understanding.

Maria Montessori (August 31, 1870) initially attracted major attention to her teaching methods when a group of poor tenement waifs, left to run wild with little or no adult supervision, came under her guidance in Rome's slums. Observing the children to discover, "the laws of their being," Montessori then created an environment in which their natural abilities could blossom. In her first school, which she called, *La Casa dei Bambini* (The Children's House), these previously neglected children with little hope of a future came into order and productivity; their skills and levels of concentration surpassed those of children their age from privileged backgrounds.

Montessori taught that each child has inner genius. The teacher's role, she insisted, was to act as the servant of the child's inner guide, to observe him and provide him with the materials he needs to engage in his work: the creation of the man he will one day become. A devout Catholic, Montessori taught the necessity of attuning to the child's soul. Some believe she captured the spirit by which Elizabeth, the mother of John the Baptist, and Mary, the mother of Jesus, educated their children. Montessori wrote, "Criticism kills the spirit." She made hands-on materials, such as the lesson of placing different-sized cylinders in holes on a wooden block, so that the child could discover for himself what works and what doesn't. The emphasis on detail, order, craftsmanship, hands-on work and the love of learning are at the heart of every Montessori classroom—all Virgo concepts arising from the wisdom of the Mother's heart. Montessori wrote:

> *In the Montessori environment, the materials are designed to be self-correcting, for the purpose of fostering self-confidence and the love of learning.*

The Mother in Virgo quietly observes each of her children. She recognizes within them seeds of potential, even when they have not yet awakened unto their own divine destiny. Patiently and wisely, deftly and with an eye for detail, she helps them strengthen their strong points and work out their weaknesses. She provides them with the tools they need and trains them in their use, for she knows one day they must leave the nest and be on their own.

Madame *Elisabeth Caspari*, a veritable disciple of Maria Montessori with whom she spent five years in India, was another Virgo educator relentless in her determination to help the world's children. Born September 5, 1899, Dr. Cas-

---

[181] "The wolf also shall dwell with the lamb, and the leopard shall lie down with the kid; and the calf and the young lion and the fatling together; and a little child shall lead them." Isaiah 11:6.

pari lived to be 104 years of age, having taught thousands of children and trained scores of teachers in communities across the globe. "Mother Caspari" was determined that Montessori's legacy would not be lost by those who learned her methods but failed to capture her message. When asked about her take on education in the Aquarian Age, she loved to quote the Bible verse, "A little child shall lead them."[181]

The child represents the soul whom the Mother has come to arouse, for the hour indeed has come to regain that which for eons has been lost.

THE VIRGO CHILD

For the little Virgo, good is hardly good enough if it's not perfect! Miguel was a 5-year-old Virgo child in a Montessori classroom. One typical day, the teacher rang the bell signifying it was time for recess. All the children ran outside to play—except Miguel. He remained, very intent upon finishing his drawing of a little house surrounded by a lovely green lawn. Miguel drew the house and a little white gate and then very carefully drew every single neatly defined blade of grass. It took the child all recess to finish. He hardly looked up. But when he did, his face was beaming.

Inquisitive by nature, Virgo children like to observe natural phenomena to discover the laws behind the manifestation. They often enjoy activities and hobbies in which they must label, paste, organize and categorize. Many children of this sign are manually dexterous or show early signs of mechanical ability or artistic skills. Many are musically talented. Virgo children typically enjoy working with crafts and cloth. Even toddler Virgos delight in handling mechanical gadgets, anything that can be taken apart and put back together. Geometrical pieces that form beautiful, intricate designs capture their interest.

Young Virgos tend to worry about the welfare of others. They respond to feeling needed. Likewise, they like taking care of things—salvaging, fixing and restoring. The Virgo child is happy when helping out; he often proves to be a real asset to his family when provided with child-sized tools that get real jobs done. As they grow, these mercurial children characteristically come up with better and more efficient ways of running the household—and everything else!

Some Virgo children are shy, often sweetly so. This child benefits when given role models inspiring him to look for the good within himself, in his work, and in others. Likewise, patient and loving caregivers do well to help the child by discouraging any tendency toward pickiness, faultfinding and complaining. Sometimes children with the Sun in Virgo can be so anxious about perceived imperfection that they decide not to try at all. Perhaps the child's perception of the expectations of one or both of his parents (represented by the Sun and Moon) awakens anxiety within him, causing him to feel frightened or ashamed. By applying himself to projects whose level of challenge is age-appropriate in a loving home and school environment that encourages joyous exploration, he sees the reward of his efforts and learns, over time, that "Rome was not built in a day"!

Virgo youth often show particular interest in the healing arts—placing a Band-Aid on a younger child's finger, peering under a microscope, concocting special herbal teas and remedies, studying anatomy and physiology. Many are naturals at science and math. Born with an affinity for reading and for learning, the Virgo child is typically at home in the classroom, especially when the material is challenging and the learning environment orderly and beautiful. Born with an innate desire to nurture and instruct others, these children usually enjoy caring for pets and younger siblings. They have a way with details, but they may lose sight of the forest for the trees. Parents may need to remind their Virgo son or daughter that, "there is a place for everything and for everything a place," lest his room become a maze of pigeonholes, books, and paraphernalia.

Virgo energy is earthy and so little Virgos are acutely aware of their bodies. Baby Virgos can be quite uncomfortable if left wet or unattended. The Virgo soul needs to be discriminating and discerning—he is the thresher destined to separate the chaff from the wheat. In this regard, toilet training is an especially vital phase for Virgo toddlers, as they learn how their bodies discriminate between what they need and what they don't need; this phase should not be forced or made unpleasant. The Virgo teenager's scrutinizing examination of every detail out of place about his person can be quite merciless. Adolescence is a key time for Virgo souls to practice seeing the good in themselves, as well as in others. Being disciplined in a work they love focuses their attention in a constructive, outward direction and helps them acquire skills and expertise as they prepare for their next step in life.

WAS MR. DARCY A VIRGO?

Was Jane Austen's Mr. Darcy a Virgo? It would seem so from lead actor Colin Firth's presentation of him in the highly successful 1995 BBC production of Jane Austen's classic novel, *Pride and Prejudice*. The role catapulted Firth (born September 10, 1960) into fame.

In fact, Firth almost turned down the role as he felt he might be wrong for it, because he wasn't anything like Darcy. Years later he told the *Daily Express*: "Darcy was this taciturn, dark, sexy guy and that is just not me. He rode horses and owned a wonderful home in Derbyshire. I ride a bike, talk a lot, and do not live in luxury." From an astrological viewpoint, however, he was made for the part! With all due respect to Firth's acting skills, I wonder if he could have pulled off the smoldering, self-absorbed Mr. Darcy so convincingly without the magnetic intensity of his Scorpio Rising! And despite all the hype, maybe it is less the haughty Darcy that connects Firth so much with the role as does the genuine, honorable Hero-in-the-making Darcy that he ends up becoming after working through torturous self-revelation, spurred by Elizabeth Bennett's rejection of his marriage proposal. Darcy realizes that if he is to win her love, he must unmask the persona he has unknowingly created— proud and conceited, character traits stemming largely from his childhood—that had served him well enough until love challenged him to take a closer look.

Acting lends itself to Firth's Virgo penchant for tweaking, perfecting, and getting every last detail down, whether that project be a character in a movie or a chapter in his own life. Indeed, when asked in an interview what was his outstanding personality trait, Firth replied, "an obsessive need for perfection." He admires people like Gandhi (Libra) who take up the fight to correct political and social injustice. And he has made it up the ladder to earn the success he now enjoys by Virgoan *stick-to-it-iveness*, regardless of challenges along the way, always improving his skills in the perfecting of his art.

Colin Firth played Mr. Darcy with co-star **Jennifer Ehle** as Elizabeth Bennet in the 1995 BBC TV miniseries of Jane Austen's *Pride and Prejudice*

Being a perfectionist goes hand-in-hand with Virgo anxiety. When asked what was his trick against stress, Firth attributed it to writing in his journal while listening to Mozart—a valid way to go from sweating the small stuff to enjoying peace of mind. Finally, when asked who are the women in his life, Firth answered: my mother, my wife, and Jane Austen!

SAVING THE PLANET & SAVING OURSELVES

Virgo rules health, hygiene, diet and dietary habits. Natives of this sign are particularly sensitive to toxins in the environment, in food, cosmetics, paint, and pharmaceutical drugs. Although they are so reactive, they tend to get over their maladies relatively quickly. The Virgo personality can be quite finicky in tastes, experimenting with one food plan after another. Certainly, correct food choices can be key in stabilizing the Virgo person's disposition and improving his general health picture. One Virgo couple's toy terrier picked up his owners' selective tastes. The puppy flatly refused the usual dog treats, accepting only the best homemade goodies!

The field of nutrition, ruled by Virgo, is being revolutionized at the onset of the Aquarian Age. Those who would save the planet and themselves are having us rethink what we eat, the way we eat, and how we grow and obtain our food and water supply. New developments are being triggered in response to the alarming genetic engineering of our crops, the wasteful erosion of our lands, and the mismanagement and pollution of our water supply. Among the exciting new frontiers: the healing power of fruits and vegetables, new ways of farming organic, live foods, the use of plants as medicine (replacing the need for many drugs), and the introduction of healthier menu choices in our public schools and other institutions.

PERFECTING FAITH THROUGH WORKS[182]

Most Virgo souls seeking greater union with God find that their natural sense of purity and restraint, their discriminating wisdom, continual efforts toward self-improvement, and their reflective and studious nature make them well suited for the rigors and simplicity of the spiritual life. Many times they already have training and experience in their *sacred labor*, the work they are destined to fulfill; perhaps they somehow have a momentum in service and self-sacrifice. Whatever the case, they almost always arrive ready to get to work and to help out where needed.

When souls diligently pursue the path of self-mastery, they often experience their personal karma lightened, allowing them to satisfy their karmic debts through prayer and service. Gifts and talents may crystallize within them, providing them the energy and skills necessary to meet what at first may appear to be a daunting task. The Virgo Aspirant will be tested through his work—as he applies himself earnestly to it, he perfects himself and strengthens his inner bond to his own divine reality.

Fulfilling one's sacred labor as a means to transmute karma is a part of each one's divine plan, no matter when they were born. Yet the Virgo Aspirant exemplifies, more than any other sun sign, the words of James, the disciple of Jesus, who said that through *work* faith is made perfect and, *Faith without works is dead.*[183]

"A HERO FOR HUMANITY"

William Wilberforce, born August 24, 1759, was a British politician, philanthropist, and a leader of the movement to abolish the slave trade in England. Like many Virgos, he was born with a strong passion to correct injustice in the world. He once said of himself, "If to be feelingly alive to the sufferings of my fellow creatures is to be a fanatic, I am one of the most incurable fanatics alive." Deeply religious, Wilberforce considered becoming a priest, but his close friend,

William Wilberforce (1759–1833)

the young Prime Minister William Pitt, persuaded him that he could serve Christ better by taking action in the political arena. And so, Wilberforce became the youngest Member of Parliament at age 21. Not all Virgos will take upon themselves an entire nation, but Virgos were born to serve. Through their efforts, they not only help others, they also help themselves! Indeed, Wilberforce came to believe that he was born to fight for the abolition of slavery in England. He began introducing anti-slavery legislation to Parliament in 1789, meeting with opposition, anger, and derision at almost every turn. It is no wonder that he suffered from debilitating and even life-threatening gastrointestinal illnesses (a Virgo ailment), often the result of stress, anxiety, and fatigue. Nonetheless, he carried on! How did he do it? He once wrote:

> *Accustom yourself to look first to the dreadful consequences of failure; then fix your eye on the glorious prize which is before you; and when your strength begins to fail, and your spirits are well nigh exhausted, let the animating view rekindle your resolution, and call forth in renewed vigour the fainting energies of your soul.*

I myself will never forget the wise counsel given to me years ago when I asked a Virgo friend why the trying circumstance in which I found myself at the time was taking so long to resolve itself. She replied, "It's a vast alchemy." (By this she meant that many things had to come into place and many lives would be affected during this scenario.) As James, the brother of Jesus, once wrote: *Let patience have her perfect work!*[184]

When all the qualities of the Virgo Hero come together, combining passion toward a higher cause, perseverance despite all obstacles, and patience, there

---

[182] "Seest thou how faith wrought with his works, and by works was faith made perfect?" James 2:22

[183] "For as the body without the spirit is dead, so faith without works is dead also." James 2:26 KJV

[184] James 1:4

almost inevitably comes the victory. In his biography on William Wilberforce, *A Hero for Humanity*, Kevin Belmonte describes the moment of major breakthrough in the cause for which Wilberforce had dedicated his life:

> *On the night of February 23, 1807, excitement grew in the House of Commons as his latest motion was debated. Speech after speech spoke in favor of abolition, and his fellow members began to pay tribute to Wilberforce. The House of Commons rose to its feet, turned to Wilberforce, and began to cheer. They gave three rousing hurrahs while Wilberforce sat with his head bowed and wept. Then the Commons voted to abolish the slave trade by a vote of 283 to 16. Prime Minister Granville called the passage "a measure which will diffuse happiness among millions now in existence, and for which his memory will be blessed by millions yet unborn."* [185]

When Parliament banned the slave trade in 1807, the tide had turned, but it would take another 26 years before the law went into effect for all of Britain, including the colonies. Wilberforce fought on as his health allowed. After three months of debate, on July 26th, 1833, the Slavery Abolition Act passed, abolishing slavery in most of the British Empire. A messenger ran to Wilberforce's house with the news. [186]

The Abolition Act—a prelude for the up and coming Aquarian Age—set the stage for the abolition of slavery in America almost 60 years later (1865), which would take the same struggle, vision and perseverance of an Abraham Lincoln (read the Sun in Aquarius) and a Civil War to accomplish.

---

[185] This scene is well illustrated in the movie, *Amazing Grace,* a 2006 American-British biographical film directed by Michael Apted. The film portrays Wilberforce's almost single-handed campaign against the slave trade in the British Empire. It also portrays his relationship with the evangelist preacher, John Newton, who had worked on a slave boat until a dramatic religious conversion after which he wrote the inspiring poem, *Amazing Grace,* later used in the well-known hymn. Newton actually had been a religious mentor for the adolescent Wilberforce when he was living in London. In the film, Newton is portrayed as a major influence on Wilberforce and on the abolition movement.

[186] He died three days later and was buried beside his friend William Pitt in Westminster Abbey.

[187] "Jesus saith unto him, *If I will that he tarry till I come, what is that to thee? Follow thou me.*" John 21:22

[188] *Aggressive mental suggestion* was first used by Mary Baker Eddy in Christian Science, is also elaborated upon in the teachings of the Summit Lighthouse and is used by some psychotherapists today.

ENOUGHNESS

Emily, a 28-year-old Yoga teacher with that subdued, earthy beauty so attractive in Virgo women, led her class through the steps of a challenging *asana* (pose): "On the next exhalation, *gracefully* raise your right leg high behind you... " Emily's students smiled; somehow, *gracefully* translated as a reminder to let their energy flow with the pose and that trying too hard would defeat their efforts. As she walked around the room, Emily continued to guide the students with her soft-toned yet strong voice: "Go within; explore what works for you; perhaps an extra stretch or, if you need to, feel free to bend your knees or use a supportive block." Almost as a side note, she added, "remember to practice enoughness." What is enoughness? Simply put: *Just enough—not too much, nor too little.*

Establishing personal boundaries is especially vital to Virgos on the path, for the economy of effort shows mastery in the use of the mother's energy. How much to save? How much to spend? When is too much work disabling? Virgos don't like to throw in the towel. Nonetheless, life will teach them the wisdom of discerning and accepting when it is time to endure and when it is time to best leave a project, even if it seems unfinished. They will learn when to accept closure in an intimate relationship or perhaps rescind their efforts to do for another what one must do for himself. The Virgo seeker of peace learns to recognize feelings of stress and frustration as red flags. He must return to center, take a breath, walk it out—dispel the anxiety that has entered his psyche before he is overpowered by it. He must practice *enoughness*!

ANXIETY KILLS ALCHEMY

The expression of anxiety runs the gamut from the slight nudge of a chronically apprehensive mindset, to the neurotic revolving of negative or confusing thoughts, to outright panic attacks. An expression every Virgo Aspirant needs to know is, *"What is that to thee, follow though me!"*[187]

Granted, some mistakes are so consequential that they alter the course of one's life, but many marvelous occurrences and discoveries are the results of so-called errors. All things happen for a reason. Elizabeth Clare Prophet, while referring to the state of anxiety so common to Virgos (also to those in the midst of Virgo cycles) taught, "The sense of struggle makes the struggle."

UNRUFFLED GRATITUDE—LET NOTHING BOTHER YOU!

Virgo Aspirants who take a critical stance make themselves vulnerable to *aggressive mental suggestion*—the unnoticed intrusion of other minds and thoughts into their own.[188]

They can learn to spot these invasive, negative and typically self-right-eous messages and thereby save themselves from later regret. As he progresses, the Virgo Aspirant is generally less vulnerable to such ploys, being more aware and less prone to the agitated states of consciousness that attract such assaults upon his peace of mind. Nonetheless, he had best be mindful, maintaining a state of unruffled gratitude, thus avoiding unthinkingly mistaking such thoughts as his own. If he allows himself to get run down or exhausted by stress or anxiety, he is essentially setting himself up for aggressive mental suggestion. When Virgo seek-ers do become caught in a whirlwind of negative energy, they need to breathe slowly and regain their equanimity. Tempting as it may be, such times are not the moment for analyzing and forcing a solution.

FORGIVENESS

That he emerges triumphant, the Virgo-Hero-to-be must recognize, come to terms with, and purge from his psyche one of the most pernicious, deeply hid-den, and widely accepted manifestations of ignorance in this sign—the belief that because he has erred he has been rejected by God! Virgo souls often sense an al-most primordial *fear of rejection*. But God never rejects his sons and daughters. Rather, when *we* reject our teacher, the experience of our karma becomes our teacher.

There can be no repentance without the confession of error, the resolution to sin no more *(no longer misuse light),* and the acceptance of forgiveness (the opportunity to learn to do better free of the burden of guilt). The Virgo Aspirant must shake out of his mind and psyche the toxic substance of shame so prevalent in this sign.

By summoning great reservoirs of love, the Virgo Aspirant assuages the fire in his mind, stills the agitation in his solar plexus, and washes out any sorrow in his heart. Ultimately, forgiveness is a choice. There comes a time when the soul must choose between remaining imprisoned within the crippling vortices of neg-ative emotions or to continue on the way. To refuse to be forgiven or to forgive is a manifestation of pride and a denial of grace that karmically binds the soul to the person or memory he refuses to let go of. Whatever action must be taken in a given circumstance, once he truly surrenders his pain, releasing the injurer to God and releasing his own resistance to forgive and be forgiven, the Virgo Aspirant continues his journey with a lighter load.

VIRGO HEROINES

Clara Louise Kieninger and *Mother Teresa* both lived lives of selfless service, constancy and faith perfected through works. Both women embodied the flame of the Divine Mother. Both Clara Louise and Mother Teresa dedicated their lives to serving God; each in their own sphere and time touched many lives of those who worked with them or who came under their care; both women inspired people throughout the world who were moved by their example.

Clara Louise Kieninger, a true Virgo Heroine, was born on September 16, 1863 to a pioneer family in Junction City, Kansas. Upon graduating from nursing school, she resolved to make the class motto, ***Ich Dien (I Serve)***, the guiding principle of her life, along with the Golden Rule, prayer and unquestioned faith in God. Clara Louise's services were held in high regard wherever she went. Her caring and capable ministration to those in need, her ability to effectively organize her staff and to train new students, her practical wisdom, compassion and no-nonsense approach to life brought her into roles of major responsibility. Often acting as Director or Assistant Director, she served in different hospitals in the USA, in Europe during two World Wars, and in Brazil, where she set up

Ich Dien (*I Serve*), the compelling memoirs of **Clara Louise Kieninger**, a woman whose lifestyle made her a true humanitarian

that country's first nursing school. In later years, she came to know and embrace the teachings of the Ascended Masters. Looking back upon her life, Clara Louise writes that she was able to meet any task before her, regardless of the magnitude of the challenge, *guided by the Father, the beloved Master Jesus, and my own beloved Guru, my Teacher.*

Mother Teresa's life is well known. Born Anjezë Gonxhe Bojaxhiu on August 26, 1910,[189] in Albania, Mother Teresa became a Roman Catholic sister and missionary in Calcutta, India. She served many years as a teacher and then the principal of St. Mary's High School until that date with destiny in 1946, when she felt Jesus calling her to serve the poorest of the poor. In 1950, she then established the Missionaries of Charity, which by 2012 consisted of over 4,500 sisters in 133 countries.[190]

---

[189] Or August 27th, the date Mother Teresa was baptized (date disputed)

[190] The Sisters of the Missionaries of Charity run centers for people with AIDS, leprosy and tuberculosis. They manage soup kitchens, dispensaries and mobile clinics, offer children's and family counseling programs, and have established many orphanages and schools. Members of the order adhere to the vows of chastity, poverty and obedience, and a fourth vow, to give "wholehearted, free service to the poorest of the poor."

Mother Teresa (Virgo) and **Princess Diana** (Cancer)—both active champions for human rights—met in 1997 at the Missionaries of Charity in the south Bronx. "Diana is my daughter," the nun often said. They both died within days of each other.

A fascinating detail of the hand of God in Mother Teresa's mission: Mother Teresa set out by requesting the municipality for a place where she could care for those whom no one wanted. She insisted that she would take care of the rest herself. Awarded an abandoned temple that had been dedicated to the Hindu goddess Kali, she changed it into a free hospice that she called, "Kalighat, the Home of the Pure Heart."[191]

Kali is revered in India as a manifestation of the power of the Divine Mother.

The Virgo Aspirant often becomes engrossed in a particular service to life that becomes his destiny and *dharma (duty)*—the central part of his individualized divine plan. By serving life, life serves him! Clara Louise and Mother Teresa drew strength, courage and faith by balancing their service with prayer. Clara Louise once commented: "I'm never tired. There is always energy all around me for the taking; all I have to do is reach out and accept it."[192]

Mother Teresa, in response to a query of whether it was hard for her to give up her vocation of twenty years to go out and help India's poor, remarked that her vocation never changed. She said, "The *vocation*[193] is belonging to Christ; the *work* is only a means to put our love into action."[194]

Let the Virgo Aspirant learn from Clara Louise and Mother Teresa that special ability of the Mother to hold the immaculate concept (vision of the divine blueprint), even in the midst of error, sickness or duress. Mother Teresa saw the face of Christ in each of those she tended. When the Virgo Aspirant is able to see the good even in those who oppose or would condemn or malign him, he will live in peace and is less likely to become discouraged or trapped in criticism or self-justification. He need not be discouraged when, as happened to Mother Teresa, he finds himself immersed in the dark night of the soul, engulfed in darkness, with questions unanswered. This, too, is a rite of purification before the ultimate victory.

Through the sacred path of redemption accelerated through prayer and the Aquarian Science of Invocation and dedicated service to life, seekers of truth may fulfill their unique mission and balance wrongs committed (karmic debts both personal and planetary). In so doing, they will recapture their true reason for being, buried under layers of karmic soot and density. This indeed is the beauty of Virgo.

---

[191] The number of people who have received help at Kalighat, which is operable even today, is incalculable. In 1974, Mother Teresa said 29,000 had been received.
[192] *Ich Dien* (p. 195), by Clara Louise Kieninger, (Summit University Press, Kindle Edition, Nov. 2010)
[193] *Vocation* can be understood a one's mission, calling or life's work.
[194] See www.YouTube.com: *Mother Teresa of Calcutta on Irish Television*, 1974.

12. ♑ Capricorn

Symbol	.... **The Goat**
Born	.... Dec. 21 ~ Jan. 19
Archetype	.... *The Father*
Key Phrase	.... ***I Am Responsible***
Element	.... **Earth**
Cross	.... **Cardinal-Power**
House	.... **Tenth:**

Career, status & reputation; sense of honor, achievement, promotions & recognition; the father or wage earning responsible parent; important authority figures, positions of power & authority, one's employer, the government; judgment

Ruler	.... **Saturn**
Esoteric Ruler	.... **Saturn**
Polarity	.... **Cancer**
Chakra	.... Crown
Anatomy	.... Joints, knees, bones, teeth

Spiritual Qualities .... **Power & dominion, productivity, responsibility, striving & honor, organization**

Vulnerable to ..... *Exaggerated ambition, domination over others, condemnation & judgment, criticism, negativity & cynicism, overly somber, skepticism*

Must Acquire ..... **Humility, confidence, conviction, sense of humor, faith**

Yogananda • Benjamin Franklin • Saint Thérèse of Lisieux • Mark L. Prophet • Joan of Arc

THE SUN IN CAPRICORN

You say that you are my judge; take good heed
of what you do, because, in truth, I am sent by God,
and you put yourself in great peril.

—Joan of Arc,
in warning to the judges at her trial

THE PINNACLE OF ACHIEVEMENT

Located at the very top of the natal chart, known to astrologers as the Midheaven, Capricorn is placed at the very point where the spiritual blueprint is brought down into physical manifestation, so that a semblance of that which is above might manifest here below. Astrologers recognize Capricorn as the gateway to the Tenth House, whose affairs relate primarily to the soul's relationship to the father, as well as to other important authority figures, and to matters concerning career, social status and reputation. Not surprisingly, most Capricorns are very much involved in managing mundane life—we typically find them established in positions of authority and command.

Whatever their field of action might be, they tend to rise the top. Indeed, Capricorn represents the crystallization of each man's unique *dharma* or destiny, as well as the height of earthly honors and achievements.[195]

But some natives of this sign are so intent upon securing worldly recognition and economic well-being that fulfilling these ambitions dominates their life. The true Capricorn, however, represents the pinnacle of achievement in character and integrity, honor and practical intelligence—the just and capable man who dedicates his life in service to humanity. Those born under the rays of this enterprising sign, then, are challenged to be strong in this world while at the same time remaining humble and spiritually attuned—a tall order, to be sure! The mystical Lebanese poet, Khalil Gibran, born January 6th, 1883, captured beautifully the means to the fulfilling of a mighty destiny in Capricorn when he wrote:

> *My Soul gave me good counsel, teaching me that the*
> *lamp which I carry does not belong to me, and the song that I*
> *sing was not generated from within me.*

THE TEST OF POWER

Souls born with the Sun in Capricorn are destined to exercise power!

Power, the harnessing of divine or cosmic energy, the very pulse of creation, brings about much good in the world when based on right motive, reason, and cause. But when employed for selfish ends, power corrupts, potentially causing grievous harm and destruction. The temptation to misuse power—whether through ignorance, or the ego's ambition to acquire great wealth, to control others, or through the sheer force of single-minded drive and relentless desire, can become overpoweringly irresistible. So much so, that many religious orders throughout the ages have required that their disciples strip themselves of all longings to be influential in a worldly sense. But the individual soul born in Capricorn may have a mighty mission to fulfill, one for which he has prepared over many lifetimes, or a karma to balance dealing with the misuse of power, perhaps affecting many people in a previous life. His destiny may require that he be in a position of command, and often of considerable means, to fulfill his calling in life and to settle his accounts.

The Capricorn person's relationship with Power takes on myriad forms, in endless scenarios. Power can be invigorating yet intoxicating, empowering yet intimidating, strengthening yet dangerously beguiling. A warning sounds forth: power laced with pride creates a volatile mix. Sometimes, natives of this sign get so charged up with self-importance that they become temporarily blinded to reason. The potent energy coursing through their veins takes over and controls them. In the ferocity of the moment, they are vulnerable to getting carried away, causing much damage they later come to regret. As is true in boxing and in the martial arts—favorite sports for many of these dynamically driven souls—the greater the individual's strength, the more crucial it is for him to be self-disciplined and self-controlled.[196]

Note that Capricornian success, characteristically, is built brick-by-solid-brick, the mortar being patient effort and earnest striving. All of it, however, can be lost in a moment of rage!

Capricorns are builders, directors, managers, governors, organizers, event planners—you name it, they make it happen! Even those among them who are more attached to home and hearth are busily executing a packed daily agenda of activities, not only in their own affairs, but also in those of their friends, family and community. But sometimes their sense of dominance, plus the plaudits of this world, cause them to erroneously suppose that they are the source of the potent vigor and strength that they experience, when in actuality they are *empowered*

---

[195] Dharma has multiple meanings. In this context, dharma refers to each one's particular and unique work and contribution to life in accordance with the divine plan for his person.

[196] Floyd Patterson, Muhammad Ali, Joe Frazier, and George Foreman are all great names in boxing history, all heavyweight champions, and all Capricorns.

Capricorn:
10th House
Cardinal-
Power Cross
Earth Element

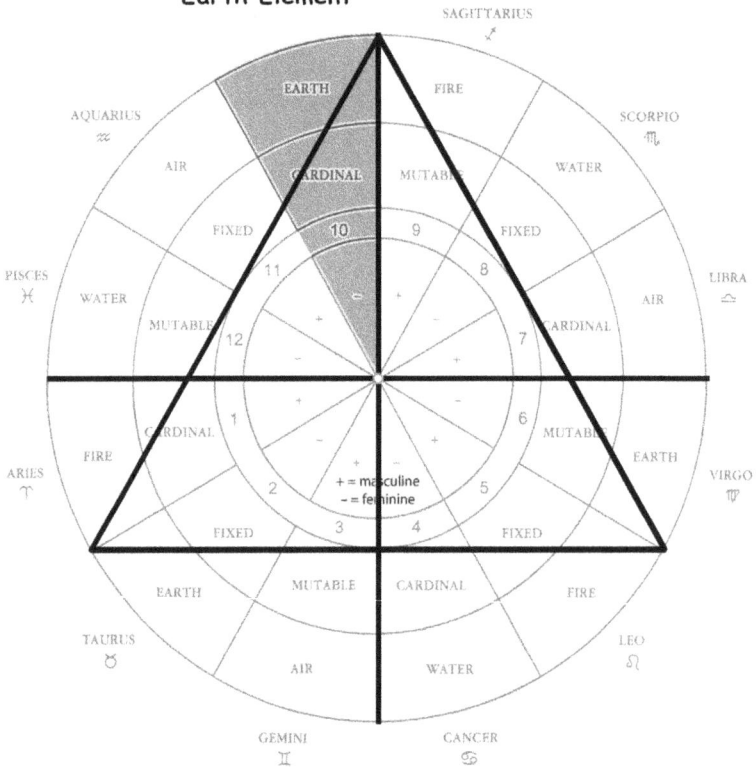

from above. Individual Capricorns experience what is essentially a spiritual question—the nature of their relationship to God—in their interactions with different authority figures in their lives; the child to the parent, the student to the teacher, the worker with his supervisor, the citizen with the government, etc. Conversely, they come to know themselves better as they take on the more dominant position within the relationship. True, in families and in the workplace, the Aquarian Age has brought about a more egalitarian lifestyle, but the chain of command—the boss is now the team leader who answers to his supervisors—remains a fact of life, somewhat reshuffled to meet the times.

Then there are those Capricorn souls who fail to rise to the occasion; because they feel they are unworthy or unequal to the task before them, because they are bowed down under the weight of past mistakes or perhaps because their willpower is suppressed by the condemnation of those who oppose them. These and other expressions of self-condemnation or low self-esteem, of feeling *powerlessness,* are but the flipside of a mistaken identity in this sign. With maturity, the Capricorn soul comes to realize that the lessons learned from failure often provide the key for future success!

Eventually, all natives of this sign are humbled and brought to their knees, which are, in fact, ruled by this sign, not out of fear, nor in defeat, but in awe and devotion.[197] Alas, so many find out the hard way that it is far better to bend the knee and remain humble than to risk being humiliated. The mysterious secret to success in Capricorn is that strength is found in humility.

THE CAPRICORN HERO

The Capricorn Hero is strong and powerful, yet gentle and kind. He is responsible and willing to take upon himself the burden of authority, but he is ever mindful that regardless of worldly offices he may assume and honors that may be bestowed upon him, he is the servant—of God, first and foremost, and then of the God-Flame within those that he governs. Like the general who fights for peace, he must fight to win, calling upon great reserves of inner strength from within himself and his men to overcome the enemy. Yet his ambition must be guided toward his ultimate goal, which is that all fighting cease. To act otherwise is to become a dictator and, as history has shown over and over again, such tyrants have their moments of glory or infamy, but inevitably fall, having brought upon themselves an inevitable judgment from an authority that is higher than any man. In reality, those who would usurp a throne not rightfully theirs are not punished, but rather returned, through Love, to their rightful place!

---

[197]Capricorn rules the knees, the teeth, the bones, and the gallbladder in the physical body.

Joan of Arc (born January 6, 1412, Julian; January 15, Gregorian) was 12 or 13 years old, alone in her father's garden, when she first heard the voices and saw the figures of three heavenly beings that she came to identify as Saint Michael, Saint Catherine and Saint Margaret. The angels instructed her that she was to drive the English out from France and restore France's rightful heir to the throne. While she cried when the heavenly visitors left—they were so beautiful—she naturally was very much afraid. Joan was directed to begin this mission by convincing the authorities of 15th century France that she was sent by God to deliver their country. She of herself had no ambition of fame or grandeur, nor would she ever have dreamt up a scheme to dress as a man, ready to engage in battle and lead armies, but such was God's direction to her. She knew his Will would prevail if she would but do her part. Although Joan was, to all appearances, a simple peasant girl who could neither read nor write, she was courageous and devout, and as is often the case in such unforgettable divine dramas on Earth, she surely was a soul of much spiritual attainment, well prepared for this mission of lifetimes!

Capricorn, the sign of the Father, is set on the Power-Cardinal Cross, which in *Transformational Astrology* is also called *The Cross of Right Identification and Right Relationship*. In her relationship to God the Father, which she strengthened through devout prayer and with every correct choice that she made, *Joan the Maid* led France to victory. Although she was condemned to death by a tribunal of the Inquisition, she was declared innocent and proclaimed a martyr twenty-five years later. She later was canonized and today, Saint Joan is recognized as France's national heroine.[198]

In greater or lesser measure, the Capricorn Hero-to-be will be called and challenged to go beyond the call of duty, to defend the right, and to choose honorably and forthrightly which way to go. Mark Twain's description of Joan of Arc might read as a primer for the requirements of any soul aspiring to be Hero in Capricorn today:

> *She was truthful when lying was the common speech*
> *of men; she was honest when honesty was become a lost virtue;*
> *she was a keeper of promises when the keeping of a promise*
> *was expected of no one... she was full of pity when a merciless*
> *cruelty was the rule; she was steadfast when stability was un-*
> *known, and honorable in an age which had forgotten what*
> *honor was; she was a rock of convictions in a time when men*
> *believed in nothing and scoffed at all things; she was unfailingly*

---

[198] Inquisitor-General Jean Brehal finally declared Joan of Arc innocent of heresy on the 7th of July 1456, twenty-five years after her death at the stake. Pope Benedict V canonized her as a saint in 1920.

true in an age that was false to the core... she was of a dauntless courage when hope and courage had perished in the hearts of her nation.

RESPONSIBLE, RELIABLE, EFFICIENT & PRODUCTIVE

As Earth sign people born on the Cardinal-Power Cross, it's no surprise that Capricorns are the producers of the Zodiac! The Capricorn key phrase is "I am responsible." A Capricorn resume might read: "Trust me to get the job done and with excellence! Count on me to be on time and to work long hours. I am reliable, dependable and hardworking, orderly and efficient. I come equipped with practical solutions to knotty problems. I work best when in charge and am capable of directing others. In great matters and small, I exercise sound judgment and common sense." The latter is a mixed blessing, however, because it really irks the typical Capricorn that most other people seem so short on the ability to see the obvious. In truth, it's not necessarily that Capricorns know better, or always that they do better, but that they are the ones who will carry on when other, less stalwart souls, will call it quits for the day.

As a rule, then, Capricorns are up and doing. Being essentially solution-oriented, they delight in challenging situations that give them the opportunity to flex their creative muscles and make use of their resourcefulness. Even so, no one person can do everything. So, natives of this practical sign must inevitably come to terms with graciously managing their interdependence with others, whether this means delegating parts of the project, making room for another's agenda, or even taking a back seat when it is someone else's turn to kick the can. The principle holds true regardless of whether their arena of operations is a family unit, a company, a social, political, cultural, or religious organization, or even a nation.

CAPRICORN, THE GOAT

Capricorn rules mountains as well as the arduous climb to the top. Just as mountain peaks pierce the heavens, the highest points on Earth, they occupy simultaneously the lower spheres of heaven, esoterically called *the etheric plane*. There is a rugged quality to members of this powerful Earth sign. Some born under its rays actually climb physical mountains to attain a sense of triumph. Others are social climbers, status seekers, and still others aspire to reach the Summit of Being.

How to get up the mountain? The Capricorn Goat is surefooted, a reminder of how to make it up the craggy heights safely and securely—step-by-steadfast-step and, like the mountain goat, steadying oneself on one's knees!

SATURN—THE TEACHER

Capricorns are Saturnian in nature—diligent, somewhat reserved, industrious, stable, dutiful, resourceful, and conservative. They command respect. Saturn is said to represent the past, tradition, and the keeping intact of the old order. Capricorns, however, while not usually apt to rock the boat, are not necessarily stuck in the past. More accurately, they study the past to learn valuable lessons that they can apply to better understand and improve the present and future. Astrologer John Soric, in *The New Age Astrologer*, rightfully calls Capricorns, "a force to be reckoned with." Saturn represents the Law. Thus, those born under its influence are endowed with an inherent regard for what should be and what needs to happen. They tend to exercise a telltale ability to look at life objectively, to organize effectively, and to see and measure what is useful, what will work, and what will not. Like the traditional father heading the household, a ruler, or a CEO, they see their role as setting and maintaining the right standards. As is true of any lawgiver, they can come off as somewhat stern and impersonal. Some Capricorns do benefit when they learn to be more merciful, flexible, less officious, and more open to new ideas. But for others, a perceived coldness is, in reality, an adherence to truth, order, and duty—period! Typically self-sufficient and independent, they may appear to be unfeeling or materialistic. Nonetheless, most desire to love and to be loved with loyalty and heartfelt affection.

In Kabbalistic Astrology, Saturn relates to the sephirah *Binah* (Understanding), a feminine manifestation of Wisdom, as opposed to the sephirah *Hokhmah* (Revelation), a masculine quality related to Uranus. Wisdom is the result of much practical experience (Saturn) and therefore, is usually seen only in mature souls. How is understanding acquired? Again, we are brought back to starting principles in contemplating the relation of man to the Creator and of the individual self to Eternal Law.

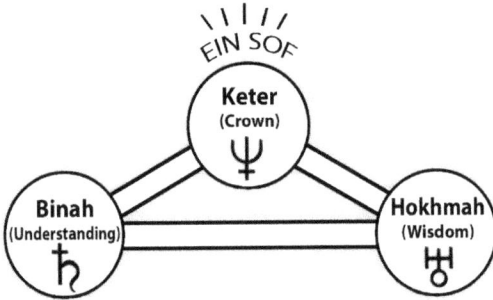

The supernal Triad at the top of the Kabbalistic Tree of Life represents the first stages of the manifestation of pure spirit (*Ein Sof* through *Keter*) as Revelation (*Hokhmah*/masculine) and as Understanding (*Binah*/feminine).

In traditional Astrology, Saturn is dubbed, *The Great Malefic*, the bearer of woes. Woe can be interpreted as, "my karma is upon me." When under much stress for prolonged periods of time, even the most stalwart Capricorn souls are apt to express Saturn's more negative manifestations of pessimism, brooding, criticism, and condemnation (of self and others), and a fear of failure. Nonetheless, despite obstacles along the way, they are patient and long-suffering. They rarely throw in the towel; they keep on keeping on when others have given up long ago.

Saturn has also earned the title of *The Tester* and *The Great Teacher*. Make no mistake about it—Saturn crystallizes our karmic accounts, bringing to our doorstep the opportunity to reap the rewards of meritorious service and years of dedicated labor, as well as the natural consequences of that which we have brought upon ourselves by past or present misuses of the light. When Saturn tests the soul, through adversity and lack or some other limitation, Capricorns who are up to the task will self-correct, do it better, resolve a problem long in the making with a practical solution, and in the process get to know themselves better. For the Capricorn mystic, as we later shall see, Saturn becomes the Guru or *Zadek*, the Great Teacher, who through love engages, disciplines, prunes and guides the Aspirant on his path.[199]

Capricorns do not expect life to be easy; most embody a certain no-nonsense, earn-your-way, and no-free-rides approach to life. As long as there is work to be done, with measurable and substantial progress along the way, they will put their hand to the plow with alacrity and determination. They expect the same dedication and conscientious striving from others. If you happen to be working for someone born under this sign, or if they are your teacher or parent, expect that you will be given what you need to get going, but you will have to earn their respect by your works and integrity to get that raise, promotion, permission (for a child), or their helping hand.

Saturn's constant exigencies and constraints can become tiresome, feeding a skeptical mindset in some Capricorns and a realistic caution in others. Spiritual leader and founder of the Summit Lighthouse, Mark L. Prophet (born December 24th, 1918), used to say, "Trust no man," a positive statement of truth when understood to mean, *It is better to trust in the [LORD] than to put confidence in man.*[200]

Saturn represents the wisdom of the ages, classic works and thinking best preserved. Nonetheless, Saturn misconstrued also characterizes stodgy individuals and entrenched institutions, many corrupt and stuck in the past, that dig in their heels to maintain control and dominance in an age of change and innovation. Fear

---

[199] *Zadek* or *Tzadik*: the true title of *tzadik* denotes a spiritual psychological description of the soul. Its true meaning can only be applied to one who has completely their natural, "animal," "vital" soul inclinations into holiness, so that they experience only love and awe of God, without material temptations.

[200] Psalms 118:8 or trust no man's lesser self, which is always subject to error.

of an unknown future may keep the less-evolved Capricornian holding onto whatever represents security to him.

For the Capricorn man or woman in the Aquarian Age intent on paying his dues and making his mark in life, charting the cycles of Saturn (with Jupiter) spells out the nature and timing of his destiny. He can foresee when the culmination of years of persistent effort is most likely to occur. For he who would enter the challenge of the spiritual path, Saturn will help him come into alignment, which is to say right relationship, with the guru or spiritual teacher and pick up where he left off—perhaps hundreds of years or many lifetimes ago—that he transmute his karma, define and manifest his unique calling in life and become the disciplined one partaking of the Wisdom of the Divine Mother.

Because he is willing to be self-disciplined that he might rid himself of the mask of the ego, once and for all, the Capricorn soul squarely on the spiritual path actually comes to welcome Saturn's tests and initiations. Saturn appears to him not as the feared debt collector, but as a wise if exacting guide, guru and friend. But for most Capricorns, the constant presence of Saturn upon them is weighty and many natives of this sign are recognizable by a certain serious cast in their disposition.

THE SELF-MADE CAPRICORN ADVENTURER

Early American patriot and Founding Father, Benjamin Franklin, was born in Boston on January 17th, 1706 (Gregorian; January 6th, Julian), the fifteenth youngest son in a family of seventeen children! Franklin embodied the Capricornian can-do spirit at its best. While born into humble circumstances, he picked himself up by his own bootstraps. By his wit and ingenuity and through his writings, legislation, diplomacy, invention and guidance, he did what he could that others do likewise. Franklin wrote:

> *To be thrown upon one's own resources is to be cast into the very lap of fortune; for other faculties then undergo a development and display of energy of which they were previously unsusceptible.*

I & MY FATHER

Saturn's position in the natal chart, and also by transit—as well as any planet in the tenth astrological house or in strong aspect to the Midheaven—takes center stage in a Capricorn person's life. While Saturn, Capricorn and the Tenth House all relate to the father and the Father Principle, they may or may not describe an actual father or masculine authority in the physical sense. Women often take the power position in families and in companies today. Likewise, although Cancer, Capricorn's polarity and the Fourth House relate to the Mother Principle, we sometimes find men assuming domestic responsibilities and acting as the primary caretakers of their children.

Critical relationship dynamics are revealed in studying these placements and the aspects related to them. Note that even the more difficult squares and oppositions in or to power points in a Capricorn person's chart, are not necessarily a death knell to a relationship. When Elizabeth Clare Prophet, an Aries (Fire on the Cardinal-Power Cross) was engaged to Mark L. Prophet, a Capricorn (Earth on the Cardinal-Power Cross), they were actually warned by an astrologer that they were heading for trouble — they were both too powerful and would inevitably be vying for being in charge. She was 20 years younger and looked up to this man not only as a companion, but also as teacher and so she concluded, "Well, if someone has to step back, it will be me." And what an exciting and loving union this couple enjoyed — together accomplishing a task (creating a worldwide spiritual movement) that neither one could have done alone).

The Capricorn individual's sense of self, his gusto for making it to the top, his self-respect and lawful ambition, and conversely, his self-aggrandizement, potential misuse of power, or fear to assume positions of authority, will almost always go back to his connection, or lack of it, to Spirit as the guiding principle of his life. Moreover, his perception of God is almost always affected by his relationship to his father, as well as his experiences with the primary dominant figure(s) in his early life, and even by relationships with his parents in past lives.

NO PAIN, NO GAIN

Capricorns typically take upon themselves a heavy load. The key symptom, however, that the weight is becoming too heavy, or that carrying on is too tedious, or that he is identifying more with the problem than with the solution, is complaining. Normally confident and in charge, complaining is a symptom of feeling first hurt, then helpless. The problem seems larger than life. A negative mental state follows. The Capricorn may defensively lash out at others or even at himself.

Constant complaining can prove to be the downfall of an otherwise well integrated Capricorn personality. The tendency to be cantankerous can be so ingrained as to be chronic, becoming a habit so unconscious that most don't even realize how much they gripe. The individual with the Sun in Capricorn can uncover this tendency within himself by listening to his inner dialog: "I could have.... would have... I should have... why didn't I?" And variations on the same theme: "You (he, she, we, they) should have... could have... would have." Fearfully asking, "but what if this happens or what if that happens?" While this may be a purposeful tool for Socratic learning, it falls into the same category of focusing on the negative.

Many people are familiar with Ben Franklin's wise counsel, *Early to bed, early to rise, makes a man healthy, wealthy and wise*. Less known is that Franklin also penned, *There are no gains without pains*.

LIGHT SHINING IN THE DARKNESS

The Sun enters Capricorn at Winter Solstice on December 21st, when the day is shorter and the night longer than any other time of the year.[201]

Indeed, the December 25th celebration of the coming of the Messiah to a darkened world is well staged at the beginning of Capricorn. It is the emerging light that shines in the darkness that is celebrated in winter, as the light of day gradually, almost imperceptibly, increases.

Capricorns, then, come into this world at a time of great darkness and of great hope. They experience very personally this juxtaposition of carrying the weight of negative karma, not all necessarily of their own making, and the joy of deliverance. After all, we are not cast into the dark night forever, but for a time, in order that we might grow. When all is dark around us, it can be challenging to focus our attention on the small seed of potentiality shining like a candle in the night. But this is precisely what Capricorn souls must learn to do—to find and to focus on the positive. Nonetheless, they instinctively know, as 19th century Swiss philosopher Henri-Frédéric Amiel wrote, reflecting upon a teaching Jesus gave to his disciples, *Work while you have the light. You are responsible for the talent that has been entrusted to you.*[202]

JUDGE NOT

Will I make it? Fear in the Earth signs often revolves around approval and disapproval—getting it, seeking it, and expressing it. When natives of this sign allow fear, fueled by an underlying sense of unworthiness, to steal into their psyche, they unwittingly accommodate the Capricorn's nemesis—shame and blame! Especially those who are sincerely trying to do their best can too readily accept the blame when things go wrong, or at least not as perfectly as they had envisioned. Taking upon themselves the heaviness of such condemnation can be particularly disabling, crippling to the soul's peace of mind, and become the underlying cause of depression. Likewise, Capricorn individuals find greater peace when they become aware of, and eliminate, the injurious habit of pointing the fin-

---

[201] On some years, the Sun enters Capricorn on December 22nd.

[202] "I must work the works of him that sent me, while it is day: the night cometh, when no man can work." This can be interpreted to mean when the Teacher is no longer with us. John 9:4

ger and blaming others. What goes around comes around!

Regardless of good intentions, such as sincerely desiring to remedy a particular circumstance, Capricorns rarely realize how damaging uninvited corrections and comments, when tinged with even a bit of negativity, can prove to be—not only to others, but also to themselves, upon whom they can be the most severe of all critics! Even when their outer achievement, practical intelligence, and other positive qualities are obvious to all around them, managing their own inner critic typically proves to be a Herculean challenge to these souls. If the Capricorn soul finds that he cannot still the inner voice that condemns him, he most likely must first heal some wound related to a close relationship (from the past, often a parental one) that is still unresolved.

How to see so much darkness, to be aware of problems that appear to defy solutions and to be painfully aware of one's own shortcomings, and those of others, and yet still stay positive in mind and in spirit? Truly, Faith is Power's natural complement and a Capricorn's greatest ally!

"GENTLE GLADIATOR"

The heavyweight boxer, Floyd Patterson, born January 4th, 1935, was a champion in the ring and a champion in life! He had risen from almost unimaginable hardship and poverty, from a childhood so chaotic that when he wasn't on the streets in New York City, he might be in 6 or 7 different schools in the same year. Even so, he became the youngest man to win the heavyweight championship title, at age 21. Nicknamed, *The Gentle Gladiator*, Patterson cared about others; he was considerate and non-pretentious. Although such compassion was considered a weakness for a prizefighter, Patterson's kind and reflective nature certainly proved to be an asset in him as a man, father and husband, and a mentor for youth. The combination of gentleness and powerful strength is an impressive combination, found in the best of Capricornians. In his autobiography,

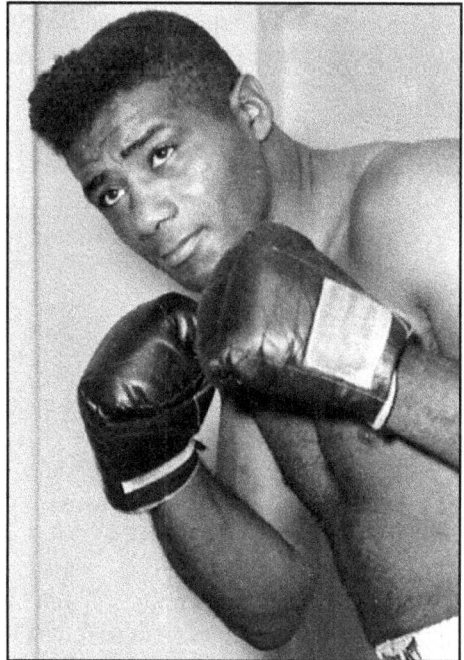

Floyd Patterson (1935–2006) American professional boxer, undisputed heavyweight champion

My Victory Over Myself, (a title thematic for most Capricorns) Patterson remarked that, although it is true, as was oftentimes reported, that he had been knocked down more than any other fighter, he had also gotten up more than any other.

THE CAPRICORNIAN FIGHTING SPIRIT

Whatever the challenge, circumstance, condition or person bearing down on the individual Capricorn soul, hinting to him that he won't make it and shouldn't even try, he has within him a fighting spirit and determination to overcome, to reach the mark, like no other!

A Capricorn teenager, whose father was a semi-professional boxer, looked forward to sparring with his dad after school as the highlight of his day. He tells that it took years before he could even return his father's fast punches that seemed to come out of nowhere. "Although I got knocked down continually," he reports with a grin, "I never stayed down!"

THE UNCONQUERABLE POWER OF WILL

The Indian guru and yogi, Paramahansa Yogananda, born January 5th, 1893, taught that failures should arouse a greater determination to sow the seeds of success. In a booklet full of wise counsel called, *The Law of Success*, Yogananda writes:

> *The bludgeon of circumstances may bruise you, but keep your head erect. Always try once more, no matter how many times you have failed. Fight when you think that you can fight no longer, or when you think you have already done your best, or until your efforts are crowned with success.*

VARIATIONS

While Capricorns may be compassionate in a general sense, many of them seem to lack emotional sensitivity. Despite the impartial and impersonal approach for which Capricorns are known, it is a mistake to write them off as being unfeeling or insensitive. Many natives of this sign feel deeply; they often are the first to offer a helping hand, a practical solution or a word of consolation. Moreover, Capricorn souls in whose charts the Ascendant or the Moon and, to a lesser extent Venus or Mars, are in any of the Water signs (Cancer, Scorpio or Pisces), typically experience emotions so forcefully that their feelings become overwhelming at times.

Nat, a Capricorn man with a Pisces Moon, is so sensitive that he protects his personal space and, as time will allow, regularly enters periods of meditation and retreat. Nonetheless, Nat has found that his perceptive sensitivity is a great asset in his role as a natural healer; his essential oil and herbal formulas, precisely determined and personalized, have been a miracle elixir to many who knock at his door. While he tends to be positive and encouraging, Nat struggles to avoid feeling downhearted (Capricorn) when he cannot solve another's problem (Pisces), and he even has difficulty charging (Capricorn) for his services, which he is tempted to simply give away. He clearly needs to put into place personal boundaries (a typical Piscean issue), but Capricorns often find it challenging to know where responsibility begins and where it ends.

THE CAPRICORN CHILD

A familiar astrological adage states, "Capricorns are old when they're young and young when they're old." Saturnian seriousness can sit awkwardly upon the youngster of this sign who is often mature beyond his years. Naturally devotional, he usually is somewhat shy and self-conscious, and he will almost always have a serious bent. Even as children, Capricorns tend to be methodical, industrious, patient, and willing to go through much preparation to reach a goal. Parents and teachers can help the Capricorn child develop a positive and balanced self-esteem by letting him know he is loved and valued not only because of what he does, but also because of who he is. At the same time, Capricorns show their love through their works, so the child born in winter benefits when receiving well-earned recognition for his efforts and his work well done. Similarly, he respects and admires those who demonstrate a confident demeanor, integrity of character and noteworthy accomplishments.

The Capricorn soul may be born into a limiting condition of some sort that weighs upon him in childhood, but which later becomes the very goad of achievement. Hannah, born with the Sun in Capricorn and the Moon in Cancer, held on to Mom's apron strings tightly even into her early teenage years. She also fought severe food allergies, a not uncommon problem with Capricorn children. Another Capricorn child, otherwise happy and healthy, refused to eat almost everything her mom put on her plate. ("Hey, Mom, I want to be in charge!") Sometimes it's tough for souls destined for dominant roles in society to take a back seat when young. These two children, blessed by supportive families, grew out of their childhood fears and dominating tendencies.

By observing their child's behavior and his likes and dislikes, the parent may perceive early signs of a Capricorn child's destined career. In his book, *Autobiography of a Yogi*, Paramahansa Yogananda describes how he repeatedly ran away from home as a young adolescent—he was searching for his Guru! Many of these children, however, pass through many cycles of learning and experience before their chosen vocation is apparent. Saturn's position in the Capricorn child's natal chart helps to map out the cycles of maturity in his life.

Capricorn children can be so naturally in charge and good at what they do that their parents may too easily put upon them tasks and responsibilities beyond their years. In an extreme example of this common tendency, one Midwestern Capricorn man tells of driving his family truck at eight years of age and picking up his inebriated father at the bar when Dad was too tipsy to drive! (In adult life, he spent many years recovering his lost childhood and became younger when he was older.)

The times we live in bring unforeseen possibilities for the Capricorn child, nurtured and raised in light, honor and truth, to take his rightful place in the building and governing of a New Age.

ALL PROGRESS IS PRECARIOUS

Earth is the densest of the four elements. All the Earth signs (Taurus, Virgo and Capricorn), by virtue of the magnetism of the physical element, tend to get caught up in their creation. Especially the more materialistically oriented Capricorns often feel compelled to manifest some form of outer perfection. In and of itself, perfection as a goal can be self-defeating. However, stretching the faculties of body, mind and soul to be able to do, think, understand and accomplish today that which before was unreachable—that works! Thus, every goal accomplished is not a final summit, but rather a plateau, a resting place affording opportunity to prepare for the next ascent to the top. The Capricorn-born civil rights activist, Martin Luther King, Jr. (January 15, 1929), expressed this well when he said, "All progress is precarious, and the solution of one problem brings us face-to-face with another problem."

THE UPWARD CLIMB

What happens when the Capricorn soul determines to transcend his former self and make it all the way home? His goal, which eclipses all lesser goals, is union with God. Perhaps he thinks of becoming one with truth, divine love, or higher consciousness; perhaps he sets out to attain Buddhic enlightenment or, as the Kabbalists say, he aspires to enter and be able to maintain an awakened state at will. Whatever the case may be, once the Capricorn Aspirant places his foot squarely on the path, his work has begun!

THE SEA-GOAT, SYMBOL OF REDEMPTION

Capricorn, by translation, means *horned goat*—both the billy goat and the mountain goat. Capricorn is also symbolized by the *Sea-Goat*, an ancient symbol that is full of occult meaning. The Sea-Goat is depicted as a goat with the tail of a fish tucked beneath it. Carvings of this strange creature in connection with the constellation Capricorn have been found on Babylonian tablets dating as far back as 1,000 BC.

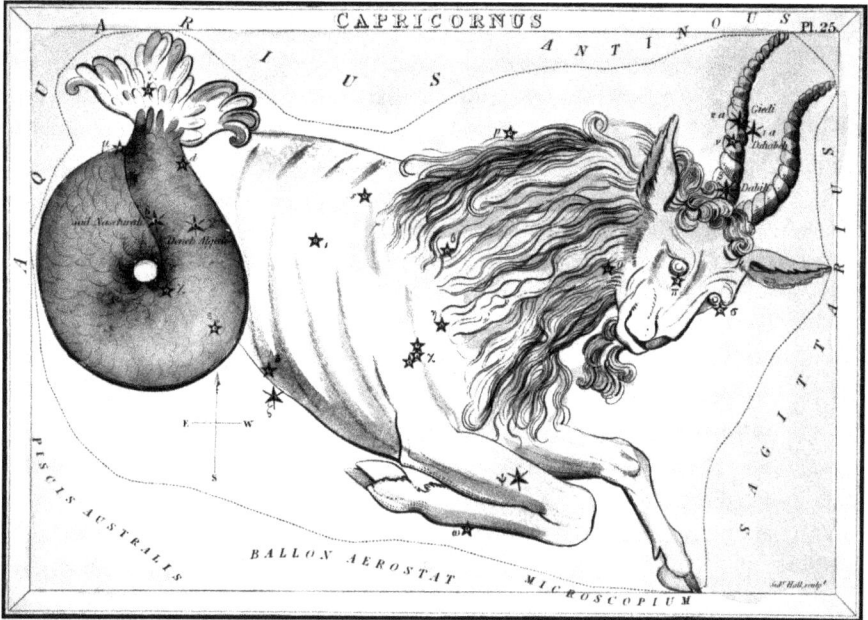

Capricorn (the scapegoat) has been interpreted to mean atonement, es-oterically decoded as *at-one-ment*—the righting of the soul's relationship to the Creator. Like the lamb, the sacrifice of the goat, can be interpreted as the sacrifice of Christ, who takes upon himself the sins of the world, that those who otherwise would be lost (through the weight of returning karma) might be able to take up the path and be saved. The Capricorn Aspirant may struggle to neither condemn nor blame himself or others, as increasing illumination reveals his and their short-comings and past mistakes; rather, in works and in the spirit of true forgiveness, let him celebrate his opportunity to put his house in order.

The Sea-Goat can also be interpreted to symbolize the seeker's conscious relinquishing of the darker, more sinful elements of self. The fish part of the goat signifies the Aspirant's willing sacrifice of the more emotional, unconscious and darker elements in his psyche, including the substance of dreams and memories from past lives. The underworld must be uncovered and purified if the Aspirant would make the ascent upwards untethered.

THE CALLING

The Capricorn Aspirant may pay his dues in the world before embarking upon his spiritual journey. Suddenly he is inspired by a vision, or like Mark Prophet as a young man, he may receive a surprise summons from an Ascended Master. Yogananda spent years searching before he found his Guru, Sri Yukteswar, at age 17. St. Thérèse of Lisieux wanted to be a saint ever since she witnessed a miraculous healing at age thirteen. [203]

Being naturally mission-oriented, the Capricorn Aspirant typically desires to leave a legacy of worth upon the planet. The Ascended Master El Morya called upon Mark Prophet to be his Messenger and to found The Summit Lighthouse, an enormous undertaking. Sri Yukteswar gave Paramahansa Yogananda the assignment to bring an understanding of Kriya Yoga to the West, a task Yogananda successfully fulfilled. Sometimes, however, the calling is quieter, on a smaller scale, but requiring no less effort from he who would transcend his lesser self.

THE LITTLE FLOWER

The Capricorn Aspirant, intent upon great accomplishments, or busily occupying himself with sundry projects, may lose sight of the little things, but it is through these seemingly insignificant actions, day-by-day, that he aligns himself with the living spirit of love. When Marie-Françoise Thérèse Martin (January 2, 1873), later to be known as St. Thérèse of Lisieux, was but 14 years of age, she asked to be admitted to the Convent of Discalced Carmelite nuns in her hometown of Lisieux, France. Three of her older sisters were already there. The adolescent girl was advised to come back when she was twenty-one. But Therese felt strongly that she could not wait so long (indeed, she would live hardly ten more years), and so she and her father made a special trip to the Vatican where she obtained the Pope's blessing. Shortly afterwards, at age fifteen, she entered the nunnery. Her circumstances and her health were such that she knew she was not called to great works, but rather, that her mission was to show the worth of living the path of Christ in the little things we do each day. She wrote:

> *Love proves itself by deeds, so how am I to show my love? Great deeds are forbidden me. The only way I can prove my love is by scattering flowers and these flowers are every little sacrifice, every glance and word, and the doing of the least actions for love.*

Thérèse set an example of being loving, even when others were jealous or cruel. The Little Flower made an effort to be cheerfully helpful in whatever task was before her, no matter how unpleasant, difficult, or insignificant it might

---

[203] On Christmas Eve, 1886, Therese tells of Jesus answering her prayer to help her sister, Celine, who was suffering from severe eczema. In 1895, in her remembrance of that night, she wrote, "I felt, in a word, charity enter my heart, the need to forget myself to make others happy. Since this blessed night, I was not defeated in any battle, but instead, I went from victory to victory and began, so to speak, 'to run a giant's course.'" (A reference to Psalms 19:5)

appear to be. She disciplined herself to refrain from gossip, to place into the flame of love all anger and to practice forgiveness, even when she was falsely accused. Thérèse chose to enter the sacred heart of Jesus, rather than to react with pride, or even with righteous indignation. She put God first; doing as she felt in her heart He would want her to do. This was her gift and the chalice that she wrought to receive His love. As tuberculosis spread throughout her body, the young Carmelite suffered beyond what even the doctors thought possible, but near the end of her ordeal, on her deathbed at only 24 years of age, she is reported to have said, "I can suffer no more for all suffering has become sweet to me." Thérèse's sisters published her memoirs in a book called, *L'Histoire d'une Ame (The Story of a Soul)*. She was canonized in 1925. Millions continue to find solace and inspiration through her words and her example. Thérèse is one of the most popular Saints of the Catholic tradition, along with Saint Francis. In 1944, she was declared patroness of France, along with Joan of Arc.

BEING LOVE IN ACTION

Putting God first—in every thought and action—requires great effort and constancy, and at the same time, it takes the surrendering of all effort to God's Will. Upon entering the path, the Aspirant must let go of any desire for applause and approbation. Jesus was accused by the Pharisees of breaking the law by healing a man of a crippled hand on the Sabbath, the prescribed day of rest. His simple and emphatic reply, *My Father worketh hitherto, and I work*, captures the mindset of he that would be an instrument of a higher power.[204]

When the Capricorn striver fills his days and nights by practicing being love in action, a sense of great peace begins to inundate his being. His aura fills with light. He feels increasingly secure in the hand of God. Love emanates forth from him ever so sweetly and compassionately—yet at times, sternly and powerfully. The climb to the top is self-transforming; each thrust upward, each simple act executed with joy, is a celebration for the gift of life. As he progresses, outer circumstances no longer dictate his sense of happiness, nor do changing astrological currents throw him off balance. *And your life is hid with Christ in God.*[205]

At the same time, the Capricorn Aspirant knows moments in which he experiences firsthand that when he moves outside the presence of peace, through doubt, anger, fear, or negativity of any sort, life quickly becomes chaotic. As long as he abides in his Higher Self, called by some the Christ Self, the karmic return predicted in his astrology is less likely to arrive at his doorstep.[206]

---

[204] John 5:17

[205] Colossians 3:3

[206] See, *The Aquarian Science of Invocation*, following, for how to transmute negative astrology.

When he does find himself in a trying situation, he is increasingly better prepared to meet it with courage and equanimity.

CHALLENGES ALONG THE UPWARD WAY

Life places the Capricorn Aspirant in situations where he meets those with whom he shares karma or who stir up from within him that which he most needs to overcome. Additionally, the more he loves, the more opposition he will meet—the more his very aura exposes the forces of anti-love, jealousy, envy, and other emotions born of fear within those with whom he comes in contact. Those who choose to remain in an illusory state of existence see the mystic as a threat. Not all are ready or desirous of having their weaknesses and their illusory beliefs exposed, nor of having to relinquish their lesser indulgences—the basic requirements for entering "spiritual boot camp."

The Capricorn Aspirant learns quickly that he must not take the barbs and slings of others personally. As long as he is reactive, his progress will be blocked or slowed. Yogananda offers wonderful, practical tips on how to be *calmly active and actively calm.*[207]

As he advances in spiritual maturity, the disciplined Capricorn devotee comes to recognize anyone who incites his anger as his teacher. Seeking to understand rather than criticize, he must be careful not to condemn nor judge others. He himself is likely to experience condemnation and false accusation firsthand at some juncture in his life. Again, he may choose to retaliate or to keep his peace.

Transits made by or to Saturn can foretell the nature of a circumstance testing the Capricorn Aspirant's faith and self-mastery. For example, a Capricorn man with Saturn in Gemini (communication and the Throat chakra) found himself to be the object of idle and at times malicious gossip. While he was burdened by this carelessness on the part of those he thought to be his friends, he himself was known to openly criticize others. The Capricorn seeker eventually realizes that it matters not whether he is the victim or the perpetrator, but rather that the energy be purified of all misqualification and returned to God. Forgiveness and harmlessness must become for him a way of life!

On the arduous way up the mountain of spiritual striving, the Capricorn Trekker will encounter his own *records* (past accounts, even from other lifetimes) and tendencies related to the constructive and the destructive use of power. He will meet the particulars of his relationship with Spirit, especially as Father, as well as any aspects of unresolved psychology with his biological father or another dominant authority figure during his childhood years. His sense of worthiness is

---

[207] *Inner Peace*: *How to Be Calmly Active and Actively Calm,* by Paramahansa Yogananda

exposed, as well as his ability to stand alone when the going gets rough. He must learn the Law, human and divine, endeavoring always that his judgments be balanced and that the law be the servant of truth.

THE THOUSAND-PETALLED LOTUS

Capricorn relates to the Crown chakra, the highest energy center at the very top of the head. The Sanskrit name for this uppermost (of the 7 major chakras) is *Sahasrara*, which means, *The Thousand-Petalled Lotus*. In Tibet and in Buddhism, the lotus, with its roots in the mud, its stem in the water, and its beautiful pads and flower floating upon the water, represents the stages of progress upon the path: from the mud of materialism, through the waters of experience, to the Light of Enlightenment. Mystics refer to the crown chakra as the gateway to Cosmic Consciousness. In Kabbalah, the crown chakra relates to the sephirah *Keter*, the divine emanation at the top of the Tree of Life, which distributes the light from the higher worlds to the lower spheres. Likewise, in mystical traditions, the light of the divine Presence descends from the Godhead through the Crown chakra, is then distributed to the other six chakras, and gradually returns back to the crown again, nourishing and spinning all the chakras in what is called the raising of the Kundalini fire.

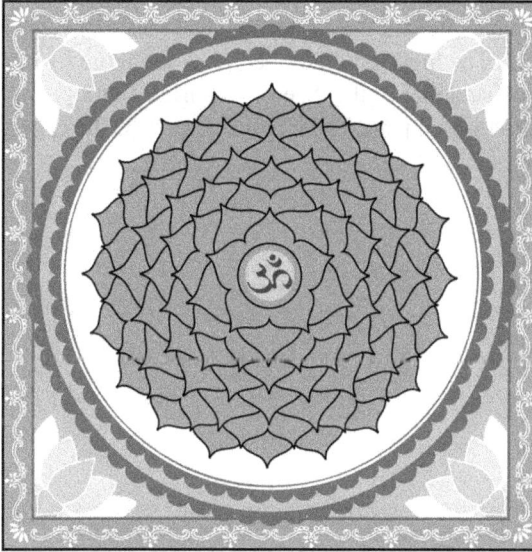

The light of the Crown chakra can be visualized as a golden, radiating flame of cosmic intelligence. It is the serene and powerful glow of wisdom depicted in the pictures of saints as a halo enveloping their heads. Buddhists visualize Gautama Buddha sitting in the Lotus at the Crown; around him shines an intense violet light. The Capricorn Aspirant uses the science of invocation and the practice of meditation to clear the Crown chakra of all misuses of the Mind of God within him. As his momentum grows, the dense, psychic substance around the brain itself, the cause of mental dullness and narrowness of thought, begins to clear. He begins to feel a tingling sensation and then a burning at the top of the head. The frequency of the higher worlds merges with his own mind and he understands and sees what he could not fathom or imagine before. At this juncture on his journey, he is cautioned against becoming so elevated in higher awareness that he neglects the needs of life and of the physical body. If not properly nourished, the brain can actually become overactive, creating short circuits and mental problems.

THE SUMMIT

The climb to greater heights never ends; the Aspirant becomes the Adept, who becomes the Ascended Master or Enlightened One. The auric forcefield of some of these great souls who have attained immortal life is so vast that it may fill a planetary sphere or beyond. The higher the climber goes, the more he can give of himself to humanity. It is said that in the Age of Aquarius, more people than ever before will take up the spiritual path. The Capricorn Hero is the expert guide on the trek to the Summit of Being.

THE AQUARIAN SCIENCE
OF INVOCATION—
DO YOU HEAR WHAT I HEAR?

What I call *The Aquarian Science of Invocation* is a reference to new frontiers that are opening our appreciation, understanding, and ability to bridge worlds through the power of sound, in all its applications—through compassionate communication, through prayer, mantras, the intonation of certain frequencies and tones, powerful decrees, fiats and melodies—even those as yet unknown. Imagine if every word uttered was conscientiously spoken, tone and pitch precisely attuned, and endowed with love. We would live in paradise, for nature herself would respond to such harmony!

It is my conviction that an appreciation of sound—of its role in creation and also its potential for destruction—as well as new developments in the art of listening—constitute integral and basic building blocks to self-transformation, and therefore, to the Aquarian Age. When I first established *The Three Magi Complete Astrological Services* in 1989, I started with a thesis that over twenty-five years of experience has confirmed, that prophecy (prognostication based on an astrological chart) is not set in stone, but can be altered by a change in consciousness. The application of the spoken word rightly employed is key to this process of self-transformation, and transcendence of one's karma (as portrayed in one's charts).

Just like Dorothy in *The Wizard of Oz,* who went hither and yon, fighting witches and having all sorts of adventures, seeking the way back to Kansas, her home, only to discover that all she had to do was to click her ruby slippers, we all have the God-given right to pronounce the words that will get us home, if we only appreciated the science and use of this science of invocation.

Anyone committed to a Higher Walk with God, no matter their age, the era they live in, or their ancestral past, *can* turn around a dire prediction. Each of us, through concerted prayer, while working on our psychology, can transform past errors into positive gains and avert negative astrological portents before they arrive at our doorstep. Yes, it is true that oftentimes we need to go through a certain experience meant to transform our understanding. But even in such instances, prayer can mitigate the severity of the event, I have seen prediction actually fall by the wayside when the soul has learned the lesson and paid his dues.

Edgar Cayce is often quoted as having said, "Why worry when you can pray?" I firmly believe in the power of prayer as an alchemical formula accelerating consciousness—the bridge between the lower and higher worlds—a major key in bringing heaven's help into life. I have seen over and over again the power of the sacred word, especially when combined with the foresight the astrological chart offers, to be an effective tool in meeting challenging situations, in resolving questions dealing with close relationships, with health and money matters, or in propelling oneself forward on the upward path.

The true and only safe means to access realms of higher consciousness and greater soul awareness is, and has always been, the exercise of the spoken word given with a clear mind and devoted heart. Thus, the seeker of truth can alter his vibration, still his being, and experience higher planes of awareness where he is receptive to greater illumination. In many instances, he is able to ameliorate or heal his diseases. Today, through different techniques of employing sound, conscientious health practitioners are guiding their patients through meditations, often using the resonance of crystal bowls, or the sounding of mantras.

The use of the *Violet Transmuting Flame* was first introduced by Godfré Ray King in the I Am Movement in the 1930s and then taught by Mark and Elizabeth Clare Prophet, of the Summit Lighthouse, as a gift and a release of light unknown since the days of Atlantis, now sponsored by the Ascended Master Saint Germain. The sounding of the violet flame in invocations and dynamic decrees is for the transmutation of karmic records and habit patterns that burden the soul and keep us repeating the same errors, as if bound to "a karmic cross."

This form of invocation is so transforming and miraculous in its effects that when used over time, especially when combined with the path and with an understanding of the astrological forces at play in your world, can truly and finally turn your life around! See for yourself—the proof is in the practice! The violet flame continues to be a magical blessing in my own life! Simply start, if you wish, with the well-known mantra:

> *I Am a being of Violet Fire!*
> *I Am the purity God desires!*

As we explore various faiths and practices in *The Hero's Journey through the Zodiac,* I speak of the chakras and touch upon different uses of prayer, mantra, invocation, and positive affirmations. I have provided links for you to explore these themes in greater depth as you are guided to do so.

Why isn't the knowledge and use of sound more widespread, since it would change our lives dramatically? I believe that even as we have harmed the Earth and now seek to undo the damage, the shift to changing the rhythm of our lives, our communications, the sounds in our daily lives, requires study, conscious decision, thoughtfulness, and momentum. Dr. Mitchell Gaynor, in his comprehensive book, *Sounds of Healing,* discusses why the Tibetan Monks have kept secret for so long their inner understanding of the therapeutic use of crystal sound bowls. It is because their destructive power is equally as great as the constructive power. In the wrong hands, they could be grossly misapplied. And even our spoken words carry the same power to create either good or to harm.

But such is the nature of the Aquarian Age, which can scarcely wait any longer for us to catch up. Evildoers and gross ignorance still exist upon this planet, but if this knowledge, some of which has not been brought forth for hundreds of thousands of years, were not to be released, the Children of Light destined to transform this planet and ultimately to ascend could not move forward as planned.

Therefore, let us know ourselves and speak our invocations of light and truth, so as to magnetize what on one level already exists. Let us not look here, nor there—for truly, the kingdom of God (the consciousness of Heaven and The New Day) is within us!

ABOUT THE AUTHOR

When Kathie García chose the name, ***The Three Magi,*** for her company in 1989, she saw the value of Astrology as a tool for understanding oneself, one's relationships, and one's world. Like the astronomer/astrologer priests of old, she was interested in the sacred science—the unraveling of the symbology and the defining of the energy of the signs and planets as keys to the unveiling of life's mysteries.

Kathie Ann Zuflacht was born on September 25th, 1951, in New York City. The Sun was in Libra, the Moon in Leo, both part of a Grand Fire Trine, and Pisces was rising. Her father was a surgeon and her mother a teacher and child psychologist. She had an older and a younger brother. She was raised with a love for the arts, for Broadway and the city's museums, and a delight in *The Melting Pot*'s diversity. This love she later passed on to her children.

As the Vietnam War broke out, Kathie began to actively seek greater understanding of life's whys and wherefores. She found inspiration in the book, *Vietnam: Lotus in a Sea of Fire—A Buddhist Proposal for Peace*, by Thich Nhat Hanh. A couple of years later, she began to study Astrology and the Kabbalah. During college, she delved into Philosophy. While making her way through volumes of Theosophical literature, she was drawn to ***The Ascended Master M (El Morya)***. By the time she was a freshman in college, she had decided that nothing mattered more than finding this master teacher. After college, she thought she would head to India to find him.

In 1973, Kathie earned a B.A. in Anthropology with a minor in Philosophy from Sophie Newcomb College of Tulane University in New Orleans. She also spent a year abroad studying at University College of London and the London School of Economics. She focused on the culture and ancient history of Mesoamerica (Mexico and Central America). Her anthropological background later proved to be a great asset in her astrological work as she learned to ask the right questions in order to understand a client's background and experience, and to appreciate how certain astrological aspects might appear differently based on the nuances of the culture into which the client was born.

Kathie says that her love affair with Mexico began when she spent the summer in and around Cuernavaca, before her 15th birthday. She felt instantly at home with the culture of Mexico and the love emanating from her people. In 1976, she met ***Manuel García*** on Isla Mujeres, a small island across from Cancun, which at the time boasted only one major hotel. The moment she set eyes on Manuel, she recognized that this was a date with destiny. Six months later, this educated woman from NYC and this fisherman/diver from the Mexican Caribbean were married. They would have four children.

A year after marrying, she felt a calling to go to New York where, she felt, a book would open the way to the spiritual path she had been seeking since a teenager. Manuel, always a good sport, assented to the trip. Two weeks later in a bookstore, she found, *The Chela and the Path,* by El Morya, published by The Summit Lighthouse. (In her dreams, she had seen the picture of the hiker from the front cover.) She and Manuel then took a bus cross-country to Pasadena to attend a Summit Lighthouse conference. This event, Kathie explains, was the turning point for the rest of her life.

After her daughter, Indra, was born in Cancun, Kathie decided to become a Montessori Teacher. When she became pregnant with her twin boys, she studied under Madame Elisabeth Caspari at the Summit Lighthouse's spiritual community near Malibu. She received her certification from the Pan American Montessori Society in 1981. When the twins were six, in 1988, Kathie turned to Astrology, which she had practiced semi-professionally in Mexico, as a means of supporting herself while she home-schooled the boys. What began as a temporary solution evolved into a lifelong passion and career.

During those years of raising her family, Kathie created astrological reports for helping children develop into their highest potential. This became **Child*Star**, the world's first astrological program designed to help parents better guide their children, and **Astro*Journey**, a forecast report for young adults. **Know Your Child**, a CD version of Child*Star, came next. As she progressed on her spiritual path, Kathie increasingly sought to discover how Astrology could prove valuable as a tool for self-realization. What was to become her astrological genre, as outpictured in this book, **Trans-formational Astrology**™, was the distilling of the wisdom of the world's mystical traditions to help define the challenges and overcomings of **The Hero's Journey through the Zodiac**.

When asked what she loved most about the spiritual path, Kathie once responded, "I love to witness the transformation in people once they apply themselves. It's awesome to behold—in the true sense of the word!" And what does she love best about Astrology?

"By knowing better what is happening and what to expect, you can make wiser choices—a Full Moon in Pisces doesn't catch you by surprise,

tumbling you into an emotional vortex of frustration. You're prepared. You pass through it in peace and you're there to help others do the same. With the astrological insight, you can take fuller advantage of a two-and-a-half-year career height and not stress it when Saturn is at the bottom of your chart. You'll understand that your work is to lay the foundation for later success."

She continues, "You realize that your astrology, your life-map, is perfect for you. You wouldn't want anyone else's chart—believe me—no matter how much better you think they have it! Life is about your opportunity to excel—we all have that! Starting with a basic understanding of the twelve Sun Signs, Astrology helps you appreciate your sameness and your differences. Parents will acquire more patience—an essential ingredient in childrearing—even if patience is not native to their disposition. Lovers will smile and be tolerant when they could have been fighting!"

And, she concludes, "I love that through prayers for transmutation, when applied directly to our astrology, we can clear up our past, which alters our present, and widens our future possibilities. If I could not present that hope to people, I would not continue in this business!" Kathie's individual counseling, her workshops, and her writing continue to impact people of all ages and backgrounds throughout the world. "Each of us has the opportunity to become the Hero," she says, "by learning how to govern our stars and chart our homeward path back to God." Astrology, for her, is a lens to clarify that Journey.

Examples of Aspects & Configurations

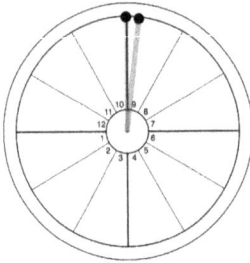

Conjunction
0-10°

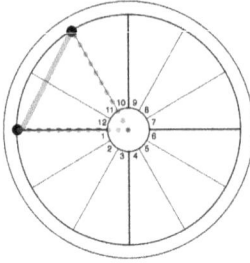

Sextile
60°

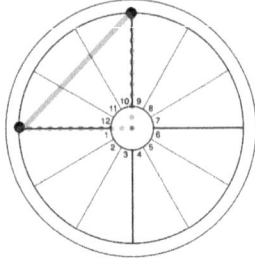

Square
90°

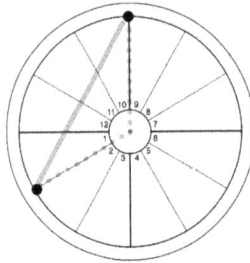

Trine
120°

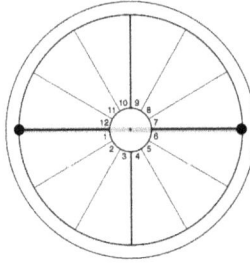

Opposition
180°

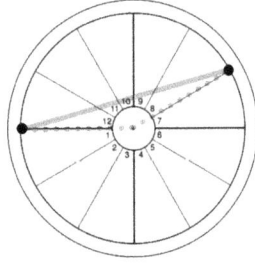

Quincunx
150°

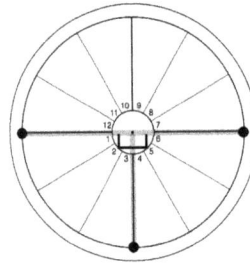

T-Square
2 opposing planets
square a 3rd planet

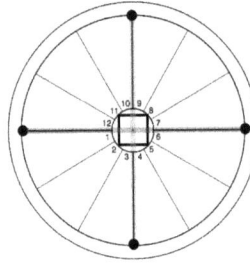

Grand Cross
2 oppositions
forming a cross

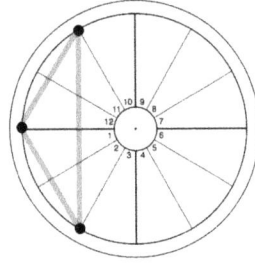

Minor Grand Trine
2 planets in trine,
both sextile 3rd planet

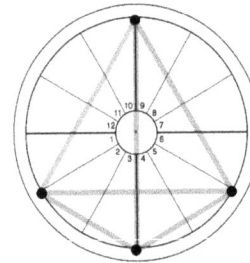

Kite
Bisected
Grand Trine

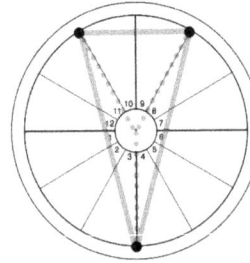

Yod (Finger of God)
2 planets sextile each
other, quincunx a 3rd

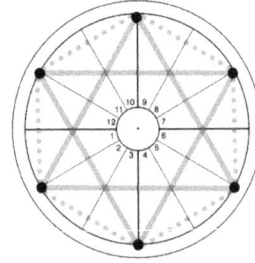

Grand Sextile
2 interlocking
Grand Trines

Glyphs for the 12 Signs of the Zodiac

Aries

Taurus

Gemini

Cancer

Leo

Virgo

Libra

Scorpio

Sagittarius

Capricorn

Aquarius

Pisces

Glyphs for Planetary Positions

Sun

Moon

Mercury

Venus

Mars

Jupiter

Saturn

Uranus

Neptune

Pluto

No. Lunar Node

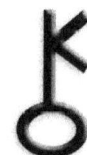
Chiron

323

Charts • Consultations & Reports • Software

For a free natal chart,
send e-mail to:

Kathie.Garcia@TheThreeMagi.com

or postal mail to:

**Kathie García
The Three Magi Astrological Services
P.O. Box 81
Emigrant, Montana 59027**

Please include the following information:

Full Name: _____

Date of Birth (Month, Day, Year):
_____ / _____ / _____

Time of birth (exact local time, if known):
_____:_____ (A.M.) or (P.M.)

Birthplace (or nearest city, if a small place):

City _____ *State* _____ *Country* _____

For personal consultations & specialized reports
and for the newsletter, contact Kathie through
www.TheThreeMagi.com

Astrologers can purchase the *Child*Star*
and *Astro*Journey* software from
www.TheThreeMagi.com

www.ingramcontent.com/pod-product-compliance
Lightning Source LLC
Chambersburg PA
CBHW060244100426
42742CB00011B/1633